THE
ALPINE JOURNAL

1994

1. HM The Queen arriving at the Royal Geographical Society on 26 May 1993 for the lecture to mark the 40th Anniversary of the first ascent of Everest. She is being received by Michael Westmacott, President of the Alpine Club, his wife Sally, and officers of the RGS and Mount Everest Foundation. (*John Cleare*) (p89)

2. HM The Queen with members of the 1953 Everest Expedition. *From L:* George Band, Charles Wylie, Nawang Gombu, Michael Ward, John Hunt, HM The Queen, Edmund Hillary, Michael Westmacott, Alfred Gregory, Griffith Pugh (seated) and George Lowe. (*John Cleare*) (p89)

THE
ALPINE JOURNAL

1994

Incorporating the Journal of the Ladies'
Alpine Club & Alpine Climbing

A record of mountain adventure
and scientific observation

Volume 99 No 343

Edited by Johanna Merz

Assistant Editors:
Roy Ruddle and Geoffrey Templeman

THE ERNEST PRESS

in association with

THE ALPINE CLUB, LONDON

IN ASSOCIATION WITH THE ALPINE CLUB

Volume 99 No 343
THE ALPINE JOURNAL 1994

Address all editorial communications to the Hon Editor:
Mrs J Merz, 14 Whitefield Close, Putney, London SW15 3SS

Address all sales and distribution communications to:
Cordee, 3a De Montfort Street, Leicester LE1 7HD

Back numbers:
Apply to the Alpine Club, 55 Charlotte Road, London, EC2A 3QT
or, for 1969 to date, apply to Cordee, as above.

First published in 1994 by the Ernest Press in association with
the Alpine Club, 55 Charlotte Road, London EC2A 3QT

Typesetting by Johanna Merz
Disc translation and repro by Arneg Ltd., Glasgow
Printed and bound in Great Britain by St Edmundsbury Press

A CIP catalogue record for this book is
available from the British Library

ISBN 0 948153 32 6

Acknowledgements

I would like to thank Prince Sadruddin Aga Khan for his article on the important work of Alp Action, of which he is founder and chairman, in promoting the conservation of the Alps. The Prince's contribution is particularly welcome, since our special theme this year is 'Return to the Alps', which has been the subject of an Alpine Club Symposium.

The *Alpine Journal 1994* reports on the Everest 40th Anniversary celebrations, and I am indebted to John Hunt, Michael Westmacott, Michael Ward and other Alpine Club members for a variety of contributions which form an important postscript to last year's anniversary volume. I am grateful to Charles and Denise Evans for a delightful unpublished drawing of Charles Evans. I would also like to thank Yevgeniy Gippenreiter and Lev Filimonov for a set of historic photographs of the 1958 Sino-Soviet Everest Reconnaissance Expedition, and Christopher Ralling for permission to reproduce a treasured photograph of Mick Burke.

My warmest thanks go to my two Assistant Editors, Roy Ruddle and Geoffrey Templeman, for their enthusiastic support; and to our member and publisher Peter Hodgkiss for invaluable help and advice during our first two years with the Ernest Press.

Finally, I thank everyone who has so generously contributed to this 99th volume of the *Alpine Journal*.

Johanna Merz

Contents

NEW DIRECTIONS

LOOKING BACK

HISTORY AND GEOGRAPHY

Contributions from:
*H Adams Carter, Lindsay Griffin, Tony Howard, Harish Kapadia, Paul Nunn,
Jósef Nyka, Bill O'Connor, David Sharman and Richard Thompson.*

---

*   *This article first appeared in the* Climbers' Club Journal, *Vol XXI, No 1, 1991.
     It is reproduced by courtesy of the editor and the author.*

MAPS AND LINE DRAWINGS
Maps 3-5, 8, 9 redrawn by Ted Hatch

Illustrations

Return to the Alps

'... The Himalaya are so vast, and there is often no sign of human activity or anything else to which to anchor a sense of scale. The Alps are smaller, but what they have is more effectively used, perhaps so effectively that it can never be bettered.'

Philip Bartlett, *The Undiscovered Country*

3. Alp Action: the programme 'Hindelang Natur und Kultur', sponsored by Riso Deutschland, aims to preserve the villages of Hindelang in the Allgäu region of Bavaria. (*Alexander Keck*) (p3)

The district of Hindelang is known for its rural charm, the natural wealth of its meadows and grasslands and for the rich diversity of its flora and fauna. (*Andreas Riedmiller*) (p3)

Left

5. Alp Action: restoring the ancient roof of Cascina Dell'Or, Ticino, Switzerland. Zschokke Holdings are currently sponsoring ancient Alpine crafts in the area. (*Laurent Guiraud*) (p3)

6. Bounavaux Chalet in the Swiss Alps was restored with a contribution from Banque Unigestion, which sponsors traditional agriculture and crafts. (*Daniel Aubort*) (p3)

PRINCE SADRUDDIN AGA KHAN
Views from the Alps

(Plates 3–6)

Prince Sadruddin Aga Khan is a leader in international environmental causes and the founder and chairman of Alp Action. The Corporate Funding Programme of Alp Action unites business and conservation to promote a positive approach to Alpine ecological and cultural issues.

Under the towering Jungfrau in the Bernese Oberland, the Timberland Company is creating the first Timberland Trail in the largest nature reserve in the Swiss German Alps – 'The best place in the entire Alps to watch mountain wildlife!', says Jacques Morier-Genoud, President of the Swiss League for the Protection of Nature which owns the park. With the support of the media and the company's retail network, this discovery path will be the basis of a public awareness campaign, helping to promote individual advocacy in daily environmental action.

This is just one example of 30 concrete initiatives launched throughout the Alps in three years by Alp Action – the International Corporate Funding Programme for the Alpine Environment. They are contributing to the preservation of a precious natural and cultural heritage. The keys to our approach are surprisingly simple: specific, diverse, results oriented. Organisations such as Major Media Partners, Reuters, Newsweek and Financial Times Television are generating worldwide awareness of action in the Alps. Each project has become the pride of corporations and employees and of the local communities who called on us to act with them. Each is a jewel where the traveller can see how people working together can achieve long-term results. Environmental consciousness cannot be stipulated by law. Rather, it begins with individual awareness and the behaviour of each one of us.

Should beauty and harmony not suffice, preserving the Alps is vital for scientific reasons: they are a reservoir that stabilises world climate. Like a huge air-conditioner, they protect us against global warming. As an ecosystem, they contribute animal and plant diversity to the whole of Europe.

Many believe that the Alps are inviolable, that they could never be hurt. But conservationists and scientists point to a steady, alarming decline in habitats, air quality and water cleanliness that is undermining the fragile equilibrium of this ecosystem. 100 million tourists visit the mountains of the Alps each year, while 73 million tonnes of goods are transported along the valleys and over the passes. Considering that transport will double by the year 2010, there is good reason for fear. Obviously a prime objective is to reduce pollution. A second is to reduce the attack of concrete and steel, the excessive and often poorly planned construction of roads, ski-lifts and other infrastructure. A third is to re-orient the focus of tourism so that people come to appreciate rather than destroy the environment and help to preserve the fabulous cultural and natural diversity of the mountains.

Leading upwards from the colourful Valley of Rhododendrons, over-shadowed by Monte Rosa, a nature reserve, or 'Panoramica', stretches for 69km through a region where wildlife thrives in harmony with human traditions. Created in 1938 by Ermenegildo Zegna, visionary founder of the world's leading manufacturer of men's ready-made garments, the 'Oasi Zegna' is now a model of corporate citizenship attracting residents and nature-lovers alike. Anna Zegna, granddaughter of the founder, says that 'with the steadfast commitment of the community, environmentalists and government authorities, and with the involvement of our own personnel and marketing expertise, we can send a powerful message for the successful preservation of the Alps'.

Over half the species of Alpine flora and fauna are threatened or dis-appearing, and Alp Action is trying to protect them all. It might seem whimsical to save an animal as tiny as a butterfly! Yet, without this essential link in the ecological chain, the entire ecosystem is upset: flower species dependent on butterflies for pollination disappear and birds which feed on their larvae starve. Nature's cycles are jeopardised. In response, Clarins – Europe's leading cosmetics firm, which has a butterfly as logo – created the first butterfly sanctuaries. After virtual eradication by hunters, environmentalists have now brought back the beaver and the ibex. A founding partner of Alp Action, Safra Republic Holdings have just co-produced an outstanding documentary with the BBC on its efforts to reintroduce the *Gypaetus Barbatus*, one of the biggest of all Alpine birds, in the French Alps.

Alp Action is also working to halt the depopulation of the mountains and the erosion of its traditions. High up, at the far end of the Lauter-brunnen valley, and in the secluded paradise of the Ticino and Pays d'Enhaut meadows, four old chalets, one dated 1433, were falling into disrepair. Yet their role – sheltering cheese-makers, shepherds who bring up cows and goats to let them graze carefully in order not to destroy the vegetation cover which protects the valleys from erosion and floods – is pivotal for the farming culture and environment. Zschokke Holdings, Switzerland's first construction group, Tetra Pak and Swiss-based Banque Unigestion have revitalised this tradition and ancient Alpine building crafts, in particular the art of *Tavillons*, a type of spruce tile that can last a hundred years.

Woodlands once represented an income for mountain communities. Today, numerous lumber trades are in the red. As a result, Alpine villages and farms are threatened by lack of maintenance of their protective forests. Moreover the number of trees that are withering is increasing. Over 25% of Alpine forests are seriously damaged. Pollution and lack of immunity to parasites are the principal causes of decline, making forests prone to devastating storms. The storm 'Viviane', which hit the Alps in February 1990, blew down 600,000 cubic metres of woodland in the French Savoie Department alone. The largest privately-funded tree planting campaign in the high Alps, funded by Kraft Jacobs Suchard, involves the planting of 400,000 trees in six countries to protect mountain communities against the threat of avalanches and landslides.

Providing financial support for foresters or work for craftsmen, even helping to create new small-scale handicraft concerns, is laudable but how can each one of us contribute to ensure long-term security and a brighter future for mountain communities? While travelling through the Alps, we should refuse tasteless, mass-produced agricultural fare in favour of regional and local, high-quality products which are the key to maintaining these communities and, through their ancestral activities, helping to preserve the landscape.

The inhabitants of l'Etivaz, in the Pays-d'Enhaut region of the Swiss Canton of Vaud, describe themselves as 'a village of indomitables who resist depopulation ... now and for ever'. There were 59 of them ten years ago and they now number 74, collectively managing 2700 dairy cows. They produce a cheese carrying the name of the village. It is produced biologically over a wood fire according to ancestral techniques, and has borne a registered quality label since 1988. This is one of the rare Swiss products which respond to European Community rules governing *Appellations d'origine contrôlées* (registered seals of origin). To market 250 tonnes of cheese per year, the l'Etivaz co-operative has opted for direct promotion at sales outlets in partnership with the Chateau-d'Oex tourist office with whom it launched its 'cheese trails' two years ago. A two-day pedestrian trail through mountain pastures allows visitors to discover the life of cheese-makers and the techniques of cheese-making.

Hindelang is a district the size of Liechtenstein at the heart of the Allgäu region of Bavaria. Its six villages and 5000 inhabitants have preserved the area's rural charm and the valley is considered a little paradise. Dominated by mountains and established along the upper reaches of the Ostrach river, Hindelang is known for the natural wealth of its meadows, grasslands and marshes and for the rich diversity of its flora and fauna. 83% of Hindelang's surface area is legally protected territory, the fruit of the labour of generations of indigenous farmers. Yet this age-old activity has been affected by ever lower subsidies from the European Community with its emphasis on intensive farming. From 200 Hindelang farmers in 1960, the number fell to 70 in the eighties. Their produce was collected and commercialised through a regional co-operative, together with that of 2000 other farmers. Certain valuable sites which had become difficult to cultivate began reverting to scrubland. The habitats of numerous species of plants, birds and other Alpine fauna had begun to disappear, threatening the

very survival of species. The three decades which witnessed agriculture decline also saw tourism boom. Today, a million yearly visitors,
attracted by the region's charm, provide Hindelang's principal revenue.

In 1991, Hindelang's authorities decided to take positive action to
preserve its natural heritage and create a rampart against mass tourism
and chaotic development by launching the Hindelang 'Nature & Culture'
quality label. Riso Deutschland, a subsidiary of the Riso Kagaku
Corporation, the Japanese multinational leader in the printing sector,
helped to launch the fund. Since last October, all 86 Hindelang farmers
have converted to methods which eliminate any chemicals noxious to the
environment. They also practise reaping techniques that preserve natural
floral diversity. The Hindelang 'Nature & Culture' label is marketed by
Hindelang's retailers, hotels and restaurants, who also inform the public
about the crucial role of agriculture in the protection of nature and the
preservation of landscape.

In balanced natural ecosystems, species' populations remain more or
less constant, resources are recycled and energy used efficiently. In the
human ecosystem, population grows continuously, producing vast quantities of pollution and waste owing to inefficient energy use and poor
recycling. Yet, the planet's resources are not unlimited! Today, a single
generation consumes more than all those that preceded it. The bright
economic prospects of recycling and recycled materials are demonstrated
in films competing for the Financial Times TV–Alp Action Awards. The
Awards document describes green technological advances which often
anticipate legislative constraints. One of the judges, Professor Klaus Schwab,
Chairman and Founder of the World Economic Forum, states: 'This is
simply a matter of survival, for industry and consumers alike ... '

The Alpine environment mirrors a fragile global equilibrium and
reflects the challenges that lie ahead.

MARTIN MORAN

Alps 4000: A Non-Stop Traverse

(Plates 21–26)

In this technological age it requires imagination to create an adventure: nowhere more so than on the well-trodden mountains of Western Europe. The linking of several ridges, faces or groups of summits in a single expedition has proved one of the most popular ideas for renewing the challenge of Alpinism, especially among the best French and Swiss climbers. Unfortunately, many remarkable *enchainements* have been emasculated as adventures by over-enthusiastic media attention, much of it encouraged by the participants themselves.

One of the less publicised yet most impressive feats in this genre was the traverse of all the summits of the Zermatt skyline over 20 days in February 1986 by the Swiss pair André Georges and Erhard Loretan. Their route included some thirty 4000 metre summits, and clearly revealed the potential for a grander traverse of all the Alpine 4000 metre peaks in a non-stop journey. But prior to 1993 the only non-stop attempt on the 4000ers was made by two British climbers, and was inspired by marathon fell-running feats, such as Lakeland's Bob Graham Round, as much as by the feats of the ace Alpinists of the day. In 1988 Paul Mackrill and John Rowlands set out to do the 4000ers in the most adventurous manner possible – on foot throughout and without high-level support teams. Beginning in early May they were beaten off the mountains several times by the snowy unsettled weather typical of the Alpine spring, and when conditions did become good in July and August they lacked the support to stay high and keep moving. Mackrill battled on for 120 days until 20 September, when he finished all fifty Swiss 4000ers with the ascent of the Grand Combin. For sheer determination it was an admirable performance, but changes in tactics were clearly needed if the 4000ers were to be traversed in their entirety in a single summer.

Forging a partnership

Any such traverse clearly demanded an intimate and efficient partnership between two equally committed climbers. Simon Jenkins and I had been aware of the 4000ers challenge throughout the late 1980s, but instead had thrown our energies into the shorter but technically harder project of a non-stop unsupported traverse of the Mer de Glace skyline from the Drus to the Charmoz.

The experience was bitter. Twice each, in 1988 and 1989, we set out from Montenvers and traversed the Drus. In each year we had installed food caches at four of the cols on the skyline. Our best effort got us as far as the

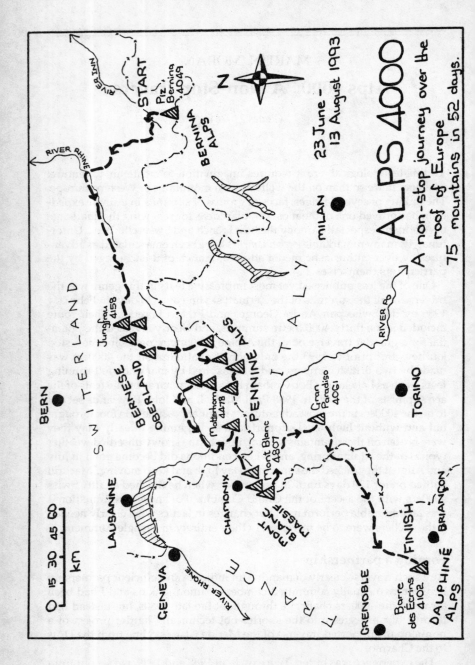

ALPS 4000

A non-stop journey over the roof of Europe

75 mountains in 52 days.

23 June – 13 August 1993

Aiguille de l'Eboulement after five days, where we had to abandon the venture owing to a worsening respiratory infection which was affecting us both. On each attempt we encountered mixed climbing more sustained than we could have imagined, rock that was shattered beyond belief and snow conditions which varied from perfect névé to abominable slush. Our lack of foreknowledge of the remote sections round the Talèfre and Leschaux basins counted heavily against us.

We emerged from these failures happy to let the prize of the Chamonix skyline fall to someone else but immeasurably strengthened as a partnership and much the wiser about Alpine climbing conditions. Meanwhile, we were individually amassing a sizeable tally of 4000ers in our work as guides, so that our route knowledge approached the level required for a rapid traverse without eliminating the novelty of the enterprise.

Tactical choices

Making the final commitment to the 4000ers implied the loss of a third of our annual earnings as guides and the personal expenditure of some £10,000 to equip and support the venture. The economic climate was not ideal for any form of financial sponsorship, even though we pledged our expedition to raise funds for Blythswood Relief Aid, a Highland charity working in Eastern Europe.

The tactical decisions were easier to make. First we had to define our list of peaks. It is annoying that none of the published lists – Blodig, Collomb, *High* magazine or Goedeke – had seemed to use an objective criterion to define separate tops. All of them appeared deficient in some areas and over-detailed in others, particularly in respect of the Monte Rosa massif where insignificant bumps abound. Simon and I decided that we would climb every top with a 35m height separation from its nearest highest neighbour. This gave a total of some 75 summits, although we would have to climb more than that in order to establish the height separation of several marginal candidates for inclusion. Our 35m rule may be seen as arbitrary, but it did ensure the inclusion of every important top in the itinerary.

Secondly, we arranged high-level support teams to keep us going during the major sections of the Bernese Oberland, Zermatt skyline and the Mont Blanc massif, as well as having our wives providing valley back-up and maintaining essential communication by radio transceiver.

We elected to begin the traverse on the Piz Bernina on 22 June and hoped to hit the expected July anticyclone during the Zermatt traverse. We constructed a base schedule of 48 days from the Bernina to the Barre des Ecrins without allowance for weather delays. Thus a time of 55 days or less seemed realistic. In constructing this schedule we had looked carefully at the routes linking the main massifs and quickly realised that the use of bicycles would save us a fortnight of hard footslogging, as well as providing a welcome change of exercise. We also planned to use skis in the Oberland.

Early successes

After six months of detailed planning we presented ourselves in the lovely Morteratsch valley on 21 June. Vague or erroneous weather forecasts were to plague our progress throughout the next seven weeks and our start on the Piz Bernina was no exception. We climbed the normal route via the Bellavista Terraces and S ridge in a blizzard which demanded navigational accuracy equal to anything we had ever applied in the Scottish winter.

There followed a two-day interlude of cycling when we saw some of Switzerland's most enchanting scenery in the Engadine and upper Rhine valleys but also experienced the crucifying effort of linking big passes. Doing the Oberalp, Furka and Grimsel passes in a day matched any physical effort we made on the mountains. Our bikes were Dawes hybrid models, light enough for road touring but amply geared for gradients up to 1 in 4.

Now fitter and a little acclimatised after our protracted ascent of the Bernina, we embarked on the Oberland, the most extensive of the 4000er massifs and the least known to us. Our entry via the Unteraar glacier had a Himalayan atmosphere. Vast untouched cirques split off in all directions and the Finsteraarhorn towered behind in impregnable splendour. In such austere surroundings, the Aar bivouac hut was perhaps the cosiest and certainly the best maintained shelter we used all summer. The Finster itself gave us an arduous ascent. Truly it is the monarch of the massif, and we struggled in gale force winds on the long climb from the Agassizjoch.

The next day we were pitted against the renowned Schreckhorn–Lauteraarhorn traverse, or the Lauteraargrat as it is better known. However, the snow conditions in the Schreckfirn were excellent and the crucial linking ridge sufficiently clear of snow that we climbed it without crampons. There are two significant tops on the Lauteraargrat, Pts 4011 and 4015, which are ignored in all the lists. Their inclusion in a 4000ers odyssey guarantees some of the finest space-walking in the Alps.

After this excitement our escape from the Obers Ischmeer basin over the Fiescherhorn on a warm foggy day was pure toil, with a significant objective threat first from serried ice cliffs and then from rapidly thawing snow. As we skied off the Fiescherhorn our edges cut a continuous wet slough that accumulated into an avalanche of disturbing scale. Near exhaustion at the Mönchsjoch hut was solved by the arrival of our support team with a mountain of food. I devoured six fried eggs in as many minutes, each with a thick slice of bread, followed by a family-sized tin of peaches; I was still ready for another meal three hours later.

The Aletschhorn was a fitting final obstacle in the Oberland – a big lonely peak with a wonderful view of our forthcoming challenges in the Pennines. We ploughed up a crusted Hasler Rib and then skied the Mittelaletsch glacier on rutted névé which left no illusions as to the consequences of a slip. Our skis were 130cm Kästle Firn Extrems with Silvretta 404 bindings. They could be easily carried up a route like the Hasler Rib, and what they sacrificed in speed and style was amply compensated for by their ease of turning when wearing ordinary climbing boots. Indeed they even managed to flatter my limited and long-redundant skiing skills!

The weather collapses

So far we had lost only one day to our ambitious schedule and now looked forward to the arrival of the big summer anticyclone. We thought it had arrived during three days of glorious weather in Saas, and our confidence tempted us to an open bivouac on the Lenzjoch at 4050m. The short but difficult link of the Domgrat would have taken us to a support team at the Mischabeljoch hut, but that night a blizzard struck. In the morning we struggled to the top of the Dom in a whiteout but further progress was impossible. It was to be three days before we bridged the 1km gap to its Siamese twin, the Täschhorn. Our detour took us back to the valley floor 3000m below, then up to the Mischabeljoch via Täschalp and the Weingarten glacier. Snow had fallen thickly down to 2400m and the Täschhorn's usually benign SE ridge proved to be a corniced monster of Andean proportions!

The Allalin–Rimpfisch–Strahlhorn linkage was scheduled as an easy day's romp, but the weather showed no mercy and we ended up taking three. Our spirits reached a nadir as we ploughed up the Strahlhorn at 5pm in a whiteout of driving sleet. Only a magnificent support operation by fell-runners Martin Stone and Mike Walford and our cameraman Martin Welch kept us going over Monte Rosa. Traversing Liskamm on a fine Sunday morning, we thought that at last we had broken the noose of bad weather, but four hours later we were nearly struck by lightning at the start of the Breithorn traverse and were forced to retreat to the Val d'Ayas hut.

The Zermatt giants

We arrived at Schwarzsee, beneath a snow-plastered Matterhorn, fully six days off the pace. 'They're definitely not joking this time,' enthused Martin Stone. 'The Zermatt guides are promising five days of brilliant weather!'

In the event it turned out to be a cool and moist anticyclone with a cloud inversion at 4200m. The Matterhorn was magnificent and totally deserted, the WNW face of the Dent d'Hérens a wonderful four-hour romp from a camp by the Schönbiel hut, and the Dent Blanche's S ridge a spectacle of ethereal winter beauty. However, our five days of grace ended abruptly just where we dreaded: the Schalijoch. We were marooned for a day without food at the bivouac hut. The storm cleared away overnight but after fresh snow we couldn't contemplate the complexities of the Schaligrat. Knowing that we had to get to the Weisshorn that very day or else face a demoralising retreat to the valley, we risked uncharted snow couloirs on the mountain's E face. In fact the climbing was fast and simple. This piece of intuitive route-finding saved us crucial hours which were immediately employed in getting down the N ridge. Snow was banked at ridiculous angles on the Grand Gendarme and its onward arête. Thank goodness there are a few easy 4000ers like the dear old Bishorn. We actually laid out full length on its summit in relief after so vertiginous a descent.

So far our knees had survived the summer without complaint, but the 2500m descent to Zinal extracted the first twinges of pain. Yet with the Zermatt ring now closed, our spirits soared and for the first time we dared to think of the finish. Surely Mont Blanc would treat us kindly.

Home ground

We compressed 130km of cycling and the Grand Combin into two days and left Switzerland five days behind schedule. Arrival on our home ground of the Mont Blanc massif coincided with a swing to the baking hot weather more typical of recent summers, and we took our helmets along for the first time. A night traverse of the Col d'Argentière and the Col des Cristaux brought us face to face with our old adversaries Les Droites and the Aiguille Verte. We knew all too much about the difficulties of the linking ridge between the two, so we did a moonlit meander up and down the normal route on Les Droites and then crossed the glacier and climbed the couloir leading to Col Armand Charlet from whence the tops of the Verte were easily accessible.

The next dawn saw us toiling out of the Leschaux basin and up under Les Périades towards the Col des Grandes Jorasses bivouac hut. Sometime during our climb the summit sérac on the south side of the mountain collapsed and engulfed eight climbers. The sight of the rescue operation, plus threatening weather, made the W ridge of the Jorasses the most nerve-racking route so far. Did Winthrop Young, Jones and Knubel really do those hand traverses under the Pointe Marguerite? We returned to the hut close on midnight and celebrated with a mouthwatering spaghetti.

The pitches needed in order to climb onto the Calotte de Rochefort impressed us equally the next morning. By the time we had traversed the two Rochefort summits and reached the Dent du Géant thunder was rumbling over Mont Blanc and flurries of hail were falling. Gripped by panic, we swung wildly up the fixed ropes past hordes of retreating Italian climbers, touched the Madonna and fled to the Col du Géant where a support camp awaited.

33 hours on the go

The stage was set for the Mont Blanc finale but the weather kept us guessing for two days. Finally a furious thunderstorm broke just as the friendly voice of the Chamonix weatherman was promising a 36-hour window of fine conditions over a crackling line from the Torino hut. After some devious route planning we reckoned we could just squeeze the mountain's 12 tops into the window, provided we climbed non-stop through the following night. The moment the wind dropped, at 10am on 6 August, we set out for the Diables ridge. For carefree aerial acrobatics the route had no comparison – a total contrast to the austerities of the Jorasses W ridge.

By 7pm we were resting in a support tent on the Col Maudit and, in between mouthfuls of soup and cheese, witnessed the best sunset of the trip. Mont Maudit was taken slowly out of respect for our digestion, but by midnight we were briskly traversing the Corridor and the Grand Plateau bound for the Aiguille de Bionnassay. True to form, the Bionnassay's summit ridge was a razor edge. Why on earth had I suggested leaving our rope back at the Dôme du Goûter? Fortified by strong coffee at the Vallot hut we joined the march of the 200 to the top of Mont Blanc. No greater contrast could be found to the warm conviviality of the crowded summit than a descent of the Brouillard ridge. By midday we were sitting on a crow's nest of solid rock high above the Col Emile Rey contemplating the guidebook's advice that 'it is essential to be well above the col by dawn' and watching stones and snow slides funnelling into the recommended couloir. With storms due that evening, we couldn't sit tight and await a frost, so we embarked on a speculative series of abseils down steep granite walls on the Miage side of the ridge in order to gain the col. Most of the old slings we had been stowing in our sacks over the weeks were now gratefully utilised.

Stumbling like a pair of zombies we crossed Mont Brouillard and the Punta Baretti and, after 33 hours on the move, gained the sanctuary of the Eccles hut. There we so amazed a French guide and his client with our route description that they promptly gave us all their spare food and departed for the Monzino, so leaving us to a blissful sleep!

Only the Aiguille Blanche de Peuterey now separated us from virtually certain success on our journey, provided that we didn't get knocked off our bikes by an Italian juggernaut. The storm held off just long enough to allow us across the Frêney plateau to its summit and back next morning. Then, in a little under 2hrs 30min, we joyously plunged down the side of the Brouillard glacier to the Val Veni and the arms of our wives.

Holding out to the end

The final five days were more relaxing mentally but still arduous. The Aosta autostrada was safely negotiated, we just beat a storm to the top of the Gran Paradiso, and then did a marvellous hike over the Colle del Nivolet and Colle del Carro into the Vanoise. A day like this striding through glorious unfrequented surroundings counted among the highlights of the journey.

Following the wheels of the *Tour de France* up the 1800m ascent from the Arc valley to the Col du Galibier was another great thrill. A tremendous view of La Meije and the Barre des Ecrins burst forth as we reached the top. It was a moment of happiness to equal that on arrival on any of our 75 summits. The Barre itself proved to be an anticlimax. We were now too tired and jaded to really appreciate the finish. From a bivouac in the boulders of the Col d'Arsine we had a 1300m climb over the Pic de Neige Cordier just to get to the start of the Barre. The *voie normale* was thronged with large voluble guided parties, piles of excrement lined the track and clouds hid the views. Happily, the crowds all stopped at the forepeak, the Dôme du Neige, and a sudden breakthrough of sunlight on the summit ridge reminded us of the unfettered glories of the mountains which we had savoured over the past 52 days.

For Simon and myself the journey rekindled the fire of true Alpinism as perhaps it was practised in the days of Winthrop Young, Knubel and their contemporaries. By following their steps in all weathers and conditions we largely escaped the crowds and discarded the regimentation and commercialism which has crept into modern Alpine mountaineering. If nought else, our 4000ers traverse has proved that real adventure in the Alps is still there for the taking.

The 75 peaks climbed: 23 June - 13 August 1993
All heights in metres

Major Mountains

1	Mont Blanc	4807	26	Dent d'Hérens	4171
2	Dufourspitze	4634	27	Breithorn	4164
3	Nordend	4609	28	Jungfrau	4158
4	Signalkuppe	4556	29	Bishorn	4153
5	Dom	4545	30	Aiguille Verte	4122
6	Liskamm	4527	31	Aig Blanche de Peuterey	4112
7	Weisshorn	4505	32	Barre des Ecrins	4101
8	Täschhorn	4490	33	Mönch	4099
9	Matterhorn	4478	34	Pollux	4092
10	Mont Maudit	4465	35	Schreckhorn	4078
11	Dent Blanche	4356	36	Obergabelhorn	4063
12	Nadelhorn	4327	37	Gran Paradiso	4061
13	Grand Combin	4314	38	Aiguille de Bionnassay	4052
14	Lenzspitze	4294	39	Gross Fiescherhorn	4049
15	Finsteraarhorn	4273	40	Piz Bernina	4049
16	Mont Blanc du Tacul	4248	41	Gross Grünhorn	4044
17	Castor	4228	42	Lauteraarhorn	4042
18	Zinalrothorn	4221	43	Durrenhorn	4035
19	Hohberghorn	4219	44	Allalinhorn	4027
20	Piramide Vincent	4215	45	Weissmies	4023
21	Grandes Jorasses	4208	46	Dôme de Rochefort	4015
22	Alphubel	4206	47	Dent du Géant	4013
23	Rimpfischhorn	4199	48	Lagginhorn	4010
24	Aletschhorn	4195	49	Aiguille de Rochefort	4001
25	Strahlhorn	4190	50	Les Droites	4000

Subsidiary tops

Defined as those summits having a height separation of 35m or over from higher adjoining summits, and an essential part of the 4000ers challenge.

51	Zumsteinspitze	4563	63	Gd Combin de la Tsessette	4141
52	Liskamm W summit	4479	64	Breithorn W Twin	4139
53	Pic Luigi Amedeo	4469	65	L'Isolée, MB du Tacul	4114
54	Parrotspitze	4436	66	Pte Carmen, MB du Tacul	4109
55	Ludwigshohe	4341	67	Breithorn E Twin	4106
56	Weisshorn N ridge gendarme	4331	68	Grande Rocheuse	4102
57	Corno Nero	4321	69	Pte Chaubert, MB du Tacul	4074
58	Dôme du Goûter	4304	70	Mont Brouillard	4069
59	Il Naso, Liskamm	4273	71	Pte Marguerite, Gd Jorasses	4065
60	Pt Whymper, Gd Jorasses	4184	72	Aiguille du Jardin	4035
61	Gd Combin de Valsorey	4184	73	Hinter Fiescherhorn	4025
62	Breithorn C summit	4159	74	Dôme de Neige des Ecrins	4015
			75	Punta Baretti	4013

Other notable tops climbed, with estimated height difference in metres:

Pt 4011, Lauteraarhorn	4011	25	
Pt 4015, Lauteraarhorn	4015	30	
Wengener Jungfrau	4089	25	
Stecknadelhorn	4241	25	
Pte Hélène, Gd Jorasses	4045	25	
Pte Mediane, MB du Tacul	4097	25	Checked with rappel rope
Aig Blanche SE top	4107	30	

NOTES

1. Top 53, Pic Luigi Amedeo, 4469m: the height was marginal and needs checking.
2. Top 57, Corno Nero, 4321m: the height differential was measured as exactly 35m with altimeter.
3. Top 67, Breithorn E Twin, 4106m: the height differential was measured as 40m.
4. Top 71, Pointe Marguerite, Grandes Jorasses, 4065m: the height differential is at least 45m.
5. The N ridge gendarme Rimpfischhorn, 4108m, was the only notable top not climbed; its height separation is c30m.
6. Other tops often included in the lists, such as Balmenhorn, Pta Giordani, Mt Blanc de Courmayeur and Il Roc, have a height differential of only 20m or less and were not considered. Their inclusion would qualify dozens of other minor bumps as 4000ers and make an objective listing impossible.
7. Some existing lists of the 4000ers, giving height differentials, were found to have several errors. An accurate survey of many of the smaller tops remains to be done.

ALISON HARGREAVES
The Big Six

(Plates 7–11 and back cover)

At the end of March 1993, I set off with my husband and two children, Tom aged five and Kate aged two, on a journey south to attempt the Big Six. I wanted to climb solo a route on each of the classic six north faces of the Alps, as first described by Gaston Rébuffat in *Starlight and Storm*: the Piz Badile, the Cima Grande, the Dru, the Eiger, the Grandes Jorasses and the Matterhorn.

I had previously climbed, with partners, the 1938 route on the Eiger, the Schmid route on the Matterhorn, and the Shroud and Croz Spur on the Grandes Jorasses. I had never before been on the Dru and had not even seen the Piz Badile or the Cima Grande. I had hoped to try and do at least one of the six in late winter or early spring after a couple of weeks getting fit but, as we arrived, the settled unseasonal winter weather changed into a very unsettled snowy spring and reluctantly we were forced to move south. Chamonix and its mountains were miserable and awash, the Ecrins was snowbound, as were the Alpes Maritimes. So Easter saw us, together with hundreds of other good weather seekers, at the picturesque Mediterranean coastal town of Cassis, for the sun, sea and rock of Les Calanques.

The weather was fair and the rock great, and I suppressed my thirst for the mountains by making long coastal approaches to brilliant spacey sea arêtes and remote hikes into the wild mountainous valleys for high brilliant routes. As my fitness and confidence increased, the weather once more took a change for the worse. Exchanging shorts and T-shirts for Gore-Tex and Polartec, I managed to snatch a few more climbs between the storms before we decided it was time to move on. It was still too early for the huge mountainous dump of snow to have settled down on the Ecrins but we decided to spend a couple of weeks at Casset in this lower Alpine area so that I could continue to maintain a level of fitness and at the same time collect some new Alpine routes.

By now the weather was starting to warm up, the wind had changed and we moved around to Ailefroide. Wild camping became a delight. Our arrival coincided with the awakening of the marmots after their winter hibernation, there was still plenty of winter's fallen wood to burn and the children experienced their first open camp fires. I was able to complete our visit with a brisk trip up the Barre des Ecrins. With plenty of rock metreage under my belt and some great Alpine routes in wintry conditions, we decided it was time to return to Chamonix where by now surely the weather must be settling down.

But no. A recent fall of snow had put another layer on the glaciers, so we drove to Zermatt to see if things were any better there. The North Face of the Matterhorn was still in horrible condition and within 24 hours we had chugged our way back to Chamonix again! Having found a wholesome yet cheap campsite in Les Bois, we made ourselves at home once more and I kept up a daily check on the *meteo*.

The Grandes Jorasses

At last there was a break in the weather – two warm sunny days were forecast before stormy patterns would move in again. I had my chance. I had kept fit with runs up to Montenvers and in the Aiguilles Rouges and now it was time to put it all to good use. In recent summers the steep lower ice pitches on the Shroud on the Grandes Jorasses have become thin and sometimes non-existent. 'Pray God for an ice age' was an exasperated New Zealander's entry in the Leschaux hut route book! One more run to Montenvers and a study through my binoculars – the Shroud appeared to be complete – and by late morning on 16 June I was steaming up through the woods towards Montenvers. I left my trainers under a boulder and, after descending the ladders, headed up the Mer de Glace.

  By mid-afternoon I was happily settled in the Leschaux hut. The great face of the Grandes Jorasses looked fine and I was happy, but soon my equilibrium was to be disturbed and the peace shattered as four more people arrived. Two were just travelling the huts and generously handed out chocolate and cigarettes. The other two were young French guides also heading for the Shroud. Now I had a dilemma. Should I let them go first and have them above me knocking snow/ice onto me, or should I go first, dangerously up the glacier in the dark, to beat their early start and then have them biting at my heels ... I decided to let them go first and was happy to lie in bed awhile after they had gone.

The early hours found me plodding monotonously up through deep snow. Once at the base of the Walker Spur, a move left and a last pull up the deep snow cone to the base of the gully and I was at the beginning of the route and it was time to start enjoying myself. The bergschrund was filled in well and I had no problem, cautiously crossing it and then up. The ice was good, I was feeling good, the movement started to flow and I moved up easily. As the gully narrowed the ice started to thin out, and as the buttress on the right gradually moved in I crept leftwards and diagonally upwards, teetering on little bits of ice left clinging to the rock between the exposed bits. This was climbing at its best. I worked out each placement, side-stepping and working my way up. Where there was ice it was generally good and it was just a matter of not thrashing it to death but working precisely from one dot of ice to the next.

The steep bit was over, the icefield laid back and I caught sight of two figures working their way up. But the cloud was coming down, I could no longer see the ridge, and just kept climbing continuously in the same direction, up and left, cursing the monotony of the slope. Conditions had deteriorated, both under foot and above, and there was a thick layer of fresh powdery snow on top of the hard old ice. Kicking hard, I was able to get a bite on my front points, but no relief for the calves. The wind had also decided to join in, with constant icy blasts. As the guides fought their way out of the final exit gully to the ridge, I sank my head into my jacket and waited for a clear run, then climbed the powdery rocks to join them. They were muttering unhappily about their original plan of continuing up the Hirondelles ridge and skiing back to Italy for a pasta supper. I was committed to descending the ridge and so returning to the Leschaux. Moments later they joined me. It was 10pm as I walked into the campsite of Les Bois, very weary, and I spent the next couple of days with the family in a peaceful daze.

The Matterhorn

Zermatt next. We decided to take as much food and kit as we could carry and base ourselves at the Zermatt campsite for as long as we needed. Another look at the face, and even though the weather didn't help, conditions on the face were definitely improving. On 29 June I made the familiar approach from the Hörnli hut. The condition of the icefield had slightly deteriorated but the ramp was now clear of wet or powdery snow, so it looked as if it should go. My problem was how to reach it. A way I had previously spotted – right and then back left – now looked desperate, but the direct line to the bottom of the ramp appeared no better. At least it was upward, so I carried on. The climbing was tricky and became more technical, a thin veneer of ice overlying chossy rock and slabs. I was grateful for my size and weight and tackled my way on up, knowing that a wrong hit would leave nothing to bite into.

As I worked to the top of the ramp I felt happier; the harder climbing should be coming to a close and I would soon be able to motor. But this was not to be. On the upper slopes fresh snow still lay in over-plentiful supply and, although the angle eased, the climbing didn't. I was tired, mentally and physically. I was now in the cloud with still a long way to go ... at last the summit. I wanted to feel relieved, but there was thunder rumbling around and I could pick out flashes of lightning rolling in from Italy, and still I had to get down. I glanced at my watch and wondered about the time: $5\frac{1}{2}$ hours I had been on the face, all that time in deep concentration. It was longer than I had hoped for, but the conditions had been much more awkward and time-consuming than I had anticipated.

The Eiger

A couple of days' rest and we drove to Grindelwald. Just to be awkward the weather improved, but the face was plastered with snow and ice – lots of it. Why not use such conditions and instead of retracing my previous success on the 1938 route go for a route up the Lauper side of the North Face? There was easily enough snow there and all it needed was a good freeze.

I decided to give it time and kept fit by running up hills and doing other routes. Rain now, and snow down to 1500m. The holidaymakers were

Alison Hargreaves soloed the Croz Spur of the Grandes Jorasses on
10 November 1993; she had already soloed the Big Six north faces
during June-August. (*Dave Sharrock*) (p16)

Left

8. Matterhorn N face. Alison soloed the Sch▮ route on 29.6.93. It follows the obvious snowfield from right to left, followed by the ramp. (*Dave Ballard*) (p16)

Below

9. Piz Badile. Alison climbed the central cla▮ N face route on 10.8.93. (*Alison Hargreaves*) (p16)

Above
Alison in the *niche* on the Dru after soloing
the Allain route on 17.8.93. (p16)

Right
The N faces of the Tre Cime de Laverado.
Alison soloed the N face of the Cime Grande
on 24.8.93. (*Dave Ballard*) (p16)

12. Dhaulagiri, 8167m, from the north. In the foreground: Rick Allen.
    (*Alison Allen*) (p43)

Dhaulagiri N face: Ivan Plotnikov (Vanya) and Sergei Efimov starting up the icefield. In the background Dhaulagiri VI. (*Rick Allen*) (p43)

Rick Allen on the summit of Dhaulagiri. (*Sergei Efimov*) (p43)

15. Cerro Kishtwar, 6200m. The climb took the L to R slanting ramp to the notch on the L skyline, and continued out of sight round the corner on the NE face. (*Mike O'Brien*) (p48)

Day 1. Steven Sustad climbing after the tension traverse. (*Mick Fowler*) (p48)

17. Day 3. Mick Fowler belaying from the bivvy ledge above the difficult pitch to the col. (*Steven Sustad*) (p48)

Day 4. Mick Fowler on the summit of Cerro Kishtwar. (*Steven Sustad*) (p48)

19. The Argentière glacier photographed in 1896. (*Gay Couttet*) (p27)

20. The same view photographed in 1993, showing the recession of the glacier and prolific vegetation. (*Nigel Shepherd*) (p27)

upset, the campsite awash, and for nearly two weeks we kept up our damp-ened spirits with family walks and long mountain runs. As families came and went, so did the rain showers.

On 22 July we checked at the weather station and there was a storm forecast; then, in a familiar pattern, it would go cold for a day, and this time might even stay cold for a further day, before it warmed up and another storm moved in. The nights of lightning had been impressive, but so too was the forecast, with so much low/fresh snow and a night of cold temperatures. Maybe this would be just the time for a route on the Lauper face? But it had been in cloud for ten days, so really I had no idea of its condition.

I packed my sack and hiked up to find a bivvy spot under the face. As the clouds teased around, I half slept and half wondered. I was fit and through the breaks in the clouds I could see that the snow was there – but would it freeze? I started breakfast in the dark but waited until dawn to leave my bivvy kit and amble up towards the start of the face. I felt no rush. I didn't want to climb in the dark and I had all day. There was only 1600m to climb and on my own I could just keep moving ...

The normal Lauper route traverses in from the right, continues way left and then back right again to finish at the heart of the face. I varied the route by continuing straight up the ice slope of the Hoheneis to its neck. A waterfall poured down the back wall and so, moving a little to the right up a precarious ramp and up through the next rock band, I stepped left to arrive directly above the neck of the Hoheneis. Straight up an icy ramp, and I was level with where the Lauper traverses across right and heads up to a gully at the left of a triangular rock buttress. Again the way didn't look the best and I decided to continue straight on up. I could see a line through mixed ground and, after a precarious mixed gully, I was into a ramp/gangway that led me quickly and directly up the face.

Although the conditions were poor and a bit unconsolidated, my line felt good and the higher I climbed the more the snow/ice improved. The wide rock band stretching from the Mittellegi was now above me. To cut through I would have to steer right a little and once through the narrows onto the Lauper Shield it was spacey and exposed. The ice was good now and all I had to do was keep climbing, motivated by the warmth of the sun that would soon put the face into degeneration.

I could see a vague gully line through the rock buttress above me and, moving slightly to the right to pass bad ground, I was soon established directly in the line and straight on up to a snowy arête leading up from the knob crack on the Lauper original finish. Unfortunately the summit ridge was a less than welcome sight, since all the recent snow and winds had built up huge cornices and it was going to be time-consuming to pass them all safely. But I set to work and crossed slowly towards the summit. The sun was blazing on the snows of the W flank. It was 2pm and time to go down. It was to be a very unnerving descent.

The Piz Badile

In 'Perkins', our 30-year-old Land Rover, we slowly chugged back to Chamonix, but the North Face of the Dru looked as if there was still too much snow on it for my liking. I wanted the granite cracks as clear of ice as possible so, leaving the crowds to fight over the routes around Chamonix, we fled south to the Bregaglia. Here we found a quiet campsite in the charming ancient village of Bondo, and there were fewer people, fewer climbers and less hassle. Climbers have written their history into the place and it felt as if the numbers have not been too great to ruin local inquisitive/helpful interest. The guardian of the village-owned campsite, who also owned the local milk co-operative, was only too keen to advise and help on weather and conditions.

Two days later I was at the Sciora hut. Spike and Suds, old Scottish friends, were resting after a great day's climbing and Steve Holland was with me to explore the area. With a reasonable forecast yet a cloudy start, 10 August saw me crossing to the N ridge to reach the start of the route. Rock boots on, down a ramp and across a brutal ice/snow slope bergschrund – then wobbly up to the start of the first corner. There were no pegs as mentioned in the topo, but slight doubts about the route were soon put to one side as the climbing became interesting and my self-confidence returned.

The next few pitches were a delight. My worries about granite slab climbing were totally unfounded and, after passing some of the early bivouacked parties in front, I was soon at the site of the 'snow patch' and the start of the main difficulties. Above me was a team of Germans, one of them stuck in the depths of the corner, while his lower mate, looking decidedly embarrassed, waited impatiently and kept shouting words of encouragement! I sat quietly on a fine ledge – and waited and ate and waited.

Nearly an hour passed before he was out, the third man raced up behind and I started to organise myself to set about the chimney/crack. Although steeper than the rest of the climb, the rock was solid, and as I negotiated my way up under the roof I was very careful to keep my back well out and avoid the downfall of the German lad with his jammed sack. At the belay ledge they were still there, muttering and uneasy. Happily they let me pass and I headed on up the slabs and cracks to lead to the base of the rightward series of chimneys. Passing the time of day with a delightful pair of contented-looking climbers, I set on up the crack and chimney. As I moved up, the clouds started to move down and, as the back of the cracks got wetter, the temperature dropped. I used both sides of the chimney or, when it widened too much, opted for the least slimy side of the green back wall. Once I had emerged from the chimney the wall dried out and after a few more feet I was able to follow a fine traverse line left onto an exposed nose, and so to finish up a brilliantly situated wall to the top. As the clouds turned damp and the lichen-covered rock turned a luminous green, I sat and thought a moment of the many parties down below with still a long way to go.

The Dru

Bondo was great, but we couldn't stay for ever; the weather was fine and, once again, the Dru was calling! Back to the crowds of Chamonix, and the *meteo* now boasted its first *beau temps* of the year. After two days of storms it would turn into four or five days of hot and sultry weather.

I decided to reduce weight by sleeping in the valley, catching the first télépherique and, after doing the climb, descend to the Charpoua hut the same day. Bumping into Marc Twight, an old friend from Nepal in 1986 who was intent on doing something on the Aiguille Sans Nom, we traversed from the Grands Montets together and, bidding him *'bonne chance'*, I left him to his route and descended the glacier to the foot of the Dru.

Three Bulgarians were still thrashing around on the awkward first wall and cracks leading off the ice. They had bivvied under the face and were not in too high spirits. To the sound of their curses, I headed up the horribly loose couloir and then, exchanging boots/crampons for rock boots, set off up the start of the Allain. The narrowing man-trap of a chimney gave food for thought until I decided to climb without my sack and then, assuming neither it nor I had fallen off, haul it up from above. That worked well, although elbows and knees were battered from a loss/lack of technique. I was soon on up and finishing the famous Lambert crack. After the body sucker of a chimney below, it paled into insignificance.

Another steep pitch through roofs and cracks and then a gully line led towards the bottom of the *niche*. After some chat and conversation with two English lads, I decided it was time to finish being sociable and carry on back to work. I had stuck on boot shells and crampons for the *niche* and now, at the top of a snowy couloir, I dispensed with them once again and aimed back towards the steep chimney above. I stopped a minute on the ledge to look down the huge walls of the W face below and, suitably impressed, I traversed left and set off up.

Working up and left I was soon at the base of the famous Fissure Allain. Deciding to use the much preferred Fissure Martinelli, I descended right and managed to get myself well and truly stuck in the Letterbox. Some entertainment later and I was free and contentedly at the top of the Martinelli, up a couple of steep pitches, more grooves, and finally the quartz band and the slab pitch to the hole and the notch. Exchanging photos with some Dutch lads from the American Direct, we set off down.

The descent was fun. We joked and laughed and teamed up again with two Americans, Dan and Dave, who were a little the worse for wear after two days on the Bonatti Pillar and without a sack of bivvy gear dropped on the first day. Once at the Flammes de Pierre, day began turning to night and, without bivvy gear, I raced on down since I wanted to see the descent to the hut in daylight.

But the hut was packed full to the brim. I was offered a can of coke and two blankets to cover me whilst sitting outside! The guardian had finished cooking and people were going to bed. I did likewise. Laid out on a flat grassy ledge, I shivered and star-gazed till the first of the early risers left and I could sneak into their warmed beds .

Back in Chamonix there was no time to rest on my laurels. I had to be in Munich for a trade fair at the beginning of September and, before that, I was keen to try and complete a route on the last of the Big Six.

The Cima Grande

So 'Perkins' was loaded up again, we chugged merrily across Switzerland, through Austria and after a hot climb over the Brenner descended into northern Italy. Soon we were heading excitedly towards the last area we had come to explore – the Dolomites. As we finally ground to a halt in the car-park of the Auronzo hut, we breathed a sigh of relief that our vehicle had made it. And now, through the clearing mist, our reward was spectacular views of rocky peaks and magnificent spires. I felt content and happy to be there.

But I had yet to see my goal: the magnificent North Face of the Cima Grande. On a walk round to look at the base of the great North Face of the Tre Cime, I wondered if I was being over-ambitious, but mentally the commitment was already made and two days later I was on the Comici on the Grande.

I had done the first pillar, which was loose and unpleasant, and now I was faced with a chimney-crack to gain the start of the climbing proper. I felt nervous, the commitment was not yet there, and I could still down climb quite easily. But no – a job had to be done and, taking stock of the situation, I continued up to a ledge and the start of the difficulties. I studied my topo (traced from a recent German guide) and after two attempts I finally established myself well into the first pitch and past the hard move. I felt wooden and awkward, the climbing was not flowing, and it was going to be a slow job. As I worked up the next couple of pitches a rhythm asserted itself and my climbing began to flow. A steep corner-crack, graded as hard as any pitch on the route, went well and I began to feel more positive and confident. As my rhythm returned, my outlook changed and, once more, I felt happy and relaxed at the way things were going. Now there were only a couple more hardish sections to the Kasparek bivouac and easier ground. Things were looking good, the hard climbing was over, but there was still a long way to the top. I studied the topo again and made sure I was on course. The route led into a huge corner system, but there were a couple of options and I was keen to make the right choice. Before long I was well up the corner and getting closer to where the route traverses left above roofs.

But now the way looked less obvious. I had come up a wet corner-crack and I was on a small cave-like ledge in front of a hideous slimy crack/roof above me. The way looked unlikely. I consulted my topo again, but surely all modern traffic didn't come up this wet and slimy corner ... or did it? Up and to my left was the lip of the roof. If I didn't traverse now I would have to go back down and traverse underneath it. But although I could see odd pegs and slings, the rock was poor, so surely they were wrong. A descent and lower traverse seemed unappealing, so I decided I would brave the slime and traverse here.

As I moved up the crack, to my relief a peg appeared and my route-finding was proved correct after all. I gained the arête above and then traversed left on a series of mini-ledges. The situation was exposed and brilliant, the climbing interesting and now I was really getting there. Just a shame about the rain. Whilst the clouds had closed in above, there was still enough clarity to see the floor several hundred metres below – an amazing situation.

The rain increased and my pace started to quicken. As the large spots soaked into the rock, I gained the edge of the traverse and climbed up the last easy pitches. As I crossed to the south side the wind was waiting to greet me; the clouds rolled, the wind roared and spots of rain turned into a torrential downpour.

But I was on my way down. All that mattered was to get down safely. As there was no thunder nor lightning, I took my time and descended with caution. The route was just as the German topo showed it, and I weaved my way, down climbing across the face to the final rock band and gully system to the screes below. As the rain turned to hailstones, my pace quickened again and before long I was bouncing lightheartedly past the sodden tourists towards 'Perkins' and my family.

Epilogue

The first part of my summer's work was over. I had set out to solo climb a route on each of the six great north faces and with the help of many other people I had achieved it. Moreover, I had climbed the routes in a total climbing time of under 24 hours, so I would be able to use my friend Steve's suggested title for my book: *A Hard Day's Summer*.

1993 was to end on a high note. When the manuscript of my book was finished and the summer drew to a close, I was tempted to do one more climb. After renewing my fitness on a route up the N face of the Midi, I waited for a window of good weather and, in November, became the first woman to solo climb the Croz Spur on the Grandes Jorasses. To me the mountains had been gentle; to many others, not so. I was fortunate enough to travel home at the end of the year and to make plans for future dreams and aspirations.

ROUTE INFORMATION

Mountain	Route	Date	Climbing time
Grandes Jorasses	Shroud	17.6.93	2hrs 30 mins
Matterhorn	Schmid	29.6.93	5hrs 30 mins
Eiger	New Route	24.7.93	5hrs 30 mins
Piz Badile	Cassin	10.8.93	2hrs
Dru	Allain	17.8.93	4hrs 45 mins
Cima Grande	Comici	24.8.93	3hrs 30 mins
Grandes Jorasses	Croz Spur	10.11.93	6hrs

NIGEL SHEPHERD

The Glacial Recession

An overview of the diminishing glaciers of the Alps

(Plates 19, 20)

During the last months of 1689 the inhabitants of the vale of Chamouny, nestling in the shadow of Mont Blanc, gathered to discuss the continuing threat posed by the mighty glaciers that intruded into their valley. For nigh on two centuries they had been subservient to the mockery imposed by this tyrant who, devoid of all compassion towards the settlers, had been consistently and steadily destroying their most noble efforts to eke out a fragile existence from farms that clung tenuously to precipitous mountainsides.

The time had come to put an end to this imposition and the misery it wrought. The solution, it was decided by the elders and the church, would be to exorcise the devil living deep within the glacier, destroying all his powers and causing the glaciers to shrivel up and die. Accordingly, a renowned exorcist, Jean d'Arenthon, Bishop of Geneva, was called upon to perform the task and over a period of some weeks the following summer 1690 he set in motion the spells that would destroy the threat for ever.

And how effective it was too. Today the snout of the Bossons glacier, for example, rests some 2km from its position at the turn of this century and is retreating at a rate of more than 50m per year. So too are the Argentière and Tour glaciers. The Bossons is no exception. There are many glaciers throughout Europe that have retreated dramatically in the last 30 years or so and some that are vanishing so quickly at the present time that they will be lost for ever within our own lifetime.

Why? Why is it that suddenly it seems that we are in danger of losing a foreboding yet beautiful part of mountain architecture? Why is it that the pristine white ice faces of yesteryear are now blackened as if by soot and the remaining ice is hard as rock? Why is it that during the summer season of 1988 the freezing level rarely dropped below 4000m? Global warming of course! It's obvious, isn't it? The 'greenhouse effect' and all that ...

The truth of the matter may indeed have something to do with global warming, but that is not the whole truth. It may only be a very small part of the truth. Geologists tell us that as recently as 7000 years ago we had glaciers in Great Britain. Furthermore, what we now know as the Alps was a massive complexity of glaciers with only a few peaks standing above the ice pack. More than that, the entire planet was once covered by ice but gradually, over the millenia, the ice has retreated and permanent snow and ice of the European Alps accounts for something like one thousandth of that found outside Greenland and the Antarctic.

It is mere common sense, therefore, to presume that the melt continues to the present day and, barring drastic climatic changes, will continue to do so until there is no ice left on this planet. It is possible that in a thousand years' time crevasse rescue technique will be a thing of the past – confined to the annals of mountaineering history.

This sad though inevitable fact is, of course, of great concern. However, what is of most concern at the present time is the dramatic speeding up of the melting process which will result in the loss of some glaciers and ice faces we are all familiar with and that some of us may have climbed. But lots of things can happen between now and then.

The most comprehensive research into the current glacial recession in Europe is being conducted by the Swiss. In recent years this research has gathered momentum owing to the important part played by glaciers in the generation of hydroelectricity. Records have been kept annually since 1880 which show that the total surface occupied by the glaciers of the Alps in 1991 was 1342 square kilometres, ie 25% less than the year of the first record.

The responsibility for this research lies with the Commission des Glaciers which was founded in 1893. Information on some 120 glaciers is gathered annually by designated observers and is assimilated at the Ecole Polytechnique Fédérale de Zurich. The information collected concerns movement of glaciers and annual variations, the volume and mass of the ice at certain points and the general topography and altitude of each glacier. The bulk of the more intensive research is concentrated on twelve glaciers that attain a surface area greater than ten hectares. These glaciers include the Aletsch, Corbassière, Trient and Rhône.

The information gathered over the years proves that the advance and retreat of the glaciers can be loosely categorised as cyclical and that the events of the recent past are not new occurrences in the grand scheme of things.

The research conducted takes into account a number of climatic factors that influence the overall behaviour of the glaciers at any one time. Observations over the last ten years or so have shown a dramatic climatic change that has never been more apparent than in the late eighties and early nineties. Winters have generally become drier and colder, with a particularly cold spell and little precipitation during the months of December and January. The latter part of the winters and the early part of the spring have seen particularly high levels of snowfall at all altitudes and regions. Though this snowfall has been higher than average it has come at a time when the ambient air temperature has risen with the change of season; and the mantle of snow, both on the high névés and lower slopes and on the steep faces, has not lingered long. Summers have become uncharacteristically hot for prolonged periods of time. There has been higher than average snowfall in June but, as with the spring snowfall, the ambient temperature is that much warmer, so that the snow does not stay around long enough to become a part of the permanent snowpack but simply melts into the atmosphere or runs off in swollen glacial rivers.

These climatic changes are significant and manifest themselves in reduced glacier movement, decreasing névés and a lack of snow and ice buildup on big faces.

The movement of a glacier is perhaps the most commonly used yardstick by which the layman measures change. Every glacier moves at a different rate depending upon a number of factors. For example, the Aletsch glacier, which is the largest in the European Alps, moves on average per year: 30m on the névés of the Jungfraujoch, 200m at the Konkordiaplatz, 60m at Silbersand and 10-20m at the snout. (This example disproves conclusively the popularly held belief that a glacier moves fastest at its snout.)

The variation in forward movement annually is determined by a number of factors, but in times of heavy precipitation and lower than average temperatures the advance will generally be greatest. Conversely, in warmer climes and lower precipitation, such as in recent years, movement will diminish. In its worst case, such as at the present time, no advance takes place and a general retreat is set in motion.

An example of this can be shown by a comparison of records over the last 20 years. During the years 1965-1970, a period of cold and heavy precipitation, the average speed of movement of the glaciers of the Alps increased by 10%. There followed a period that conformed to the average and then, in the years 1977-1981, the movement increased by about 40%. In some cases, such as the Corbassière glacier below the Grand Combin, the average speed increased by 75%. This corresponds with a period of intense cold and high snowfall in the Alps and is testified by the vast upsurge in the popularity of winter sports in Europe, particularly the sport of skiing and the growth of a lucrative package holiday market and associated business.

The general retreat of the glaciers is now well established and has increased dramatically since 1987. Within Switzerland, the Commission des Glaciers records that out of 110 glaciers observed in 1987 there were 27 advancing and 74 in retreat. In 1990 there were 90 glaciers in retreat and 14 advancing. Taken over the whole number of glaciers observed, the average retreat was 5.1m in 1987 and a massive 9.8m in 1990.

These figures are the quantifiable ones – the ones that are obvious to the casual observer and that can be seen at glacier termini all over the Alps. Other evidence is not quite so apparent. At annual intervals the thickness and density of the glaciers is also measured. To the visitor this decrease is less obvious, though in the case of the Griess glacier, any *habitué* of that area could not fail to notice the dramatic reduction between the years 1988 and 1990, when the thickness of the ice diminished by a massive 227cm overall. This can be compared to the Aletsch at 115cm and the Silvretta glacier at 65cm during the same period. Taken over a term of 20 years, the annual reduction of the Swiss glaciers comes out at 9 million cubic metres per year, though in some years it has reached a high of 16 million cubic metres.

Enough of the figures! What does all this mean to us poor climbers – those of us who hope to preserve the hard-won skills of crevasse rescue and safe glacier travel. In my own short experience of the Alps since the mid-seventies, I have noticed a few significant differences that I am quite sure others have also observed. I remember distinctly the coldness of the nights in early forays to the Alps around 1975. Even camping in the valleys, the water would freeze in billy cans outside the tent and it was almost unheard of to walk out to a climb in the small hours without being wrapped snugly against the cold bite of the crisp air.

I remember, too, being able to walk onto the Bossons glacier along the path leading from the entrance to the Mont Blanc tunnel – a feat totally impossible today, though nonetheless attempted by many tourists. Often the retreat is drastically accentuated; for, once a glacier retreats to steeper ground, gravity plays its part in the overall recession and a miserly retreat of ten metres per year rapidly amounts to many tens of metres as vast amounts come crashing down. The Glacier du Trient which until 1988 had seen very little retreat has now begun to recede with alarming rapidity. This is nowhere more apparent than on the descent from the Cabane de Trient on the Chamonix to Zermatt traverse.

Glacier retreat on the faces is equally alarming. The Welzenbach route on the Grands Charmoz no longer exists, having been reduced to a sliver of ice high up on the face. The lower part, which was testimony to the perfection of the art of stepcutting, is reduced to a grotesque and suicidal heap of rubble. Gone also are the magnificent mixed face routes on Mont Blanc de Cheilon in the Pennine Alps. The sparse grey ice clinging tenuously to the rock is a trivial remnant of a past era.

More striking changes can be seen when comparing old photographs with new scenes taken from the same vantage point. Photos of the Argentière glacier are a remarkable example of this. In the Couttet photo of 1896 (Plate 19) the snout of the glacier encroaches to within a kilometre or so of the village. The rock feature immediately left of the church spire in the recent photo (Plate 20) is clearly evident in the old picture. In comparing the two, the aspect I find most remarkable of all is the prolific way in which the vegetation has established itself in the 97 years between the two photographs. How different the mountains must have been 500 or 1000 years ago ...

Earlier in this study I stated that the changes taking place in the European Alps can be regarded as cyclical in that similar events to those currently taking place have occurred at other times during the last 100 years. The early 1920s was one such period. Statistical analysis of ice samples from other regions of the world shows that there have been mini ice ages in between ice ages; there have been periods of extreme cold lasting as little as 200 years, but enough to give the global ice cover a bit of a boost.

From a core sample taken from near Camp Century in northern Greenland in the early 1970s (a core, incidentally, 4500ft long), scientists were able to ascertain by measuring the weight of oxygen present, that if the patterns of the past were to repeat themselves, we would be at the beginning of another ice age by the 1980s. Current trends disprove this then popularly held opinion which was expostulated convincingly by Nigel Calder in his BBC series *The Weather Machine and the Threat of Ice*.

There is a tendency to become obsessed with blaming the climatic changes and ultimately the glacial retreat and lack of snow in the Alps in recent years on the 'greenhouse effect'. For the time being, though, we can only bide our time to see if it is a short-lived period of warming or if indeed it is a continuing trend. That the glaciers are generally in retreat and have been that way for a couple of centuries cannot be denied. We can only hope that the process of melt will slow down for a while and give us back the pristine white mountains of yesteryear. If not, we will have to change our Alpine seasons to a different time of the year ... or maybe we could just call the present incumbent of the post of Bishop of Geneva to reverse the spell.

LINDSAY GRIFFIN

In the Playground of the Porcellizzo

The majority of British visitors to the head of the Bregaglia's Porcellizzo valley arrive tired but outrageously happy. They have just completed a much sought after north-south traverse of the Piz Badile, either via its elegant and ultra-classic North Ridge or the world famous Cassin route on the NE face.

Most will make the lengthy journey back to the campsites of Bondo or Vicosoprano in a bit of a daze, having failed to notice the somewhat shorter though equally fine climbing to be found on the sunny Italian side of the range. Here the granite is almost universally golden brown and has none of the rockfall scars that are clearly visible on several peaks above the Swiss Bondasca or Albigna valleys. Indeed, on a number of routes the granite is of a quality rarely surpassed elsewhere in the Alps.

In high season the Gianetti hut will generally be full of gregarious Italians; for the Badile, although by no means the highest peak in the region, exerts an overwhelming magnetism towards the majority of visiting Alpinists, and the S face, which begins less than one hour's gentle boulder-hopping above the hut, provides the easiest route to, and descent from, the summit. Its original ascent in 1867 also marked the first of many significant contributions to Alpine history by a certain W A B Coolidge, when he was a mere 16 years of age. In contrast to the hustle of summer, the joys of autumn in the Bregaglia can include the apparent non-existence of other climbers and an atmospheric clarity rarely encountered during July and August.

With this reasoning I persuaded non-Alpinist but experienced rock-climber and close neighbour, Peter Hargreaves, to forsake both his wife and the comforts of the Miner's Arms, in order to travel to Milan in late October. Subsequently, we were ferried by public transport to a pleasantly lifeless San Martino, after which we had to walk. Limited to only eight days on the hill, our sacks should have felt manageable. In retrospect the combined amount of food and spirit carried (the latter for Peter, you understand) would probably have kept us in good shape for well over two weeks, and not surprisingly we had made little impression on the lower Porcellizzo before darkness fell.

We slept out that night under a clear, still sky. Despite an altitude of merely 1800m our water bottles (though not the duty-free whisky) were well frozen by the following morning, but the brilliant sunlight, truly enhancing the autumnal colours, soon warmed our bodies as we soldiered northwards towards unfamiliar granite spires. Only a lavishly constructed path gave any hint of the popularity of this location during the summer months.

We had been enjoying this marvellous solitude for more than an hour when, much to our surprise, snippets of conversation came floating down on the cool breeze. A few minutes later and we were off-loading our sacks onto some convenient lumps of granite and engaging in cheerful conversation with a thirty-something German couple. They were on their way home to Stuttgart after a cold night in the hut and an early morning spent taking photographs for a forthcoming magazine feature. The woman was attractive and quiet, letting the man do the talking in almost perfect English. He seemed eager to impart his extensive local knowledge and swamped us with facts, only two of which stayed in my mind.

'The superb granite slabs of the Mello valley may attract a wide international audience,' he stated with Teutonic authority, 'but very few climbers other than Italians make it up to the mountains on this side of the range.'

We talked loosely around vague objectives, but I could see he had something more positive in mind. Suddenly his eyes narrowed and he looked at me with an expression that implied I should take his next statement very seriously.

'If the weather stays fair, you must, *you simply must*, do the Vinci route on the Cengalo: it's one of the finest rock climbs in the Central Alps.'

I should add that, part-way through our conversation, he had delved into his sack and produced a plastic bottle, three-quarters full of Italian red wine. We accepted out of politeness, of course, but the result, on almost empty stomachs, was devastating. It took another four staggering hours to reach the haven of the Rifugio Attilio Piacco which forms the small but comfortable winter refuge for the rather grandiose edifice of the CAI's Gianetti hut.

The weather did indeed remain fine and an ascent of the easy Piz Porcellizzo rewarded us with stupendous views of autumn clarity along the whole Alpine chain; from glimpses of the Brenta rock towers and Adamello ice cap, through the Pennine and Ecrins massifs, to the faintly discernible form of distant Monte Viso. We began next day with an ascent of the Direct SSE Pillar of the Punta Torelli, making a classic British Alpine start by leaving the hut shortly after midday. In late October the amount of daylight is limited: so, not surprisingly, twilight descended whilst we were stumbling back across the moraine.

The Pillar is a highly recommendable outing, given to us by the well-known local activist Carlo Mauri in 1955. Originally V+ and A1, it has long been climbed without aid, and the hardest move – a left-facing layback round a small roof – now just warrants VI. The entire crux pitch is steep, intricate, on wonderful rock and finishes with an exposed belay. Best stop here, even though the stance is hard to find; to continue would lead to serious rope drag. The penultimate pitch is a steepish slab on typically compact, knobbly Bregaglia granite. I suppose it is about 20m high, but it feels more and was avoided on all the early ascents. It may be only V, but there is not a glimmer of protection, so don't even contemplate falling.

South of the Torelli and quite close to the hut lies the dramatic monolith of the Torre Vecchia. Who could resist an ascent to its spectacular summit? The appearance of utter inaccessibility when viewed from the hut is deceptive. To the north an almost horizontal ridge runs into the boulder slopes of the Torelli and gives an easy scramble to the top. Not surprisingly, there are lines all over its steep faces of clean golden granite, but the classic is still the 150m SE Pillar climbed solo in 1954 by Giulio Fiorelli from San Martino. It gives four pitches of excellent climbing with maximum difficulties of V.

The next two days were frustrating. Cloud shrouded the peaks, though fortunately produced little more than a slight snow flurry. By the second afternoon the sun was beginning to break weakly through the murk and we ventured south on the *Sentiero Roma* – the popular high-level route that makes a magnificent west-east traverse below the frontier ridge, crossing no less than seven cols. An hour and a half later saw us and the slowly improving weather reach the Barbacan South Pass. Below lay the locked and shuttered Omio hut, and close by the local *aiguille* – Punta Milan. The latter had always appeared quite spectacular in photographs, bearing a strong resemblance to the more famous Dibona or Aiguille de la Tsa. At close quarters it seemed surprisingly small and not a little vegetated. Yet it is still an elegant, airy summit and should be reached via the classic *Ho Chi Minh route* (IV+) on the SE face.

We turned to the Cima del Barbacan and reached its exposed summit via a frightening series of fearsome moves over large wet blocks and slippery grass. They tell me it's II+ in the dry.

A starlit night gave way to a crisp clear morning and we took this opportunity to head for the Cengalo. The S ridge presents a magnificent fin of golden granite leading to the south summit or Punta Angela. It is possible to climb the entire ridge from its base: a 25-pitch undertaking that few parties complete. Normally the crest is reached at about one-third height, leaving 13 pitches that include both the main difficulties and the finest climbing. This section was first led directly along the crest by the brilliant but little known Italian Alpinist, Alfonso Vinci, at the start of the Second World War. A short career in high-standard climbing resulted in several major Bregaglia and Dolomite routes, before he turned his adventurous instincts towards other forms of exploration and headed off to the Amazon jungle in search of diamonds.

Vinci used aid, but the climb is now free with an overall grade of TD and a technical crux of VII–. Actually, there are only three pitches of VI or above, making this a route that will appeal to the mountaineer rather than the rock athlete. What *is* unusual for a route of this type is that every pitch, irrespective of grade (and the easiest is a mere III+), is superb and gives varied climbing that is often sensationally positioned.

I carried a vaguely drawn topo which I kept carefully hidden, juggling the lead so that I arrived nicely below the crux. Tying firmly into the belay anchors I beckoned my man to the front. This seemed a most sensible move at the time as the first 25ft or so looked totally runnerless. The pitch was superb – a succession of delightfully precarious moves that I thoroughly enjoyed with the rope above. Unfortunately, I paid for my cowardice by later having to lead the other two tricky pitches. Although half a grade less in standard, one of these actually contained the hardest move on the route.

Do go and climb it, but remember that flared and shallow cracks are typical of this part of the world, and a selection of Friends 1-3 will prove extremely useful. We wore light windproofs and were warm whilst climbing in the sun, but a hand feeling for holds on the shady flank of the ridge rapidly became chilled.

Reaching the top after seven hours, we quickly embarked on the rappel descent. It turned out to be complex, serious, and judging by the gear in place seldom used, though I suppose the fact that it was pitch dark for much of the way may have influenced my feelings. Ascents of the S ridge tend to be infrequent and, despite reports of a partially improved line of rappel anchors, a recent party still felt the descent rather unsafe. In retrospect, with the current paucity of snow on the normal W ridge descent, we would have been far quicker going over the top, even in rock boots. The only other thing you ought to know, should you ever be returning at around the same hour, is that the Gianetti hut in the middle of the night bears a remarkable similarity to any one of the multitude of large boulders that litter the surrounding area.

Winter arrived dramatically the following day, allowing us only to dream of what might have been. As we passed our bivouac spot of seven nights earlier, almost nine inches of snow lay thickly on the sagging roof of the old cowshed. The many other attractive objectives, accessible from the Gianetti hut, would have to wait for another year.

The greatest exposure on the *Vinci route* had occurred when perched high above the sheer E face, and in 1992 two fine lines were added to this area of splendid rock. Both routes were climbed by parties which included the current local hotshot, Gianluca 'Rampikino' Maspes. *Dalai Lama* more or less follows the right side of the prominent pillar (400m: VII), and the huge dièdre to the left is taken by – you guessed it – *Gran Diedro*, also at VII.

In contrast, the SW face of the Cengalo is a little too disjointed to provide any major lines, although the most direct, put up in 1962 with 50 pegs and 32 bolts, is now reported to give a fine, nine-pitch free climb at VI+. To the SE of the Cengalo the *Sentiero Roma* reaches the wild upper cirque of the Ferro valley by crossing the Passo Camerozzo. South of this pass lies the Pizzo Camerozzo – a nice little peak in its own right – and from its summit a long and almost horizontal ridge continues south for some distance to the Punta Bertani. The crest is quite narrow in parts, the climbing often exposed, and the flanks offer no escape. Locally it is considered a very worthwhile medium-grade expedition (IV), but this sort of climbing is no longer fashionable and nowadays it is attempted much less often.

Impressive lines on the W face of the Bertani prove on closer inspection to be disappointingly easy and rather lichenous, but the steep smooth walls overlooking the Ferro valley have recently been scrutinised by two of the most prolific modern activists of the region – Sonja Brambati and Paolo Vitali. This dynamic husband and wife team, who live just down the road alongside the limestone spires of the Grigna, has created many new routes in the last ten years. *Asterix* (VII–) and *Obelix* (VI and A1), which take parallel and bolt-protected lines up the 300m SE face of the Bertani, are just two of their many fine offerings.

The Bertani and, to its south, the Punta Moraschini are topographically referred to as Monte Scione or 'Whirlwind Peak'. The Moraschini is a striking summit with a conspicuous rounded pillar on the NW face. Seen from the Gianetti hut the pillar looks remarkably blank and is guarded at its base by overhanging yellow walls. This inhospitable appearance no doubt put off any serious inspection until the first ascent in 1979, when local guru Giuseppe 'Popi' Miotti, partnered by two other well-known names in Bregaglia climbing, Madonna and Merizzi, took a closer look. They were amazed by the relative ease of the ascent and the quality of the climbing, which went completely free (mainly IV and V with a crux – a delicate traverse round a roof – of VI). Despite successfully climbing this feature at the height of summer, the team found that the peak really did live up to its name and they christened their climb *The Pillar of the Polar Wind*. It is now considered a modern classic of the valley, although it still receives relatively few ascents.

So, what of the Badile? The shortest and, together with the sombre NW face, least frequented side of the mountain is the SW wall. It was first climbed in 1904 by a disgusting couloir towards the left side of the face, but the most alluring feature is a steep and conspicuous pillar rising above the central amphitheatre. It was left to local boy Giulio Fiorelli to make the first ascent in 1957 and so create the best route on the wall. Again, some aid was used, but the crux pitch, turning a yellow roof on the right side of the pillar, is now climbed free at VI– .

The sunny SE wall is a much more attractive prospect and sports the very popular *Molteni route*, which finishes fractionally to the left of the bright yellow Radaelli bivouac hut close to the summit. Mario Molteni created a number of worthwhile routes before his demise after the first ascent of the NE face, but this is often considered his finest – linking the weak points on the wall by a splendid piece of route-finding. Several local experts feel it is equal, if not superior in quality, to any other route of a similar standard on the Italian side of the range. The last four or five pitches leading onto, then up, the crest of the pillar immediately right of the normal route are simply superb.

There are now six lines on this face, though more than half use the Molteni start, owing to the difficulty of creating an independent line through the barrier of overhangs that characterise much of the base area of this wall. The most difficult free climbing is currently found on *La Muchacha de las Bragas de Oro* – a 1991 route by José Maria Jimeno (a visiting Spaniard who appears to have spent a large part of his active life on the bold slabs of the Mello valley) which climbs the small pillar at the right extremity of the face (300m: VII). However, one or two of the existing routes still contain sections of aid and must nowadays be prime targets for high-standard, all-free ascents.

Almost 160 years ago, Douglas Freshfield, that great explorer of peaks and passes in this wild region, spoke of 'granite buttresses so bold that grandeur is the last element the scenery could be accused of wanting'. Climbing standards may have risen, but the sentiment remains unchanged.

1. Alps 4000: Simon Jenkins and Martin Moran basking in contentment back
at the Schreckhorn hut after the 16-hour traverse of the Lauteraargrat.
(Ian Dring) (p7)

Left
22. Spacewalking on the N ridge of the Weisshorn. (*Martin Moran*)

Below
23. Traversing the Kanzel on the Zinalrothorn. (*Martin Moran*)
(p7)

The Aiguilles du Diable. (*Angus Andrew*) (p7)

The final steps: Simon nearing the summit of the Barre des Ecrins,
13 August 1993. (*Martin Moran*) (p7)

26. Martin Moran and Simon Jenkins on the top of the Aiguille du Jardin.
(*Martin Welch*) (p7)

27. Avalanche on the S face of K2. (*Roger Payne*) (p54)

28. Julie-Ann Clyma climbing up to Camp 1
on the Abruzzi Spur.
(*Roger Payne*) (p54)

29. Roger Payne climbing on mixed ground
between Camp 1 and Camp 2.
(*Julie-Ann Clyma*) (p54)

30. Julie-Ann Clyma at 7000m on the Abruzzi Spur. (*Roger Payne*) (p54)

Left

31A. The North Tower of Paine:
Andy Perkins on pitch two.
(*Jerry Gore*) (p58)

Below

31B. The Towers of Paine.
(*Jerry Gore*) (p58)

ANDY MACNAE
Avoiding the Chamonix Trade Routes

This article is a sequel to a talk I gave at the Alpine Club Symposium 'Return to the Alps' held at Plas y Brenin in November 1992. My topic then, as now, was crowd avoidance in the Mont Blanc massif and the pursuit of mountaineering routes of high quality and accessible grade. Here I am going to take a potter about the range, restricting myself to the major peaks and pointing out some little gems of strangely low popularity.

I'll start on Mont Blanc – where else? The Miage face, huge and lonely, gives a number of good, but serious, routes and is bounded by one classic, the *Tournette Spur* (PD) which leads directly to Mont Blanc's summit. It's 1000m long and, with some danger both from stone and sérac fall, not to be underestimated in spite of its lowly grade. You will almost certainly have this beautiful route all to yourself.

Moving round, we come to the Frêney and Brouillard faces which to many epitomise remoteness and commitment. Only on the Central Pillar of Frêney and perhaps on the Innominata are you likely to see other parties. For the full experience, approach via the Eccles hut which can be reached in 7-9 hours from the Val Veni. Having walked up from the valley (overnight is best) one has the great satisfaction of crossing the range under one's own power. From the Eccles hut, the Brouillard is the more accessible of these two faces. An early start is essential, since stonefall often rakes the base of the pillars. The Central Pillar gives splendid rock-climbing on both the *Original* (1965 TD+/ED1) and the more recent *Etica Bisbetica* (ED1), whilst on the Red Pillar the *Gabarrou/Long Directissima* (ED3) looks very, very good but distinctly testing. On completing these routes, to gain its full flavour, the Brouillard ridge should be followed to the summit. But this makes a long day and it's no place to get caught out.

The Frêney is a little awkward to reach from the Eccles hut and the approach can suffer stonefall, but it's well worth the effort. The classic Central Pillar is the best route here, but sadly often busy. For the honed, the *Jori Bardill* (ED2/3) offers an excellent alternative, with most people finding a liberal use of aid essential.

On the right-hand pillar is the fine *Gervasutti route* (TD+). The approach is threatened by stonefall but once you are on the pillar the climbing is very good. Just around the corner from the Frêney is perhaps the finest crag of them all: the Eckpfeiler or *Grand Pilier d'Angle*. Admittedly I have something of a soft spot for this crag, but few will disagree that here 'real' climbing is to be found at its best.

The *Cecchinel/Nomine route* and the *Dufour/Fréhel* might attract a bit of traffic but you would expect to be alone on the brilliant *Bonatti/Gobbi* (ED1).

True it has a little loose rock but that doesn't mean you need to pull on it. And of course there is the grand prize: *Divine Providence* (ED3/4). This has become something of a Brit playground, with three (or four) of the first dozen ascents, including the first complete winter ascent, being British. There's life in the old dogs yet. Note I said complete – by that I mean going over the summit of Mont Blanc. It's what the Grand Pilier routes are all about. 900m of techno climbing, then 600m of often gnarly snow leading to the top of Europe's highest mountain.

At this point the mighty Peuterey ridge must be mentioned. Climbed in its entirety, it's still one of the greats, whilst routes on its component peaks, particularly the Aiguille Noire, can be distinctly adventurous experiences. Continuing on, we pass the Brenva face, but I won't dwell on that except to note that *Route Major* (TD–) is amongst the less travelled of Rébuffat's *100 Plus Belles Courses*. Instead, I'll move on to Mont Maudit's SE face and the splendid *Crétier Direct* (TD). Definitely another 'real' route and when the snow mushrooms are in bloom a rather exciting one. A word about the routes immediately to the right (including the *Polish route*). Current summer conditions seem to leave them increasingly exposed to stonefall, so be careful. The *Kagami Spur* (Polish start) is a safer and very good option.

On Mont Maudit's E face the *Androsace Pillar* is a totally compelling line with a couple of excellent variations and I can't understand why it is not climbed more often. If the ED2 grade puts you off, how about the *Central Spur* (TD–)? The rock is good but be sure to be on it early.

I'm going to skip past Mont Blanc du Tacul and its satellites on account of the summer crowds. In a similarly controversial vein, I'll also avoid the Aiguilles, since they are basically rock climbs. There are exceptions: *Nostradamus* (ED2) is a big tick and the new *Twight/Parkin* (1992), also on the Pèlerins, is certainly not mere rock-climbing – but I can't mention everything.

And so to the Drus. Firstly, the Petit Dru, where the good routes are mobbed and the less good are downright dangerous (for most of the summer I would include the classic N face in the latter category). But have you considered the Grand Dru? Check out its south side; you might be both surprised and impressed.

Just next door is the Pic Sans Nom. All the routes on its NW face are good but pride of place must go to yet another Gabarrou route – the *Directissima*, at EC3. It's hard, both on rock and ice, but quite superb and one of the very best. Dominating the Sans Nom is the Aiguille Verte. Its *Nant Blanc Face Direct* (TD), when in condition, is one of the finest mixed routes around. On the whole the Verte is a very quiet hill. The fact that getting off can be more nerve-racking than getting up probably has something to do with it.

On Les Droites the *NE Spur Direct* (ED1), whilst not being exactly untravelled, is still a must and a lot quieter than the Walker (and, I think, better). To the left is the *Bergland Pillar* (TD) which gives apparently good rock-climbing and, considering its fine line, this would be an exceedingly cunning choice for the aspiring TD climber.

The Courtes is of course very well travelled, but I must point out the NE spur (D+). It's a wonderful line and remarkably quiet. The rock is a bit poor at times, but you can't have everything. Challenging at the grade.

And so on to the Grandes Jorasses. The E face is one of the least frequented major walls in the range. Its best route is Gervasutti's greatest creation. At ED2 it was truly ahead of its time. The face is bounded by two major ridges. The SE or Tronchey (TD) is very long and very much a wilderness experience and a big undertaking. Shorter, but no give-away, is the Hirondelles (NE) ridge (D+), better known but still likely to be a lonely experience. On the wonderful N face, only the Walker and Croz are busy. In a normal summer, ie with *The Shroud* out of condition, the best alternative is probably the *Croz Direct* (ED2) which is actually much safer than the Croz, being sheltered from stonefall once the crest of the spur is reached.

Whilst in the area the Petites Jorasses must be covered. On its W face the *Czech route* (TD) gives an excellent and adventurous contrast to the overused *Classic route*. No pegs and the odd dubious belay add to the atmosphere. On the E face there are a number of superb slabby rock climbs, with the original *Bonatti route* (TD+) being the best. The S ridge (D–) gives a lovely climb which, if it were in a more frequented part of the range, would be mobbed. The same could perhaps be said of the *British route* (D) on the W face and SW ridge of the nearby Aiguille de Leschaux. The rock might occasionally be suspect, but it's a worthwhile route to a rarely visited summit. Another is the Aiguille de Talèfre. The routes on its NW face are reminiscent of those on the N face of Les Courtes. The *Dufour route* (TD) is particularly recommended.

Mont Gruetta, together with its satellite Petit Mont Gruetta, hosts a high concentration of excellent rock climbs on good granite. Approaches can be long and complex and as such they are very much mountaineering routes. On Petit Mont Gruetta, three routes are recommended: the *British* (TD), the *Barthassat/Emery* (TD) and the *Grassi/Meneghin* (TD–). On Mont Gruetta itself how about *Pilastro del Sorriso* (TD) and the E face *Original route* (TD+)?

At this point I'll begin to draw to a close, otherwise I might go on for ever. There are a lot I haven't covered – the Chardonnet, for instance. Perhaps I should mention its quieter S side where the *Capucins Buttress Direct* is the best line. And what about the Petit Clocher du Portalet, a uniquely impressive bit of rock, and its steep, steep rock climbs? Or the NNE face on the Aiguille d'Argentière, or ... But no, I'd best stop there.

I must finish with a word about objective dangers. I have been careful to list routes which, unless I've said otherwise, are likely to be *relatively* safe. But conditions change, especially in recent years, and so a degree of judgement must be exercised when going for these less travelled routes; just the sort of judgement that should be used on any mountain route but which seems too often forgotten on the over-equipped and over-used trade routes. So keep eyes and mind open and enjoy the massif as it was meant to be enjoyed.

JERRY LOVATT

Thomas Ford Hill: An Alpine Footnote

While the name Thomas Ford Hill is not entirely unknown to Alpine historians, it is only recently that the full picture of his involvement in the story of the first ascent of Mont Blanc has come to light. Hill's extensive manuscript diary has been in the possession of the family since his death in 1795 and his descendant Dr Edward Ford has recently started work on transcribing it. I am indebted to Dr Ford for supplying the relevant sections of the journal and for permitting their use in this article.

Brown and de Beer, in their definitive work *The First Ascent of Mont Blanc*,[1] provide a tantalising glimpse of the activities on the mountain of Thomas Ford Hill, one of the earliest of its British explorers. Their account is tantalising in the sense that it introduces this otherwise totally unknown traveller, gives him an interesting supporting role in the story of one of the greatest events in the history of mountaineering but, through lack of documentation, is unable to offer confirmation even of the month in which Hill's activities on the mountain were taking place.

In 1786 Hill made his second visit to the Chamonix valley. Two years earlier, he had ascended to Montenvers in the company of a large party including one M. Le Cointe, a banker from Geneva. From Montenvers, Hill and Le Cointe climbed further towards the base of the Charmoz. On their descent, it would appear that they took too direct a line, straight towards the Mer de Glace; while Hill recognised the danger and retraced his steps, Le Cointe insisted on continuing. Sadly, he did not return and his body was found the next day in what Hill identifies as 'a valley called the Grand Chenot'.

Nothing daunted by the tragic experience of his first visit, Hill returned to the valley in 1786, arriving in Chamonix on the 1st of August. On the 2nd he ascended the Brévent, and on the 3rd he paid a visit to M. Jaquet (Exchaquet) of Servoz to inspect the latter's celebrated model of Mont Blanc. It would appear that a plot was hatched at this meeting to make an attempt to cross the Col du Géant to Courmayeur, and on the 5th they set out via Montenvers for a bivouac at the Couvercle. The following day they ascended the Glacier du Tacul to an unspecified point where 'the chasms became too numerous to permit us to proceed'.

Brown and de Beer note that Exchaquet blamed their failure on the slow climbing of Hill. The latter's journal, however, takes a somewhat different view, indicating that 'Mr. Jaquet' maintained that it was too difficult and that they should return to Chamonix.

Thus, Hill descended to the valley and passed through or close to Chamonix on the day before Paccard and Balmat set out for their bivouac on the Montagne de la Côte. He continued via Bionnassay to Contamines, where he found his companions Hardy and Hillyard. Together, the three of them proceeded to Courmayeur on the 7th. Hill only identifies one of the guides who accompanied him on this trip to Courmayeur. This was the celebrated Jean-Marie Couttet, doyen of Chamonix guides of the period and regular guide to de Saussure. Brown and de Beer indicate that one of the other two was Pierre Balmat and the second probably Jean-Laurent Jordanay.

On the 9th of August, totally unaware of the momentous event taking place on the other side of the mountain, Hill, accompanied by his friend Hillyard and the three guides, set off to attempt Mont Blanc. He wrote in his diary: 'Mount the mountain or Aiguille called here the Montagne de Friti (Mont Fréty), one of the points of Mont Blanc on this side, with Mr Hillyard of Lincolnshire. Took three guides and provisions to lie a night, to mount the Mont Blanc if possible.'

In 1786 it was clearly something of a forlorn hope that one might ascend Mont Blanc from the south side. However, on the same day as the mountain was being climbed for the first time, Hill and his party did achieve the distinction of making the first known ascent by travellers of the Col du Géant from Courmayeur. A later section of the journal indicates that Hill, while recognising the impossibility of anything like a direct ascent from the Col, felt that it would still be feasible 'by making a large circuit, and lying on the mountain among the rocks, for which we were prepared ... '. Hillyard, however, was apparently having none of this. Thus, after two hours of exploration of the Col, they descended to Courmayeur and relative obscurity, while two explorers on the north side of the range were descending to Chamonix and their unique place in the history of mountaineering.

REFERENCE

1   T Graham Brown and Sir Gavin de Beer, *The First Ascent of Mont Blanc*. Oxford University Press, 154-156, 1957.

Expeditions

RICK ALLEN

Dhaulagiri on Cabbage Soup

(Plates 12–14)

I first caught a glimpse of the 'white mountain' in 1980, walking over from the valley of the Kali Gandaki to enter the Annapurna sanctuary. Above the trees a great white trapezoid hovered on the horizon in the early morning light. Twelve years later I was congratulating Sergei Efimov on the success of his team on the E ridge of Cho Oyu and suggesting that we put together a joint expedition to Nepal, when he mentioned Dhaulagiri. The mental picture returned and I said yes.

Along with most other visitors to central Nepal I had seen the S face of Dhaulagiri, a prodigiously dangerous wall of snow and ice which repulsed Messner and Habeler. Our aspirations were directed at the N face, lying between the normal route of the NE ridge by which Diemberger made the first ascent in 1960 and the much tried NW ridge which eventually succumbed to siege tactics a decade later.

Hard currency was probably not going to be one of the major contributions of my Russian friends, and I knew that I would need to be more organised and better focused in my drive for financial support than ever before. The net result of my efforts was absolutely zero for sponsors, media interest, grants and, virtually, gear. Who had ever heard of Dhaulagiri anyway? Fortunately, Sergei did find some companions who were able to share the costs and we assembled in Kathmandu in March 1993.

Nepali liaison officers know that most British and all Russian expeditions are low on tangible reward and a joint Russian–British team was sure to be a shoestring outfit. Mr Ram came to eye us up at the offices of Mustang Trekking but accepted his charge anyway and proved to be a resilient companion as far as Base Camp.

Our approach from the roadhead at Baglung took us away from the busy trekking route of the Kali Gandaki and up the little frequented valley of the Myagdi Khola. The villages have a subsistence economy and our Tamang porters hired in Kathmandu needed their own food supplies. One night we observed huge hillside fires burning out of control. These appeared to have been started deliberately as a quick and wasteful means of making charcoal for sale in Pokhara, a very disturbing development for the area. After a week we encountered late snow lying at the treeline at about 3500m and we paid off 50 porters, retaining 10 to carry our gear in relays onto the Chondarban glacier. Gear and bonuses were not enough to retain the loyalty of our remnant; they needed food and fuel and our carefully calculated supplies were decimated in three days.

Base Camp was established on the glacier beneath the N face on 8 April and we examined our objective. The northerly aspect of Dhaulagiri which greeted Herzog's reconnaissance party in 1950 as they crossed French Pass is forbidding. A great ice shelf at about 6000m cascades down the bottom third of the face in a jumble of icefalls. Above the shelf an icefield rises to meet a 400m rock barrier. Above the rock a fringe of séracs threatens most of the face, barring access to the summit snowfields. A French party had reached the ice shelf a few years ago but no other attempts on the face are recorded. However, Sergei had done his homework and we thought that we could trace a line up the centre that was neither too dangerous nor too technical. The rock wall is seamed by a prominent rightward-slanting ramp leading to a horizontal break which forms a characteristic '7' shape. Above this the sérac barrier is absent, eliminating the major danger on the face. A sharp, snow-covered moraine arête appeared to offer a route through the lower icefalls and after a day of camp construction we embarked on the face.

Our team consisted of six Russian climbers, two Georgians and one Brit, plus our Russian doctor and my wife who accompanied us as trekking members. Although I was nominally joint leader, Sergei was unquestionably in charge. He would discuss plans with us all and take differing views into account but he had the final word. Expeditions to Alaska, Everest, Kangchenjunga, Cho Oyu and Nanga Parbat, as well as all the 7000m peaks in the former USSR, gave him a depth of experience matched by few of his contemporaries. Two seasons climbing with him had given me respect for both his abilities and his judgement but on Dhaulagiri he also demonstrated mastery of budgets and diplomacy – a truly great expedition leader.

All the climbing members set off on the rib winding up amongst the icefalls. As the moraine narrowed into an acute arête, which shed snow and rubble alternately to right and left, I wondered why my companions seemed less ill at ease than I was. I suspect that the Caucasus consists largely of material like this. During a two-day excursion we were able to get tents to the edge of the zone of séracs where the ice shelf breaks up and felt satisfied with our progress.

We could not claim to be a truly alpine-style expedition but for our numbers we were certainly light-weight. Dhaulagiri was the only permit we had so that was where we acclimatised, pushing our tents higher on each excursion and leaving behind snow-holes or tents at the previous high points. Ropes were fixed only on séracs and crevasse walls. Reascending these ropes was a revelation, as my companions used one jumar and one hand and simply walked up the ice walls with full rucksacks. The sole representative of British mountaineering was reduced to sack hauling when the walls began to impend and was in danger of developing an acute sense of inferiority.

Four excursions over three weeks took us across the ice shelf and up the icefield to a narrow ledge hacked out below the rock wall at 7300m. One severe afternoon squall caused us to bivouac early but the weather generally remained stable, in spite of radio reports from the Everest region of climbers disappearing in storms. We climbed as three ropes of three much of the time and divided between two home-made hoop tents at night.

Russian mountaineering seems to have developed on the basis of strong regional clubs, overlaid by a system of training and competition at a national level. A strong competitive element was present in the selection of teams for major expeditions in the past. Some of my companions were exceptionally gifted products of that process: Valery Pershin, now a rock-climbing trainer, Sergei Bogomolov, a sports coach, and Ivan (Vanya) Plotnikov, who leads climbing and rafting excursions in the Siberian Altai. While Western and especially British alpinists focus on the 'pair' as the basic unit in the mountains, my Russian friends were more team orientated, happy to function in ropes of three, four or five as the terrain changed or someone wanted to drop back for a rest. There was no subtle jockeying for a chance to go for the summit; it was assumed that we would all go for it together. This goes a long way to explaining the formidable success record of Soviet expeditions in the 1980s on which a very high proportion of members summited.

A different climbing culture is not assimilated overnight and occasionally I simply managed to blend the worst of my rope management habits with the worst of theirs but for the most part things went smoothly. I was undoubtedly considered lazy for not getting up early to dig the tents out but a brew in the morning was always my first priority.

Therein lay the source of a running argument which we never satisfactorily resolved. I am utterly convinced that the more liquid I can consume at altitude the better my body will like me and the further it will go. This is anything but an extreme or eccentric view amongst my acquaintances but to Sergei it was a Western fad.

'You want more tea?', he would ask, as Oliver Twist stretched out an empty mug. 'This is not necessary.' In vain I watched for signs of weakness in my dehydrated companions as we gained height, while I survived by drinking the washing-up water (sic).

Our food on the mountain was basic but substantial, almost identical to food at Base Camp with a few nuts, raisins and smoked Volga fish thrown in. A consignment of gas canisters had vanished in transit from Llanberis so we relied entirely on petrol stoves and lightweight pressure cookers to prepare a stew of cabbage and potatoes or rice each evening. This Tilman-esque existence suited me well and I had to agree with Sergei when he said that he couldn't understand how British climbers survived on a diet of muesli bars.

After four days of rest we packed our sacks on 5 May with food and petrol for nine days and straggled out of Base Camp under our burdens. Nights in snow caves at previous high points gave me welcome hours of sleep, a sure sign of effective acclimatisation. However, Merab, one of our Georgian friends, passed the night at 7300m in pain and anxiety and he decided that he could not risk continuing. His countryman Gia renounced his chance of the summit to escort his friend down in the morning.

Seven of us moved on into the ramp system that cut across the lower rock wall, moving quickly at first on ropes fixed the previous evening by Sergei B. and Vanya. The back pair recovered the ropes and fed them up through the chain of climbers to the leader who fixed each pitch after leading it. In this way we moved almost continuously up the mixed pitches of Scottish III to a horizontal break. Here the petrol stove was fired up for a midday brew. The lead was then taken by Alexei Lebedikhin, a metallurgist from Sverdlovsk, all of whose gear with the exception of his boots was home made. He adjusted the laces which held on his personally welded crampons and set off on snowy rock which steepened into Scottish IV. His *tour de force* that afternoon took us to a rocky ledge at 7600m and while we dug out boulders and gravel for two tents he calmly descended the ropes to recover his sack.

The next morning Sergei E. led us almost horizontally towards a tongue of the summit snowfield which bypassed the hanging séracs to the left. In one and a half days we had cracked the crucial rock wall by the 'route of 7' and, as we sat in the snow to brew up, the summit seemed suddenly within our grasp. I pushed on up the snow, breaking trail in a slow rhythm towards a shelf that would accommodate our tents.

Sergei E., Sergei B., Alexei and I set off early towards the rocky ridge and after an hour Vanya caught up with us. Valery was still in his tent, apparently discussing with Boris Sedusov the merits of continuing. Boris was our least experienced high-altitude climber and had already suffered cold problems in his hands and feet. However, he did not lack strength or determination and the pair eventually set off in mid-morning. Our group of five reached the summit of Dhaulagiri at 11am on 11 May in gathering cloud and strong winds. We snatched some photos in the intense cold and descended quickly, meeting Valery and Boris at the crest of the ridge. In spite of the fierce winds, they were also able to reach the summit and descend to the tents safely.

That night the wind shook our home-made tents in paroxysms of cracking fabric and I was convinced that it would burst into our precarious cocoon. Boris moved over to share the warmth of a full tent because he was deeply chilled and I dozed with my boots on in case the fabric ripped.

The storm moderated in the morning enough to begin the tricky descent of the wall but there was much delay as ropes were passed down the chain. Boris's crampons repeatedly came loose and he lost all feeling in his hands as he attempted to fasten them. By mid-afternoon we had only reached the foot of the rock wall but Boris was in a state of exhaustion and four of us remained with him there while Vanya and Sergei B. continued down. We had left our single bottle of oxygen at this ledge and Boris was able to regain some strength with its help. The descent continued for another day and a half, as we helped our frostbitten companion off the mountain and fought to retain our own concentration against creeping fatigue.

Porters were already waiting for us at Base Camp, where the food had virtually run out, and most of us simply changed our boots and started walking down the glacier. The doctor and three others remained with

Boris who was subsequently evacuated by helicopter after attempting unsuccessfully to walk out. His toes were eventually amputated in a Russian hospital, but he seemed to have no regrets about his decision to go for the summit.

Our expedition, culminating in the ascent of the 'Route of 7' on the N face of Dhaulagiri, was profoundly happy and rewarding for me. It was almost completely devoid of the dissension and divisions which have so often marred multinational trips. Good weather helps but old-fashioned commitment to the team was evident in everyone. Special food, fancy gear and media coverage were, strangely, absent.

Summary: An account of the first ascent of the N face of Dhaulagiri, 8167m, via the 'Route of 7', by a joint Russian–British expedition. The joint leaders were Sergei Efimov and Rick Allen. Seven team members reached the summit on 11 May 1993.

MICK FOWLER

The One That Nearly Got Away

(Plates 15-18)

Food at Base Camp was becoming boringly repetitive. Rice and dahl. The only things that varied were the proportions. Day 1: 40% dahl, 60% rice. Day 2: 60% dahl, 40% rice. And so on.

Dolardrum, our second cook (the first clearly couldn't stand the prospect of three weeks with us and ran away!), suggested he introduce some variety into our diet by returning to the nearest village and buying greens, potatoes, chickens, etc. And so we ended up with two chickens strutting boldly around Base Camp pecking purposefully and generally looking remarkably healthy. But Dolardrum was a Buddhist. He would not kill them. Mike Morrison and Mike O'Brien were equally firm in their stand. Eating yes – killing no. I was the one most keen for a varied diet but was new to the techniques required. Steve Sustad was a vegetarian who in one of his previous (American) lives had chicken-killing experience. It was, he assured us, simply a matter of swinging the poor creature round by the neck until it broke. I looked uncertain. The vegetarian offered to demonstrate. The two Mikes made friends with the chickens and suggested they might make good pets. Dolardrum caught one and presented it to Steve. The other ran off into the mist, not to be seen again until the following morning.

Some vigorous swinging had a sudden and surprising result. The head came off. An effective if not entirely expected result.

The resultant meat provided one or two mouthfuls of variation from the normal diet, but it was clear that for food that was actually enjoyable to eat we would have to get onto the mountain and justify breaking into our closely guarded supply of chocolate bars and baby food.

We had been in India for three weeks now: one week arguing with bureaucrats in Delhi, one walking in via Manali, Udiapor and Atholi (rather than the direct route via Kishtwar which was classed by the Home Affairs Ministry as out of bounds to mountaineering trips – although, ironically, the area was open to unsupervised trekkers) and one week struggling to acclimatise in more or less torrential rain.

The weather was appalling. I had been here before, in 1989. Then I remembered the weather as being continually good. Now it rained – and rained, and rained. Deepak, our liaison officer, was the Indian bouldering champion, but the boulders were mist-shrouded and dripping with water – much like his tent and sleeping-bag. He looked miserable. Eventually the Mikes decided to cut their losses and head for home. Deepak professed himself keen to head down to meet Dolardrum's family, and Steve and I began to get that uncomfortable feeling of being on our own. On the bright side, though, the departure of the other two meant that there were considerably more chocolate bars available between Steve and me. The delays had cost us time and, with our days at or above Base Camp strictly limited by my return to work, some urgent activity was indicated.

A slight clearing in the weather provided the necessary impetus and soon we were weaving our way up the moraine-covered glacier, stumbling under the weight of our sacks. Although it was only about seven hours' walk to the foot of the face, the soft upper glacier necessitated either a very early start or a two-day approach. Neither of us liked the prospect of a sufficiently early start, and so two days it was – one across the glacier and up steep boulders and grass to avoid an icefall and the second mainly plodding up soft snow to the flat bowl at the foot of the face. In 1989, on Cerro Kishtwar, illness in the team had prevented us from even crossing the bergschrund. It was not too difficult, therefore, to beat our previous high point. Crisp front-pointing up impressively deep and narrow avalanche runnels allowed us to keep clear of the time-consuming powder snow out on the slopes.

Thirty minutes after we had crossed the bergschrund, a series of expletives from above suggested that something was wrong and my fears were confirmed when Steve waved an ice axe devoid of a pick. To go down now would risk missing what promised to be a good weather-break, but to go on would mean making do with only three tools between us. The decision was immediate; we could pass an axe between us as required. Using an adze to climb steep ice did present problems though. It was necessary to flick the corner in – a motion which almost inevitably resulted in a chip of ice finding its way down the climber's neck. Noticing Steve's discomfort, I refrained from mentioning the subject hoping (successfully) that no suggestion of sharing the tool on this relatively easy ground would be made. We were aiming for a diagonal ramp cutting prominently across the face which could now be seen not far above us. Powder snow clung stubbornly at an amazingly steep angle, effectively keeping us guessing as to whether it would be relatively straightforward or involve desperately insecure scrabbling on powder-covered rock. At one point we could see that it narrowed so much that some pure rock-climbing would be necessary, and high up it clearly steepened into an horrific overhanging section to reach a col high on the N spur.

Picking our way on upwards, the ground became increasingly awkward. The ropes came out and, after a total of seven weeks trying to climb this mountain, my first roped pitches were done. The difficulty at this stage consisted of short steps of Grade IV, but even on this ground it was easiest to swap a broken axe at every stance, so that at least the leader had two good tools.

The powder snow accumulation did a remarkably good job at disguising the difficulty of the ground ahead. What looked to be straightforward snow/ice invariably turned out to be hard ice or rock covered in twelve inches of powder. The whole ramp was set at least at 65 degrees and it was a source of continual amazement that so much powder had built up on it. This ground, though, appeared to be Steve's forte. Scraping the snow away with his adze and teetering gently up the precarious ground beneath, he left a clear trail like a giant slug. A pendulum pitch to cross a particularly blank section led to a convenient projecting flake where our progress ended for the night. We had brought a small two-man Gore-Tex tent with us but we didn't manage to find even one site above the bergschrund on which to pitch it. Instead, I always slept wrapped in the tent fabric, whilst Steve made use of a bivvy-bag that he had fortuitously brought along.

Steadily more challenging ground led to the overhanging section at the top of the ramp. Arriving at 3pm there were only three hours or so of daylight left. Benightment was looking a definite possibility. After an initial effort on my part saw my sack becoming inextricably stuck in the main fault line, Steve led a fine mixed pitch, impressing me enormously by braving the cold temperatures without gloves, whilst I froze in the back of the fault line. The warming powers of adrenalin-surging activity never cease to amaze.

This section had been one of the uncertain areas of the route. From beneath the face the problem looked to be a deep vertical gash with a couple of large chockstones. Ever hopeful, we had convinced ourselves that it would be possible to squeeze behind these obstacles and get easily up to the col. Now that we were actually here it was clear that our thoughts were perhaps a little over-optimistic. The bulk of the fault line consisted of impressively crumbly material which was distinctly not conducive to good protection placements. There were two chockstones neither of which had a through route. Steve had effectively outflanked the first one but the second still loomed above us through the evening mist. A challenging pitch followed, with sky-hooks and ice axe clips allowing progress bolstered by protection from dubious rock pegs. It was my turn to warm up, whilst Steve could do little but shiver and watch my faltering progress in the failing light. A final difficult traverse and a swim through bottomless powder saw me arrive at the col at 7pm in the last rays of the light.

We had hoped that the col would provide a reasonable site for the tent, but the reality was disappointing; not only was the col only 15ft wide but it consisted of a knife-edge of bottomless powder overhanging at the far side. Fortunately I had managed to place a sound belay peg before the light faded completely. I had left my sack hanging midway up the pitch and, being unable to haul it up in one go, I now stood in gently falling snow, cooling down rapidly and waiting for Steve's assistance in manhandling it round the overhangs. Every time he freed it I could pull it up for a few feet until failing strength or another snag prevented further progress. Tying it off to the belay each time became increasingly challenging as the light faded completely. The problem was that my head torch was in my sack and I dare not unclip any knot whose function was not

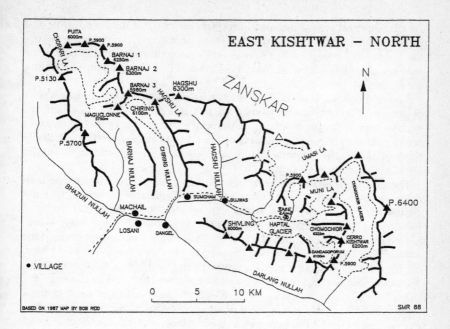

one hundred per cent clear. The result was an impressive tangle of knots and a very cold Fowler by the time Steve hauled himself up onto the col.

A precarious night on separate ledges, with a pulley system ferrying food and drink back and forth, gave way to another cloudless morning and the sight of more horrors ahead. Our proposed line now moved round onto the NE face which we hoped would allow rapid progress. Closer inspection, however, confirmed our worst fears: very steep smooth granite slabs smothered in powder snow. The day passed slowly, with long hot precarious pitches in the morning sun and a series of cold grovels in the afternoon. A final mixed rock and snow aid pitch of the most memorable sort led out to a patch of powder snow on the N spur. Placing the last belay peg of the day (in the dark again!), my hammer head broke. Only one axe and one hammer between two. Such is life. We tried to look on it as providing 'additional interest'.

Across to one side of our two sleeping 'ledges' was ... a sling. It could only have been left by one team. In 1991 Andy Perkins and Brendan Murphy had made a spirited attempt on a line climbing the centre of the NW face and exiting onto the N spur at this point. After 17 days of capsule-style climbing they climbed away from the end of their fixed ropes, doubtless hoping for easier ground around the corner on the NE face. They were, of course, disappointed and ground to a halt a mere 150m from the summit.

Our situation was different. Being five days up from Base Camp and three days from the bergschrund we were feeling relatively strong. Before the light faded completely, I saw enough to be thankful that this was the case and sympathised with Andy Perkins and Brendan Murphy for failing when they were so close.

Above us, the crest of the N buttress reared up as a smooth bulbous nose of granite. The obvious way lay to the left up a distressingly steep groove system capped by an overhang of dripping icicles. Forty metres of awkward powder snow scraping and a short desperate wall led to a belay at the foot of the groove proper. Here, an abseil sling suggested arrival at the Perkins/Murphy high point.

The groove was just off vertical with an eggshell layer of ice one inch away from the rock. It was one of those difficult areas where it was not clear which way would be the best – smashing the ice away and climbing the rock or hooking up the ice hoping that it wouldn't come away. Working on the basis that I could always fall back on the former technique if the latter failed (but not vice versa) I proceeded to cross my fingers and head off up the ice. A section coming away in the first 20ft almost ended this technique but instead revealed a fine nut placement. And so it went on ... one of those fantastic pitches where everything went right for a change. Every time I bashed away a piece of ice protection, possibilities appeared; every time I climbed the ice, it stayed in place. Perfect. A short aid section led to a small bay beneath a particularly nasty overhanging crack. Time to belay. Steve came up and professed himself unhappy with the way ahead. I could see the problem. Blank granite on either side of the crack offered no protection and the crack itself was completely ice-choked with a very large Himalayan icicle formation hanging dangerously down on the lip.

The great thing about climbing with Steve is that, happy or not, once he has convinced himself that there is no alternative route, he can be relied upon to do everything he possibly can to get up. Here he was true to form. Demolishing the icicle with care (only bruises for me, as opposed to breakages or death) he proceeded to aid on screws, an upside down knifeblade, Friends between ice and rock, and finally étriers on the picks of axes. None of the gear was much good and I watched with a not inconsiderable adrenalin flow myself – especially when a placement pulled at a crucial moment and the Sustad body fell a full 10ft onto the tied-off pick of an axe. Not to worry, the system worked and a second try produced the desired result. Steve floundered onto relatively easy ground, consisting of his favourite combination of 75 degree ice and 18 inches of powder.

Seconding was a fiasco with the ice in the crack splitting and me dangling spider-like inspecting the line from six feet away. An ignominious series of awkward heaves and pulls (fortunately without anyone looking!) saw contact with the mountain re-established and a very heavy-breathing Fowler being landed on the stance and directed at the (probable) top pitch. The most challenging powder yet. Three feet of it just plastered onto rocky slabs, with a jutting cornice 50ft above. Feeling somewhat like an insecure mole, progress was tedious and slow. Protection was uncomfortably sparse but the sun could be seen sparkling on the edge of the cornice and success seemed close.

A lot more effort was required but with almost surprising suddenness my carefully excavated channel through the cornice was complete and a blinding panorama of magnificent mountains was on display. The other peaks of the Cerro Kishtwar massif could be seen below us, whilst Sickle Moon, Hagshu and the Brammah peaks dominated a cloudless horizon. Never had I been on a Himalayan summit in such flawless weather. The frustrations of Delhi, the incessant rain earlier on ... all the masochism of a Himalayan trip suddenly seemed worthwhile.

Having soaked up the splendour of a perfect summit scene, we turned to descend. One blow to the first abseil peg from the remaining hammer and the whole atmosphere changed – the entire head unit snapped off. One adze was left between us for a 1200m abseil descent. An adrenalin pumping prospect.

To quote a well-known proverb 'You can't count your chickens before they are hatched', or – put another way – 'You can't tick your Himalayan peaks before you get back down'.

We had to delay our tick for two days. By this time we were back at Base Camp and the alloy head on my vaguely functional hammer was not looking its best. But then life is good after a Himalayan success and this was not the time to worry about what might have been.

Summary: In September 1993 Mick Fowler and Steven Sustad made the first ascent, in four days, of the 1000m NW face of Cerro Kishtwar (c6200m) in the Haptal Nullah of the Kishtwar Himalaya.

ROGER PAYNE

Summer on the Savage Mountain

(Plates 27–30 and front cover)

Our small expedition to K2 was the culmination of a two-year project that combined industry, development and mountaineering. With support from Eastern Electricity the expedition oversaw the installation of micro hydroelectricity systems in two mountain villages on the approach to the Baltoro glacier. The hydro systems were requested by the villages; they work with the Aga Khan Rural Support Programme (AKRSP) which is a development charity. The technology is simple and manufactured locally (these types of schemes have been developed by Intermediate Technology). The villagers provided the necessary labour, and the turbines and generators were installed by AKRSP Engineers who received special training and assistance from Eastern. Our job was to liaise with the different interested parties and to try and resolve any local problems that might arise.

Our journey to K2 was punctuated by stops related to the development objectives. At Skardu we met AKRSP Officers and toured current initiatives. At Shigar our expedition doctor, Caroline Williams, visited the small but very busy hospital and delivered a donation of medical supplies. We stopped at Mango to inspect progress on the new micro hydroelectricity scheme and at Hoto to check that the installation carried out in 1992, as part of the project, was in good order. Progress at Mango was very good and the Hoto scheme was running as expected. Valuable discussions took place at both villages with village leaders and AKRSP representatives.

We arrived at Base Camp on 29 June, which coincided with a period of weather and conditions that were about as perfect as it is possible to get. After only eight days of our lightweight attempt on the Abruzzi Spur of K2, Alan Hinkes, Victor Saunders, Julie-Ann Clyma and I had already established Advanced Base and two camps on the ridge itself (at c6150m and 6800m): we were fit and acclimatising fast. The climbing to this point was interesting throughout, with quite a lot of mixed ground and the difficult House's Chimney leading to Camp 2.

On the last and probably the best day of this fine spell three members of an American/Canadian expedition reached the summit. During their descent one of the summit climbers tripped and lost control in the Bottleneck; moments later he was tumbling out of control down the S face. This was the second of five fatalities on K2 during the summer of 1993. The other members of the team arrived back at their high camp on the Shoulder (c8000m) in strengthening winds and poor visibility. From

Camp 2 Julie-Ann and I watched a wall of black cloud engulf the southern horizon and then the peaks near us. The Americans had to draw on all their strength and experience to descend in deteriorating conditions.

The summer's first fatality was a 35-year-old mountaineering instructor from Slovenia. His expedition had made very rapid progress on the mountain. Only 21 days after setting up Base Camp four members of the expedition reached the summit ridge in bad weather on 13 June. During the descent, in which one member almost failed to relocate Camp 4, three suffered serious frostbite and one succumbed to oedema.

Until the beginning of 1993 only 78 individuals had recorded ascents of K2 by one of the seven routes that lead to its summit. In 1986 Julie Tullis and Alan Rouse reached the summit but – in a year that claimed the lives of 13 climbers on the slopes of K2 – they both perished at Camp 4 on the Shoulder having been trapped by a ferocious storm. Despite almost 30 attempts since 1986, there had been no ascents of the Abruzzi Spur during the intervening years.

Throughout mid-July the weather was very unsettled with almost daily snowfall. Strong winds roared on K2. The summer seemed to be following the same pattern as in 1992 when our plans for a new route on the SW face of Broad Peak were thwarted by midsummer storms bringing high levels of precipitation, with rain at Base Camp and avalanche conditions up high. However, there were still three other expeditions trying for success on the Abruzzi and, like them, we tried to make progress with optimistic forays onto the spur.

It was not until 21 July that it was possible to pass our previous high point of the 7th when Julie-Ann and I climbed above the Black Pyramid and left a dump of equipment and food just below Camp 3. This section of the climb has several steep steps and the Black Pyramid itself was compact slabs littered with very old fixed ropes.

Ideally, five days is the minimum amount of good weather necessary for a summit bid: four to get to the top and back to Camp 4 and then, crucially, a fifth to find the way down to Camp 3. As over half of the previous ascents of K2 had been in the early part of August we were confident we would soon be making final preparations for our own summit attempt.

Another period of bad weather followed, with very strong westerly winds that accelerated between K2 and Broad Peak North. Although the weather was far from perfect, on the 27th we were moving again. Members of the German and Swedish expeditions had set off before us to discover that for the third time tents at Camp 2 had been seriously damaged by the wind. One of the Swedish tents and all its contents had simply been blown off the mountain. They contacted us by radio and we gave them permission to use our tents that had stood firm during the storms. Despite strong winds and poor visibility on the 30th we all ascended the Black Pyramid and crossed the sérac band to reach the site of Camp 3 and the snow slopes leading to the Shoulder. We arrived in the afternoon and started to dig a snow cave, just big enough for four, by 10pm. But a Swedish climber, who had been unable to locate his team's camp, and a member of the Dutch International team without bivouac equipment, sought shelter in our snow cave. Hence, Alan and Victor spent the night in their Camp 4 bivvy tent.

Next morning our radio contact with Base Camp revealed that from the German and Swedish teams ahead of us, six climbers had reached the summit the previous day. Three members had died during the descent. Alan and Victor started to move up the wide snow slopes above to the site of Camp 4, but stopped at c7700m to assist the surviving member of the Swedish summit team who was frostbitten and exhausted. They brought him down to Camp 3 and then descended back to Base Camp. He was physically and emotionally drained. He had spent the whole of the previous night trying to get his team mate down from the summit. By morning when his own life was in serious danger he left his partner who was suffering from cerebral oedema.

Overnight Julie-Ann and I looked after the exhausted climber at Camp 3, and next day (1 August) we lowered him down the mountain. Visibility was poor and very strong winds again battered the Abruzzi Spur. There was a heart-stopping moment when one of the old fixed ropes on a steep section of the Black Pyramid broke while the injured climber and I were simultaneously abseiling. Fortunately some quick footwork meant a serious fall was just avoided. After 13 hours' continuous effort Advanced Base Camp and other members of the Swedish expedition were reached without further incident.

After the rescue and helicopter evacuation of the Swedish team member there followed a long spell of continuous bad weather. During this period two very unusual discoveries were made. Almost exactly 40 years after the epic descent of the Abruzzi Spur, during which American climber Art Gilkey was swept away in an avalanche, some of his remains appeared on the glacier only 400m from Base Camp.

The eight members of the 1953 expedition had spent ten days at their Camp 8 (7700m) in bad weather and Gilkey had developed thrombophlebitis. They lowered Gilkey down in a storm and at one point one man fell and pulled five others off. Incredibly, various ropes became entangled and Pete Schoening held them all on one belay. Gilkey was left belayed to two ice axes while tent platforms were dug for the night. When they went back to move Gilkey he had disappeared, apparently having been swept away in an avalanche. It seemed imperative that we should try and make contact with the members of the 1953 team and, through them, any surviving relatives, to ensure that the remains were disposed of in accordance with their wishes. Next day a few remains of a very small Asian person were found. We speculated that these were probably one of the three brave Sherpas who had died trying to save Dudley Wolfe who became stranded high on K2 in 1939. After our return it was established that these were almost certainly the remains of Sherpa Pasang Kitar.

The 1st to the 13th of August, our planned summit attempt period, brought the longest spell of unsettled weather of the whole trip. Each day the snow continued to fall and as the winds raged up high it seemed less and less likely that we would ever get back on K2. However, on the afternoon and evening of the 13th, the weather did appear to clear, the pressure started to rise and we returned to Advanced Base Camp. The following morning everyone moved up to Camp 1, but by 7am we could see that the weather was closing in again rapidly. Victor moved on up to Camp 2 that afternoon, but the rest of us stayed at Camp 1 for the night. On the 15th we were all together at Camp 2, but we became trapped there in continuous bad weather with very strong winds. Each evening the clouds would part for half an hour or so, raising our hopes for the next day; but each night the wind roared and whipped fresh snow around the ridge to reveal another day of continuing storm.

Finally on 19 August, in just marginally improved conditions, we moved up to Camp 3. Although in strong wind and cloud it was a joy to be moving again on the Black Pyramid. However, despite our down suits the cold was penetrating. On the slopes above the sérac band we found thigh-deep snow. Climbing to the site of Camp 3, only a few inches of our 15ft marker wand indicating the entrance to our snow cave was visible; a blanket of at least six feet of fresh snow covered the entrance. We dug out the cave only to discover that the roof had collapsed. With darkness approaching and the prospect of climbing above on avalanche-laden slopes it was decided to retrieve our gear and descend. We reached Camp 2 at 10pm that night and spent all of the day of the 20th clearing the mountain to reach Base Camp at 7pm. We did not fix any rope on K2 and, along with rubbish from other teams, we cleared all our equipment and rubbish from the mountain and Base Camp. Our porters had already arrived and so we were up again at 4am on the 21st to pack our loads and start the walk-out.

During the day of our departure huge avalanches swept both the S face and Abruzzi Spur of K2. The walk-out was concluded with a visit to Mango where the new hydroelectricity scheme was in full working order and greatly appreciated by the locals.

Obviously it was a great disappointment that none of us reached the top of K2. Unfortunately the expedition was plagued by bad weather associated with the worst monsoon on the Indian subcontinent in 50 years. However, we had an enjoyable time, worked together very well and showed that a lightweight approach to climbing on the world's second highest mountain can work. Through our development project during the summer of 1993, a sustainable and positive impact was made on the mountain environment.

Summary: Prolonged bad weather thwarted the efforts of the 1993 British K2 Expedition to reach the summit via the Abruzzi Spur. However, in a summer which saw five fatal accidents on K2, the team suffered no injuries or illness and rescued an injured climber from high on the mountain. The expedition also oversaw the installation of two micro hydroelectricity schemes in villages on the approach to Base Camp.

JERRY GORE

Windmills in the Mind

(Plates 31A, 31B)

Alpinism is changing fast. An obvious statement, perhaps, as most of us are aware that classic routes like the North Face of the Eiger are now climbed solo in well under ten hours, and that standards must have risen dramatically if two men can climb a new line on K2 in pure alpine style where many large-scale expeditions have failed despite the use of fixed ropes, bottled oxygen and the choice of the easiest line on the mountain.

The question I would like to ask is: how truly in touch are we with real alpinism today? I would argue that on our protected and closeted island we find it difficult to comprehend what alpinists are doing amongst the world's Greater Ranges, even if we have the basic details in front of us. After talking to mountaineers up and down the country, as I do on a weekly basis, I have reached this sad but inescapable conclusion – sad because we used to lead the world in this game of climbing. The talent is there amongst the young and brave, but it seems to be far too narrowly centred on very small pieces of rock or ice, rather than on the massive unclimbed walls littered across the globe.

As a result of these thoughts, and in an attempt to inspire discussion and controversy, I have set out in this article my own thoughts on alpinism in the nineties by citing a few examples. I hope that these will give some indication of the motivation which lay behind my own attempt, with Andy Perkins, on The Shield in the Paine National Park, an account of which follows this introduction. But first a word on alpinism as I see it: I am differentiating here between pure alpinism and all the other associated games. I am not talking about traditional mountaineering, pure ice climbing, or even the siege game. No. Alpinism, to me, is very simple. It normally involvees two people, total commitment, a fair proportion of very technical ice and rock, and involves starting at the bottom of the climb and going to the top in one continuous unsupported push.

An excellent example of modern alpinism is *The Grand Voyage*. This route lies on Great Trango Tower (6286m) in the central Karakoram and was climbed by John Middendorf and Xavier Bongard over 19 days in 1992. The route is graded VII/5.10/A4+. So what does all that mean? Grade VII indicates a long and committing climb. This route took well over two weeks of continuous climbing, all at altitudes in excess of 5000m, with every night spent in a hanging tent called a portaledge. 5.10 is the technical grade for the free rock-climbing part of the route, ie British E2, of which there was only one pitch on this 1381m route. The greater part of the climb was made using artificial techniques on vertical or overhanging rock.

So what is the big deal about A4 when people were doing A5 in America way back in the 1970s? The answer is that this is New Wave grading and so, by most people's understanding, John and Xavier were doing old grade A6 at 6000m over many days through storms and snow. To give an example of what this standard of artificial climbing involves, New Wave A4 typically can result in a fall potential of up to 130ft. Despite all their problems, these climbers were also extremely ethical. For instance, Xavier, on one of the crux A4 pitches, despite numerous pieces of protection that were all marginal, only put in one tiny rivet (a small bolt designed to hold bodyweight only) in the entire 60m pitch. This was only to avoid a broken limb.

During the climb they encountered pitches of grade VI Scottish rotten ice and a four-day storm, but were entirely unsupported, with no helicopters, no porters and no pre-placed ropes. They started at the bottom and kept going.

Another example of modern alpinism was the attempt on the S face of Annapurna by Jean-Christophe Lafaille and the late Pierre Beghin. Basically they tried a very technical mixed route straight up the middle of the face, became storm bound after three days and decided to retreat. Beghin fell soon after initiating a series of abseils, leaving Lafaille still high on the mountain to make it back alone over many days of tortuous descent, with a broken arm and no equipment.

Though that particular expedition ended in tragedy, it is the concept adopted by this team that illustrates my point. Beghin was a 'super alpinist', able to climb steep ice solo at 8000m, fast and without oxygen. He was not a brilliant rock climber. So he asked Lafaille to partner him because Beghin reckoned he would come in very useful on the rocky bits of the route. In Britain Lafaille would be regarded as a fantastic rock climber. He has soloed without a rope up to French 8b (E8), succeeded in numerous indoor competitions while in the middle of his military service, developed whole sport crags single handed, and was responsible for *Patience* at the Roche des Arnauds, graded French 8c. This is still one of the hardest sport climbs in the world. These feats alone are inspirational. He also happens to be an astounding solo alpinist doing multiple new route *enchainements* by himself, with nothing to help him but his own body and mind. Combine all these abilities into one person, partner him to an equally gifted climber, and one can begin to realise what modern alpinism is all about.

So what sort of skills does one need to climb today's harder alpine routes? The first requirement is a leading grade of E5 6a on natural protection, and 7a/b on bolts. These are bare minimums and ideally one should be at home on both crack and face routes. Technical expertise up to grade V Scottish on both ice and mixed routes is essential, with a few East Coast VIs under your belt to ensure efficiency on steep rock with crampons.

Thirdly, knowledge of big-wall techniques and experience of Yosemite A3 nailing always pays dividends when aiding sections to maintain speed. Finally, you will need 100% commitment, combined with a high level of organisational ability. These are prerequisites.

So what about the routes? The following are just a few of my personal favourites. There are plenty more waiting to be done!

1   The Ghilini/Piola Directissima on the N face of the Eiger (1300m/ Abominable/A4/6b)
2   The W face of Gasherbrum IV (7980m) by R Schauer and V Kurtyka
3   The NW ridge of K2 (8611m) by C Profit and P Beghin
4   The NW face of Cerro Kishtwar (c6200m) by M Fowler and S Sustad (Scottish VI/A3/1000m) (See 'The One That Nearly Got Away', pages 48-53.)
5   The E face of Cerro Standhart (2800m), in Northern Patagonia: Exocet VI by J Bridwell, J Smith, G Smith
6   The E face of Aguja Poincenot (3036m), in Northern Patagonia, by D Anker and M Piola (600m/ED/6b+ obligatory)

On that note let's go to Patagonia for a complete rest and, by comparison, a real holiday! To climb among the Towers of Paine in Southern Patagonia had been a long cherished dream of mine ever since I attended an Alpine Club symposium on South America. I had been captivated by an old black and white film taken during one of the early flights over the range. In August 1992 I had still not managed a trip abroad, and the N ridge of The Shield (2400m) seemed to offer everything I wanted – a good alpine objective with a bias towards rock, a new route and one that might yield to a lightweight approach. All I needed was a partner.

Andy Perkins was an obvious choice. A seasoned campaigner with a predilection for the cold and wet stuff, Andy could be relied upon to stay focused through the appalling weather we anticipated. Practically every account I had ever read about Patagonia mentioned the hideous winds, but one quotation stuck in my mind. It was Toni Holdener's comment on the Swiss attempt of 1973/74 on Fitzroy's E pillar: 'During the subsequent retreat – which would have been impossible without fixed rope – everyone had to give his all to escape those elements of hell.' He was one of six, we were two, and we were not taking any fixed rope.

15 December
Breakthrough. After four days of carrying, digging, stashing kit and bitching about it, we made the 'Windmill' col and saw the ridge for the first time. Climbing alpine-style in Patagonia is rather like juggling with mercury – hazardous to your health and every bit as frustrating. It is a specialist's game with only a few taking part, and even fewer succeeding. All the other teams we met in the Paine were sieging the Towers with fixed ropes, heaps of ironmongery and a lot of vino. Most were at least four-man teams or larger.

An Argentine group operating on the dihedral to the right of the *South African route* on the Central Tower of Paine seemed to have a weekly change around, with an assorted team of South Africans, Argentines, and Chileans. While one unit was bashing away on the face, another would be off leading treks around the park to raise money so that they could maintain their assault on the wall. Theirs was a strange existence but it did mean they could spend most of their time at camp partying.

Not for us the easy life of wood huts and smoky fires. Like banished monks, we retreated to our Advanced Base: a large boulder perched under the Gothic vastness of The Shield's E face. Our route took its long, curving N ridge, elegantly describing the mountain's right-hand sky-line. The Shield was first climbed in 1968 by two Italians, M Curnis and M Dotti, from the Rio Frances side. That expedition encountered the usual hurricane-force winds and great technical difficulties on a route that required 1000m of fixed rope and 200 pitons.

Andy and I arrived at the col leading to the summit ridge armed only with a basic rack, fifteen pitons and two 8.2mm ropes. Up to this point we had climbed a 5.7 rock band just above Advanced Base, grade II snow and ice slopes to the approach gully, and then a series of interesting mixed pitches up to the col. These involved strenuous IV/V climbing, loose rock, waterfalls, A1 nailing and vertical snow. I felt like a mountaineer again.

It was so windy that when I heard it cracking like a whip above our heads it reminded me of the little explosions from a Chinese festival dragon. I considered attempting to climb technical rock in this sort of wind and shivered.

I remembered talking to Alan Kearney, the American Patagonian expert, in Yosemite a couple of years back. He had raved about the N ridge then, saying it would probably go. He is a great promoter of alpine-style climbing in the region, making the first true ascent of the S face of the Central Tower without recourse to fixed rope. He completed the ascent after four major attempts over two months and ended up spending two nights on the wall with only minimal clothing and food. His subsequent account of the climb was full of shredded rope, frozen and bleeding hands and the sheer savagery of being in a full-scale Patagonian storm with no place to hide.

Alan's story came back to me as Andy and I stood doubled up on the col, peering at the huge sweeping arch that formed The Shield's northern battlements. I clung hard to the rock, my fingers already beginning to freeze, and looked up at the serried ranks of granite towers that stood between us and the summit. It was late in the day and the weather was deteriorating – certainly no place for a couple of alpine rats!

'Rack your gear and let's piss off!' Andy yelled against the furore.

23 December

At 3am it was fairly clear and we decided to go for it. After seven days of gales and sleet huddled under a rock, it was good to get moving again. We were climbing by 4.15am, up the ropes of the first rock band, across the snow and onto the ice that leads to the approach gully. Halfway up on jumars, covered in spindrift and sodden Pertex, the wind roared and the world seemed to be closing in on me. I went to clip my top jumar above the belay piton and suddenly I was falling. There was a jerk on my harness and I was stopped by the thin line linking my second jumar to the rope.

The wind held its breath as I hung motionless by a thin strip of tape. There was silence for a split second – just the drip, drip, drip of the melting icicle above me. My jumar system, invented by Geoff Hornby, had worked and I was still in the game. Cursing deeply at my own stupidity, I offered up a quick prayer and determined to be more careful next time. At the col the wind was so strong I couldn't hear Andy even when he was yelling in my ear. Dejected, we descended.

24 December

Weather shit – lost at chess twice today. Christmas Day tomorrow and then it would be practically New Year. I thought of home, hot water, good food, clean sheets. Then I prepared the freeze-dried; another tin of tuna, the inevitable noodles all washed down by tea and the mandatory Mars bar. Four bars per person per day – our diet had a startling variety. I zipped into my bag and drifted off as the wind picked up and the snow started falling.

29 December

At 3am the skies were clear, so we went back up to Windmill col. We arrived at 8am, to be blown flat by the winds. The weariness of defeat surrounded me as I accepted that the conditions were too bad to continue. The delicate face-climbing we anticipated above would simply be suicidal; so it was back to Advanced Base. Wandering along the glacier, I stopped under a large boulder and watched the falling snow as the wall shimmered and the sun's rays pierced the light cloud to pick out streaks in the meltwater. I trudged back to the tent to listen to Frank Zappa and crawl inside my protective shell.

Andy woke me at 4pm, very agitated. The vario was singing; the pressure was going up fast. Outside it looked clear but still windy. He was sure the weather – coming now from the south instead of the west – was getting better. We checked at 6pm and again at 8; the pressure was still going up. Axes were sharpened, food packed and spare clothing sorted and stowed. We lay back, but sleep came only fitfully.

30 December

At 3am the alarm buzzed and I practically sprang to attention – old habits die hard. Outside the sky was clear and still. Brews, a packet of Alpen and I was out into the night, as a well-rehearsed ritual unfolded itself perhaps for the last time. I cleaned the pans. Andy donned his Buffalo suit and packed his sack. Ice tools attached, head torches secured firmly on helmets, we moved out into the darkness.

In four hours we were back at the col. Though cold, there was no wind. Plastics were swapped for rock shoes and Gore-Tex socks. I led off up the short, strenuous section onto the easy ground leading to the ridge proper. Despite our big rack and 60m ropes, we were quickly moving upwards on pitches that gradually became harder and steeper. Across slabs, up cracks and grooves, and we were doing the bastard in style. Rough granite onion layers, three-quarters peeled, hung above us like daggers as Andy laid siege to a blind crack off to the left. It was choked with ice and he had to clear it with his axe to make progress. He took a hanging belay near the top of the crack system.

Panting hard from bringing up the sack, I moved past and immersed myself in what proved to be the first crux. I tore my frozen hands jamming up the ice-filled cracks, my shoes now sodden and useless. I reached the roof and dithered for a few moments before stepping gingerly across to another system. It led through the overhang and onto easier ground.

The route continued tortuously to the Big Shelf, signalling the halfway stage. Andy led off on the second crux, bridging delicately up a rotten corner-cum-chimney. It emerged onto friable and loose flakes and he took an awkward stance on slabs. I raced off and found myself climbing cracks on the very edge of the ridge. I could look straight down the E face, a vertical drop of 2000ft. I quickly popped another Friend in.

I could see easier terrain above and after the 25th pitch we stood on the summit rubble anxiously looking at the weather. I paused for an instant, glancing across to the E face of the Fortress, reviewing the Yugoslav route carved out over a two month period of sustained aggression in 1990. The irony of this hard-won route to a Patagonian summit was reflected in its name: *One Minute of Wisdom*.

We started down. At 1am, exactly 22hrs after waking, we were back in the tent. *The Adventures of Don Quixote*, in places both dangerous and exciting, had been a long wandering journey set against a Spanish backdrop. On New Year's Day the weather was perfect and, as a bonus, we climbed the N ridge of the North Tower of Paine. Last year it took six Italians five weeks to climb this route. On the summit, it was so still I could have flown my paraglider back to Base Camp. The whole of the Patagonian ice cap was spread out before us and the Central and South Towers spiked the horizon like burnished spears painted on a blue canvas.

Perkins finished his fourth bottle of wine – and I was on my third. I switched off the movie as the drink took effect and dozed fitfully through a dream world filled with huge spires of rock torn apart by the explosive howl of violent winds: Patagonia – Land of Tempest. I was glad to be going home.

Summary: An account of the first ascent of *The Adventures of Don Quixote* (ED1/5.10/A2/28 pitches) on the N ridge of The Shield (2400m) in the Paine Group, Southern Patagonia by Jerry Gore and Andy Perkins on 30 December 1992.

GRAHAM LITTLE

Gneiss and Ice: Greenland on the Rocks

The 1993 British Lemon Mountains Expedition

(Plates 39–42)

'How do you fancy a trip to Greenland? – we're going to the Lemon Mountains – I sailed there with Robin Knox-Johnston in 1991 – I'll send you a copy of the book – you must come – it's only for a month – it will be a fabulous trip!'

The famous Bonington enthusiasm left no place for a negative response. The other two members of a four-man team were to be Greenland 'old hands': Rob Ferguson who had taken part in Stan Woolley's Northern Group Greenland expedition in 1990 and Jim Lowther who, at the relatively tender age of 29, had already been to Greenland on ten previous occasions. I had climbed with Chris in the Indian Himalaya in 1992 (making the first British ascent of Panch Chuli II by a new route), so I knew that we would be compatible climbing partners.

The characteristics that allow two individuals to function well together as a climbing team are difficult to specify. The closest that I can come to a definition is to talk about complementary strengths, intuitive understanding, similar aspirations and a respect for one's partner's 'gut feelings'. But compatibility is only truly tested during periods of danger and stress. Harmony between all members of an expedition is even more difficult to predict (and achieve). Given the sheer diversity of human nature and the general strains of expedition life, it is not surprising that friction sometimes occurs between expedition members and that there is as much scope for antipathy as there is for friendship.

A first meeting with Rob and Jim promised good company and the probability of a cohesive team despite our varied backgrounds, and age differences that spanned 30 years! The opportunity for some good games of bridge, once we had tutored Rob into the skills of this most noble of card games, provided us with an alternative, non-climbing focus.

I can't remember whose idea it was to take a global positioning system (GPS) with us but it fell to me (being the 'surveyor') to obtain one at nil cost. I also hastily volunteered to draw up the food list, knowing of the dietary masochism traditionally associated with Arctic exploration. This fear proved well founded when Rob sent me a menu from his previous trip – dehydrated mince and green beans for every main meal didn't sound exactly mouth-watering fare!

So it came to pass that the 1993 British Lemon Mountains expedition left Glasgow on 20 June *en route* for the Chisel glacier via Keflavik and Akureyri in Iceland and Constable Pynt (sic) in East Greenland, clutching a hand-held GPS, courtesy of Garmin (Europe) Ltd, with plans not only to make first ascents but to obtain three-dimensional positional fixes on the peaks climbed. Our short stopover at Constable Pynt coincided with a traditional Greenland midsummer feast. While Jim and Chris tucked into whale meat, seal blubber and raw narwhal, Rob and I declined such gastronomic adventures and nibbled on a little dried fish.

The chartered Twin Otter flies south under the control of a couple of very cool dudes wearing leather jackets and the kind of shades that only pilots and poseurs can wear. Jim's complexion turns pale, which he claims is due to the altitude. We know better! Chris, his digestive tract obviously better acclimatised than ours, dashes around the small aircraft in camera-happy mode, looking in the best of health.

Sharp granitic teeth pierce the swirling clouds and wide glaciers are glimpsed far below. We are 250 miles from the nearest human habitation. 'Where would you like to land?' one pilot asks in the casual manner of a taxi driver asking where one would like to be dropped off. A massive rock and ice peak suddenly looms into view. Jim recognises it as Mejslen (Chisel).

'Just to the north of that peak,' he replies, managing to sound almost as cool as the pilot. One dummy run to check out the glacier for big crevasses and we are bumping along the slush-covered ice, spot on target.

'This is the first plane ever to land on this glacier,' somebody says. Shortly afterwards, we are the first people to stand on it. The Otter is soon a fading speck on the horizon. We are left, surrounded by our supplies, in the heart of an incredibly beautiful mountain world – one of the remotest places on the surface of the earth.

Soon tents are erected and our first Base Camp established (at N 68 29 03, W 31 49 36). There is no need to acclimatise (the peaks reach a maximum height of 2600m) and I'm keen to get to grips with our first mountain. A unique feature of climbing north of the Arctic Circle in June is 24-hour daylight which usually allows the mountaineer to dispense with bivouac gear on a climb. However, on the negative side, it can have a strange effect upon the body clock and, with little night time freeze, produce some very worrying snow and ice conditions. Our first climb has to be the N face of Mejslen, which we identified from the plane – a complex 1000m rock and ice wall due south of Base Camp. We tackle this as a four-man team to get the feel of the place and to consolidate group dynamics prior to splitting into two-man teams with separate objectives.

Mejslen proves a magnificent introduction to Greenland, with technical mixed climbing via a series of ice arêtes and rock traverses giving difficult route-finding and an uncertain outcome. We reach the summit ridge by a pitch of hard ice, then top out at 02.30 in the low glow of the Arctic sun,

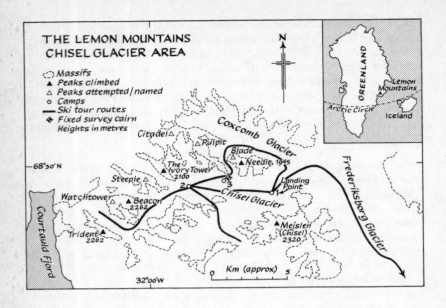

only three days after leaving Scotland. The true summit is a small split rock tower perched at one end of a short level arête. I set the GPS tracking and in a matter of 40 seconds it has observed four orbiting satellites, producing latitude and longitude values. The height value readout (a less reliable aspect of a 'stand alone', hand-held GPS) eventually settles at 2320m (for the technically minded, the GPS was set to WGS84 and Geoidal Height). 'Official' duties over, I soak in the grandeur and vastness of this frozen land, gazing out to the great ice cap (which we were to learn later, from Danish scientists, has recently been drilled for ice core extraction to a depth of over 3000m!).

The descent, reversing our ascent route, is interrupted by a three-hour rest on a scree-covered rock ledge at half height while we wait for the slopes below to creep into shadow. I sit contemplating a cramping pain in my left foot and the nature of our fine madness; the others sleep blissfully! We arrive back at Base Camp, tired but happy, after a 29-hour round trip, Jim and Rob skimming in on skis over sodden snow, with Chris and me plodding behind.

Our plan to move Base Camp further up the glacier leaves me no option. This is the moment of truth! Donning telemark skis and strapping myself into the harness of my pulk (a smooth-based fibreglass and alloy sledge) gives me a powerful feeling of apprehension, as if preparing for some strange initiation ceremony. 'You'll soon pick it up,' Chris assures me, but during the course of the expedition I can't say that I ever really enjoyed the experience. From our new Base Camp, 6km further up the Chisel glacier, Jim, Rob and I snatch an ascent of Beacon, 2262m, by a long icefield and a rock ridge of biscuit-like consistency, before several days of heavy snowfall pin us down at Base Camp. This period of bad weather gives us the excuse for a good rest and some major bridge sessions. The whisky supplies also see some serious activity!

A metre of fresh snow has fallen but the hot sun soon melts it down, encouraging a spot of ski-touring. This involves the crossing of a hitherto unexplored col to the west of the Needle massif and down onto the Coxcomb glacier. A stunning blade of grey gneiss takes my mind off my skiing incompetence and I join the others line-spotting and swapping superlatives. It is a truly eye-boggling wall – a clean 300m sweep of perfect rock. The mist descends as we ski back around onto the Chisel glacier and damp snow begins to fall as we skin back towards camp on a compass bearing.

When the weather clears, Chris and I head off to climb a magnificent tower of pale gneiss, the highest on a many-towered mountain spine lying at the head of the Chisel glacier between the much greater bulks of Steeple and Citadel. Dumping skis, we solo up steepening snow to cross the bridged bergschrund and then clamber up mixed ground to a ledge at the toe of a long, slim tongue of rock descending from the right edge of the NE face. Exchanging double plastic boots for rock boots and leaving ice tools and crampons on the ledge makes us feel slightly vulnerable but greatly enhances the pleasure of climbing. Following a distinctive fault line we gain height quickly on dry rock.

Strange cries above demand our attention. Dark silhouettes wheel high against a cloudless sky, their almost human screeching and aerial antics drawing closer. They are the first birds we have seen in this empty land. We feel a curious empathy, as we share with them our common affinity for high and lonely places. (We confirmed later that they were Ivory Gulls. Little is known about these enigmatic birds, which are among the very few larger forms of wildlife in this Arctic wilderness.)

A skin-mincing cracked corner slows our progress. It is strenuous and technical (5b) and I'm relieved to take a belay below a capping overhang. Using aid, Chris soon climbs over the overhang and shouts down: 'We've cracked it!' This seems a premature assumption, but three pitches on find me in a small rock bay with little but blue sky above. Chris brings me up onto the broad summit platform and we exchange broad grins. The views are so captivating that, despite enjoying nearly an hour on top, we forget to build a cairn.

Jammed ropes and loose rock test our composure as we descend The Ivory Tower (it could have no other name) but soon we are reunited with our ice gear and then with our skis. We arrive at Base Camp, drenched with sweat, to a generous welcome from Jim and Rob, which means a lot after their disappointing retreat from the vast S face of Pulpit. Although we are now operating as two independent teams, there is a powerful feeling of cohesion and mutual support.

After a day's rest, I persuade Chris to have a go at Steeple by the long thin gully that we had spotted from the summit of The Ivory Tower. Although still tired, he agrees to the plan. 'You're the greyhound, I'm the labrador,' he adds with a wry smile. I think this is intended as a compliment but I'm not sure! Jim and Rob have left in the early hours of the morning to attempt a fine looking peak that we had explored on an earlier ski tour. After a substantial lunch of salmon and oatcakes, we head off at 1600, intending to climb the gully on Steeple during the 'night' when the snow and ice should be in its most stable condition. As we ski up to the col the clear skies give way to flat grey clouds. A chilling wind blows, yet it isn't really cold. Our gully terminates well above the base of the face so we climb diagonally up from the right, following a snow/ice ramp. The snow is dreadful and after three pitches Chris says he thinks we should go down. I suggest another pitch but agree that the omens are not good. Suppressing disappointment, I soon accept that Chris's gut feelings are common sense and I fix up our first abseil anchor. Three spectacular abseils down a compact, vertical wall take us onto the snowfield again. As we return to camp, the wisdom of our retreat becomes evident, as heavy wet snowflakes fill the darkening sky. Crawling into the security of our tent, we feel concern for the well-being of Rob and Jim. If anything goes wrong, we are the rescue team. Our isolation is complete.

I am awoken from a restless sleep in the early hours of the morning by the welcome sound of two voices. Though snow-plastered and tired, Jim and Rob smile broadly as they tell of their successful climb. While Chris makes a brew we hear of many pitches on good ice and excellent rock. Collapsing séracs and a nightmare descent with frozen ropes and nil visibility were mere details. Trident has been a total experience!

Ever since first seeing it I have harboured an overwhelming desire to attempt the stunning rock monolith that dominates the lower Chisel glacier. Fortunately Chris shares my passion. The SW pillar of Needle (1945m), as we named the peak, is by any standards a magnificent objective and one that will demand a special commitment. Another move of Base Camp puts us in the ideal position to make an attempt.

The slabby lower wall of the SW pillar gives climbing of a high standard and quality, five pitches on immaculate gneiss. I take the first pitch, a glacier-polished and strenuous 5b, but Chris gets what turns out to be the crux – a soaring, cracked corner and ramp above (5c). He leads this in perfect style under the warm Arctic sun. One more pitch and we return to camp, leaving fixed ropes for a racing start in the morning. We spiral up and around the great grey pillar, carrying with us the minimum of gear and a determination to top out. Eventually we gain the W face of the mountain, where the upper pitches carry ice and banks of unconsolidated snow. Feeling rather foolish and ill equipped in my rock boots, I swim up a slope of slipping slush to finger-jam a crack in a bald wall streaming with meltwater (5b). I slump, wasted, on an island of dry rock above.

A couple more pitches and we are on the summit, gazing out over golden glaciers, mesmerised by the array of jagged peaks casting long, ragged shadows far below. It is shortly after midnight, yet we are bathed in the low light of the sun; there is not a breath of wind. I experience a feeling of utter contentment, knowing, for these few moments, why I climb.

Chris and I share the ritual of photography before commencing the long descent. The elation of the summit slips away as we settle into the broken rhythm of abseiling and down climbing, forcing mind and body to move with deliberation, to rebuff the seductive voice tempting careless action. Elated at having made what is probably the most difficult climb yet achieved in Greenland, we ski back to camp after a 24-hour round trip. Rob gives us a warm welcome, but it is obvious that all is not well. The story of their attempt on Citadel soon unfolds – a fast ascent to the upper tower, the cannonball-sized falling rock glancing off Jim's helmet and impacting upon his collar-bone, followed by the epic self-rescue. Jim is very disappointed at having to retreat from so high on Citadel (probably the highest peak in the Chisel glacier area) and is clearly experiencing considerable pain. However, he is very much alive and mobile and it soon transpires that, even with a broken collar-bone, his skiing ability is still far superior to mine!

The weather is still very settled, with cloudless skies and a chill breeze. I spend the morning listening to my Walkman and luxuriating in the buzz that a good climb gives you. I potter around in the afternoon, skiing over to a rock outcrop to build a cairn and get a GPS fix. This innocent diversion nearly ends in disaster when one ski breaks into a hidden crevasse. I throw my body to one side to avoid following it. Rob, showing his usual consideration, skis over from the tents with a rope to belay me on the return journey.

In a characteristic fit of over-optimism I convince Rob that the route that Chris and I attempted on Steeple would now be in condition. Rob falls for it and we set off late that same evening. The weather is certainly better than on my earlier attempt, but sadly the conditions are not. We gain the narrow lower reaches of the gully, to be confronted with steep, soggy ice. Rob squelches up a pitch, as copious floes of iced water are released by every axe placement. I lead on through, up steepening rotten ice reminiscent of Point Five Gully about to fall down! Ten metres up with no protection, and sanity suddenly returns.

'Let's get out of here,' I shout, above the sound of flowing water. Rob concurs.

Now the great pulking experience is imminent. We must bid our farewells to the Chisel glacier, which has been our home for the last three weeks, and head down to the coast to rendezvous with our pick-up plane. Much of the first day's pulking is almost pleasurable as we cover many kilometres down the wide, smooth Frederiksborg glacier. Jim, scouting out the route with one arm in a sling, is constantly ahead of the rest of us. The monotony of the journey is broken by frequent references to the dominant nature of the true Cathedral (c 2600m) which stands with embarrassing grandeur in the heart of the Lemon mountains. That peak, the highest in the range, is the one that Chris and Jim failed to locate in 1991!

The mighty Frederiksborg glacier is forced to bifurcate by an inconveniently placed peak. We take the left fork and are soon ensnared in a maze of crevasses, then brought to a standstill by an area of unfriendly pressure ridges. We camp. A short section of backtracking allows us to gain a sinuous route through the ice maze to a lake on the fringe of the glacier. Ethereal silver light and pewter-grey clouds reflected upon its surface compel us to try to capture its magic on film. A snow-filled runnel, caught between the tormented glacier and the ravished cliffs on its E bank, gives us swift, safe passage for a while, but not for long. Numerous obstacles make it necessary to carry the pulks and ferry individual loads. Jim, still in considerable pain, is heroic.

After crossing several meltwater channels, we reach the head of Watkins Fjord, choked with pack ice. Abandoning the pulks (an act that has played upon our environmental consciences ever since), we spend a couple of days carrying the rest of our kit over the hills, past Twin Lakes, to our pick-up point on a glacial outwash plain at Sodalen. Unseasonally, the 'airstrip' is snowbound and, although our skiless pick-up plane lands spot on schedule (interrupting a critical game of bridge), an hour's energetic digging is required to clear enough snow for it to take off.

Soaking in the thermal springs back in Iceland, I reflected upon what had been a very enjoyable and successful expedition. As Chris had promised, it had been a fabulous trip, with magnificent mountains, memorable experiences and, most important of all, the best possible company.

Summary: The 1993 British Lemon Mountains Expedition made the first ascent of five peaks in East Greenland during June/July 1993:

Mejslen (Chisel), 2320m, via the N face	1000m	D sup
Beacon, 2262m, via the NE face/E ridge	750m	D inf
The Ivory Tower, 2100m, via the NE face	590m	TD
Trident, 2350m, via the NE face	900m	TD
Needle, 1945m, via the SW pillar	765m	ED

Expedition members: Chris Bonington, Rob Ferguson, Graham Little and Jim Lowther.

HARISH KAPADIA

Exploration in Western Spiti

The Kullu-Spiti-Lahul Expedition 1993

(Plates 76, 85, 86)

Spiti has always fascinated me: the stark barrenness, the grey hills with green patches of cultivation and the deep gorges. I had explored the valleys east of the Spiti river – the Lingti and Syarma valleys – in 1983 and 1987. In 1993 I returned to explore the western valleys of Khamengar and Ratang to complete the Spiti experience.

The area west of the Spiti river is now open to Indians without permits for entry or photography, and with minimum formalities to foreigners. Thus after many years we could roam freely, with cameras. This year, the whole of northern India experienced one of the heaviest monsoons ever. The Kullu valley was flooded, the roads blocked and daily afternoon rain was a common occurrence. The rain had damaged tracks and destroyed large stretches of mountain and we had to cut new tracks over the scree slopes in many places. In the light of the havoc caused by the rains everywhere, we were lucky not to be seriously delayed, though it made things tougher and involved a lot of hard work.

Approaching Spiti from the south, we reached Manikaran in the Kullu valley on 15 July and travelled along the Parvati river. It was one of the most beautiful treks I have ever experienced – first through forest to Pulga and Khirganga and then via open meadows, crossing delicately poised bridges to the lovely Lake Mantalai at 4150m. There were *gaddis* (shepherds) all along the way and solid rocky peaks rising to the south. We turned east to enter a steep nala for our first pass, Pin Parvati (5400m), which was crossed from Spiti in 1884 by Sir Louis Dane and in 1906 by F Skemp; it was crossed from Kullu in 1921 by H Lee Shuttleworth. In 1939 Col J O M Roberts was unable to locate it and crossed to Spiti by another pass. Now the Pin Parvati pass is crossed by many parties and by the shepherds too. It was steep but we climbed it without difficulty on 22 July. Descending to the east, we entered Spiti and camped at the junction of three nalas which join to form the Pin river. We trekked along the Pin for the next three days to reach Sagnam, one of the largest villages in the Pin valley. On the way, the village called Mud was a sight to behold, with its striking situation and green fields. At Sagnam we replenished our supplies. The new openness was evident: foreign groups roamed freely at the Ghungri monastery. Even the villagers were wondering why there was no police post this year at Sagnam. How different from my last two

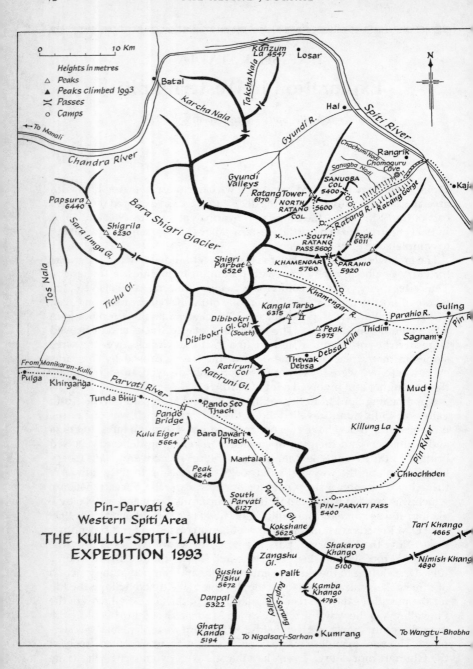

Pin-Parvati &
Western Spiti Area

THE KULLU-SPITI-LAHUL
EXPEDITION 1993

visits, when a piece of paper – our permit – defined the freedom of the hills. There were many other changes evident too: Spitians now have supplies of cooking gas and electricity, and many have television and other modern gadgets. They have been propelled into the consumer age.

Khamengar valley

After a rest day we turned west, up the Parahio river which joins the Pin river at Sagnam. Ratang valley was first explored by two British expeditions. In 1955 T H Braham and P F Holmes entered the gorge and camped halfway up the valley, climbing some peaks. Holmes returned here in 1956 with G W Walker; they climbed a number of peaks and explored the valley to its head. On their return they crossed the South Ratang Pass to Khamengar valley and reached the Parvati river after struggling through a pass to the Dibibokri nala. These were remarkable explorations and climbs, when maps were non-existent and a walk of many days was needed to reach the Spiti valley. We were the first party to explore these valleys again, after 37 years. The 1956 expedition had climbed both the peaks we climbed, and had walked out through the Ratang valley.

The Debsa nala and the Khamengar river join to form the Parahio river which, after a short run, joins the Pin river. Turning NW from Thidim we entered the Khamengar valley, where we stayed until we had studied its head and all the peaks. Kangla Tarbo (6315m) in the Khamengar valley is a beautiful, sharp peak, worshipped locally. It is the highest peak in Western Spiti (not counting the peaks on the Lahul–Spiti watershed). The Pin, Parahio, Khamengar and Debsa valleys have been declared the 'Pin Valley Ibex National Park'. We turned north up a side nala to reach the South Ratang Pass (5600m). It is situated between peaks Khamengar (5760m) to the west and Parahio (5920m) to the east. We climbed both peaks. The descent into the Ratang valley was steep and exposed. We had to guide the porters through it to the main Ratang river which we reached the same day.

Ratang valley

On 4 August we moved to the Upper Ratang valley to camp at the foot of the Ratang Tower. I went ahead to explore the head of the valley and saw the snow and ice pass leading to the Bara Shigri. We also saw a large herd of ibex. In the meantime, a party had climbed up to the North Ratang Col (5600m) at the western shoulder of Ratang Tower (6170m). No route was available to descend to the Gyundi valley. We returned to the Ratang valley and despite a further search could not find a suitable pass by which to cross over to the Gyundi valley with our laden and ill-equipped porters. By 5 August we had returned down the Ratang valley. On the 6th we moved up the unvisited Sanugba valley formed by a tributary of the Ratang river. We climbed up for two days and finally reached the Sanugba Col (5400m). We could observe and photograph many unclimbed peaks on the Gyundi divide, but no crossing was possible.

Ratang Gorge

We decided to return along the Ratang river. It took us three days and several river crossings. For two days we passed over a stupendous, high wall which was frightening and perhaps geologically and geographically significant. It was tiring but a great walk and we saw many *bharals* scrambling fearlessly on the rock walls. Finally, we reached a maidan at the foot of the ancient Chomoguru cave (named after a legend) on 11 August. After more river crossings we suddenly came upon a pukka metalled road *inside the gorge*. The road was built to go along the 5km-long water-tunnel of the hydroelectric project on the Ratang river, which supplies most of the electricity to Spiti. Soon we were in the broad Spiti river valley and at Kaja.

Thus ended our 222km trek in 28 days. From Kaja we travelled by the daily bus to Manali (via Kunzum la, Chandra valley and the Rohtang Pass), a 12-hour journey, and proceeded to Bombay.

Summary: The Kullu–Spiti–Lahul Expedition 1993. The expedition was sponsored by The Mountaineers, Bombay. The Khamengar and Ratang valleys were explored from 11 July to 15 August, 37 years after they had first been visited.

Peaks climbed:

2 August	Khamengar (5760m) 2nd ascent	Harish Kapadia Kesarsinh
2 August	Parahio (5920m) 2nd ascent	Kaivan Mistry Yog Raj Thakur Surat Ram

Passes crossed:

25 July	Pin Parvati Pass (5400m)
3 August	South Ratang Pass (5600m)

Cols reached:

5 August	North Ratang Col (5600m)
8 August	Sanugba Col (5400m)

Team members:
Harish Kapadia and Kaivan Mistry. (Vijay Kothari, Kekoo Cola and Saif Bijliwala joined for the first part.)

Supported by:
Harsinh Sr, Harsinh Jr, Kesarsinh (Kumaoni), Yog Raj Thakur and Surat Ram (Manali).

NOTES

Naming of peaks and passes

Many passes and peaks in these areas are named after their explorers: for example, Gunther's Col, Abinger Col, Snelson Col and Holmes' Col. The Survey of India, and some later maps, would not accept individual nomenclature. Sometimes such names have scanty links with the area: for example, A E Gunther never reached 'Gunther's Col', but only mentioned the possibility of its existence. It is suggested that these passes should now be named after the terrain or area, so that one day they will be incorporated on the maps and any confusion about the area will be dispelled. No disrespect is meant towards the early explorers.

Gyundi valleys

Though we could not cross over into the Gyundi valley north of Ratang, we were able to gather some first-hand information about it. The energetic *gaddis* of Kangra have penetrated deep into the valleys and they stay there for the summer. The popular routes which they take with their horses and supplies are from Batal up the Karcha nala and across a pass into the Gyundi, or from Losar up the Takcha nala across a different pass into the Gyundi, or from Hal in the main Spiti valley along the Gyundi gorge. All these routes are in regular use. There are high passes leading to the Bara Shigri from the Gyundi valleys. The riddle of the Gyundi gorges has been solved by the energetic *gaddis*.

BIBLIOGRAPHY

Trevor Braham, *Himalayan Odyssey*. Allen & Unwin, 1974.
Peter Holmes, *Mountains and a Monastery*. Bles, 1958.
Harish Kapadia, *High Himalaya Unknown Valleys*. Indus, 1993.
Soli Mehta and Harish Kapadia, *Exploring the Hidden Himalaya*. Hodder & Stoughton, 1990.
Himalayan Journal, Vol 20, 79. (Exploration of the western valleys, 1955 and 1956.)
Himalayan Journal, Vol 40, 96; Vol 44, 96, 120. (Exploration of the eastern valleys, 1983 and 1987.)

DAVE WILKINSON

Not the Soviet Union

For the summer of 1992, my early plans for Pakistan or Greenland had fallen through, so I was at a loose end. Then I remembered seeing a note in the Alpine Club Newsletter about a trip to the Pamir. I picked up the telephone and made the necessary last-minute arrangements. The trip was to be a joint one: four British and sixteen from the former USSR. My three compatriots were Tony Park, an excellent rock-climber and one of the younger generation of Alpine Climbing Group members, Phil Thornhill, well-known for his international soloing exploits, and Gordon Dyke, who is even older than me. He used to climb with Peter Harding in the 1940s, now lives in Switzerland, and has only recently taken up high-altitude mountaineering.

This motley team were to join up with sixteen climbers from the city of Minsk, capital of the former Soviet state of Belarus* ('White Russia'). They had fairly simple objectives: ascents of the ordinary routes on Pik Kommunisma (7400m) and Pik Korzhenevskaya (7100m), highest and fourth highest mountains in the former USSR, and conveniently accessible from the same base camp. Over the phone we tacitly let them think that we would be joining them on these ascents. However, I mentioned to Tony that perhaps when we got there we could do our own thing, and bring a bit of free enterprise into ex-Soviet sport.

We flew to Moscow by Aeroflot. The food on the plane was exactly what, in total ignorance, I would have expected from Russian *haute cuisine*: meat and three veg – solid, nutritious and uninspiring; as if some committee of the supreme Soviet had purpose-designed the menu for maximum solidity, nutrition and lack of inspiration. Subsequent meals in their cities and mountains for the next five weeks did nothing to change that impression. At Moscow airport we were welcomed by our host, Tolya, and a few of his friends. They took us for another solid meal in a restaurant, then on to the station and the night train for their native Minsk. Before we boarded the train, they gave us an enigmatic piece of advice: 'Don't talk loudly – if they know you are foreign they might charge you extra money'. What sort of bribery and extortion was this? Later on, we realised what it was all about. Under the old Soviet system, foreigners had to pay for all accommodation and transport within the USSR in hard currency and at a cost much greater than Soviet citizens would pay. This part of the system

* The citizens of this country do not like to be confused with Russians. They have recently changed the spelling of their country from the better-known 'Byellorussia' to 'Belarus' which is an older version and sounds less like 'Russia'.

had survived the recent reforms intact, but our guardians were passing us off as locals, which further reduced the cost of our trip. In fact, so low is the rouble on the exchange markets, that the whole five-week trip cost us only £650 each, including the £250 air fare from London to Moscow.

After our journey as honorary Russians, our friends took us to their parents' dacha in the woods outside Minsk. Every middle-class Russian seems to aspire to such a country retreat. Most of the recent ones are DIY-built, in whole villages of dachas, with gardens abundant with fruit and vegetables. Later we met the rest of the team. One of these was Leonid, a short stocky man with a ruddy complexion and a smiling face – a sort of Belarussian Don Whillans. He was introduced as their 'trainer'. I recalled accounts of Russian climbers' early morning PT sessions. What sort of people had we got involved with? But we needn't have worried. Leonid's 'training' also matched Whillans', his favourite exercise being a sort of 'one arm lift', but using smaller weights – vodka rather than beer.

We were treated with the greatest possible hospitality by our Russian hosts – whoops, Belarussian hosts; calling them 'Russians' is rather like accusing a Welshman of being 'English'. Forget past images of cold-war Soviet leaders saying '*nyet*'. These people are as friendly as any in the world – especially so now that the Communists are out of power. Under the Soviet system all foreign parties were accompanied by a KGB minder who made sure that none of their own people behaved in a friendly way towards these capitalist decadents. Now that the KGB have gone, there are 50 years of repressed international friendship to be made good; but they do also have their own interests: hard currency. No doubt they made a little profit from us, which would have helped to cover the cost of their own trip. We did not begrudge that, since the cost to us was so trivial.

We flew from Minsk to Dushanbe, capital of Tadzhikistan, a journey further than from London to Moscow, again posing as locals. The four of us were easily lost amongst sixteen genuine Belarussians. We travelled on to the last small town, Djurgital, some by light plane, others by truck with the baggage. Somehow I had imagined that this Muslim country would be similar to others I had visited – Pakistan, Morocco, etc – with their bustling markets and distinctive culture. But alas, Soviet conformism had laid its heavy hand even on this far-flung corner of the empire. Dushanbe and Djurgital alike had drab workers' flats and near-empty markets.

Djurgital was the last town before the mountains. In the Karakoram or the Himalaya we would have been trying to hire porters for the walk-in to Base Camp. But things were different here. Our baggage was put in a big heap on the airstrip. In flew the biggest helicopter I had ever seen. We piled in the luggage. This was no flimsy alpine mountain-rescue machine, but a huge throbbing monster, with rotor blades 40ft across and strange pod attachments to the body. I bet this had seen service as a gun-ship in Afghanistan. Forty minutes later we were disgorged into a huge ablation valley at 4200m – the Moscvina Glacier Base Camp.

This place used to be an international mountaineering camp run from Moscow. Foreign visitors were housed in big permanently-sited tents with full board. Now it is run by the Tadzhikis themselves. You can still get the fully laid on accommodation or, as we did, you can pitch your own tents and do your own catering. For this we paid a small 'camping fee' for which a rubbish collection service was provided and a small wooden porta-loo erected near our camp. Half a mile away was the old international camp which boasted such facilities as a couple of shops and a bar (high prices and limited stocks) and a very efficient sauna! All this was at one end of the ablation valley which formed a large triangular plain bounded by the lateral moraines of two glaciers. Parties from various nations, ex-Soviet and otherwise, had their camps around its edges. The flat central part was left clear for helicopter landings, which occurred most days as various parties came and went. Most of the time there seemed to be about 150 to 200 people in residence – quite a little village.

Our large dining tent, complete with tables and benches improvised from wooden packing cases, was the centre of social life, with much noisy vodka-oiled singing and raucous merriment in the evenings. The ever-present threat of high-altitude weight loss was thankfully reduced by our hosts' dietary custom of three solid meat and veg meals per day. Whatever the truth of the western media's tales of Russian food shortages, we were cer-tainly at no risk from undernourishment. We were also well entertained by Gordon, who had an endless supply of stories of life in the British Navy in the Pacific during the Second World War, and subsequently working for British intelligence in eastern Europe.

This international village of a base camp had one other British party: a commercially guided group from 'Out There Trekking' who aimed to get their clients up Pik Kommunisma. In fact they did not do this, owing to the heavy snow cover in 1992, but managed the next best thing and guided most of them up Pik Korzhenevskaya, the other seven thousander nearby. Although the concept of guided climbing may not appeal to everyone, it did seem that these folk had a good time, and certainly a successful one, under the guidance of Jon Tinker and Mark Miller. (Sadly, Mark died a few weeks later in the Kathmandu air crash.)

The objectives of most Russian and east European teams were ascents of the big peaks by their ordinary routes. The big peaks also have many harder routes, and there is plenty of scope for new routes on all but the highest peaks. Most smaller peaks have been climbed by their ordinary routes. During the summer of 1992 many parties did the ordinary route on Pik Korzhenevskaya; later, when the heavy snow had consolidated, they also did the ordinary route on Pik Kommunisma. 'Peak of Four', one of the easier six thousanders, had several ascents as a training peak or for 'winding down'. Hardly anything else seemed to have been done.

One exception was Pik KGB (c5600m) just across the glacier from Base Camp. It had an attractive NE face which looked across to us. The face was about 1100m high and similar to many an Alpine D/TD ice face. The centre of the face had a formidable sérac barrier which gave it an initially off-putting appearance, but this could easily be avoided on the left. It looked so obvious that we thought it must have been done before. We asked Leonid and some others. They pointed to the ridge on its left and said that was the way. Our Doctor had a radio. We asked him if he had heard a weather forecast. 'Tomorrow the weather will be bad. But maybe it will be good.' He seemed to have little confidence in forecasts. We took a small Gemini tent across the glacier and camped below the face. Not being well acclimatised, we doubted our ability to get up and down in a day, so we took a stove and sleeping-bags, the extra weight guaranteeing that we would have to bivouac, but making this tolerable. As a concession to lightweight tactics, we left the tent behind.

North-east faces get early morning sun, so we started at midnight, climbing unroped by head torch. We were halfway up by dawn. Then we gradually slowed down, suffering the combined effects of fatigue, under-acclimatisation, enervating and dehydrating exposure to the sun, softening snow and steeper terrain. Most of the ground was typical 50 degree snow and ice, with several minor bergschrunds thrown in, and one longer steep pitch, about Scottish grade 4, near the top. We reached the summit in the late afternoon and descended the upper part of the E ridge to a bivouac. Next morning, the promised snowfall came a day late. We completed our descent by a 'mystery tour' down the SE face. Tony took half my load on top of his and took it back to Base Camp, while I went round the corner to retrieve our tent.

Back at base, the Minsk lads were generous with their congratulations. Leonid in particular had a hug like a bear. They now admitted that it was probably a new route. But they did have a few uncomprehending questions: 'How did you move so fast at the start?', 'Why did you go so slow near the top?'

Meanwhile, they had started to move on Korzhenevskaya. It seems that they get a lot of kudos for ascents of all the four 7000m peaks of the former USSR, and they were very keen to bag these two. They seemed strangely unconcerned about acclimatisation. They laid great emphasis on fitness, as if mountaineering were yet another Olympic sport. Most of their equipment was primitive: paraffin stoves on the hill, home-made rucksacks, various species of bendy boots, and overweight crampons without front points, looking like something from an Alpine museum. They certainly needed to be fit with all that excess weight to carry. But they got up Pik Korzhenevskaya at only their second sortie, after just one 'acclimatise and carry' trip. Phil, as always operating alone, also succeeded on this peak, but not without signs of fatigue. A few days later, Tony and I followed in their footsteps, along with several other parties. It was not just a snow plod – there were two or three slightly technical sections – but the local guides had previously put fixed ropes on these, so reducing the route to a level suitable for all and sundry. Gordon had trouble with an old-injured knee, so was disappointed.

Back at base, we took a two-day rest and the good weather ended. The Minsk lads were on Pik Kommunisma and had an exciting couple of days descending in a whiteout. Phil was also caught out after his first solo ascent of the N face of Pik Korova (6220m), an impressive, if somewhat sérac-threatened face. He finally staggered into camp looking like a latter-day Captain Oates, much to the Belarussians' relief – they had given him up for dead.

On a clearer day our return helicopter landed, but then departed without us in an attempt to help a French party stranded by the storm high on Kommunisma. Unloaded, it flew to over 7000m in a vain mission to drop them food, fuel and medical supplies, an attempt which was foiled by strong winds – a stern reminder of the risks inherent in climbing high mountains without enough time to acclimatise, exacerbated by rapid access by helicopter.

The high mountains of the former USSR are well worth a visit at present. There are no permission requirements or peak fees, the bane of visits to high mountains elsewhere in Asia. Little English is spoken so, unless you speak Russian, it is best to go as some sort of combined party with a team from an ex-Soviet country. But you had better go soon, for who knows how the politics of this volatile region will change in the next few years.

Summary: In July-August 1992 Tony Parks, Dave Wilkinson, Phil Thornhill and Gordon Dyke joined a party of sixteen Belarussians for a five-week stay at the Moscvina Glacier Base Camp in Tadzhikistan. Pik Korzhenev-skaya (7105m) was climbed by the normal route. Pik KGB (c5600) was climbed by the NE face – a new route by Tony Parks and Dave Wilkinson (D/TD). Phil Thornhill climbed a new route on Pik Korova (6200m): the N face.

CHUCK EVANS

The Other Side of Nepal

(Plates 70–75)

In memory of Carlton Freeman who was due to share this adventure, but sadly was killed in the Alps shortly before our departure.

To the Karnali

Across the Terai long stretches of road lead into the warm smell of Indian night. I am awoken as our bus lurches to the side of a bumpy ungraded track and we stop on a bridge over the Babai Nadi to let the drivers sleep before venturing into the hills. The stars are bright and mosquitoes are abroad. Taking a stroll to stretch my legs, I beat a hasty retreat at the sound of uproar from the local village dogs, and then, with each returning step, wonder if I have turned my back on a tiger.

The road ends at Surkhet and early in the morning of 9 April 1992 we begin our trek. The first day is an eye-opener; no breakfast and a 5000ft climb, with the thermometer on John's sack reading 40°C. We struggle awkwardly between patches of shade and curse the descending mules, which kick up dust and aggravate our already parched throats. There is little water and only one tea stop all day, but *daal baht* works wonders and the songs and laughter of our 63 porters help us up to a ridge-top village at about 7000ft. We experience the joy of the first camp fire, eat masses of food and then settle down to what, for me, is the best sleep I've had for months.

A day of deep red rhododendrons and a knee-wrenching descent leads down to Dungeswor in the Koltila Khola. Caroline and Julia muster an audience of 20 or 30 children as they go for a swim whilst Matt, John, Frank and I are left to wash in relative peace! No requests here for sweets, for 'one rupee' or 'school pen'. We learn that back home John Major is re-elected, but domestic politics slips the mind; it has no relevance.

Over the next few days we gain height gradually, passing west of Dailekh and east of Dulu, site of the winter palace of the ancient kings of Jumla. We get to know our Sherpas (Tenzing Tashi from Khumjung and Nuru from Solu) and also our mobile kitchen. This is led by Nawang Kharsang from Rimishung with Mila from Ghorka and two Rai boys. Their names are difficult so we call them Jimmy and S-B. Roshan Sharma from Terai acts as general factotum. We settle into the freedom of expedition life, where all is new and of the moment. Uncomplicated by the events of yesterday or the troubles of tomorrow, there is no meaning beyond the next horizon. Our preoccupations are confined to food and porters, with

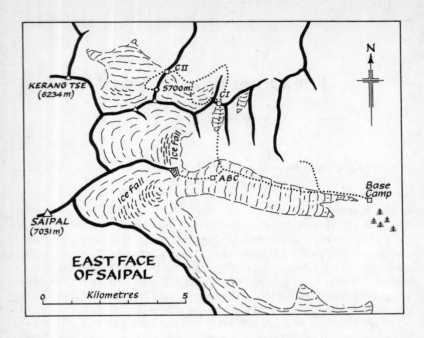

EAST FACE OF SAIPAL

WEST NEPAL

Saipal remaining, beyond comprehension, 14 days' walk to the north. Only the occasional Mugu man and his goats hint of another world beyond the mountains we can't yet see. Even the Karnali river is a dream.

To reach Manma, district capital of Kalikot, we must climb through dense jungle over the 3000m Haudi Lagna. In contrast to the heat of the day, the cool of the woods on the skin is refreshing and revives senses numbed by sun and dirt. I often wonder at the age of the paths through these hills, and here the creepers, white orchids and hanging lichens add a primeval quality. In 70 days away from roads we meet only one Westerner: a Dutch eye surgeon who works in the Karnali zone for three months each year. She tells us that here in these woods she has met a nomadic jungle people. Keeping themselves apart from the local Nepalis (who don't regard them as human) they wear few clothes and build no villages. They live in small encampments for two to three months at a time before again vanishing into the trees. In a land already primitive by Western standards it is strange to be confronted with shadows of yet older times.

Through the haze from Haudi Lagna we are elated by our first and only view of Saipal during the walk in. We place pink rhododendrons on a little shrine and plunge into the Tila Khola. Our excitement leads to renditions of French climbing songs and 'Hills of the North Rejoice' – which are answered by all manner of hoots and catcalls from the Sherpas far below. Food is scarce from now on and so at Manma we buy government rice for our porters. It isn't available to the locals and, although of inferior quality, costs the same as in Kathmandu (20p/1kg). For a week we follow the west bank of the Karnali northwards. At times we walk close to the river for hour after hour, now deafened by a roaring torrent, now a little astonished as 1000 tonnes of glossy blue-green water slide silently by. On other days we traverse hillsides, 1000m above the golden ribbon which, far below, carves relentlessly down to the Ganges plain. It is hot, arid cactus country and somehow claustrophobic – we can't see where we are going nor where we have come from. We turn in on ourselves and have the sense of passing through an underworld. The people are poor but high-caste Hindus and the villages have flat-roofed Tibetan-style houses. We take an occasional swim or watch monkeys prowling the cliffs on the far bank, and one morning an owl the size of an eagle is chased by crows out of an enormous banyan tree.

At last we come 'down to a temperate valley', the Kuwari Khola, our secret back door to Saipal and Humla. We leave behind the Karnali zone and enter fragrant pine forests and, deep in the river valley, a wet and wonderful jungle of walnut and bamboo. This constricts to a narrower gorge before opening out into a mythical land of alpine meadows with one or two small Bhotia settlements. Here the goats, previously seen through clouds of dust and laden with bags of rice, are grazing contentedly on green grass. Potatoes, chang and curd are available. There is a freshness in the air and for me a sense of homecoming.

The Mountain

In 1963 the Japanese climbed Saipal by its S ridge and in 1985 the Spanish by the SW face and the W ridge. Both these and previous expeditions had approached the mountain from the Seti river system. Following exploration by Denis Bertholet in 1988 two separate expeditions, Austrian and Swiss, flew to Simikot, capital of Humla, and managed to establish a base camp on the NW side of Saipal from which they succeeded in climbing the N ridge.

We were the seventh expedition to reach the mountain, but the first to approach from the Karnali. Base Camp was established in front of the E face on 26 April at the foot of the terminal moraine of a short flattish glacier which led to broad open meadows. It was low (3650m) but very beautiful; trees covered the hills on either side and the Sherpas were quite as taken with the place as we were.

The summit was seven miles from Base Camp and at 7031m was still 11,000ft above us. Whilst distant and ethereal, this massive cascade of icefall and rock seemed at the same time immediate and compelling. It had already taken hold of our imagination and now stood no longer a dream, but a tangible barrier between us and our aspirations. To our left the serrated E ridge extended towards us for two miles at over 6000m and then dropped sharply to a col. On our right two peaks at 5940m and 5760m were joined by a complicated ridge system (the NE spur). Ahead, a massive cornice stretched along the N ridge, surmounting a magnificent double-backed amphitheatre.

We made Advanced Base at 3850m in the middle of the glacier and directly below two large icefalls, which were separated by a rock buttress. A continuous barrage of sérac avalanches from both sides and stonefall on the buttress rendered any direct assault on the face inadvisable. We therefore turned our attention to circumventing the right-hand icefall to the north, and climbed a gully and bowl to reach Camp 1 (4800m) on a hitherto uncrossed pass. From here our attempts to reach the main N ridge along the NE spur proved unfruitful, and so we decided to push further into Humla.

From Camp 1 we descended into a bowl and, skirting west round Peak 5760m, were forced to climb avalanche-prone slopes up to a ridge on which we placed Camp 2 at 5200m. Progress from here was blocked by an arête running between the mountain and Kerang Tse (an unattempted 6000m satellite of Saipal). We traversed towards this, but retreated at the prospect of another descent and reascent under an unpleasant icefall. Our final effort was to climb to a high point of 5700m on the N side of the mountain.

Whilst a little disappointed at our inability to find an acceptable route, we were looking forward to a big feed at Base Camp and hoped to explore the approaches to the E ridge on the S side of the amphitheatre. Unfortunately, descending with heavy sacks from Camp 2 on 16 May, Nuru Sherpa and I were involved in separate falls down the same gully. We gathered speed on unstable snow, hurtled down an avalanche runnel and flew over a large bergschrund to land painfully on its lower lip. Relieved not to be seriously injured, I hobbled across to Nuru who had broken his ankle and cracked a vertebra. With some difficulty and suffering considerable pain in his back, Nuru was lowered and then carried down to an emergency camp. From here, John Holland and Roshan made a marathon journey over the Chote Lagna (4700m) to Simikot in order to radio for a helicopter. Five days later, Nuru was evacuated from the N side of the mountain and, back in Kathmandu, had an operation to pin his ankle.

It was perhaps fortuitous that we were delayed by this accident, as at some time on the same day a huge avalanche thundered down our route between Camp 1 and Advanced Base. Having fanned out 200yds onto the main glacier, the tumbled blocks of ice still involved us in a 20ft climb down to our old trail to Base Camp.

Humla

When we left the Kuwari Khola on 26 May it was covered in spring flowers, and yaks from the nearby Humla village of Chala were grazing in the summer pastures at Sain. However, the north-facing slopes of the 4560m Sankha Lagna were still deep in snow. We struggled down through mist into a canyon and next day crossed the Kerang Khola to reach Chala – a primitive collection of flat-roofed houses huddled together below a broad ridge separating the Humla Karnali and Kerang Khola rivers.

Enjoying being on the move again, we travelled deeper into Humla and rejoined the Karnali at Muchu, a village of apple orchards on the Tibetan trade route. The region was much more alpine and less arid than we had expected. A panorama of several unnamed 6000m peaks was visible to the north of the Karnali and we had exceptional views back to Saipal and on to the S side of Gurla Mandhata in Tibet.

Humla was also less poor than we had been led to believe. The people clearly led a subsistence life-style, but the Bhotia settlements we passed following the Karnali back east to Simikot were well ordered and prosperous compared with the Thakuri villages further down river. We waited a week for our Chala porters to recover from festivities following a local election and complete the journey from Base Camp. Their in-bred characteristics did not impress our kitchen boys, who called them 'spider-monkeys', and when finally they arrived at Simikot they seemed ill at ease even in this remote outpost of Nepal.

Return via Rara Lake

We paid them off and succeeded in air-lifting most of our gear direct to Nepalganj to enable us to travel light on the walk out to Jumla. On 8 June we dropped back into the Humla Karnali gorge, and followed it south and east for three days, slightly disconcerted by reports of cholera further downstream.

At Darma we left the river and began a climb to the Chankheli Lekh, a delightful pine-forested pass leading over into Mugu. After a long hot day we reached Rara on the evening of 13 June just as it was getting dark. Whilst not particularly impressive by European standards, Rara, at an altitude of over 3000m, is the biggest lake in Nepal. Its isolation gives that restful tranquillity which, after weeks in the hills, can only be provided by a mile or two of level water. It is fresh and clear and surrounded by wild roses and pine trees. A strange feature is that hardly any streams flow in or out, despite a 4000ft drop to the Mugu Karnali as it bypasses the lake on its N and E flanks.

From Rara a day and a half took us over the Churchi Lekh and down to the Sinja Khola, where we were eaten alive by midges. Another day over a final pass and a long descent brought us to Jumla, a veritable metropolis. We camped by the airfield and gazed with mixed feelings at the Kanjiroba Himal.

Summary: In April-May 1991 the six members of the British Saipal Expedition, led by Chuck Evans, carried out a first reconnaissance of the NE side of Saipal (7031m), reaching 5700m on the NE spur. They also travelled through the little-known region of Humla.

Celebrating Everest

MICHAEL WESTMACOTT

The Everest Anniversary Celebrations

A Personal Account

(Plates 1, 2 and 67)

'The Queen will be wearing a cocktail dress,' said the Palace Official, and Her Majesty's intention was duly recorded in the Minutes for the benefit of ladies attending the celebrations. Clearly we were now down to basics. Indeed, the planning seemed at times to be more elaborate than it had been in 1952/53, perhaps because then there had been but a single objective, whereas now there were several, depending on who you talked to. The Mount Everest Foundation wished to replenish its coffers, publishers saw an opportunity for new titles, films were promoted, exhibitions mounted, T-shirts designed, and special supplements planned for the weekend newspapers; the bandwagon was overloaded. Forty years ago *The Times* soberly covered the progress of the expedition; the rest of the media (a term then scarcely invented) only became interested late in the day, and were held at arm's length by the expedition. How different now! From the beginning, the 1953 team themselves had said that they did not wish to promote any great show nor have a great fuss made, but would do their best to co-operate with the organisers. By the end, they were in much the same gratified but bemused state of mind that they had experienced after the return to Kathmandu all those years ago.

The centrepiece of the public celebrations was the 'expedition lecture' at the Royal Geographical Society, introduced by Chris Bonington and admirably delivered by John Hunt, Mike Ward, George Band and Ed Hillary. There were three performances, before a total audience of some 1800 people, the third and last in the presence of Her Majesty the Queen and other members of the Royal Family. The enthusiastic applause which followed the account of a forty-year-old adventure was quite astounding. It was a moving experience for all those involved.

After the lecture, Her Majesty the Queen, with the Princess Royal and the Duke of Kent, attended a reception to which a number of distinguished British and foreign guests and about 120 members of the Alpine Club and Fellows of the RGS had been invited. It was most gratifying to receive afterwards a letter from the Palace making it clear that Her Majesty had much enjoyed the evening; the lecture, we knew, had gone very well, but we wondered whether the reception afterwards had not been altogether too crowded, in spite of the ruthless pruning which had been applied to the guest list.

The arrangements for these lectures had been made in the context of a fund-raising exercise for the Mount Everest Foundation conducted by its ex-Chairman Charles Clarke and current Chairman Patrick Fagan. The organisers had realised from the outset that it would not be possible to match the generous, and very successful, Annapurna celebrations in 1990, when all the surviving first ascensionists of 8000m peaks and many other distinguished mountaineers had been invited, at Chamonix's expense, to a party lasting several days. We were well aware that no government or municipal help would be available in the UK. The lecture programme was, incidentally, a financial success, contributing substantially to the 40th Anniversary Appeal.

The evening at the RGS was a high spot. For me, however, other events were more simply enjoyable. On the previous day there had been a reception for the 1953 team at the Alpine Club, attended by some of the foreign guests who were in London for the RGS affair, and by as many AC members as could be accommodated. A fine exhibition of photographs from successive expeditions adorned the walls of the lecture room. Exhibits from the archives and other memorabilia were on show upstairs. Food was provided by a volunteer team, the wine flowed freely and speeches were kept to a minimum. The occasion was relaxed, bringing together many old friends and acquaintances. It was good to have with us Charles Warren who was Medical Officer on the Everest expeditions of 1935, 1936 and 1938. The Sherpa community was represented by Nawang Gombu, Tenzing Norgay's nephew, who was with us in 1953, by Tenzing's son Norbu Tenzing, and by Pertemba.

Earlier in the year six members of the 1953 expedition had met in Khumbu, originally with the idea of attending the opening of the new Thyangboche monastery, the previous building having been destroyed by fire a few years ago. But the work had not been finished on time and, whether coincidentally or not, the planned opening date had been declared by the monks to be inauspicious. It was a relief not to have to join the crowds that were bound to arrive for that occasion. As it was, there were at least two 'anniversary' expeditions in the area and several TV teams, as well as the usual complement of trekkers and climbers. Some of us arrived on foot from Jiri on 31 March to find those who had come by air ensconced in a large camp in a sloping meadow near Lukla. It quickly became clear that this was also something of a fund-raising occasion, this time for Ed Hillary's Himalayan Trust. The time spent at Lukla provided a pleasant rest after ten days walking, but was much taken up with TV, group photographs and interviews. I wondered more than once how Ed Hillary had survived the past 40 years of fame. All honour to him that he has used it for the great work he has done with and for the Sherpas. He and John Hunt were whisked away by helicopter one day for a party at Thyangboche, a celebration and a 'Thankyou' for all they have done.

So the six expedition members did not have a lot of time together, dispersing after two days in various directions. In spite of poor weather, the walking party had enjoyed their journey to Lukla, following much of the route of 40 years ago. Times had changed, but the country and the people are still most attractive. There are tea-houses and lodges at intervals; no longer are Europeans a curiosity, nor is an empty tin or a polythene bag snapped up by the locals as soon as it is abandoned. But the litter situation is a lot better than in London, and there are very few signs of serious erosion, though there are more villagers and no doubt fewer trees. I had a particular interest in butterflies, having collected some in 1953 and recorded a migration, mainly of long-tailed blues and diptera, over the 3000m Lamjura Bhanjyang. This year, there was no such movement over the col. Generally, there seemed to be fewer butterflies around. Whether that was due to a late and snowy spring, to deforestation or just to the rose-tinted memories of youth, I cannot say.

After Lukla, most of the party walked to Namche Bazar, where it then split up, some going on to Kala Pattar, while the original walking party went to both Thame and Gokyo. *En route*, we were interested and impressed when we visited one of the tree nurseries set up by the Himalayan Trust. Then more of us went home, leaving George Band and me, with our trek leader Steve Aisthorp and David Murdoch, the doctor from Kunde, to attempt Imjatse (Island Peak). The weather on our approach was abysmal, dumping quantities of fresh snow on the peaks. It cleared brilliantly for our attempt, but we ran out of time on the final ridge, reaching a respectable 20,000ft but unwilling to face the descent in the dark that would have followed a few further hours of work to reach the summit. It was, however, a splendid mountaineering day with which to round off our trip.

There was one more great pleasure for me, in meeting again Pasang Phutar, my personal attendant during the walk-in 40 years before. He is now an old gentleman of over 80, a great age for a Sherpa of his generation. He lives comfortably in his son's modern home in a suburb of Kathmandu. How good it is when the benefits of 'development' go to the right people.

The final phase of the 40th Anniversary celebrations was, appropriately, at the Pen-y-Gwryd Hotel during the weekend which included the 29th of May. We began by attending a party at Plas y Brenin as guests of the British Mountaineering Council, which was also host to the annual assembly of the UIAA. At this party, Ed Hillary was made an Honorary Member of the UIAA, in recognition of his work for the Sherpas. Then, next morning, on the anniversary of the first ascent, the press were in attendance for a short time at the PyG. But after that we were able to be alone at last, with our families and friends. We walked round the Snowdon Horseshoe, we dined sumptuously as guests of the house, and we relaxed together. It had been a memorable celebration.

BUCKINGHAM PALACE

27th May, 1993.

Dear Lord Hunt

On our return to Buckingham Palace last night, The Queen
asked me to write to thank you for your very special part in
yesterday's celebration of the Fortieth Anniversary of the
first ascent of Everest. I do not think I need tell you how
much Her Majesty enjoyed the evening because it was so evident
throughout. The riveting account of the events of forty years
ago during your lecture re-awakened for The Queen, like every
single member of the audience, the thrill and excitement of
your achievement all those years ago. Her Majesty
particularly enjoyed the chance to meet members of the 1953
team after the lecture. She also was most grateful to you for
presenting her with the commemorative edition of your book
which she has asked should find a special place in the Royal
Library at Windsor.

I should be grateful if you would pass on The Queen's
thanks to all members present of the 1953 team for a truly
unforgettable evening. This letter comes with Her Majesty's
warm good wishes to you all.

Yours sincerely

(ROBIN JANVRIN)

The Lord Hunt, KG, CBE, DSO.

JOHN HUNT

The Everest Reunions

(Plates 63–67)

For the first ten years after 1953 we all used to meet annually to celebrate our climb. From 1965 onwards we spaced the reunions at intervals of five years. But it is an indication of our fellowship that in 1980 Alf Gregory suggested that five years was too long a gap; in that year, and again in 1990, he hosted a most enjoyable interim meet in Derbyshire. All our other reunions, except the one on Skye in 1955, took place in Snowdonia at the Pen-y-Gwryd Hotel, by tradition the meeting place of British rock-climbers since the nineteenth century.

There have also been Everest reunions elsewhere than in Britain. In 1963 the Swiss Foundation for Alpine Research generously convened a gathering, at Meiringen in the Bernese Oberland, of Swiss and British alpinists who had been on Everest in 1952, 1953 and 1956. Tenzing and I represented the 1953 team and Noel Odell was invited as an honoured guest. In 1973 the Indian Mountaineering Foundation hosted an international conference in Darjeeling, both to mark our twentieth anniversary and to celebrate their own success in 1965. Three of us – Alf Gregory, Charles Wylie and I, with my wife Joy – took advantage of this opportunity to travel to the conference the hard way, by trekking across Nepal from Khumbu. We timed it perfectly, taking 19 days to reach the Singalila ridge on the eve of the conference, with the lights of Darjeeling twinkling below us. Ed Hillary and Tenzing were there to greet us. In 1978 that route was reversed when a larger party of 1953 veterans and some of our reserves, accompanied by wives and Tom Bourdillon's widow Jennifer, made the return journey across Nepal to Khumbu after celebrating our Jubilee with our Sherpas, and sharing it with a large gathering of distinguished mountaineers from around the world.

Photographs of our reunions at Pen-y-Gwryd provide evidence, year by year, of the changes which time has imposed on us, but they cannot record the unchanging nature of our relationship. It has endured, undiminished, through all these forty years. Against a background of twenty reunions at home and abroad, it is not surprising, therefore, that 1993 was a very special year for us. It was Ed Hillary's happy idea that we should gather once again in Khumbu; he had hoped to combine a reunion with a formal opening ceremony of the rebuilt Thyangboche monastery, but, in the event, the building was not completed in time. In March most members of the old firm, with some of the 1953 reserves, wives and two daughters, set off for Nepal. One group, including my wife Joy, travelled out a week earlier in order to follow part of our original trek in 1953. The departure of the second group was timed to ensure that we would all meet at Lukla.

As a member of the latter party I travelled with my daughter Prue, Charles Wylie, George and Mary Lowe and their friends. We were joined in Kathmandu by Ed and June Hillary and were fortunate to take part in celebrations in the capital. Our Ambassador gave a magnificent reception, attended by over one hundred guests, including Chris Bonington, Reinhold Messner and other well-known mountaineers. The Nepal Mountaineering Association gave a party at the Everest Hotel attended by the Minister for Tourism and several Ambassadors, at which splendid memorabilia were presented to each member of the 1953 expedition. Seated beside us on the dais was Pasang Phutar, one of our old Sherpas living in Kathmandu.

Most joyous of all was another reception, also held in the Everest Hotel, which was organised by Sherpas from Solu and Khumbu to express their gratitude for the benefits bestowed upon their people as a result of our first ascent. This was primarily a tribute to Ed Hillary, whose work in building schools, hospitals and bridges has so much improved the quality of life in those two districts. The reception was a most generous and touching gesture, for which much financial sacrifice had been made by the two local communities.

At Lukla, our two groups were reunited at a private campsite bedecked with mauve primulas and surrounded by rhododendron bushes, among which a few early blossoms gave a touch of colour. There were many other people on the site, including four television crews and various visitors. Unfortunately, the presence of so many people somewhat diluted our reunion – Ed and myself, in particular, sometimes found ourselves separated from our families and old comrades. But this did not entirely spoil a unique episode in the Everest story.

A highlight which, sadly, only a few of us were able to enjoy was a reception by the monastic community at Thyangboche. We were flown there by helicopter and were offered a demonstration of gratitude and affection by the monks and the community they serve. Ed and I were privileged to receive this welcome on behalf of the rest of the team, and everything combined to make it a magical experience: the orchestra of monastic mountain horns, the trumpets, cymbals and conch shells, the dancing of Sherpas and Sherpanis, the showering upon us of gifts, the adornment with scarves (with Ed and me almost submerged under a mountain of silk!). And there, peeping beyond and above the great ridge of Nuptse, was Everest's summit, holding so many memories for us all.

It was just as well, amid such moving ceremonies, that a note of the ridiculous was also struck: the sight of Ed and me, after we had inspected the new building, seated in the courtyard of the monastery, surrounded by spectators, endeavouring to look dignified as we ate the lunch offered by our hosts. Ed fared better than I did, for he was given a tin of Dundee cake, while I struggled to extract the contents of an outsize sardine tin with a knife.

The reunion was followed by various treks. Mike Westmacott and George Band (nearly) climbed Island Peak, one of our original first ascents in 1953. My daughter Prue reached 19,000ft on the ridge of Kala Pattar and had her first close-up view of our mountain: it was a supreme moment for her. I draw a veil over my own performance.

On the very date of the fortieth anniversary – 29th of May – we gathered at Pen-y-Gwryd for our sixteenth reunion. Predictably, the media journalists and cameramen were in keen attendance. We were royally entertained at Plas y Brenin ('Palace of the Kings'), formerly the Royal Hotel, by the British Mountaineering Council. I enjoyed enormously the opportunity to meet old friends from Europe and beyond, especially Yevgeniy Gippenreiter, with whom I have shared so many experiences: in Moscow and London, in the Caucasus and Pamir, and here in Snowdonia. The last time he and I had been at Plas y Brenin we had tried our skill in a canoe on Llyn Mymbyr dressed in mountain kit, and had capsized in the middle of the lake!

On Sunday 30 May, a very wet day, Jane and Brian Pulley put on a superb meal at the Pen-y-Gwryd, washed down, as tradition dictated, by Bouvier champagne. We missed the company of Charles Evans and Griff Pugh, but welcomed Tenzing's son Norbu Tenzing and his wife, and Nawang Gombu, Tenzing's nephew and our youngest Sherpa in 1953. We were also delighted to welcome Jo Briggs who, with her husband Chris, had entertained us so generously at every previous reunion at the hotel. After the dinner John Jackson gave us all great pleasure with an exhibition of his photographs. We enjoyed a good laugh – and maybe a tear or two – over a film which recorded our reception in Delhi on our way home 40 years ago, which had been presented to me by an Indian photographer.

It was on that happy note that the curtain came down on 'Everest 1993', and the latest of so many memorable Everest reunions.

MICHAEL WARD

The Exploration and Mapping of Everest

(Plates 43–47)

From its inception in the middle of the 19th century, the Royal Geographical Society (RGS) took a keen interest in the mapping of the Everest region. This formed an integral part of the many Everest expeditions, some of which had individual surveyors or survey parties attached to them. Many mountaineers took part in this work, particularly those with a scientific background. But it was not until 1961 that a comprehensive map was produced of the Everest region.

The Identification of Everest

The identification and naming of the mountain we call Mount Everest had begun much earlier. Since circa AD 750 the Rongbuk valley monastery and the surrounding region of south Tibet had been considered by Tibetans as places particularly suited to the highest intellectual attainment, since they were within sight of the peak named Chomolungma.[1] This must have been the peak, now known to all as Mount Everest, which dominates the whole region and can be clearly seen from the trade route to Lhasa that runs north of Rongbuk and south of the Tsangpo valley. A mountain in a similar position and with a similar name, Chomo-Kankar, is mentioned in an early Tibetan geographical text; Chomo Uri was another local name. As mountains played an important part in Tibetan culture, being seen variously as ladders by which their ancestors descended from heaven, or as pegs or pillars supporting the sky or fastening it to the earth, any outstanding peak would have held great religious significance.

Although a number of Jesuit missionaries visited south Tibet in the 17th century in search of Nestorian Christian colonies, it seems unlikely that any of them saw Everest, as they were in an area too far west. However, in 1661 Johannes Grüber and Albert d'Orville left Lhasa and travelled west along the Tsangpo valley, crossing the Himalaya at Tengri Dzong by the Nyelam valley and reaching Kathmandu in January 1662. Though Everest would have been visible along much of their route, neither of these missionaries mentioned in their writings having seen a particularly high peak; nor did Father Desiderei who reached Lhasa from west Tibet in 1716, returning by a similar route to Tengri Dzong.

The first survey of the Everest region was made by the Chinese between 1708 and 1716 in the course of a general survey of the Chinese empire. From this survey Jesuit fathers in Peking drew a map that was published in 1717-18 in the reign of the Emperor Kangshi. On this map a mountain group named Jumu Lungma Alin can be found in the position of Everest. The map formed the basis of the earliest European map of Asia, d'Anville's *Nouveau Atlas de Chine* published 20 years later in 1733. [2,3]

The first attempt to make a formal survey of Nepal, which was not covered by d'Anville's map, was made by Charles Crawford, a member of the staff of the first mission to Kathmandu, between 1801 and 1804. He calculated the latitude and longitude of the capital and produced a large-scale map indicating the height of some peaks seen from the city. He also completed a small-scale map of the rest of Nepal based on information supplied by native travellers, but on this no high peaks were recorded. Anglo–Nepalese relations deteriorated soon afterwards and Nepal was to remain closed to Europeans for the next 150 years.

In the early part of the 19th century, officers of the newly formed Survey of India began mapping that vast and little known country. In 1818 George Everest, who had gone to India as an artillery cadet in 1806, was made chief assistant to William Lambton, the founder of the newly formed Great Trigonometrical Survey (GTS) of India. From 1830 to 1843 George Everest combined the posts of Surveyor-General and Superintendent of the GTS, and it was during this period that he conceived and put into effect the grid-iron system of triangulation which eventually reached the foothills of the Himalaya; he was unable to go further north owing to the political difficulties presented by the independent kingdoms of Sikkim, Nepal and Bhutan.[4] However, altitude measurements were made of all the peaks visible from the plains of India, and first Dhaulagiri (Peak 42) in central Nepal, and then Kangchenjunga (Peak 8) on the borders of Sikkim and Nepal, were considered to be the world's highest peaks. At the same time, ignorance of the topography of the Himalaya was so profound and widespread that Joseph Hooker, the botanist, was able to write in his *Himalayan Journals* of 1854: 'It was not then known that Kangchenjunga, the loftiest mountain on the globe, was situated on my route and formed a principal feature in the physical geography of Sikkim.'[5]

With further routine measurements it became apparent that an insignificant looking peak in NE Nepal, about 70 miles west of Kangchenjunga, was extremely high. First observed around 1848 it had been designated Peak 15 and appeared to be one of a number of seemingly minor summits. Eventually, between November 1849 and January 1850, the highest mountain in the world was discovered at 27° 59.3' north latitude and 86° 54.7' east latitude from Greenwich. An average height of 29,002ft, or 8840m, was computed from six different stations.[6] This information was conveyed to a meeting of the Asiatic Society of Bengal. On 1 March 1856, Andrew Waugh, who had succeeded George Everest, wrote to Sir Roderick Murchison, President of the Royal Geographical Society, giving him the coordinates and estimations of height. He suggested that the name 'Everest' be given to the peak to commemorate his outstanding predecessor and because there was neither a local name nor a native appellation.[7] In this he was wrong, because the Tibetans knew the peak as Chomolungma or Jumu Lungma Alin. Moreover, Hooker mentions in his *Himalayan Journals* that

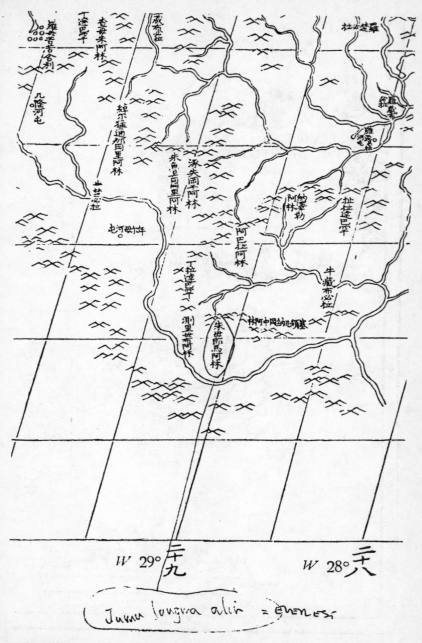

Detail from a map drawn by Jesuit fathers in Peking from a survey
of the Everest region made by the Chinese between 1708 and 1716.

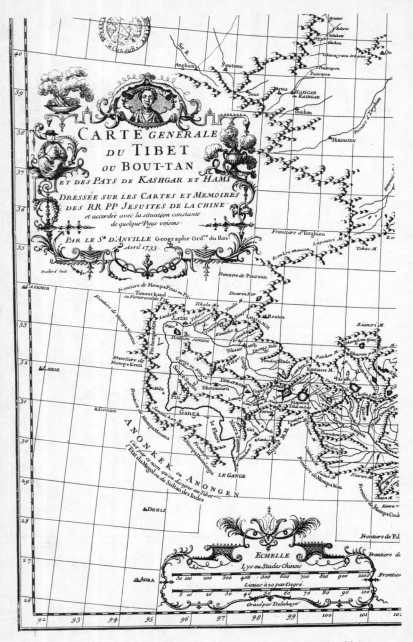

Part of a page from d'Anville's Nouveau Atlas de Chine,
published in 1733, the earliest European map of Asia.

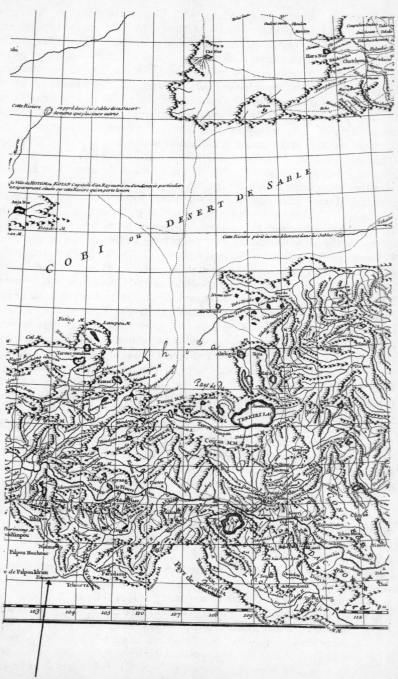

Tchoumour Lancma M = Everest

the Nepalese called a 'stupendous white mountain mass' in this area 'Tsungau', and comments in a footnote that this is 'better known as Everest, the loftiest summit on the globe. Its position is latitude 28°N and longitude 87°E. It cannot be seen from Kathmandu' (which is correct). This last piece of information probably came from Brian Hodgson, former Resident in Kathmandu, with whom Hooker was staying whilst in Sikkim. A letter from Hodgson, quoted in the Proceedings of the RGS 1855-57, states that Peak 15 already had a name, 'Devadhunga', a claim later investigated and found to be incorrect. The controversy over a name for Everest has continued to the present day, and current local alternatives are 'Qomolungma' or 'Chomolungma' (Chinese) and 'Sagarmatha' (Nepalese).

Among the first Europeans to attempt to establish the identity of Everest were the Schlagintweit brothers. In 1855 Hermann Schlagintweit painted a mountain from Phalut on the Singalila ridge running south from Kangchenjunga. The title of the painting (Plate 64 in the Alpine Journal 97) is 'Gaurisankar or Everest'; Schlagintweit believed that these were alternative names for the same mountain. Two years later, in 1857, while on a visit to Kathmandu, Schlagintweit climbed a small hill, Kaulia, in the Kathmandu valley and from there saw the mountain called by Hodgson, the British Resident, 'Devadhunga'. Schlagintweit identified Devadhunga as Everest, but certified the local name as 'Gaurisankar'. But the Survey of India never accepted the name 'Gaurisankar' as an alternative to 'Everest'. The correct identification from Nepal was made in 1903 when Henry Wood of the Survey of India also visited Kaulia and clearly showed that the peak visible from there was Gaurisankar (Peak 20) and well known to the Survey. Peak 20 was 35 miles west of Everest, and the peak which Schlagintweit painted in 1855 was, in fact, Makalu. The first close-up inspection and identification of Gaurisankar and its higher neighbour Menlungtse was made from Tibet in 1921, and by Shipton and Ward from Nepal in 1951.[8]

Since Europeans were forbidden to travel in Tibet and Nepal during the latter half of the 19th century, Hari Ram (the pundit M-H, or No 9) was the first to circumnavigate the Everest region, crossing the Nangpa La in 1885. However, he left no record of having seen a particularly high peak.[9] Natha Singh, an Indian surveyor, reached the Khumbu glacier in 1907 but was unable to carry out a survey and just sketched the lower end. In 1898 Dr L A Waddell, later a member of the 1904 Younghusband mission to Lhasa, obtained a Tibetan picture map of the Himalaya south of Tengri. But the group of peaks shown are more likely to be the Menlungtse–Gaurisankar group than Everest.[10]

The 1904 mission to Lhasa provided an opportunity to identify Everest from the north and make certain that there were no higher peaks. This task was carried out by a survey party consisting of R H D Ryder, C G Rawling, F M Bailey and Henry Wood. Wood, who had been in Nepal the year before, identified Everest with certainty from Kampa Dzong, and a good and closer view was obtained by Rawling from the Kara La pass 50 miles to the north of the mountain.[11] But the immediate neighbourhood of Everest still remained unexplored and unmapped. However, H H Hayden, attached to the mission as a geologist, took a number of photographs of the mountain and sent them to the Secretary of the Royal Geographical Society. Previously, photographs of Everest had been taken from the south and east, by Vittorio Sella in 1899, and by J Claude White in 1903 from Sandak Phu, 10 miles south of Phalut on the Singalila ridge. Kellas took further photographs in 1920 from the Kang La, 25 miles north of Phalut.

Although Col John Noel reached Tashirak on a tributary of the Arun, 40 miles east of Everest, in 1913, he had only a poor view of the mountain.[12] An aerial survey of Everest was considered but never carried out at that time.[13]

Thus, by the outbreak of the First World War, Everest had been clearly identified and photographed but only from a distance. The whole Everest region between the Rongshar and the Arun, and between the Tsangpo river and Namche Bazar remained to be explored and mapped. This process was to be completed between 1921 and the end of 1953.

Mapping of the Tibetan (north) side of Everest

The mapping of Everest from the north was carried out between World Wars I and II in the course of seven expeditions. As soon as the First World War was over, in December 1918, the RGS and Alpine Club jointly considered obtaining permission from either the Tibetan or Nepalese governments to explore Everest and find a route to the summit. As the world's last major geographical challenge (now that both the Poles had been reached) it was felt that every effort should be made to do this. Permission for a Nepalese approach was refused, but with the backing of the India Office and the Government of India the Dalai Lama gave permission for an expedition to visit the Tibetan side of Everest in 1921. It had two objectives: to survey and to find a route to the summit.[14]

The 1921 Everest Expedition[15]

The members of the survey party were Major H T Morshead, Major E O Wheeler, Lalbir Singh Thapa, Gujjar Singh, Turubaj Singh, a photographer Abdul Jalil Khan and 16 porters. Their task was threefold: to carry out a general survey, at 4 miles to the inch, of the unmapped area to be explored by the expedition; to complete a detailed survey, at 1 mile to the inch, of the immediate environment of Everest; and to make a revision of the existing quarter-inch map of Sikkim on their way from Darjeeling to Tibet.

At this time, knowledge of the Everest region depended on the work of the pundits, in particular Hari Ram, and on rough notes and sketches made by early Jesuit travellers. The survey made by Col Ryder and others on the Tibet Mission of 1903-4 had approached no closer than 50 miles from the mountain, leaving the area west of Kampa Dzong and south of the Ladak range (now known as the Gangdise range), together with the main Himalayan boundary peaks, as *terra incognita*. This region extended to 15,000 square miles and at its centre lay the Everest group with four of the world's ten highest peaks: Everest, Lhotse, Makalu and Cho Oyu. This area offered one of the last great prizes of mapping and mountain exploration.

Six weeks before the arrival of the main expedition in Darjeeling, three members of the survey detachment started work on the revision of the Sikkim survey. 2500 square miles of southern Sikkim were completed, whilst northern Sikkim was later covered by Turubaz Khan after the main party had left for Tibet. Morshead concentrated on the general survey at 4 miles to the inch and covered a vast area of unmapped country essentially from the sources of the Bhote Kosi (Rongshar river) in the west to the Arun river in the east. Each river cut through the Himalaya in deep, narrow, precipitous gorges about 60 miles apart. Meanwhile, Wheeler surveyed the immediate Everest region using a Canadian method of photo survey which he had developed in the Rockies. Despite poor weather (for much of the survey work was carried out during the monsoon), all the main objectives were achieved and the first reasonable map of the northern part of the Everest region was made.

The expedition's most important contribution to the first ascent of Everest over 30 years later was that the main configuration of the glaciers and ridges on the Nepalese side of the mountain were defined, and that Mallory looked into the Western Cwm and took the first photo of this mysterious high valley. On the north side of the mountain, the approach to the North Col by the East Rongbuk Glacier was discovered by the surveyors and the North Col was reached by Mallory and Bullock.

The expedition produced a remarkably good photographic record and a map available in three sheets at 1 mile to the inch. A geological survey of the whole area was made by Dr A M Heron of the Geological Survey of India. Additions to the map were made in 1922, particularly in the region of the Arun gorge,[16] with further valuable additions in 1924 when an Indian surveyor, Hari Singh Thapa, was attached to the party. The 1933 expedition carried out no exploration in the immediate region, but Professor L R Wager subsequently drew a geological map of the drainage areas of the Arun, Teesta and Ammochu rivers based on work by J D Hooker, F R Mallett, E J Garwood, H H Hayden, A M Heron, N E Odell and by Wager himself.

The 1935 Reconnaissance Expedition

In 1935 a lightweight expedition visited the north side of Everest.[17, 18] Under the leadership of Eric Shipton its purpose was to assess whether the monsoon season was suitable for attempting the mountain despite the poor weather experienced at the same time of the year in 1921. Its other objective was to make a detailed map of the north side of Everest so that a precise route could be planned for an attempt in 1936.

Michael Spender, the surveyor, had developed new methods of photographic survey in Greenland; throughout the expedition he was assisted by Shipton, Charles Warren the medical officer, and Edwin Kempson, a mathematician and housemaster at Marlborough College. Spender borrowed a Zeiss photo-theodolite adapted for rapid work by the use of roll film and used by him in Greenland. In addition, the Wild photo-theodolite belonging to the RGS and used by Kenneth Mason in the

Karakoram (Shaksgam) in 1926 was taken, together with a third, very portable instrument of great simplicity – the Watts-Leica photo-theodolite. This had been made from a Leica camera mounted on a Watts mountain theodolite, and was intended to be used by climbers more interested in climbing than in surveying.

The 1935 Everest expedition was exceptionally successful, since it achieved the ascent of more 20,000ft peaks than had ever been climbed before. Though primarily a reconnaissance expedition, its members reached a higher point on Everest than was to be achieved by the formal attempt, plagued by atrocious weather, in 1936. Finally, Spender completed a 1:20,000 photo-grammetrical survey of the North Face in which accurate measurements of height and distance were made. He also commented, very pertinently, that there was little point in spending a great deal of time, energy and money on field-work unless there were adequate back-up facilities for processing and writing up the results – a point that is still relevant today.

The 1936 and 1938 expeditions carried out little significant exploration or survey work. However, N E Odell made many observations in the Earth Sciences.

Mapping the Nepalese (south) side: the 1933 flight over Everest

The Nepalese side of Everest was examined in detail for the first time in 1933, from the air.[19] The aim of the Houston–Westland expedition was to fly over Everest from Nepal – as Tibetan airspace was forbidden. Two flights by two planes were made from Purnea in India. Both vertical and horizontal photographs were taken and were processed by A R Hinks, a mathematician and cartographer who was secretary of the RGS, and H F Milne, the chief draughtsman for the Society.

By incorporating Spender's map of 1935, the first (Hinks–Milne) composite map of the north and south sides of Everest was completed in 1945. A photostat of the final drawing was taken by Ward on the 1951 reconnaissance expedition, as there was no lithographed copy available until 1952.[20]

The 1951 Reconnaissance Expedition

Although no formal survey work was carried out on this expedition,[21] Ward made a compass traverse of the area west of Everest that had not been covered by the photographs and mapping of the 1933 Everest flight. This included the Ngozumpa glacier in the Nimagwa region and, further west, the Gaurisankar–Menlungtse basin. In the course of these explorations, Cho Oyu and Gyachung Kang were seen clearly from the south, and the Nangpa La was visited by Murray and Bourdillon.

These explorations yielded data around which the 1952 Cho Oyu expedition was later planned. The area east and south of Everest (the Imja and Upper Hongu), visited by Hillary and Shipton during the 1951 reconnaissance, was already well depicted on the Hinks–Milne map, of which Ward had a copy. Hillary and Riddiford crossed the Tesi Lapcha pass and descended the Rolwaling valley.

The 1952 Cho Oyu Expedition

Though again no formal survey was carried out on the Cho Oyu expedition,[22] the party completed a formidable amount of exploration: in particular, the area on the Nepal–Tibet border, north of the Tesi Lapcha pass and south of the Menlung La, was clarified. This contained a group of peaks, clustered around the Tolam Bau glacier, that ended in the Upper Rolwaling valley. This area was later surveyed by the Merseyside expedition in 1955.

The party then explored east towards the Barun glacier and Makalu. This major glacier, which drains the south and west side of Makalu, was discovered from aerial photographs taken on the 1933 Houston–Westland expedition, and in 1952 it was followed throughout its whole length from the Tibetan border just west of Pethangtse to the junction of the Barun Khola with the Arun river.

1953 Pre- and Post-monsoon Expeditions

No survey work was carried out during the successful 1953 Everest expedition, and the maps used were based on the Survey of India, in particular a map of the immediate Everest region at 1:126,720, printed in 1930. Concurrently with that expedition J O M Roberts, who had brought in the extra oxygen cylinders, made the first exploration of the peaks immediately south of Namche Bazar: the Numbur–Karyolung group. He then clarified the area of the Upper Inukhu Khola, made the first ascent of Mera Peak, crossed the Mera La on 19 May, and established the position of the Hongu Khola which was wrongly depicted on the Survey of India quarter-inch map.[23] After Everest, Charles Evans stayed on and surveyed the Kang Cho group, just west of Everest, which had been climbed during their acclimatisation period by the main Everest party. He also climbed Kang Cho (6038m) and then extended his survey to the peaks between the Ngojumba glacier and the glacier leading to the Nangpa La and the area which had already been explored in 1951/52.

Charles Evans now decided to explore the Numbur–Karyolung group where J O M Roberts had only spent two days. Following Roberts's route onto the Lumding glacier, Evans found it impossible to cross the ridge running north from the summit of Numbur (6959m), the highest peak in the group. He therefore had to retrace his steps down the glacier and go a long way south to a small hamlet, Thangu. From here he went west and north onto the Dudh Kund glacier which rose from the south and west faces of Numbur and Karyolung (6511m). Ascending this glacier, he again had to break out west into the next valley, in which lay the Zurmoche glacier. Going west again, he managed to cross a ridge running south from the summit of Bigphera Go Nup (6666m) and finally descended into a group of glaciers running into the Rolwaling valley west of the Tesi Lapcha pass. At last he was in familiar country again.[24]

In accomplishing this difficult piece of mountain exploration, Charles Evans had finally filled in the last 'blank on the map' of the Everest region. As a result, by the end of 1953 not only had Everest itself been climbed but all the main peaks, passes and glaciers of the whole region had been seen and photographed and a considerable amount of both ground and aerial survey work had been completed.

1954 to the present

On the 1954 New Zealand–British expedition to the area east of Everest, Charles Evans consolidated his explorations with a photo-survey which was incorporated in the Holland maps of 1961 and 1975.[25]

In 1954-55 the Federation Française de la Montagne produced a 1:50,000 map of the area between Makalu and Everest, whilst in 1957 Erwin Schneider, the Austrian cartographer, drew a map at 1:25,000 of the south side of Everest. In 1963 this was extended and reissued at 1:50,000.

In 1961 the first comprehensive map of the whole Everest region, from Rongbuk to Namche Bazar and from the Tesi Lapcha pass to the Barun valley, was drawn by G S Holland of the RGS.[26] At 1:100,000, this incorporated work from all previous expeditions. In 1975 Holland's map was revised and extended and further detail was added. It is now the landmark map of the area, against which all others are judged.

In 1977 Chinese cartographers from Lanzhou University under Professor Chen Jiaming printed a map of the Everest region in Chinese. Survey work had been carried out between 1966 and 1975. In the copy in the RGS archives, the Chinese names have been translated into English [Wade–Giles system] and placed on the map.

In 1980 Bradford Washburn, Director of the Museum of Science in Boston, wished to increase the accuracy of the maps of the Everest region, so that glaciologists and geologists could have a large-scale 1:10,000 detailed base, with 20m contours, on which to work. To this end he obtained permission to overfly Everest at 12,000m. The resulting map at 1:50,000 was published by the National Geographic Society in 1988. It was drawn by the Swiss Federal Office in Berne and place names were decided in consultation with Nepalese and Chinese cartographers. A second edition was published in 1991 showing the names and dates of ascents of Everest made over the years by different routes.[27] The larger scale maps are to be found in the map archives of the RGS.

Of all the mountain areas of the Himalaya and Central Asia, the Everest region is the one that has received the most attention from mountaineers and cartographers. In the course of many pioneering expeditions, these dedicated men worked together to produce a succession of maps of the region that are as delightful to look at as they are nostalgic and informative to study.

REFERENCES

1   E G H Kempson, 'The Local Name of Mount Everest' in H Ruttledge, *Everest, The Unfinished Adventure*. Hodder & Stoughton, London, 1937.
2   W R Fuchs, *Der Jesuiten Atlas der Kanshi Zeit*. Monumenta Serica. Monograph Series IV. Fujen University, Peking (Beijing), 1943.

3   J B Du Halde, *Description Géographique Historique ... de l'Empire de la Chine et de la Tartarie Chinoise. Vol 4*. Paris, Le Mercier, 1735.

4   K Mason, *Abode of Snow*. Hart-Davis, London, 1955.

5   J D Hooker, *Himalayan Journals* (2 vols). Murray, London, 1854.

6   L A Waddell, *Among the Himalayas*. Constable Westminster, London, 345, 1899.

7   A S Waugh, letter in *Proceedings of the Royal Geographical Society 1*, 345-347,1855-57.

8   M P Ward, 'The Exploration of the Nepalese Side of Everest'. *Alpine Journal 97*, 213-221, 1992/93.

9   'Work of the native explorer M-H in Tibet and Nepal in 1885-86' in *Proceedings of the Royal Geographical Society (New Series) 10*, 89-91, 1888.

10 L A Waddell, 'The Environs and Native Names of Everest' in *Geographical Journal 12*, 564-569, 1898.

11 C G Rawling, *The Great Plateau*. Arnold, London, 1905.

12 J B Noel, 'A Journey to Tashirak in Southern Tibet and the Eastern Approaches to Mount Everest' in *Geographical Journal 53*, 289-308, 1919.

13 A M Kellas, 'The Possibility of Aerial Reconnaissance in the Himalaya' in *Geographical Journal 51*, 374-389, 1918.

14 M P Ward, 'Northern Approaches : Everest 1918-22' in *Alpine Journal 99*, 1994.

15 C K Howard-Bury, *Mount Everest. The Reconnaissance 1921*. Arnold, London, 1922.

16 C J Morris, 'The Gorge of the Arun' in *Geographical Journal 62*, 161-173, 1923.

17 E Shipton, 'The Mount Everest Reconnaissance' in *Geographical Journal 87*, 98-112, 1936.

18 M Spender, 'Photographic Surveys in the Mount Everest Region' in *Geographical Journal 88*, 289-303, 1936.

19 Marquess of Clydesdale, D F McIntyre, *The Pilots' Book of Everest*. William Hodge, London, 1936.

20 M P Ward and P Clark, 'Everest 1951: Cartographic and Photographic Evidence of a New Route from Nepal' in *Geographical Journal 158*, 47-56, 1992.

21 E Shipton, *The Mount Everest Reconnaissance Expedition 1951*. Hodder & Stoughton, London, 1952.

22 E Shipton, 'The Expedition to Cho Oyu' in *Geographical Journal 119*, 129-139, 1953.

23 J O M Roberts, 'South of Everest' in *Himalayan Journal 18*, 59-64, 1954.

24 C Evans. Personal communication, 1992.

25 E P Hillary and W G Lowe, *East of Everest*. Hodder & Stoughton, London, 1956.

26 G S Holland and G R Crone, 'A New Map of the Mount Everest Region' in *Geographical Journal 128*, 54-57, 1962.

27 M P Ward, 'Sagarmatha–Mount Everest–Chomolungma. Map by the National Geographic Society'. Review in *Geographical Journal 155*, 433-435, 1989.

YEVGENIY B GIPPENREITER

Mount Everest and the Russians
1952 and 1958

(Plates 32–38)

In 1952 there were rumours circulating in the press and published in *The Times* that the Swiss team, led by G Chevalley, which was making a second attempt to climb Mount Everest in the autumn of 1952, were not the only climbers hoping to 'win' the highest mountain in the world from the British. While the Britons were conducting a training expedition to Cho Oyu, a third force had appeared in the Mount Everest arena – the Russians.[1] The press reports stated that on 16 October 1952, after a training meet in the Caucasus, a big Soviet expedition consisting of 35 climbers hurried to the Himalaya. Led by Pavel Datschnolian, the rival team included five experts: Anatoli Jindomnov, a geologist, Joseph Dengumarov, a physician specialising in high-altitude physiology, together with Vladimir Kashinski, Alexei Metzdarov and Ivan Lentsov.

The climbers and their equipment were transported from Moscow to Lhasa, via Novosibirsk and Irkutsk, in five military aircraft, but it took them longer than they had anticipated to cross Tibet and reach the foot of Mount Everest. At Base Camp all the Tibetan porters were paid off, and the Russians started climbing without a period of acclimatisation. They followed the pre-war British route from the north. From Camp VIII at 8200m the leader radioed that the assault party, being in good condition, expected to reach the top within the next two days, weather permitting. This was their last message. On 27 December a search lasting 18 days had to be abandoned because of the onset of winter and the last search party returned to Base Camp. No traces of the six missing men, including the leader Pavel Datschnolian, were found and it was assumed that they had all been swept away by an avalanche above Camp VIII. The following spring, while the British were climbing on the southern side of the mountain, the Russians resumed their search. However, the attempt did not produce any new information.

In the summer of 1954 Sir John Hunt (as he then was) visited Moscow to give a lecture on the successful ascent of Mount Everest. When he made diffident enquiries about the 1952 Russian expedition he was informed, unofficially, that it had never taken place. Even today, I recall with shame how some top Soviet and Party dignitaries deemed it 'undesirable' on political grounds for Sir John to be given a big Russian audience for his lecture on 'the achievement of British imperialists'. Sir John had to deliver his talk with slides at the British Embassy before only ten carefully vetted Soviet climbers. Owing to my knowledge of English I was one of them and

Sir John presented me with a copy of his book *The Ascent of Everest*. I was very happy to have the opportunity to return this kindness two years later when I sent him my Russian translation of it issued by the Foreign Languages Publishing House in Moscow.[2]

Later that summer, 1954, I paid my first ever visit to Britain, as interpreter to our national rowing team at the Henley Royal Regatta. I was pleased to accept an invitation from Sir John and Basil Goodfellow to visit the Alpine Club – the first visit by a Russian climber. Afterwards the three of us had dinner at the Reform Club – an unforgettable experience for a Soviet citizen accustomed to a quite different political and economic system. Those first contacts have since developed into a warm friendship of many years' standing.

On a number of occasions we were questioned about the Russian attempt to climb Everest in 1952. Some of us climbers suspected that such an expedition, inadequately planned and rashly implemented, might well have taken place in an attempt to gain political prestige and glory from this outstanding mountaineering achievement. But when the undertaking suffered such an abject defeat, all the information about it would have been hushed up and buried in the best tradition of Communist secrecy.

Some of us tried to find out the truth by making enquiries through the national mountaineering federations and personal channels. All other possible sources were investigated including government departments, sports associations and trade unions. We carefully examined the archives, studied mountaineering journals of the forties and fifties, checked every single name mentioned in foreign press reports – and discovered nothing. None of us knew or had even heard of the climbers and scientists mentioned in the reports. Finally we reached the conclusion that the whole story was nothing but a 'high-altitude duck', as we say in Russian – in other words a *canard*.

Nevertheless, we continued our efforts to clarify the picture whenever and wherever possible. In January 1962 I visited Tenzing Norgay in Darjeeling. One of his other guests, Captain H P S Ahluwalia, raised the question. Tenzing replied that his uncle, at that time Head Lama of the Rongbuk monastery, had told him that he himself had seen some Russians there. But no concrete data was mentioned and I think he was probably referring to the three Russian members of the joint Sino-Russian reconnaissance expedition to Mount Everest in autumn 1958. More recently, in autumn 1991 when I happened to be in Lhasa, I met Mr Konbu (or 'Gong Bu' as it is written on his visiting card) who climbed Everest in May 1960 with the Chinese expedition and who is now Deputy Director of the Physical Culture and Sports Commission of Tibet Autonomous Region and also Deputy President of China and Tibet Mountaineering Associations. I asked him if he had ever heard anything about the ill-fated Russian expedition of 1952. His answer was firmly negative.

In a personal letter to Walt Unsworth, dated 24 November 1974 and quoted in Unsworth's *Everest*, Kiril Kuzmin, then President of the Mountaineering Federation of the USSR, wrote that neither that organisation nor any other sports bodies of his country had ever sent expeditions of Soviet mountaineers with the aim of climbing Jomolungma (Everest) in 1952. He pointed out that at that time Soviet mountaineers lacked the opportunity to organise expeditions either to Everest or to any other eight-thousander. I would add that, even if we had been given such a chance, we would have been ill-prepared. At the beginning of the fifties, Soviet climbers did not have the necessary experience to tackle such formidable objectives and lacked suitable equipment such as oxygen apparatus. It was only in 1958 that our experts started developing modern climbing gear in connection with preparations for the Sino-Soviet expedition to Everest scheduled for 1959.[4]

The following brief account of the 1958 Sino-Soviet reconnaissance expedition tells the story as it was narrated to me by its Russian participants, together with my comments. In May 1958 the All-Chinese Committee of Physical Culture and Sport officially invited Soviet alpinists to take part in a joint expedition to Mount Jomolungma (Everest) from Tibet.[5] At a meeting in Beijing attended by a Soviet representative, decisions were taken on the planning and organisation of the future venture. The ascent was to take place in the pre-monsoon period of 1959. However, the Soviet representative tactfully suggested a preliminary reconnaissance of the northern approaches to Jomolungma, in particular the state of the Rongbuk glacier, the eastern slopes of Chang La (North Col), and those above the main Rongbuk glacier. The last major expedition to visit the area was that of the British in 1938 and after 20 years conditions there could have changed considerably.

In August-September 1958 a joint Sino-Russian training meet took place in the Soviet Pamir during which successful ascents were made of Peak Lenin (7134m) and other summits. There had already been good co-operation in the Caucasus and Pamir in 1955, and in 1956 the highest mountains of Xinjiang – Muztagh Ata (7546m) and Kongur Tiube Tagh (7595m) – were climbed by joint parties from the USSR and China.[6] But it was not until the beginning of October 1958 that the Chinese informed us that a reconnaissance of Jomolungma would indeed take place and Soviet mountaineers were invited to join the expedition. On 15 October three Russian climbers – Yevgeniy Beletski, Lev Filimonov and Anatoli Kovyrkov – flew to Beijing to discuss with their Chinese colleagues detailed plans for the forthcoming reconnaissance. It was to be led by Chuj Din, a distinguished Chinese climber, aged 30, whom we had already met on the joint climbs of 1955 and 1956.

On 19 October Chuj Din flew to Tibet with an advance party and was joined there by the rest of the expedition members on 23 October. It was planned to proceed by trucks to Zhigatse and then move 350km with a caravan of riding horses and pack animals via Shekhar Dzong and Tingri to Rongbuk. On 29 October the reconnaissance party left Lhasa in eleven lorries and escorted by soldiers and officers armed with pistols, automatic rifles and machine guns. One group was even guarded by a mortar platoon, for Tibetans are particularly afraid of mortars, mines and grenades.

According to their religious beliefs a soul will not find peace if the body is torn to pieces. The Chinese made use of this circumstance to economise on guards for the march-in.

The Chinese insisted that the entire party should be clad in the officers' winter uniform of the People's Liberation Army. Our Russian black sheepskin coats were rejected and the climbers were issued with long uniform sheepskin coats with a green fabric cover, huge fluffy three-cornered fox fur hats and high fur-lined boots. The Chinese also required the expedition to be called a 'Visiting delegation of the Committee of Physical Culture of the People's Republic of China with the participation of three Soviet experts'. Moreover, all the correspondence between the sports bodies of China and the USSR on these matters was 'classified' and we were asked not to make public any information about it.

On 30 October the party reached Zhigatse. In order to take full advantage of any periods of good weather near Everest, the mountaineers went on ahead with a minimum number of porters, using riding horses, two *árabas* (two-wheel bullock carts) and donkeys. The soldiers followed on foot. The mountaineers covered 25-30km daily, and the group reached Shekhar Dzong on 10 November, Tingri on the 13th and Rongbuk on the 16th. They visited the Rongbuk monastery where they found about 70 monks in residence. Base Camp was established about 500m below the snout of the main Rongbuk glacier. Here, on 17 November, it was decided to divide the party into two groups of eight persons each (five climbers plus three porters) in order to reconnoitre both slopes of the North Col. Lev Filimonov was assigned to the group led by Chuj Din and on 18 November they went up the right bank of the Rongbuk glacier. The group was accompanied by two soldiers armed with automatic guns who also helped with load carrying. The group used a map which had been produced by E O Wheeler (surveyor on the 1921 British expedition) and they went to the head of the main glacier to an altitude of about 5900m. They saw that a route to the North Col was accessible from here but that the approach up a steep 400m snow slope might become dangerous after fresh snowfalls. The group bivouacked at 5300m and at 5575m (or 5830m according to Wheeler's map). At the end of the moraine two hollow aluminium poles were found sticking out of the stones. On 21 November the group returned to Base Camp.

The second group, led by Yevgeniy Beletski, carried out their reconnaissance from 18 to 24 November. They followed the route of the previous expeditions up the East Rongbuk glacier, encountering tins, pieces of rope, packing materials and other remnants. They bivouacked at 5950m and at 6300m-6400m, a little below the site of the pre-war British Camp III, where rotten oxygen bottles were found. On 21 November an altitude of 6500m was reached. From here all the key pitches of the climb to the North Col could be seen. Having taken photos and filmed the route, Beletski started the descent. About 100m from Camp III the body of a porter from a previous expedition was found. When both groups met at Base Camp they reached the conclusion that the route via the East Rongbuk glacier and the North Col should be the one chosen for the 1959 expedition.

On 28 November the entire party left Base Camp, staying the night at the Rongbuk monastery. Beyond Tsoola La the party continued by trucks to Zhigatse, using the new road still under construction, which took them just a few hours instead of four days as formerly. They reached Lhasa on 9 December and from 10 to 15 December they worked on the results of the reconnaissance and on plans for the main enterprise the following year. On 16 December the party left Lhasa and returned to Beijing where they finalised their report of the expedition.

To sum up: the reconnaissance party worked for 46 days at altitudes above 4000m, 14 days above 5000m. It included 10 Chinese and 3 Russian mountaineers, 3 meteorologists, 4 topographers, 10 Tibetan porters, 4 radio operators, a considerable number of teamsters and accompanying persons, about 50 horses and 350 pack animals. The expedition successfully fulfilled its aim. Yet it received no coverage either in the world press nor even in the Soviet press of the time. Why? Because the Chinese requested that there should be no publicity. Why again? Because of the political situation in Tibet which was unstable and unclear. From time to time there were clashes between groups of Tibetans and the regular Chinese army. When the deputy chairman of the Party Committee of Tibet received the participants of the reconnaissance, he told them frankly: 'The people here do not understand us.'

In February 1959 all the Soviet candidates for the joint expedition went to the Caucasus for a training meet at Shkhelda Mountaineering Camp. This provided an opportunity to test people and equipment, including oxygen sets, in severe conditions during climbs to both summits of Mt Elbrus. Strong winds, snowstorms and temperatures down to -40°C were encountered. In the middle of March the Soviet team for the forthcoming expedition came to Moscow and were invited, on 18 March, to the All-Union Committee of Physical Culture for a final meeting and instructions. The plan was to reach Base Camp at the snout of the East Rongbuk glacier by 1 April 1959 in order to have ample time to make three acclimatisation ascents.

I was present there, sitting happily with Mikhail Khergiani and Joseph Khakhiani, my close Svanetian friends from Georgia who were also in the team. I well remember the atmosphere of elation and expectation which swept the entire audience. No wonder: the long cherished dream of Soviet mountaineers to try to tackle the highest summit in the world was about to come true. We were waiting for some senior official to come and say farewell words of encouragement and good wishes, among them an appeal to hoist the Soviet flag at the highest level possible on Earth for the glory of the Socialist Motherland. After a long delay two men entered the hall: Dmitri Postnikov, 1st Deputy Chairman of the USSR Committee of Physical Culture, and Kiril Kuzmin, prospective leader of the Soviet part of the expedition. Kuzmin's head was bent and his eyes were brimming with tears. Postnikov ascended the rostrum: 'Comrades,' he declared, 'I have a grave mission to report unexpected and very unpleasant news. We have just received an official notification from Beijing: the 1959 Jomolungma expedition cannot take place.' And without giving any reasons he left the astounded audience.

Later we were able to ascertain that the Chinese authorities had cancelled the joint expedition because of a big revolt in Tibet which had started on 10 March 1959. In 1960, when the situation in Tibet had become more stable, the Chinese again invited us to undertake a joint ascent of Mount Jomolungma. This time, however, it was the Soviet side that rejected the proposal and again politics was at the bottom of it – a growing ideological difference between China and its 'elder brother'. So the Chinese, making use of some of our equipment sent to Beijing for the 1959 expedition, had to carry it out by themselves in spring 1960. But that is another story ... [7]

As for the 1958 Sino-Soviet reconnaissance expedition,[8] the two sole publications about it in Russian appeared only in 1963. A brief report, entitled 'Through Tibet to the foot of Jomolungma' by Y A Beletski, appeared in the *Transactions of the National Geographical Society* of which he was a member.[9, 10] Another participant of the reconnaissance, Lev Filimonov, told me that he tried many times to write about the expedition but his manuscript was always rejected without explanation. Unofficially, he was told that 'it was deemed undesirable' to publish it, but never by whom or why.

The situation remained unchanged until Mr Gorbachev's visit to China in May 1989, the first Sino-Soviet 'summit' in 30 years, after which at last Lev Filimonov's diary notes, 'A Road to Everest', were published in a monthly youth journal in 1991.[11] It had taken 33 years for his story to reach the climbing world.

REFERENCES AND NOTES

1   The first ever attempt of that kind was made by A de Naranovich, a Russian consul in Milan, who sent an application to the Everest Committee asking to be included in the 1921 expedition but his request was rejected since, from the very inception, it was intended to be a purely British undertaking. See Walt Unsworth, *Everest*, 2nd edition. The Oxford Illustrated Press, 35, 1989.

2   The last foreign book on Mount Everest translated into Russian was Sir Francis Younghusband's *The Epic of Mount Everest*, Arnold, 1926, which was published in the Soviet Union in 1930.

3   Y B Gippenreiter, 'Chronicle of Everest' in *Everest 82, the ascent of Soviet mountaineers to the highest summit of the world*, composed by P P Zakharov. Physical Culture and Sport Publishing House, Moscow, 353-363, 1984.

4   *John Hunt writes*: 'On leaving Spartak Camp beneath Elbrus on Sunday 13 July 1958 to continue our climbing programme in the Central Caucasus, I presented a pair of British-made mountaineering boots to Josef Khakhiani, Master of Sport and one of the Soviet members chosen for the joint Sino-Soviet expedition to Everest. Other gifts included air mattresses and a watch.'

The 1958 Sino-Soviet Reconnaissance Expedition: the North Face of Mount Everest seen from Camp III at 5575m, according to altimeter measurements, or 6830m according to the map produced by E O Wheeler, surveyor on the 1921British Everest Expedition, which was used by the group. (*Lev Filimonov*) (p109)

Yevgeniy A Beletski, Honoured Master of Sport of the USSR in mountaineering, leader of the Russian party, riding a saddled Tibetan horse covered with a sheepskin coat issued by the Chinese. (*Lev Filimonov*) (p109)

34. Anatoli Kovyrkov, aged 30

35. Lev Filimonov, aged 39

Members of the Russian party were dressed in high fur-lined boots, down clothing with windproof anorak and trousers over it. The huge three-cornered fox fur hat was issued by the Chinese as part of the officers' winter uniform of the People's Liberation Army. (*Lev Filimonov*) (p109)

36. Two soldiers from Sichuan province who carried their sacks and automatic guns to the highest point reached. They are seen near Camp II, *c* 5300m, on 18.11.1958. (*Lev Filimonov*) (p109)

The Rongbuk monastery, reached by the party on 16.11.1958, and the North Face of Mount Everest, with Changtse, 7550m, in front of it and Peak 6882m on the left. (*Lev Filimonov*) (p109)

The Rongbuk monastery was later destroyed in the so-called 'cultural revolution'. It was possible to ride a horse through the main entrance on the left. At the top of the picture are the premises where the party stayed overnight on their way back from the reconnaissance. (*Lev Filimonov*) (p109)

39. East Greenland: Mejslen (Chisel), 2320m, and Base Camp I on the Chisel glacier. (*Graham Little*) (p64)

40. Graham Little on the summit ridge of Mejslen. (*Chris Bonington*) (p64)

The Needle massif from Base Camp II. (*Graham Little*) (p64)

Chris Bonington on the summit of Needle, 1945m. (*Graham Little*) (p64)

Some map-makers of Everest:

Left

43. Major E O Wheeler, a member of the surv[e]
party on the 1921 Everest Expedition,
carried out a general survey at 4 miles/in[ch]
a detailed survey at 1 mile/inch
of the immediate environment of Everest,
and a revision of the existing quarter-inch
map of Sikkim. (p103)

Below left

44. Michael Spender, surveyor on the 1935 Ev[erest]
reconnaissance, made a 1:20,000 photo-
grammetrical survey of the N face. (p104)

Below right

45. A R Hinks completed, in 1945 with H F M[ ]
the first composite map of the N and S sid[e]
of Everest. (*Hugh Ruttledge*) (p105)

Above
Charles Evans, in 1953 after Everest, carried out some difficult but essential mountain exploration N and S of Everest to fill in two 'blanks on the map' of the Everest region. (*John Merton RA*) (p106)

Right
G S Holland, in 1961, completed the first comprehensive map of the whole Everest region. At 1:100,000, this map incorporated work from all previous expeditions. It was revised and extended in 1975. (p107)

48. The Aletschhorn, 4195m, seen from the summit of the Gross Fiescherhorn, 4049m. Summer 1982. (*Rupert Hoare*) (p196)

49. Ibex at the Gleckstein hut above Grindelwald in 1982. (*Rupert Hoare*) (p196)

5   The expedition was to take place between March and October 1959 and would be given unrestricted funds in accordance with a special resolution of the Central Committee of the Communist Party of China. It was evidently timed to be one of the events celebrating the 10th anniversary of the Chinese People's Republic.

6   K K Kuzmin, 'To Jomolungma from the North' in *Conquered Summits 1958-1961*. Geographical Literature State Publishing House, Moscow, 239-244, 1963.

7   *John Hunt writes:* 'A group of Soviet alpinists visited Britain in 1960, and were climbing with some of their hosts, including myself, in Snowdonia in June of that year. They expressed disbelief when the news reached us that a Chinese expedition, including their intended colleagues for the joint Sino-Soviet expedition, had been successful. Their opinion was that the Chinese lacked the experience and equipment which could have been supplied by the Russians.'

8   The participants of the 1958 Sino-Russian reconnaissance expedition, together with all the members of the successful Chinese 1960 expedition, were awarded a special memorial medal in the form of a gilded star with contours of Jomolungma. This was the only official recognition on the part of the Chinese authorities of our participation and contribution to their final success. Lev Filimonov has shown me this medal which he treasures as a very memorable insignia.

9   Y A Beletski, 'Through Tibet to the Foot of Jomolungma' in *Transactions of the National Geographical Society No 3*. Leningrad, 203-212, 1963.

10   *John Hunt writes:* 'Yevgeniy Beletski came to lecture before the Alpine Club in 1956, and was one of our hosts at Spartak Camp in July 1958. Yevgeniy Gippenreiter came as his interpreter.'

11   L N Filimonov, 'A Road to Everest' in *Young Guard No 12*, Moscow, 65-96 and 129-176, 1991.

CHRISTOPHER RALLING

Filming on Everest

(*Plates 62–69*)

After making two documentaries on the subject, I thought I had finished with Everest. But when my daughter Jo suggested we should put in a bid through my small company to make a film for the 40th anniversary, I realised that I hadn't. The memories, the tug at the heart, the awesome fascination were all still there.

Down the years since 1975, when my own involvement began, I have got to know and greatly admire a good number of Himalayan climbers, without ever really understanding why they take such risks. Too many of them have died in that time: Dougal Haston, Nick Estcourt, Pete Boardman, Joe Tasker, Julie Tullis, Al Rouse and, most painful of all for me personally, Mick Burke, who was our cameraman on the South West Face expedition. A photograph that I took of him in the Khumbu Icefall hangs on my study wall. Three weeks later he had disappeared somewhere on the summit ridge. I can't explain it, but Mick was the main reason why I wanted to go back.

As with climbers, so with film makers – there's little left to be done on Everest. To date, well over fifty documentaries have been made. We have had dramatic pictures from every ridge and face. We have had action pictures from the summit, canoeing, ballooning, skiing and hang-gliding. In 1988 the Japanese actually erected a satellite dish high on the summit ridge and sent live television pictures around the world.

Considering the extreme conditions, the standard of filming has been extraordinarily high. Among the pioneers, I would give pride of place to Captain John Noel, whose vivid images from the 1922 and 1924 expeditions belie their age. A generation later, Tom Stobart and George Lowe made a unique record of the first ascent in their remarkable film *The Conquest of Everest*. In more recent times there are many to choose from, but I would pick David Breashears who made the first microwave transmission from the summit in 1983, and for sheer versatility Leo Dickinson, who seems to be equally at home whether he is operating his camera from a kayak, a parachute or a balloon.

This is not the place for a detailed discussion about film equipment, but there are two very obvious problems to be overcome when filming on Everest. One is weight and the other is extreme cold. In the course of 70 years, cameras and sound recorders have got steadily lighter. We have moved from 35mm to 16mm, and now to miniature video cameras. These changes have not always meant an improvement in picture quality, but on Everest mobility counts for much more. If a lead climber can take a small camera in his rucksack, he is likely to produce much more dramatic stuff than a professional cameraman working with a long lens and a tripod thousands of feet below. For best results I would recommend a combination of the two.

But problems of a quite different kind await the documentary maker on an Everest expedition. Ideally, one would like to film everything of interest which happens, while remaining as unobtrusive as possible. In the highly-charged atmosphere of a major expedition, poised on the brink of success or failure, that isn't always possible. During the 1971 International expedition, which was supposed to reflect world fellowship at its best, members of the BBC documentary team became embroiled through no fault of their own in the personal conflict and rivalry which finally destroyed any hope that Norman Dyhrenfurth's fractious team ever had of reaching the summit.

The BBC had exclusive filming rights and were, in fact, major sponsors of the expedition itself, which raised suspicions in the minds of the European members of the team. They managed to convince themselves that the film's producers were only interested in a British success. Matters came to a head when a vote was taken on whether the team should devote all its energy and resources to tackling a new route on the South West Face, or whether some of them should stick to the well tried South Col route. By that stage individual members were spread out between Base Camp and the top of the Western Cwm, and some of the results of the ballot had to be relayed back to the leader, Norman Dyhrenfurth, on the BBC radio link. When the vote went against the South Col attempt, Pierre Mazeaud, a member of the French Chamber of Deputies, accused the BBC of rigging the result. In a famous outburst he shouted 'They expect me ... to work as a Sherpa for Anglo-Saxons and Japanese. Never! This is not me, but France they have insulted.' (How quickly passions boil over in such a cold climate!) All the Europeans, Mazeaud himself, Carlo Mauri from Italy, and the Vauchers from Switzerland walked off the mountain. Allegations in a Swiss newspaper that the film team had been taking drugs brought the BBC to the brink of an ugly libel suit. Wisely, perhaps, they decided to let tempers cool.

There is much more to this story which need not concern us here. But for film makers, the events of 1971 raise an important question. Of course the BBC team were completely innocent of trying to influence the course of events, or of taking drugs. But on a major expedition, how integrated should the two groups, the climbers and their chroniclers, become? At sea-level, there would not be much doubt about the answer. But high mountains, I believe, present a different set of criteria. Inevitably you are all thrown together, often battling with the elements and sometimes depending on each other for survival.

I have been involved in the making of three films about Everest: in 1975, in 1982, and now in 1993. In each case the problem of trying to give an accurate account of events presented itself in different ways.

Everest the hard way

In 1975, Chris Bonington, anxious perhaps to avoid a repetition of 1971, decided to make all of us, climbers, reporters and film makers, full members of the expedition. I don't remember balking at this at the time. We were duly flattered, and in any case one of our BBC cameramen, Mick Burke, had already been chosen as a lead climber. Apart from myself the other members of the film team – producer Ned Kelly, cameraman Ian Stuart and sound recordist Arthur Chesterman – had all been to Everest before on the ill-fated 1971 expedition, which Bonington himself had wisely avoided.

I think it is true to say that there was virtually no friction between ourselves and the climbers in 1975, which is not to say that they trusted us to produce the goods. Neither of the two stars, Dougal Haston and Doug Scott, really believed that a documentary film could come anywhere near the actual experience of an expedition, or even a true distillation of it. On the walk-in, Dougal would make elaborate detours rather than pass one of our cameras. After about a week of this, I had a serious chat with him, pointing out that we were in danger of filming 'Hamlet without the prince'. He took the point and became much more co-operative. But his remoteness always remained part of his star quality. Doug said he couldn't help noticing that while a large proportion of British climbers came from the north, the films were almost invariably made by people from the south. It was true enough.

The first bone of contention between the climbers and their chroniclers involved *The Sunday Times* reporter, Keith Richardson. I found him a rather unbending figure, who found it hard to participate in the general banter which is the common coinage of all mountaineering expeditions. But the heart of the problem was Richardson's dogmatic refusal to show his reports to anyone, even Chris Bonington, before they were despatched. 'If I interview the Prime Minister, I don't show him what I've written before publication,' he said. 'What is the difference out here?' The difference, I think, has to do with the altitude and isolation of major Himalayan peaks. If you're not first and foremost a band of brothers, everything can fall apart. Richardson's first report, sent back from Kathmandu, caused a flurry of letters from home, which had a very unsettling effect on the expedition.

As it happened, Richardson was obliged to go down to Namche Bazar with acute altitude sickness, never to return, and the job of reporting for *The Sunday Times* was passed to me. In the mess tent, I made a point of telling everyone that a despatch was going off next morning in case anyone wanted to read it. A couple of climbers read the first one, and after that nobody bothered. Access was all they wanted. There was just one occasion when Chris Bonington was worried about what I might write. Hamish MacInnes, the deputy leader, disappointed that he had not been given a major part to play in the final assault, decided to leave the expedition. It was a serious enough matter to cause repercussions back in the UK. I told Chris that I must tell it as I saw it, and he never pressed the point.

Chris Bonington has a reputation for strong, decisive leadership. But his emotions are never far below the surface. Ned Kelly and I wanted to get his spontaneous and highly personal thoughts on a daily basis, so we equipped him with a high-quality miniature tape recorder to use as a spoken diary in the privacy of his tent. In due course this would form part of the voice-over for the film. However, it was always understood between us that Chris himself would have a say in what was used. It was not the kind of arrangement one makes very often, but on that occasion I think it was more than justified. Chris felt no inhibitions about using the recorder, and when one recalls that there were two heart-breaking disappearances in the course of the expedition – the Sherpa boy Mingma Nuru in the early stages and Mick Burke at the end – there was very little that he asked us to exclude. I shall never forget his prophetic forebodings about Mick on the night before he made his summit bid.

The last picture of Mick, taken by Pete Boardman, shows him clutching his auto-load camera and wearing his Union Jack woolly hat. At that moment he was probably only 20 minutes from the summit, and no power on earth would have made him turn back. We will never know for certain, but the probability is that he did indeed make the first solo ascent of Everest, and shot some historic film that was never recovered. By the time he began his descent, the weather had deteriorated drastically. Unable to see through the driving spindrift, it would have been all too easy to miss the route round a gaping hole in the cornice, which is clearly visible in Doug Scott's picture taken a couple of days earlier. Significantly, Mick had given up wearing his contact lenses a week before and reverted to spectacles.

Undoubtedly the most moving moments in the 1975 film came when Pete Boardman and Martin Boysen gave their account of Mick Burke's last hours before he disappeared somewhere on the summit ridge of Everest. They were scarcely back in Camp 2 themselves and still in a state of shock. I was inclined to hold back, but my colleague Ned Kelly, who has an instinctive empathy with climbers, seemed to know that they were ready to unburden themselves.

Here are some of their words:

BOARDMAN
Anything that anybody says when they're 6000 feet lower down – it's apart from you, and there's nothing really from down there that could stop you if you really wanted to go for the top.

BOYSEN
I struggled and struggled, and I just wasn't working at all well, and eventually I noticed a crampon had dropped off – and then I noticed my other foot was also without a crampon. So I'd lost two crampons on this rock step. One I picked up, but the other one I saw gently rolling down the slope. And I thought Oh God – that's it ... I might as well turn back. And Mick saw this and said 'Hard luck old son ... cheerio.' I wished him good luck with as good a grace as I could manage.

BOARDMAN

We plodded up to the summit. I sat down about ten feet below it and I waved up Pertemba. We both felt very pleased and happy up there, and after about half an hour we started back down again, very confident that we were going to have a nice leisurely, safe descent. And all of a sudden we saw Mick. I thought it was Martin at first. I hadn't expected Mick to be going so strongly and keenly. He wanted us to go back to the summit to film, but we were moving roped, taking a bit more time, and we also wanted to conserve our energy for the way down. We said, 'Well no'. He filmed us a bit and we said 'D'you want to come with us?' but he said 'I'm so near now. I'll just go up towards the summit.' In fact he said 'Will you wait for me at the South Summit?' So we said 'Sure, we'll wait for you down there.'

BOYSEN

It was a howling gale. The snow was really rattling down, the tents were rattling, and I began to get extremely worried at that point because I was thinking well, if they don't actually get back, or if they miss the fixed ropes due to the whiteout conditions, or anything else ... if they have to stay a night out in that weather, then I thought it's going to be extremely serious. They could very easily die ... the probability is that they would die.

BOARDMAN

We could see about five feet at this time. The snow was icing up our eyes, and we just felt we had to go. We just couldn't wait any longer because, the weather being as it was, we could never have survived a night out ... there.

Mick, more than anyone, would have appreciated their candour.

Everest: the unclimbed ridge

My own involvement with the 1982 expedition, seven years later, began when it was all over. Pete Boardman and Joe Tasker had vanished on the North East Ridge, while tackling the formidable Pinnacles. The circumstances were just as mysterious as Mick Burke's disappearance, and the effect on the survivors equally shattering.

The expedition was a small one. Chris Bonington and Dick Renshaw were the other two high-altitude climbers, with Adrian Gordon as Base Camp manager and Charlie Clarke as the doctor. Instead of taking a professional film crew, Joe Tasker had volunteered to undergo a few day's training at ITN in the use of lightweight camera equipment.

It was Charlie who phoned me up on their return, asking me to take a look at the footage they had managed to retrieve from the mountain. He was afraid it might all be useless; and at our first viewing I was of the same opinion. Most of it, especially the high-altitude material, was so over exposed that you could scarcely make out the climbers in the bleached whiteness of their surroundings. The only hope was to send the negative to a specialist laboratory, and have the whole lot reprinted. The result was a revelation. Not only was the film perfectly transmittable, but Joe Tasker had shown himself to be a cameraman of real talent and insight. The resulting film, though much simpler in construction than *Everest the Hard Way*, was just as moving and in some ways more powerful and immediate. Of course there were no on-the-spot interviews. Instead, we all met one evening in Charlie's basement kitchen, where the survivors recalled their experiences. In spite of a gap of several weeks, they lost little in the telling.

BONINGTON
I know I was afraid quite a lot of the time, and I didn't admit it. And in the same way, when Pete and Joe actually went for the summit, I'll always remember during the whole lead-up period, they were almost conning themselves that it was going to be a pushover going over the Pinnacles. And I, because I'd actually pulled out, was then of course saying to myself well ... God they look desperately difficult! And I didn't dare say it to them because I didn't want to discourage them. And I'll never forget the night before they actually set out for that final push, they were quite incredibly tense ...

Return to Everest
And so to 1993, and the 40th anniversary of the first ascent. Six of the original team, including John Hunt and Ed Hillary, were planning to hold a reunion in the Everest region, accompanied by families and friends. The others from the original expedition who were going back were George Band, George Lowe, Mike Westmacott and Charles Wylie. It looked like a marvellous opportunity for any documentary film maker. The competition was quite fierce. Our own opening bid was a proposal to tell the whole story of Everest in four episodes. But this appeared to get lost in someone's pending tray at the BBC.

I ended up with a commission to make a single programme for Channel Four. The programme editors were quite clear that they wanted a simple film, re-telling the story of the original climb through the reminiscences of the returning veterans. The use of archive film on television is very expensive, and I knew that my budget would run to no more than twelve minutes from *The Conquest of Everest,* which originally ran for an hour and a half. But with a bit of luck and good weather, it looked like a highly feasible proposition.

The first task was to pick the right team. As all Himalayan climbers know, altitude sickness is not just a matter of fitness. It can strike one person and not another in the most arbitrary manner. To replace anyone on a Himalayan expedition is a very expensive business. The best insurance is to choose people who have worked at altitude before, and in this respect we were lucky. The cameraman John Davey, the sound recordist Phil Streather, and the location manager Bruce Herrod had all been high in the Sola Khumbu before. The exceptions were my daughter Jo, the Associate Producer, and Charlotte Moore who joined as our Production Manager.

In London, Charlotte looked at me plaintively as she said 'I'm tougher than I look.' She was. After a few days, both of them were scampering about like mountain goats. Back in London, the redoubtable Joanie Blaikie acted as our belay. In other respects, I think one looks for the same qualities that all good expedition members need: endurance, temperament, and a sense of humour. John Davey needed all three. Unknown to any of us, he broke his arm early in the shoot, but kept on working until the end.

I would be the first to admit that film crews can be an obtrusive nuisance, and sometimes ruthless in pursuit of a story. Even before we left England, I sensed that some members of the anniversary party were more than a little apprehensive that too much media attention might spoil the whole occasion. My main worry was that several teams would all be closing in at the same time. Chris Bonington would be in the offing for Yorkshire TV, a New Zealand crew were making a profile of Hillary, and the Germans were coming in strength. We knew, too, that we would only have a few days before the group set off in different directions, giving us an insuperable problem in deciding whom to follow. Of the original team only George Lowe was planning to retrace the route up to Base Camp itself. After long deliberations, we decided to go with him, even though it meant losing contact with the other five. In retrospect I think it was the right decision.

We managed to get a splendid scene as John Hunt and Ed Hillary arrived by helicopter for a ceremonial welcome at Thyangboche monastery, and another when Hillary dropped out of the sky once again to be greeted by the pupils of Khumjung school, the first to be built with money from the Himalayan Trust. In the short time we spent with them, George Band, Mike Westmacott and Charles Wylie all revealed those honest, friendly, down-to-earth qualities which seem to have been a hallmark of the 1953 expedition. Meanwhile, in his tent one night, John Hunt had given us a most vivid and revealing interview. (If there is a nicer mountaineer in captivity, I have yet to meet him.) As for George Lowe, he revealed himself to be a sharp and witty raconteur who should really be hosting his own TV show. Here he is in an extract from the film, doing a double act with Ed Hillary. They are describing the day the Himalayan Trust was born:

LOWE

We came back with a storm chasing us, and we literally ran up the last couple of thousand feet. It was incredible that we did it, but we got to the top. We were all very tired and then we had that long descent, didn't we ... ?

HILLARY

I remember we came down on a very long rope, because we really just couldn't see anything, and there were masses of crevasses; and I was on one end of the rope up front, and George was on the other end at the back, and I was constantly falling down crevasses, and George, who I must admit had very quick reactions, would jerk on the rope and stop me from going down more than five or six feet ...

LOWE

... and I had three Sherpas anchoring behind me. The idea was that we strung ourselves out in that emergency situation, and this was really the first time those Sherpas had been involved in really hard mountaineering.

HILLARY

There were avalanches tumbling down all around us from the fresh snow and we were absolutely exhausted, but we got to the bottom of the glacier onto the clear ice where it was safe, and we sat down.

LOWE

We had a tent there ...

HILLARY

That's right, and the Sherpas insisted on George and me just sitting down; they almost made us sit down while they prepared the whole camp, and then they more or less put us inside our sleeping-bags, while they got the primus going and brewed up some tea for us. And we just lay there in comfort. We had a very warm feeling about our three Sherpas that day who, even though they were just as tired as we were, insisted on us resting while they looked after us.

LOWE

And we had this big-hearted moment, which was really true. We said we really should try to give something back to these chaps.[1]

Back in London, to catch the date of the 40th anniversary, we had just over three weeks in the cutting room, instead of the more usual eight, to complete the film for transmission. Most directors take the view that it is asking for trouble to show a rough-cut to one of the protagonists, but there are exceptions to the best of rules. For John Hunt and his team, the original expedition had become, willy nilly, the most important event of their lives. The style, flavour and balance of a documentary are often determined during the editing process. It's all too easy to get these things wrong in the closing stages.

John and Joy Hunt with their daughter Prue, who had all been with us out in Nepal, came in to the cutting room to see the rough-cut in the middle of May. Their response was very positive, but they thought there was one jarring note. This was a remark of Charles Wylie's early in the film. 'There was one Sherpa,' he said, 'who I think was politically inspired. Unfortunately there were Communist influences in Darjeeling. He was a Darjeeling Sherpa and we had reason to believe that the Communists tried to get him to disrupt the expedition. He had to be dismissed, I'm afraid, and after that there was absolutely no trouble at all.'

I thought long and hard about this, but finally decided to leave the sequence in. For one thing, it was news. I had never read about it in any of the books. Also, it was interesting, to say the least, that not even that most famous of Everest expeditions had escaped the tentacles of the Cold War. The second reason, a more personal one, was my firm conviction that every good documentary needs one or two jarring notes. Otherwise they run the risk of looking bland, safe and predictable. Needless to say, John took the point.

So much for *Return to Everest*; it was not the most daunting, but perhaps the most satisfying of the three films about Everest I have had a hand in. It was just the latest in that long line of documentaries which began in 1922. But how many of them 'got it right'? By Doug Scott's stringent standards, the answer must be none at all. You cannot capture the essence of one climber's individual experiences, even if he, or she, really wishes to share them. I suppose I have seen a good many of the fifty or so Everest films, and looking back it is easy to see where most of them went wrong. The two ingredients which 'date' most quickly are music and commentary. It may have seemed a good idea at the time to get the poet Louis MacNeice to write the words for *The Conquest of Everest*. But it was not. It may have seemed a good idea to get Orson Welles to read the commentary for *Americans on Everest* in 1963. But it was not. It may have seemed a good idea for the Chinese to turn their film of the 1960 expedition into a hymn of praise to Mao Tse-Tung. But it was not.

I don't have the slightest doubt that my own three efforts will look just as dated in the years ahead. If I had to give advice, banal and obvious though it may sound, to future documentary makers on Everest, it would be, quite simply, to let the sound and the pictures do the work for you, and as far as possible let the climbers tell the story in their own words. Then, at the very least, the film will be true to itself and to its own time.

NOTE

1   *George Lowe writes*:
We were on the Nup La in 1952. We crossed back from the West Rongbuk glacier chased by a storm. The three Sherpas were Ang Puta and Tashi Puta and Angye – all from Khumbu. Tashi Puta was the younger brother of Angtharkay, the famous sirdar who travelled with Eric Shipton. Within two years of the journey Ang Puta and Tashi Puta (both in their twenties) had died of illness. No one could tell us the reason – other than pointing to their abdomen, grimacing with pain and saying 'they died quick'. Angye I always searched out in Namche on my visits – saw him in '91 – but he died in 1992. I guessed his age as similar to mine!

REBECCA STEPHENS

A British Woman on Everest

On 17 May 1993 Rebecca Stephens became the first British woman to climb Mount Everest. She was accompanied by Sherpas Ang Pasang and Kami Tchering.

It was our last chance, our last attempt on the summit of Everest. The season was drawing to a close – the monsoon encroaching – and talk was of cold beers in Namche Bazar. This was it. Our last moment – and the Sherpas thought it too dangerous to climb.

'Guys, don't give up on me now. Please not now.' These were my thoughts as Sherpas Ang Pasang and Kami Tchering lay huddled in a small, domed tent. Tchering Zhambu and myself were in another, positioned for a summit bid from the South Col. 'There's black cloud in the valley. Not good weather. We're young,' they cried.

'Well,' I mused, 'the perfect excuse.' A large part of me thought: 'I can go back to bed, put my head down, forget the whole bloody thing.' But another part of me wanted that summit. Was making a decision always so impossibly hard? To go or not to go. It had seemed that way for as long as I could remember. Choice is a terrible thing. Until Everest I had thought climbing easy – not physically easy, necessarily, but simple. There was only one aim: to climb to the top. No buses to catch, timetables to meet; no finances to juggle, bathrooms to clean, taxmen or editors to appease. No clutter.

Everest put an end to that. Everest, by virtue of its sheer size, makes complicated all things that should be simple. Camps need to be established: tents, sleeping-bags, stoves, billies, food and drinks put in place. Oxygen, too – for those who use it – needs to be positioned. And teams are large: nine Westerners in our case, and seven Sherpas. A lot of people. A lot of variables – before counting the biggest variable of all: the weather.

I was tired of decision-making. Twice in the last week I had thought we should have made a bid for the summit when, in the event, circumstances for our team dictated otherwise; and twice I had watched tens of climbers ascend, and descend triumphant.

But one more chance – just one, a slim one – presented itself. We had been to Camp 4 on the South Col, retreated, and were now at Camp 2, 22,500ft, at the foot of the Lhotse Face.

Was it only yesterday, Camp 2? It felt an age. I remembered John Barry, the expedition leader, saying: 'It'll be a monumental test of will.' He was referring to the climb, to having to retrace steps from Camp 2 to Camp 4; and he was right – almost. The hard bit was not the climb itself; it was summoning the energy to pack my rucksack, put on my harness, my boots and crampons and set off, again. So nearly I didn't bother. The forecast was for 45 pushing 50 knot winds and I convinced myself I would be walking into failure. I would climb to the Col – that ghastly, inhospitable, frightening place – only to have to retreat once more. My chance of success, I thought, was no more than one in a hundred.

'You're a realist,' said Sandy Scott, our doctor. 'I'd have said three to four per cent.' I was scared, too. Suddenly I found myself in a situation in which I was talking in the first person singular. I would be alone. I had assumed that John would be making a second attempt with me. But he had made his choice. He had stayed a third night on the South Col to look after Harry Taylor, who was snowblind after his oxygenless ascent.

'But you won't be on your own,' Sandy said gently. 'You'll be with Ang Pasang and Kami Tchering, and Tchering Zhambu.' These Sherpas were twice as strong and twice as fast on the hill as any man I had met, and always smiling. But I had never actually climbed with them – and it would be me making all the decisions.

'They know this mountain better than anyone,' said Sandy. Ang Pasang and Kami Tchering both had been to the South Summit several times. 'And they're cautious,' he said. I felt ashamed. Sandy was right. The Sherpas would look after me.

The four of us set off together from Camp 2 at 5am. Dawn was just breaking. Once on our way we travelled quickly, across the head of the Khumbu glacier in the Western Cwm and up the steep Lhotse Face. I was hugely advantaged. On our first attempt we had used oxygen from Camp 3, at about 24,000ft, a little over halfway up the face. The oxygen bottles were British, solid and strong to meet British standards, which was great, except that each bottle weighed a hefty 6.5kg, and that was without the brass attachments, regulator and mask. For the second attempt we had handed over an astronomical sum of money to the New Zealanders for their spare titanium bottles, made in Russia. They were the best: small, simple to use and, most important, light. I had plenty of them.

I plugged in at Camp 2 and shot up the fixed ropes to Camp 3 in under four hours. Previously, my best time, without oxygen, had been $5^1/_2$ hours. We stopped for a quick brew in our tent at Camp 3, perched on the tiniest snowy shelf between séracs, and then went on our way, across the Lhotse Face – just a walk really – and up and over the Geneva Spur to the South Col. Tchering Zhambu and I were on the Col by 1pm. Ang Pasang and Kami Tchering had raced ahead and were already ensconced in their tent, brewing us tea.

I loved watching them. They were so dextrous. They were small – Tchering Zhambu was tiny, about 5ft 2in. But the efficiency of their movements amazed me. The tent I shared with Tchering Zhambu was full of snow, littered with food wrappings, and sort of crescent-shaped. It had been domed once – in fact the last time that I was in it – but the poles had buckled in the wind and the canvas had collapsed. It was chaos and yet Tchering Zhambu managed to sort the oxygen, dry his feet, man the radio and lean out of the tent to collect snow for a brew; all without knocking over the 'boil-in-a-bag' warming on the stove in the corner . I did nothing. I was not allowed to.

Seven pm and we put our heads down, just for a couple of hours. Didn't sleep, just rested.

'Tchering Zhambu,' I whispered. He stirred. 'Tchering Zhambu, there's no wind.' I could hardly believe it: the forecast was as wrong as it was possible to be.

Tchering Zhambu sat bolt upright – it was 10pm, we planned to leave at 11pm – and immediately lit the stove for a brew. It takes a while, all this brewing, collecting and melting snow, but an hour or so passed and I got the distinct impression something was up. The Sherpas – Ang Pasang and Kami Tchering in the other tent, and Tchering Zhambu in mine – were talking among themselves in Nepali.

'What's up?' I asked Tchering Zhambu.

'Weather not good.'

'But there's no wind,' I retorted. I stuck my head out of the tent: the mountain was clear, the sky full of stars.

'Ang Pasang says black cloud in valley. Too dangerous.'

There was only one thing for it. I put on my boots, tripped out of my tent and into theirs.

'Ang Pasang?'

'Black cloud dangerous,' he said, 'We're young.' What to do?

'Ang Pasang, pass the radio please.'

John and Sandy were sleeping in the cook tent that night, by the radio, so I could call them at any time. I was touched. The boys at Base Camp were doing the same.

I explained: 'John, Ang Pasang says we may not find our way. And there's lightning. You have a view on that?'

'I don't know, Becs.' This was desperate.

'The weather's going to get worse, not necessarily in the next two hours, but it's going to build up. Whether it will hold off long enough I wouldn't like to say,' said John.

The discussion went round in circles: Camp 4 to Camp 2, Camp 2 to Base Camp, back to Camp 4. '

Talk it over very gently with Ang Pasang and let him make the final decision,' said John. 'It's his life too.'

We waited an hour. The wind did not pick up and the stars still crowded the sky. And then I saw three lights making their way up the hill from the Col. I do not know how the decision was finally made, but one thing was for sure: if those three people thought there might even be the slightest chance of making the summit, I could not go back to bed. At 12.30am we were ready to go.

'Get on those fixed ropes,' said John, 'Get on to the South Summit; reassess the situation there. And good luck. I think you're going to be OK. Over.'

I heard him switch to Base Camp: 'The beauty of fixed rope,' he said, 'is that you can't get lost. If the worst comes to the worst they can rattle down the ropes, back to the tent.' I wonder if he would have been happy to let us go if he had known what we were to discover? There were no fixed ropes. They must have been buried in the snow.

There were just three of us now. Tchering Zhambu had a cough, and was forced to turn back after climbing only a couple of hundred yards from the Col. It was dark, very dark. And to add to the fun I had let my head torch batteries run flat, as had Ang Pasang. Kami Tchering led, turning his head every few paces so we could follow. It was much steeper than I had imagined; icy in patches. In other places rock lay camouflaged under the thinnest powdering of snow. I wondered at times how the hell we were going to get down again. But for the moment we were heading up and, I thought, going rather well. The Sherpas apparently felt otherwise. It was about 4am, still dark. They sat in the snow and refused to budge.

'What's the matter, guys?' They were chatting away madly on the radio, in Nepali. 'Nawang says you've got two cold, scared Sherpas,' said John. Nawang was the cook at Camp 2. Thin cloud now engulfed us and there were no longer stars visible in the sky.

'Maybe if you can persuade them to keep going until dawn, that might do the trick,' said John.

Maybe. 'Look, Ang Pasang, let's just keep climbing until we catch up with the three ahead. We can discuss it with them.'

I tried everything: Take my jacket. (I had a spare one.) 'If you get to the top? Of course you can come to London.' There was a reluctance, but they – we – moved on. We never did discuss the matter with the three climbers ahead. We caught up with them, said our hellos and climbed on past (they had no oxygen, so climbed slowly). It was hard work – harder for the Sherpas than for me. I was on three litres of oxygen per minute, they on one. That made a big difference. We would take seven paces, maybe eight (ten was always beyond our reach) and rest for a minute, another six, and rest again. And when the snow deepened, we took it in turns kicking steps.

Up and up. The dawn broke and light snow blew in our faces from the east. The whole of Tibet was one ominous snow cloud, and yet somewhere – somewhere along the SE ridge leading to the South Summit – the Sherpas' attitude changed. They wanted that summit too.

I don't know why: I had read hundreds of books and talked to countless people, and yet when I stood on the South Summit, the view along the final ridge to the true summit staggered me. Everything we had climbed thus far was snow, or ice. This was rock, mostly: angular lumps falling away sharply left and right.

'You can go first Kami Tchering,' I said.

'No, you can go.'

'No, you go.'

Kami Tchering led. It was not difficult by Alpine standards; perhaps *peu difficile*. But it was exposed. Best not look down. There were fixed ropes, in parts; but where there were not, one slip and it would all be over.

I was happy when I left the rock behind for the broader snowy ridge that led to the summit. I knew it was the summit: it had lots of flags on top. It was not very dramatic. But the joy on the Sherpas' faces made my heart near burst. They grabbed the radio: 'Summit, summit, summit. We make summit.'

I suppose it is fear that forbids one to bask in such moments too long. The cloud cleared for a moment to reveal a view across the Tibetan plateau that stretched for miles: to China and Mongolia, no doubt. But I only glanced for a second. It was cold, and the wind had picked up a little.

Going down was exhausting: I knew it would be. And dangerous. The five people who had died this season had died here, descending from the summit to the Col. I concentrated hard, and the Sherpas were wonderful: 'Slowly, slowly.' Kami Tchering led, while Ang Pasang paced himself just behind me.

It took about five hours down, and for an hour of that time the snow cloud that had filled Tibet invaded our path and masked our vision almost completely. But I felt calm, and when it cleared, there, far below, was a small, red figure on the Col, excitedly waving his arms. It was Tchering Zhambu.

A half-hour later he was unstrapping my crampons and rubbing my hands warm because, casually, I had remarked that I was chilly. He boiled some noodle soup, but I was not hungry. Gently, he insisted I should crawl into my sleeping-bag and rest; but I could not sleep.

It didn't matter; nothing mattered that night. I was content. It was a feeling I had never before experienced.

Summary: Rebecca Stephens was a member of the DHL British 40th Anniversary Everest Expedition which aimed to climb the mountain by the route of the first ascent and to raise money for Sir Edmund Hillary's Himalayan Trust. The joint leaders were John Barry and Peter Earl. Four people stood on the top: Harry Taylor, who on 10 May became the second Briton to climb Everest without bottled oxygen, and, on 17 May, Rebecca Stephens, accompanied by Sherpas Ang Pasang and Kami Tchering.

(*This article first appeared in the* Financial Times, *19 June 1993. It is reproduced by kind permission of the Editor and the author.*)

Above and Below
the Snow-line

JIM CURRAN

Fifty Not Out

(Plates 79, 80)

It happens to me every year on January 8th, the same birthday as Elvis Presley. But 1993 was the great five, oh. There is no denying that now I have to accept that even if I live to be ninety I'm well past halftime and almost certainly a lot nearer the final whistle than I would choose to be. (There wasn't much consolation, either, in knowing that just up the road from me Paul Nunn was, as usual, two whole days older.)

So I resolved that 1993 must be a good one. It got off to a promising start with a quick foray to Nepal to shoot a documentary with Chris Bonington at Everest Base Camp to coincide with the 40th anniversary of the first ascent (was I really only ten then?). I have to say that despite or because of a brief and personally unmemorable trip to Everest from Tibet in 1988, I had never harboured any great desire to go there again. I had no great expectations that I would ever really enjoy doing the most famous trek in the Himalaya.

But I couldn't have been more wrong. It was a wonderful, if hectic, time, and brought home to me the realisation that even with all Nepal's much publicised problems of exploitation, pollution and overcrowding, the approach to Everest is still a fabulous experience. In fact many of the clichés are simply not true. For instance, most of the litter is now being buried; yes, of course there *are* many other people on the trail but it's not as bad as one is led to believe. It's still a very big landscape to move through and if the sight and sound of other trekkers offends, well, just look up, and be stunned.

For me the memories are of chance meetings with several old friends along the way and the making of new ones as Everest itself loomed nearer. In particular, Pertemba, who was masterminding our trip, was a wonderful companion as he gave us the benefit of his knowledge and insight into Sherpa customs and culture. For Chris, of course, this was a trip down memory lane and frequently he would be greeted with sudden recognition and affection by Sherpas and porters dating right back to the early sixties.

At Lobuje we met John Barry and Rebecca Stephens as they approached Base Camp after warming up (if that is the right phrase in a particularly cold spring) on Island Peak. They looked fit and confident, as did Harry Taylor, and it was no great surprise to hear of their success. Gorak Shep and Base Camp were marked by a near terminal power crisis to our main video camera and only the presence of a solar-powered battery, loaned by the Brits, saved us from humiliation. My own arrival at Base Camp caused Bill Barker to ask, with studied innocence, how long had I been interested in photography!

Despite Chris getting a nasty throat infection sending him temporarily and uncharacteristically speechless, and some very poor weather, we eventually snatched the opportunity for Chris to do his pieces to camera against a theatrically stormy background on Everest and Nuptse. With relief at having justified the expense, we turned for home. I decided on the plane to use the loot to fund two more trips during the year.

Four months later I again left Heathrow with Chris, this time to Moscow to film and climb in the Caucasus. With us were Jim Fotheringham, Chris's secretary Louise Wilson and Gerry her husband, and the filmmaker Richard Else. It was a happy and relaxed little group, united in our desire to film/climb Elbrus, 5633m, but at heart we were more interested in experiencing a wider spectrum of climbing in the Caucasus, as well as imbibing a varied range of alcoholic beverages but invariably based around champagne and vodka!

It was a hectic three weeks. We first camped in the Adylsu valley where, from the romantically named Green Bivouac, we climbed Via Tau 3820m and Gumatchi 3810m. Chris and Jim, the 'A' team, bagged Cheget Tau 4110m and Jantugan 3931m, all four being Alpine scale peaks.

Then we all set out for the Ushba plateau. It took two gruelling days to get there but, to my relief, the Ushba icefall was in reasonably friendly condition this year, even if the weather wasn't. We spent three nights camped on the plateau, marvelling at the spectacular Shkhelda Towers across the way, as they floated in and out of the clouds. We also managed to snatch two easy routes and almost, but not quite, a hard one. The easy ones were the W summit of Chatyn Tau 4368m and the SE ridge of Pic Shchurovsky 4259m. (This is the normal descent route used by hard men who have climbed the major N face of the mountain.) Chris and Jim set out with Sacha and Vocca, our two delightful Ukrainian guides/interpreters/friends, and in vile weather they made a valiant attempt to climb the classic NE ridge of Ushba 4696m, eventually getting to within 50m of the summit before beating a prudent retreat to avoid a stormy bivouac. The next day, in gentle drizzle, we wobbled gingerly down the icefall and plodded the few hundred miles or so down the valley to hot showers, food and more champagne.

Which only left Elbrus. It was by no means an anti-climax, far from it in fact, for it was a wonderful cloudless day and we were all acclimatised enough to do it with a bit to spare. The view from the top was every bit as good as we had been told. Given the unfortunate publicity Elbrus has had recently, it would seem to be, in the featureless vastness, a very serious place in bad weather. It's also not a good place to learn to use compass, crampons and ice axe. I can't help feeling that inexperienced trekkers could be biting off a lot more than they can chew in anything other than the perfect conditions that we experienced. But it provided a nice finish to our three-week foray, though the two final days in Moscow were also interesting for different reasons. (OK, mainly alcoholic ones.)

The return coincided with the end of my teaching career, for I had managed to get early retirement from the University of the West of England

as a 50th birthday present. With gay abandon I marked the occasion by
lashing out on yet another huge airfare, this time to join the larger than life
President of the BMC (yes, we're talking Big Mac here) in Santiago, where
he was attending a UIAA meeting. Mac proposed a trip up to Northern
Chile to visit the volcanoes of the Atacama desert, the driest place in the
world. A flight to Antofagasta and the hire of a four-wheel drive Toyota
made this a reality.

We spent a few days walking and exploring around the oasis of San Pedro
de Atacama with Licancabur 5916m always piercing the horizon. But neither of us was really acclimatised enough to attempt it and with mixed
feelings we drove north to the wonderful scenery of the Lauca National
Park right on the borders of Peru and Bolivia. Here the volcanoes are
bigger and snowier and the altiplano higher. We camped by the shore of
Lago Chungara, looking out across the lake at billowing storm clouds over
the Bolivian border, with the perfect volcanic cone of Parinacota 6330m
dominating everything. At least we were camping high and getting some
mileage in, but after a pleasant ascent of a large hill called Guaneguane
5099m, we reached an impasse. It seemed a very long shot to get up
Parinacota, and anything else was either too remote or not worthwhile.
Mac, thinking laterally, suggested a return to San Pedro de Atacama and I
agreed whole-heartedly. Licancabur was calling me back.

So after a near heart failure caused by almost running out of petrol in the
most desolate part of northern Chile, we arrived back in San Pedro. It was
Sunday afternoon. Our flight back from Antofagasta left on Thursday
morning and my flight home was on Friday. That gave us Monday and
Tuesday to reach the foot of the volcano through a maze of lethal dirt
tracks made, all too obviously, by the army, get some way up to bivouac,
and then climb the thing. It would have been a good move to bring with
us Graham Little's 1992 *AJ* article on the subject, but we forgot.

The first part of the plan went OK and by Monday evening we were
ensconced by a small snow patch optimistically imagining we were nearly
halfway up the W face. Next morning brought an early setback. Mac had
suffered a slight chest infection since he arrived in Santiago. Now at around
5000m he felt as though one lung was barely working and wisely decided
to descend. Rather unwisely he urged me to carry on, and very unwisely I
agreed.

I set off at 7.30am, giving myself until 2.30 to get to the top. I followed a
long rib of lava blocks, slabs and towers, preferring to scramble and even
climb little buttresses and cracks than fight up the interminable scree slopes
surrounding them. I spent most of the day thinking about Lindsay Griffin's
accident in Mongolia. At least, I thought, I'll be able to make a quick descent
down the scree. The day seemed never ending and, judging my height
against the skyline ridges, the top seemed miles above me. By midday I
was beginning to flag; by 2 o'clock I was getting faintly alarmed. 2.30
came and went, with the top still apparently far away. Then, just before 3,
the angle abruptly relented and I stepped out onto almost flat ground. The
summit was only about 30m higher and suddenly I could see down to the

amazing vivid waters of Laguna Verde and across into Bolivia. I plodded up to the crater rim and took a quick picture down into a little frozen pond at the bottom, followed by a precautionary remote snap of yours truly (you've got to get the evidence these days!).

Then it was off down the central scree slope we had spotted from the bivvy site. Horror of horrors, it was almost immobile. After ten minutes I had descended only a few metres and had fallen over on my nose about twenty times. Wearily I leant against a boulder and tried to think. Only about four hours' daylight and I had to get not just back to the bivvy site, but all the way down to the truck, over 2000m lower. Necessity being the mother of invention, I resorted to starting a huge avalanche of scree, jumped on, and by lying down on the shifting, bouncing rocks, descended slowly in state and a huge cloud of dust. Shattered and suffering what felt like a terminal asthma attack, I reached the bivvy site at 5. Stumbling, cursing and stopping for wheezy rests, I got back to the point where I could signal Mac with my head torch in the last glimmers of daylight. At half past eight I arrived at the truck where Mac cheerfully took a flash photo of my ripped and dusty salopettes. I looked as though I'd spent six months in Hope cement works.

Two weeks later I was climbing in the Wye valley with Stephen Venables, gleefully recounting my adventures in my customary self-effacing way. But despite legs like tree-trunks, my performance on rock was undistinguished.

'Let this be a lesson to you,' advised Stephen kindly. 'All this mountain climbing is just another step down the road to old age. You'll be joining the Austrian Alpine Club next and learning to yodel.'

This, coming from a man who had climbed Everest and fallen down Panch Chuli, was advice that could not be ignored. 1994 will be a good one too, I hope, but this time more climbing and less summits!

GUY SHERIDAN

The Albanian Alps and Korabi Massif

The European Community Monitor Mission to the former Yugoslavia has its headquarters in Zagreb, Croatia. As a member of the United Kingdom Delegation to the Mission, I arrived in Zagreb for monitoring work in July 1992. This was relatively early in the existence of the Mission to the former Yugoslavia and much of the work then was centred on monitoring the fragile cease fire and attempting to disengage the two opposing sides – Croatians and Serbs. Many people might conclude that what was achieved by the Mission did nothing to stop the Serb/Croat war spreading into neighbouring Bosnia Herzogovina. Perhaps that supposition is correct and history now confirms how impotent the European Community and the United Nations have been in trying to find a formula for peace and, for the latter, to impose it. However, not many people know that while hatred, slaughter and double-dealing were playing their part equally with Muslim, Croat and Serb, the European Community had despatched teams of Monitors to peripheral States to the former Yugoslavia in an attempt to prevent a spill-over of the conflict to them. Bulgaria and Hungary have minorities in Macedonia and Serbia respectively and Kosovo has a majority ethnic Albanian population.

I had been working for five months in the Serbian Republic of Krijena (those areas of Croatia which had a Serbian majority population who had ridden on the back of the breakup of Yugoslavia to gain, by force, political and military control of them and had pronounced the three regions independent Republics) when, in early January 1993, the Danish Presidency of the Monitor Mission despatched me to Tirana, Albania, to establish the Mission there and to start monitoring Albania's borders with Montenegro, Kosovo and Macedonia as soon as was possible.

My delight was undisguised. Not only was one heading for a country that had been closed to foreigners, particularly Westerners, for almost half a century but one was also going to remote mountainous frontier regions with unrestricted remit to walk, sleep, eat and drink there. In the words of the Head of the Mission: 'Our business of being seen by the border forces of those three Republics of the former Yugoslavia, at any time and any place, in our conspicuous white clothing and unarmed, would hopefully deter the spread of this evil ethnic conflict.' I could hardly believe my good fortune. Perhaps this is an over-simplification because, whatever inter-pretation I put on the job of an EC Monitor, our business was serious, in remote and unforgiving circumstances and often dangerous. A mountain-eer's specific requirements one might say!

Albania is a small, mountainous country which lacks infrastructure and bears the marks of decay and repression imposed upon it by almost fifty

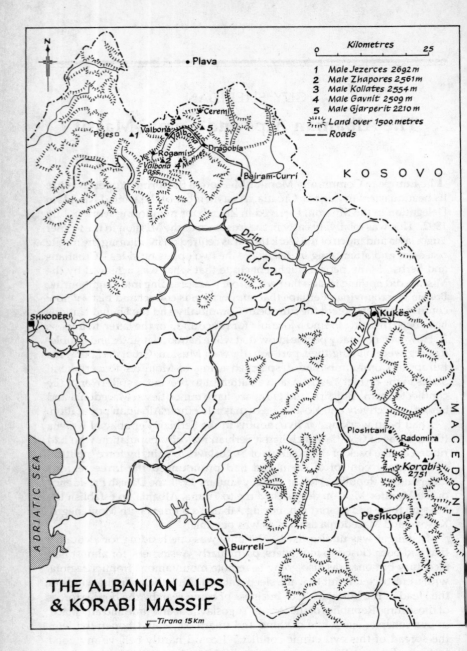

THE ALBANIAN ALPS
& KORABI MASSIF

years of Communist rule. The new democratic era arrived in 1991 and
with it came expectations of instant benefit and riches. These hopes dig
deep in the cities and towns where they are fuelled by a dozen or so television channels beaming across the Adriatic from Italy. Yet a nine-hour
drive to the top north-eastern corner of the country on tortuous roads

brings you into high green valleys where the trees have not been cut down, where grey spires of rock soar into the Balkan sky and where life for the scattered population has not changed for decades. This is the Valbona valley, the very heart of the Albanian Alps. The frontiers with Montenegro and Kosovo form the NW to NE fringe of the Alps and danger along the marked frontier is never far away. In Enver Hoxha's day, a fear of revisionist influence on the conduct of his 'pure' communism was manifest in the paranoic construction countrywide of 800,000 concrete bunkers and a regularly patrolled devegetated belt close to the actual frontier: the bunkers to keep the invading West (or East for that matter) out and the belt to keep the population in. These are the marks which disturb the eye, here and all along the rugged frontier, in what is otherwise a pristine, unvisited mountain paradise.

The Valbona valley is entered through a narrow gorge some ten kilometres from the small town of Bajram-Curri. It is cut off by deep snow for the four months of winter and it is only from late April that a vehicle can reach it. A dirt road follows the river's edge and gradually climbs through beech and pine forests to arrive at the small hamlet of Dragobia. The altitude of the hamlet is not great, a little under 600m, but its position at the confluence of the Motines and Valbona valleys is the herald of greater things to come. At the head of the Motines valley lies the bulky, grey E face of Male Gavnit, 2509m. It towers over steep snow slopes which, even at these southern European latitudes, lie thick until mid-June. On the opposite side and to the north, the ramparts of Male Gjarperit, 2210m, stand sentinel to a steep-sided valley a little further up towards Valbona village itself. An atrocious dirt road finds a twisted line to Ceremi, a scattered village which nestles under the frontier with Kosovo. Ram, the resident interpreter with the Monitor team in Bajram Curri, whom I, as the boss, had stolen for two days, was born here. A better man for my short visit in May 1993 would have been hard to find; his knowledge of English is excellent and he possesses a similar energy for the hills. My plan for the visit to the Alps was modest and centred on the desire to see these remote mountains which have, in the past 50 years, rarely had a foreign visitor, probably never felt the tramp of modern climbing boots nor heard the tinkle of the latest mountaineering ironmongery.

Valbona village is crowned by an ugly brute of a 'chalet'-style concrete building which was built for use by the Party faithful. It now sits abandoned with windows broken and, together with the numerous bunkers on the fringe of the village, is the only eyesore in the length and breadth of the Alps. In the ten kilometres from Dragobia the road climbs to 1000m and the snow-line is closer. Each corner turned reveals another colossus with great grey cliffs and gullies full of snow and ice. The pyramid summit of Male Jezerces, 2692m, the loftiest in the Albanian Alps, is visible from Valbona and on the jeep track a little way out towards Rogami the N face of Male Zhapores, 2561m, could be called the 'Eiger' of the valley. Two or three kilometres further on is the well dispersed village of Rogami with a border post forming the final metre of the jeep track. Attractive two-storied houses with tiles of beech wood are surrounded by apple and cherry trees, in May just coming into blossom, and herds of goats and small cattle out enjoying the new growth. Higher up, the beech trees still had the mauve hue of winter and patches of snow lay up on the Valbona pass, our destination that day.

There is a good path up to the pass and, once above the beech forest, the only thing that lies between you and the frontier with Kosovo, some six kilometres distant, is the grey and white bulk of Male Jezerces. The Valbona river rises from beneath the scree and cascades over a cliff to disappear once again in the stony flood plain at Rogami. The track meanders up through high pastures and up steeper shale before it emerges from beneath some cliffs onto the pass at 1965m. On this day in May, with the snows of winter still lying deep on the surrounding peaks, we really felt that we were in high country. We enjoyed a picnic lunch on the pass until an early afternoon thunderstorm rolled up from the north-east and rumbled away for the rest of the day. The storm put paid to a plan to walk round the flank of Jezerces to a summer border post at Pejes, so that the Kosovo border forces could be reminded that we EC Monitors had the ability to pop up anywhere and at any time.

We spent that night in Rogami as the guest of a farmer who barbecued a lamb for dinner. The next day we walked above Ceremi and after climbing through beech forest onto open mountain we strolled in hot sunshine, through scattered patches of snow, for five kilometres along the watershed that formed the frontier with Kosovo. For the best part of the day we walked above 2000m in the shadow of Male Kollates, 2554m, following the pyramid markers of the border. Far below in Kosovo lay the town of Plava where the Albanian population were being harrassed by the Serbs. There were many people in the Valbona valley who, in generations gone by, used to walk over the high passes to visit relatives down there. Ram mentioned that he had some remote cousins there but, since the borders of the Austro-Hungarian Empire were redrawn after the First World War and had carved away about 50% of Albanian territory, those people living behind the new frontier were given another nationality overnight. He had spoken with feeling and it gave rise to sombre thoughts on the walk. The views to the south and to the Alps were made more memorable by the notion that we were the first foreigners to have been able to walk along this remote frontier of the country for nearly half a century; memorable, too, because we were accompanied by an armed escort!

More adventurous plans had been made earlier in the spring to ascend Korabi mountain, at 2751m the highest peak in the Balkans west of Bulgaria. Unfortunately they had been thwarted by the weather but not before I had gained a good feel for this isolated peak. That first attempt had convinced me that return I must, but at that time I had no idea that very different circumstances would take me to the region for a second try.

Korabi is a complicated mountain with ridges, spires, faces and a dozen or so subsidiary peaks forming a massif of about ten square kilometres. The frontier with Macedonia follows the eastern edge of the massif with many pyramid markers cemented into the steep ridges. It is remote, although a dirt road and a three-hour uncomfortable jeep ride will take you from Peshkopia to Ploshtani and Radomira, two small villages from which one launches off on foot. Radomira is the lower of the two villages and lies at a little over 1000m. At this altitude snow lies deep in winter and to venture further towards Korabi would require skis. In early April I had encountered a group of four Italians, with their Alpine touring skis, on the steps of the hotel in Peshkopia. They were heading for Korabi and I wished it had been possible to join them. They would undoubtedly be the first men to venture on skis onto the slopes of the region's highest mountain and any mountaineer would confirm that when a 'first' eludes one it is natural to be dismayed. Perhaps my chance would come at some future date and I wished them *'bon courage et bon voyage'*. In fact the weather broke during that night and luck ran out for the Italian team.

It was at about 9 o'clock in the evening on 26 June that our liaison officer in the Ministry of Defence at Tirana came running into the Mission villa to ask for a team to be sent to Peshkopia immediately since an Albanian army officer had been shot dead and a sergeant wounded, high up on the frontier with Macedonia – and close to Korabi. There was no point in leaving before daybreak. I elected to deal with the incident myself and to start at 3am with Ludovic, a tall French signaller. We gathered up rations and sleeping- bags, because it was sure to be cold up at the foot of Korabi, and a satellite transmitter which we would use to send our report of the incident to Zagreb.

We were in Peshkopia by 6.45am. It was a Sunday so there was little traffic on the twisting road through the mountains east of Tirana and the town itself was deserted at such an hour. We breakfasted in the hotel before going over to the divisional headquarters to obtain more details of the incident and exactly where it had occurred. There we met the head of border security with whom we were now to drive to Ploshtani and further up into the mountains. I knew the lower part of the track from Ploshtani because we had tried it in the course of our first attempt on the mountain but beyond that point it had hardly been used even by four-wheeled drive vehicles.

It was gorgeous weather with good visibility and the Land Rover went up the rocky and eroded track with ease. We soon found ourselves at 2200m on open grassy slopes that seemed to stretch from horizon to horizon. The views were spoilt by the profusion of bunkers that littered the mountainside and each had a connecting trench to the next which had left deep zig-zag scars across the hills. One such trench barred further progress with the vehicle, but I was delighted by the prospect of a long walk and decided that our escort should stay behind at the Land Rover with the French signaller who had a minor injury from swimming the previous day at a beach on the Adriatic. Taking Moisi, my interpreter, with me, we joined the director of border security for the gentle two-hour walk to the scene about seven kilometres distant.

We soon gained the line of a ridge which took us parallel to and above the high valley up which we had been when we had turned back in bad weather a few weeks before. It was interesting to be able to peer down into that valley now and see how far we had been able to advance up it. Beyond and high above our level on the ridge sat the bulk of Korabi mountain, now almost bare of snow except for pockets in the couloirs and gullies. It was known that the two Albanian army men had ascended the valley on their horses before gaining the ridge that we were walking along and they would have shared this view although probably not with the same enthusiasm. Although I had a poignant but important job to do this day, it did not stop me from admiring the scene and making mental notes of a route up the mountain.

When the investigation of the incident was over there was just time to make a fast ascent of Korabi. We returned to Ploshtani where, under a threatening sky, we prepared for a night under the stars beside the parked Land Rover on some flat ground close to the border post. While Moisi collected firewood, security from the post was arranged for the night. I cooked supper for the four of us and, after I had announced that we would be starting at 04.30, we crawled into sleeping-bags.

At 01.30 the first peal of thunder shook us and it was not long before the first spatters of rain fell. Reaction to this was a dive for the Land Rover by my three friends, while I decided to strike for cover and crawled underneath the vehicle to stretch out between the axles. This would be preferable to a contorted position inside, as I knew that real rest in such circumstances was difficult. The rain increased and soon run-off from the upper surface of the Land Rover was beginning to flood the ground surrounding my sleeping-bag. It was time to quit the spacious bedspace even though the penalty would be cramped discomfort for the rest of the night. But a major imponderable lay ahead. 'Did the sentry whose beat was around the vehicle know that I was underneath?', I asked myself repeatedly. As the flood water penetrated my sleeping-bag, I stopped worrying about the sentry and his probable adverse reaction on seeing me emerging from under the vehicle. My first priority was to get out. I began to ease sideways from under the bulging axle differentials to below the front offside door where I knew Ludovic, the Frenchman, was sitting. I had reached the point of sitting half out and half under and was knocking on the door window when the first challenge from the sentry rent the air. I knocked harder on the window, appreciating that I now had a serious situation on my hands. There was no sign of any response inside and I realised that perhaps the sound of heavy rain was drowning the rappings. I knocked even more urgently. At the same time the sentry delivered a second verbal challenge, louder than the first. There was still no flicker of movement from inside the Land Rover and I could see my life in peril. I struck even harder as I heard the sentry cock his Kaleshnikov. And then he shouted his challenge again. I trusted in my Monitor's white T-shirt which must have been visible to him in the dark and shouted 'Ingleesi' several times. The sentry dropped down onto one knee. I shouted 'Ingleesi' again and thumped on the window. The light in the rover went on and a door opened. It was Moisi. He said to the sentry in Albanian: 'It's OK he is one of us.'

I clambered out of the wet bag and into the back seat. The memory of the cold tacky flesh of the dead Major had gone through my mind and I wondered whether I would see the flash from the muzzle three metres away or whether it would be so quick that there would be no time for even a thought. During the remainder of the night, that close encounter with terminal danger kept my mind overactive and obstructed the rest needed before the attempt on Korabi. With the storm continuing, the decision was made at 05.30 to abandon the attempt. I wondered if there existed a spell on me and this mountain. Any further try would have to wait until my return to Albania as a tourist.

I recall Ram, my interpreter in the Albanian Alps, telling me that in the summer of '92 he had accompanied a Belgian alpinist into the Valbona valley. Shortly afterwards the Belgian had sent him a copy of an article he had written for a mountaineering journal. In it he had richly applauded his 'discovery'. Thus it may only be a matter of time before thousands find their way to what can only be described as the last virgin mountain playground left in Western Europe. I have no doubt that readers of this article will show respect for these wild and beautiful places so that others who come later can also enjoy them. But I do have an underlying fear that soon the Valbona valley, and Korabi too, will be subject to the development so evident in the European Alps, the odours of unburied rubbish and the unwelcome changes that will be inevitable to the lives of the agrarian folk who live there. In spite of this sentiment, my visits to the Albanian Alps and Korabi have convinced me that a return, one day, must form part of more adventurous plans than I was able to achieve as a European Community Monitor.

Epilogue

On relinquishing the appointment as head of the EC Monitor Mission to Albania in July 1993, I made several courtesy calls on government ministers and the President of Albania. To them I proposed that two national parks with supporting legislation be established specifically to preserve the natural beauty of the alps of the Valbona valley and the Korabi massif. Perhaps the legislation is already being prepared. I hope so.

MAPS

1:50,000 scale maps of Albania are exceedingly difficult to obtain. Great suspicion exists, still, over enquiries from a foreigner for detailed maps. This is not surprising considering the isolation that has been imposed on the country by 50 years of repressive communism. I have one set each of the Albanian Alps and the Korabi Massif and would be only too happy for them to be copied by AC members contemplating a visit to the country.*

* I have copies of these maps and members are welcome to borrow them. Ed.

JERZY W GAJEWSKI

Discovering Chornogora:
A Sentimental Journey

(Plates 77, 78)

Anyone who lived in L'vov and the area north of the Ukrainian Carpathians before the Second World War will remember with emotion the beauty of the region: the windswept mountain meadows (*poloniny*) with their waving grasses; the view from Goverla, Chornogora's highest mountain; the creak of snow under their skis when descending from Goverla's summit (2061m). There are not many people left now who can still remember that golden landscape of their youth.

Chornogora is part of the Eastern Beskidy in the Eastern Carpathians. The mountains of the Chornogora range are not exceptionally extensive or high, but to understand their unique appeal it is necessary to know something of their historical background. The Tatra Association, the first Polish tourist group, was founded in the 19th century far away from Chornogora, but some of its first sections were organised in Kolomyia and Stanislawów at the feet of the Eastern Beskidy. For many years both the Tatras and the Chornogora were a magnet for hikers and skiers. But in 1945 the region of the Eastern Beskidy became part of the Soviet Union and was closed to visitors from abroad. Only rarely was this region visited, always illegally, during the following decades and it was not until 1980 that the first semi-official expedition was organised by students from Warsaw.

Since 1989, however, it has been possible to travel freely to the area, the arrangements being organised by newly created Ukrainian travel agents. But although it is invariably the Polish participants who have the best maps, guidebooks and general knowledge of the area, it is still necessary to use the services of a local 'liaison officer'. So it was that the Eastern Beskidy were opened again to visitors and the legend of Chornogora was sufficient reason to explore the region. In particular, it was Goverla, the range's highest peak, which tempted and lured me there in the hot, dry summer of 1992.

The trip started badly with an extremely tiring train journey from Przemysl to Kolomyia via the Polish–Ukrainian frontier. Past Soviet habits still ruled on the Ukrainian railway, so that the windows remained hermetically sealed in spite of the hot weather. The only air that was allowed to enter the carriages was through jagged holes of broken glass in the doors. Muddles and misunderstandings over seats and tickets still had to be

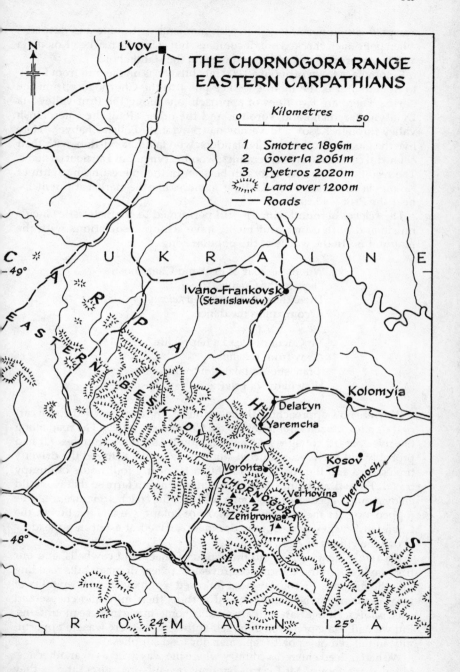

N

L'VOV

THE CHORNOGORA RANGE
EASTERN CARPATHIANS

Kilometres

0   50

1 Smotrec 1896m
2 Goverla 2061m
3 Pyetros 2020m
 Land over 1200m
—— Roads

C
-49°
U K R A I N E

Ivano-Frankovsk
(Stanislawów)

Kolomyía

Delatyn
Yaremcha

Kosov

Vorohta
CHORNOGORA   Verhovina

3 2
Zembronya
1

-48°

R O 24°M A N I 25° A

accepted as the norm, together with moments of trouble and suspense when policemen checked our documents. But at last we reached Kolomyia and much-needed rest and refreshment at the station hotel.

Kolomyia, a town of about 60,000 inhabitants, is on the trail from L'vov to Romania; it is the main entrance point to the Chornogora from the north. There are two lines of approach: one along the Prut valley via Delatyn, Yaremcha and Vorohta, and the other along the Cheremosh valley through Kosov and Verhovina (previously Polish Zhabye). Here live the Guculs, Ruthenian highlanders, who fascinate visitors with their colourful costumes, music, ceramics, wood-carvings, and ancient customs. The results of their creativity can be seen in the interesting museum of Kolomyia or, in a less formal setting, at places like the market at Yaremcha, near the Prut waterfalls.

The *kolomyika* round dance is still performed to characteristic Guculs music and both dance and music have strong associations with the mountains. In the words of the popular song:

> Where the roar of Prut and Cheremosh
> Plays to the Guculs,
> There the sound of joyful *kolomyika*
> Accompanies the dance.
>
> No Gucul can lead a happy life
> Away from *poloniny*;
> If fate should take him to the plain,
> He will die of grief.

We were now approaching the mountains. The overcrowded coach carried us a few dozen kilometres up the Cheremosh valley. The road along the river passed cottages and several rebuilt Orthodox churches. It had probably not been reconstructed since the war. We admired the driver's tirelessness and the coach's durability after nearly four hours of bumpy travel. From time to time the bus would stop near a farm so that we could enjoy a much-needed drink from a well and the coach's engines could be topped up. As the sun set in a blaze of colour, we left the bus in the Cheremosh valley and, in grey darkness, arrived at a hut in a meadow above the village of Zembronya.

We awoke next morning to the sound of sheep and cowbells, and our first daybreak in the Chornogora revealed a view of misty hills receding into the distance. In the days that followed we enjoyed the hospitality of local herdsmen, who gladly shared with us their milk and cheese and even *palinka*, Hungarian vodka, probably home-made in these mountains. But we had come prepared to be self-sufficient, as there was no opportunity, in this remote spot, to replenish our food supplies.

We had indeed entered a country where life was lived as in another age. Here, at the foot of Mt Pyetros, smiling raven-haired girls sang as they milked the cows, and herds of small, robust Gucul horses roamed free over the hills. Only the sight of an occasional tractor or truck brought us back to the reality of the present.

During that week we walked along the main range of Chornogora, from Mt Smotrec (1896m) westwards to Mt Pyetros (2020m), over a number of well-known summits: Pop Ivan (2022m), Brebyenyeskul (2037m), Turkul (1932m), Dancezh (1850m), Pozhyzhevska (1822m), Breskul (1911m) and, of course, Goverla, the highest at 2061m. Below the rounded silhouettes of the main summits, covered with *poloniny*, were the steep cirques of Gadzhina, Breskul and Zaroslak; while lateral rocky ridges rose to the distinctive tops of Shpyci and Kozly. At the foot of Turkul there was a small lake, known as Strange Lake. Delighted by the fine weather and beautiful surroundings, we bivouacked here and made a fire with branches of the dwarf mountain pine, and relished our freedom and carefree companionship.

From time to time we found relicts from the past: rusty barbed wire running along many of the hills, just below the ridge which once marked the main defensive line of the Austrian and Hungarian armies during the First World War. Few people realise today that the region of Eastern Beskidy was vitally important to Hungary in the years 1914-18. If the Russian armies had succeeded in crossing this mountain barrier, all the plains of Hungary might have been overrun by the invaders. The defenders retained this line, but at a high cost; the Great War took its relentless toll here as well as in the Dolomites, East Prussia and the fields of Flanders. Here too we found the remains of some of the old Polish/Slovak border posts (with numbers and the letters P and S) along the main ridge of Chornogora. These posts are useful guides for hikers, especially as they are noted on the old maps.

What is it about this region which attracted our forebears and yet still retains the power to fascinate today's visitors? Perhaps it is the open aspect of the landscape, backed by the hills and mountains of the Carpathians stretching away into distant Romania. Perhaps it is the unspoilt isolation of this wilderness area where foresters' lodges are hidden deep in the valleys and where even shepherd's huts are rare. Whatever its appeal, this beautiful, unspoilt mountain region of the Chornogora, together with the other ranges of Eastern Beskidy, offers new possibilities of nostalgic travel into a landscape of the past.

New Directions

Competition Climbing: A Debate

At the Alpine Club on 26 October 1993

The President, **Michael Westmacott**, introduced the three lead speakers: **Ivor Delafield**, President of the UIAA's Commission of Rock-Climbing Competitions, **Ed Douglas**, Editor of *Mountain Review*, and **Hugh Harris**, British Mountaineering Council Development Officer with responsibility for Climbing Walls, Youth and Competition Climbing.

The President said that there had always been competition in climbing, and he recalled an incident 40 years ago, after Everest, when Alfred Gregory was asked by a reporter how high he had got and he said well he had helped to establish the top camp at something under 28,000ft.

'Oh, so you came fifth,' said the reporter.

The President commented drily that if there is no competition in the normal way, it gets invented for people. But we were talking here of more structured competition: primarily rock-climbing, but also ice-climbing and ski-mountaineering.

Ken Wilson raised a point of order: 'It seems to me that this debate, taking place in what is in fact the major club in the land, could be seminal. People should not take it lightly. This is the first genuine debate that has taken place *in a club* in this country and people should realise that what is discussed here and the conclusions we come to could have resonance throughout the whole country.'

Ivor Delafield opened the debate by admitting that during the past six years he had become deeply committed to competition climbing. As President of the UIAA's Commission of Rock-Climbing Competitions, his present task was to co-ordinate all the UIAA federations which represent countries engaged in competition climbing. He emphasised, however, that he was speaking as an ordinary member of the BMC rather than in his UIAA role. He laid a number of facts before the meeting which demonstrated the extent to which competition climbing had already taken hold. For instance, in 1994, competitions would be held in Germany twice, Switzerland, Austria, Russia, the Czech Republic, France twice, Italy, United States, Japan, Spain and Britain. We were now recognised by the International Olympic Commission as a sport, and there was a very good chance that competition climbing would feature at Sydney 2000.

Ivor Delafield described the current role of the BMC in competition climbing: to administer the British team, to promote and develop training courses for team members and others and to promote and develop youth activities. They were also responsible for organising and running an international World Cup competition each year. But if the BMC were going to continue to run competition climbing in this country it was vital that they should do it well and not underestimate the resources, effort and energy needed to carry out their obligations. If the BMC failed in their efforts or if it was found that the membership did not want competition climbing, that would be very sad but it would not be the end of the game. As with expeditions, enthusiasts would get the necessary money together somehow.

Ed Douglas said that he had followed competition climbing since its inception in this country without ever really liking it very much. The history of competition climbing was an interesting one, and of urgent importance because it, and its attendant culture of sport climbing, was an imminent threat to the type of climbing that most of the people in this room grew up loving.

'We had, until the mid-1980s, been rather dismissive about competition climbing in this country. The Russian form of the sport – speed climbing – is not the precursor of the modern game, which originated more on the sun-drenched limestone walls of southern France. Once bolted routes became accepted there in the late seventies and early eighties, several things inevitably happened:

• People could practise routes, thus allowing standards to rocket – which they have, and by four or five grades in a decade.

• A lot more people would go climbing because it was now safe. And they do. More than one research agency has claimed climbing as the fastest or one of the fastest-growing sports in Britain.

• It would evolve from being something bearded wierdoes do into something that scantily clad boys and girls do.

• This massive influx of youth would make it image-strong and ripe for exploitation on the TV.

'All of these things have happened in the last ten years and now give the impression that they were inevitable evolutions that could not be resisted by the few manic traditionalists like Ken Wilson and myself who complained. The result is that climbers are now chipping routes quite regularly, bolting and retro-bolting widely, and even gluing on additional holds where nature has failed to provide.

'Vast indoor crags have been, or are, in the process of being constructed so that inconveniences like bad weather, loose rock and other tiresome intrusions into the gymnastic ideal are expunged from the memory. It used to be the case that climbers rock-climbed to prepare themselves for the mountains. Nowadays, gymnasts use fibreglass panels to prepare themselves for the rock.

'If you have a lot of people doing something all at once for the first time together, then it builds up a tremendous energy which is very enjoyable to share in or, if you're a journalist, to watch. It also tends to frighten some of the older generation, like those running the BMC, into acting quickly so that "youngsters" will think them cool and trendy and in touch. The BMC thus found itself having to do big U-turns in the late 1980s when its initial distrust of competition climbing was overtaken by events. At the 1987 General Assembly of the UIAA, a decision had been reached to establish the current World Championships, although many "non-official" events had already been held as a sort of crest to the wave of sport climbing that was rapidly spreading across Europe. The BMC registered its opposition to the UIAA going down that road and announced that it had no mandate to support climbing competitions. Within six months, however, the BMC's Management Committee had done a complete *volte face* and was now supporting them.

'In the intervening period a maverick organisation called the Independent Sport Climbers Association had organised a speed climbing event at Malham. The key word there, of course, is *independent*, that is to say something beyond the control of the BMC: a youth-driven group that had no time for committees and the old traditions. These people couldn't care less what the BMC thought, so the Council, fearful of competitions taking over crags and of sport climbers moving beyond their jurisdiction, held its nose, shut its eyes and jumped in with both feet. There was nothing wrong in adopting this point of view (although I don't agree with it) since the BMC has always been a body representative of all climbers. But bear this in mind:

'At no stage did the BMC consult the broad mass of climbers about what it should do; indeed it didn't even know the questions to ask them at that stage, beyond whether anybody minded if they went ahead and allowed competitions to happen. So, in a frenetic six-month period, the BMC had changed its course by 180° and has since steamed resolutely towards that golden land where competitions appear on the telly every month, everybody makes money and the BMC remains as a kind of benevolent uncle, overseeing the development of all climbing into the next century.

'Except, of course, that it hasn't happened like that. What the Americans have already discovered – and the rest of the world is rapidly finding out – is that large-scale international competitions on custom-made walls are monstrously expensive. There is only one way to make these work and that is to secure formidable sponsorship deals from companies with nine-digit turnovers; and the only way you can get those boys interested is by getting TV coverage. The problem with the World Cup is that it is even struggling to get *climbers* to come and watch it, let alone persuading ignorant TV executives that they should back *this* sport ahead of others that are chasing the television dream. The upshot of this shortfall of interest has been the regular cancellation of World Cup events. The World Championship has become an ailing behemoth that blunders round the planet, too expensive to feed and house for anyone to give it a permanent home.

'You can't get round the problem that something that does not come from within climbing itself won't work if the climbers themselves don't want it. The initially attractive idea of having the best climbers in the same room on the same route, fighting it out like vertical gladiators, had some fundamental flaws. The vast majority of the walls used in competitions mimic steep limestone climbing, which suits those who love Verdon but makes a nonsense of the term "World Champion". The great appeal of climbing, surely, is in its variety, the triumph of technique over brute strength, the psychological challenge that each of us face. If it's just a question of how strong you are, then interest dwindles.

'You may well be asking, what has this got to do with me? The youth of today can do what it likes to its tendons, can spend as long as it wants in cellars doing one-finger pull-ups. *My* sport – the thing I do with my friends – is untouched by all of this. Well, you're absolutely right. You can carry on doing whatever you want for as long as your karma allows you and you need never clip a bolt. But – and, for me, it is an Everest-sized "but" – if you care about the future of climbing then you will seek to change things. At the moment the strongest impression young climbers get of mountaineering is that of the competition and sport climbing world. The slow, methodical accumulation of experience has been abandoned in favour of a rapid rise through the grades on bolted routes.

'We are in danger of producing fewer and fewer climbers at the cutting edge of alpinism. Young climbers do not get the same exposure to adventure as we did when we began. They are exposed to something which is fun, athletic, enjoyable, and what their friends are doing – but which isn't climbing. Climbing is about uncertainty, risk, discovery, joy, doubt, fear. It is also hugely rewarding.

'One of the sport's great strengths is its anarchy, its freedom to do as one pleases. But remember also that its anarchy is also its great weakness. It allows those of fixed resolve to do whatever they please and justify it, whether that be retro-bolting or organising competitions that nobody wants to watch.

'What I hope to do in my activity as a journalist is to try to suggest to people that there are alternatives; that a cold February day spent in the cloud on Ben Nevis may not do your training schedule much good but it's a jolly good day out and there may even be sandwiches.'

Hugh Harris recalled some of the more important events which had led to the BMC's present role in the competition climbing scene. The first recorded BMC involvement was a paper presented by the late Peter Boardman, then National Officer, in 1976, in which he had outlined all the concerns about competitions on natural crags that still worry the BMC today and form part of our policy. Peter Boardman had also made the point that these objections did not apply with the same force to climbing walls.

'During the 1980s competition climbing grew in popularity in Europe and many of the UK's leading climbers were taking part, mainly on outdoor crags. In 1986, the UIAA decided to take over the organisation of world competition climbing. Only the BMC, of the UIAA Council, opposed this. During 1987/88, interest among UK climbers increased and plans were put together for an "extravaganza" at Malham Cove complete with TV coverage, sponsorship and attendant crowds – everything the BMC feared. After strenuous objections from them, the project was dropped. The issue was now centre stage and was discussed at the BMC's AGM in April 1988. The

Council was almost unanimously advised by those present to take competition climbing on board, but only on artificial walls. On 15 June 1988, after a long and full debate, the Committee of Management voted by 14 to 1 to accept and implement this policy on artificial structures only. This view was accepted by the UIAA in 1990.

'The following year saw the first formalised competition in the UK in Leeds. A month later, also in Leeds, the first ever UIAA World Cup took place with Jerry Moffatt winning in outstanding style. The BMC received £20,000 per annum for four years from the Sports Council in 1990 to fund the British team. This was money which would not have been available for other purposes.

'The popularity of competition climbing increased during 1991 and the number of good climbing walls also increased. During the autumn of 1992 the first British championships were held at The Foundry in Sheffield, at Bristol and at the Sobell Centre in London. In December 1992 the World Cup competition was a great success with over 7000 spectators. In January 1993 the BMC's Committee of Management voted by 15 votes to 2 for the BMC to organise the 1993 World Cup event but this eventually had to be cancelled owing to a dispute over international TV rights. If this dispute can be resolved, then the BMC are confident of being able to run World Cup events successfully and profitably in the UK for at least the next three years. In May 1993 the BMC received funding from the Sports Council for a Development Officer for Competitions, Climbing Walls and Youth; and Reebok agreed to sponsor the British team, initially for a three-year period. It is wrong to misrepresent the facts by saying we are in dire financial straights, for this is just not true.

'The actual philosophical case for the BMC being involved in competition climbing is more difficult to argue, but the BMC does have credibility with the vast majority of active climbers because of our policy concerning competitions: namely, to keep them indoors, to be involved with their organisation, to protect the crags and, hopefully, to influence some of the younger climbers. All the leading competition climbers are, or have been, "traditional" climbers: Jerry Moffatt, Simon Nadin, Ben Moon, Tony Ryan, Felicity Butler, Ian Vickers and a number of the younger climbers coming up now.'

Hugh Harris then explained how he himself had become involved in competition climbing. Originally from Northumberland, he had climbed since 1982 and during the late eighties and early nineties he had played a major role in developing hard bold new routes in Northumberland. At the same time, he had found it perfectly natural to enjoy the emerging sport climbing in Yorkshire and Wales and to practise the dubious pleasures of winter mountaineering in Scotland. He still participates in all these styles of climbing. Late in 1990, the Berghaus Wall opened in Newcastle and proved an instant success. To Hugh, it seemed the ideal opportunity to transfer a natural outdoor competitiveness to an indoor environment. He teamed up with Stephen Porteus and between them they convinced everyone that bouldering competitions were a good idea. The 'Boulder for Fun' competition proved a huge success. Many other bouldering competitions had started at the same time, encouraged by the provision of new walls and a large demand from climbers. Hugh had also played a major part in organising and running introductory climbing courses on the wall. From their inception, the courses aimed to put across all aspects of climbing including ethics and the environment. It had seemed perfectly natural for those people who had done one of these courses to develop their climbing in a traditional style and yet also to enjoy taking part in bouldering competitions.

In March 1992 Hugh Harris had taken over the management of The Foundry in Sheffield. This was the first permanent climbing wall suitable for holding a major national competition and in October 1992 the first round of the three-event British Championship was held there and proved very popular, attracting over 100 entrants and at least 400 spectators. It had been the most atmospheric event he had ever attended.

Hugh Harris continued: 'As an average climber who, over the years, has accumulated many different experiences of all the myriad areas of our sport, I feel I can sympathise with the different viewpoints and bridge the gap between traditionalists and new-style climbers. In my opinion all areas of the sport can co-exist. Competition climbing is just one part of the grand tapestry.

'We must stand back and ask ourselves if we, the policy writers and power-brokers of our sport, can deny to the climbing public the opportunity to take part in competitions. To do so would make us bigoted and selfish. After all, if we do not want to take part in them, we don't have to. What is wrong with enjoying one particular area of a sport? There has not been a threatened clamour from competition climbers to bolt up every crag in sight. Times change – what was anathema to some people in the climbing world is now a flourishing part of the grand and ever-changing heritage of climbing. Providing that this emerging branch of our sport respects the existing status quo of ecology, environment and tradition, surely we dare not act as Luddites – for otherwise competition climbing will decide it does not need us and we will be left as bystanders!'

Ken Wilson: 'I think that the contributions of our three colleagues have been outstanding and I hope they are recorded in the *Alpine Journal*. It is absolutely essential that we start looking at this thing under the microscope, not only in this club but in clubs all over the land. This is what has *not* happened; and this is where the BMC were fundamentally wrong in all the decisions they took, because they took decisions without this matter being properly debated – and we should debate it now.

'All over Europe crags are being covered with bolts, and what we have to decide in this country is: do we want it to happen here? If you look through the old journals, particularly the Rucksack Club journals, you'll find that a huge debate took place in the thirties about whether or not hills should be waymarked with paint. Just imagine what our hills would be like now if there was paint all over them!

'As you know, all over the Continent the hills have got paint on them. We decided not. Some sort of subliminal debate took place in the Wayfarers and the Rucksack and the SMC or wherever, and paint didn't get put on the hills. A similar debate was going on about whether pitons should be put in cracks , with exactly the same result – no pitons in cracks. These two things are linked, because they show that we didn't want to reduce our hills and our crags to something that was pathetic and easy. And, as a result, we've got the sport that we all know: something that's challenging. When you go onto a small crag in Britain you're in an adventure area.

' I climbed on a crag in the Inn valley two or three weeks ago – a wonderful granite crag covered in cracks. The whole thing was riddled with bolts. I talked to an ageing climber who was there with his son – a guy in his mid-fifties, like many of us – and I said 'What's all this nonsense?' He says 'Oh it's just exercise. We do normal climbing in the hills.' That is the spectre that we're facing. We are on the brink of a holy war, and competition climbing is part of that equation. If competition climbing takes root, particularly if it gets on television, we'll be swept away and everything we know and love in the mountains – the Idwal Slabs, for example, just to name an easy area. There'll be bolts all up it, bolts on the stances, bolts halfway up the pitches, and the Sports Council and Roger Orgill, who is here tonight, will aid and abet it, because the one thing that the Sports Council want to see is our sport dragooned into a nice, neat, competitive, organised institution, just like all their other sports, and we should take pride in the very fact that we're not like that – we're a square peg in a round hole and we should stay there.

'On the political side, the BMC has got three basic choices. It can choose non-involvement, maintaining fraternal relations with any specialist organisation that might emerge and preserving our link with the UIAA. A middle ground would be to provide referees, rather like the FA in relation to the football league, and again to provide a link with the UIAA. This was the ground that the BMC adopted between 1989 and 1992 and for which they had a mandate (though ununanimous and undebated). The third option appeared in 1992 when, all of a sudden, the sponsor dropped out and the BMC suddenly decided that they had got to run competition climbing because there was £49,000 worth of funding available. And all of a sudden, the policy suddenly changed and they became impresarios overnight.

'Now let's just run through the advantages and disadvantages of these policies. The first , non-involvement , stands or falls under its own strength; the BMC preserves its position but it doesn't become tainted by commercialism. Disadvantages: it loses touch with an emergent group, and perhaps loses touch with young people.

'By adopting the second possible policy, the middle ground, the BMC would keep close involvement and maybe control and influence with the UIAA without ever getting involved with full organisation; and it would be seen to be keeping in touch with the young people. Disadvantages: in practice, it would be sucked in and compromised by commercialism and organisation. Like all bureaucratic organisations, the BMC loves to organise, and when it's aided and abetted by the Sports Council just watch them! And it would also get pushed along the Olympic road by the UIAA.

'The third option, full involvement, has the advantage for the BMC that it keeps control of the whole shooting-match and there may be financial gain. The disadvantages are, first, that it becomes more and more bureaucratic in character, more and more bureaucrats get hired, and the BMC gets more and more out of control by us, the Club members. The bigger it becomes, the more faceless it becomes. And that's happening. The second thing is, it changes its whole culture. Can you imagine what the BMC would be like if it had to run and adminster an Olympic sport? Have you any idea of all the litigation that takes place? All that wormwood of international sport? The BMC would get sucked into all that if competition climbing ever became an Olympic sport. The final thing, and this is the big crunch, is that if it forcefeeds this thing into Olympic existence, we'll have bolts all over the crags in Britain within a generation.'

Derek Walker: 'I think I'm a fairly traditional climber. I became a Vice-President of the BMC at the AGM in April 1988 when it was decided, almost unanimously, that the BMC should act and take control of competition climbing. This business about no debate having taken place is absolute bullshit frankly. The AGM discussed it, thrashed it out, and there were representatives of the Climbers' Club, the Fell and Rock, the Wayfarers', the Rucksack, the Alpine – all the national clubs thrashed it out and the strong advice given to the Committee of Management in April 1988 was that we had to get a grip of competition climbing before it was taken away, the climbing world was split and the youngsters would be off and do what they wanted and perhaps bolt up where they wanted and hold competitions where they wanted outside. That was the view on the day I was elected to become a Vice-President of the BMC. Two months later, in June, taking the advice of that AGM, the Committee of Management accepted, by 14 votes to 1, the principle that the BMC should take control of competition climbing and assist in the organisation and promotion of future World Cup events.

'I think that the decision in 1988 was right. It would appear that the vast majority of British climbers and mountaineers are behind us in this, and every survey that the BMC has conducted since then (and we've conducted many – at Buxton and at many many lectures and other events) has shown that at least 80 per cent of the membership approve the BMC stance on competition climbing: that we take control, we look after it, we keep it on indoor climbing walls. That is the clear message we've got from our fraternity out there.

'If we had *not* taken control at that time, I believe that the climbing world would have been split asunder. The young climbers would have gone away. We would have lost them. I think we would have seen competition climbing taking place outdoors and we would have had not the slightest effect on the worst excesses of bolting. So the BMC Committee of Management, in my opinion, handled the situation well and has also exerted great influence with the UIAA on the international competition scene. It was the BMC view that prevailed when they insisted, and the UIAA agreed, that all international competitions should take place on artificial structures. As far as the BMC membership is concerned, we have had no clubs resign on the issue, in fact the club membership has increased, and the individual membership of the BMC has doubled from 5000 to 10,000.

'Ken talks about the Jehad – the holy war – but let's remind ourselves who these barbarians are: Felicity Butler, the leading female competition climber in Britain over the last three years, enjoys both the competitions and normal proper climbing as well. She has just joined the Climbers' Club. Ian Vickers is the leading young lad climbing in the competition scene at the moment, and he comes from a background of hard traditional Lancashire climbers. There's nothing he likes better than soloing and climbing on the normal crags as well as climbing in competitions. [DW gave several other examples of competition climbers who also enjoy traditional climbing.] So they are not some sort of alien breed, these folk, and I find it hard to differentiate them.

'Finally, I think it was right for the BMC to be involved, as there's a whole load of people out there who enjoy competition climbing and, had we not been involved, I think the situation might have been very much worse.'

Roger Payne: 'I am one of those horrible faceless bureaucrats that Ken was referring to earlier, but I'm going to ignore all the previous contributions regarding competition climbing because I think the *real* threat from competitions is much wider and has barely been touched upon this evening. There are running competitions, from our own fells to running races up Mont Blanc, climbing in a variety of forms including ice-climbing, high-altitude races on 7000m peaks in the former Soviet Union, ski-mountaineering and cross-country skiing races, there's snow-shoeing races, there's canyoning, and there are other events that take place in the mountains such as the winter Olympics (the hideous village that was built at Albertville). There's mountain biking, hand-gliding and parapenting, downhill skiing and various he-man, abseil, canoeing, adventurer go-go sorts of things [laughter]. These types of events are usually organised by commercial rather than sporting interests, one example being this spring's so-called Adventure Olympics in the Pyrenees, organised by the French and Spanish Olympic committees and tourism bodies. It all happens in the mountain environment and has an impact on our sport.

'Now I agree with Ken and deplore a lot of the things that he was talking about – the impact of retro-bolts on crags, and competitions outdoors – but I don't think that making competition climbers into some sort of scapegoat is really the way forward. In Europe they have lost the war about retro-bolts. If we want to continue to do what most British climbers do every weekend – on-sight climbing with leader-placed protection – if we want to protect that, we should fight against competition climbing outdoors and remove retro-bolts wherever they appear. That's my personal view. And if this meeting is serious about trying to protect the mountains from competition climbing, then we need to shift the focus away from what was said in 1976 or what wasn't said, or whether it was unanimous or one vote against and start looking at the other issues I have mentioned very briefly.'

Roger Orgill, Senior Development Officer for Countryside & Water Recreation, was introduced by the President as 'the man in the grey suit from the Sports Council' [laughter]. He said: 'I came along to listen tonight, but I am moved to say something, particularly in response to the comments from Ken. It's good to hear you again in full flight, Ken, and thank you, Mr President, for this opportunity.

'Ken has warned you of the danger of an agency like the Sports Council, which seems to be only interested in competitive sports and games, getting hold of your sport, or our sport, and pursuing vigorously that element which it can most closely identify with. However, over the last five years and since Ian McNaught-Davis and Chris Bonington came to introduce themselves to our new Chief Executive, David Pickup, in 1989, and explained to him in great detail the emergence of this new branch of the sport and the dangers it presented, we have been alerted at Headquarters and I have laboured the point to the grant assessment panel that we must only move at the rate at which the British Mountaineering Council wishes us to move.

'The Sports Council recognises the BMC as a democratically elected body to take care of the sport of mountaineering, and therefore the views conveyed through the BMC are seen to be the views of the mountaineering fraternity at large, and not of some isolated body.

'The BMC has a very high reputation in the field of promoting good practice in mountaineering, including the conservation of that finite resource of mountains and crags. I do assure you that there is no danger, in the next four-year period, of competition climbing stealing an advance over anything else, and the priorities are still for access and conservation of our mountains.'

Stephen Jones: 'I think there are three interrelated issues which are going to become problems for us. One is something Ken mentioned but which needs more attention – that if you put competition climbing on TV, that will be the shop window for new people coming into the sport, and it's bolted and it's indoors and it's dry and you're not going to fall off and hurt yourself. But it's not a good introduction for people going rock-climbing and going on to the Alps and hopefully going on to the Greater Ranges in an exploratory way. It will also be a shop window for bolting up crags.

'A second point relates to access and a scenario where access to crags is banned because without bolts it's not safe, and if it's not safe then the owner is at risk from you suing him because there is a safer alternative to placing your own protection, and that is bolts.

'Thirdly, we might try to emulate the Mountain Club of South Africa by setting up an access fund to secure traditional climbing in perpetuity by literally buying the crags. Perhaps the only way to guarantee traditional climbing is for the climbing community to try to put some funding aside towards buying the crags, because they are either going to become covered in bolts or we are not going to be able to go climbing there at all.'

Roger Payne made the point that the BMC have a policy on crag owner-ship and is against being involved in acquiring crags. If we were to start buying crags a price would be put on them. In any case, we would never be able to raise enough money to buy crags in Britain.

David Hamilton: 'We are talking as if climbing is a static sport, that it exists in a certain form and that either we choose to change it or we choose to preserve it. We should be aware that the world that climbing inhabits is changing. Thirty or forty years ago there was nobody in Britain who made a full-time living out of mountaineering. Now there are thousands of people. Whether you're selling books, whether you're a staff member of the BMC, whether you're manufacturing clothing or equipment or whether you are leading treks around the world, there is now a large industry in Britain. France is lucky in that there are huge amounts of rock and if somebody bolts one place and you don't like it you can always go and climb somewhere else. Britain is fundamentally different as there is a sub-stantially smaller amount of rock. Yet people manufacturing climbing equipment in Britain want to double, every couple of years, the number of people participating in the sport, and this is one of the influences on the increase in climbing walls, competition climbing and all the changes we're seeing. It is now a commercial activity and we risk being like King Canutes trying to stem the incoming tide. The shop window of this sport is compe-tition climbing and that's bringing in a new and different type of person and increasing the number of people going into the shops and buying equipment. Any debate on this issue has to understand that there are many people whose business and livelihood depends on getting more and more people into the shops buying harnesses, karabiners, helmets. Many of these people don't like the idea of risking their necks.'

Ken Wilson: 'And once the education world gets hold of the idea that climbing doesn't have to be dangerous, then you're going to get school-teachers, outdoor centres, Uncle Tom Cobbly and all wanting those crags to be bolted up. So it's not only the equipment manufacturers who want to expand the sport. Let's face it, I'm a publisher so, on paper, I want to expand the sport! We have got a real uphill struggle if we want to keep the sport exactly as it is – in other words, no bolts in the Llanberis Pass, no five or six bolts up Cenotaph Corner, no bolts on all the climbs on Cloggy, no bolts on the Idwal Slabs, no bolts on the Milestone Buttress. That's what we're talking about and if we don't really bend every sinew, that's going to happen and it's going to happen soon. Any bolts that appear must be cut out, and cut out immediately, under the aegis of the BMC. What we need is a strong "no retro-bolting" policy, pushed home by the BMC, and with cordless hacksaws to back it up!'

Sally Westmacott: 'Could I say a few words as a very ordinary, non-talented climber very much of the old school? I hate competition climbing, I don't like competitive sports very much, I hate the media, I hate the television, but I do think that if you've got, as Ken said, an enemy out there that you're waging war on (in other words the bolters) then it's no good burying your head in the sand and hoping it will go away. I think that the BMC probably *has* done the right thing in trying to take charge of climbing competitions in this country. But when it comes to things such as bolting up routes that have always been climbed free, then it's up to the ordinary climbing public to police it. It's no good expecting everybody else to do it, or even expecting the BMC to do it. We *are* the BMC. It's up to all of us to keep an eye on this sort of thing. I personally am appalled at the use of chalk [loud applause]. So it's up to all of us to police these threats.'

Glyn Hughes said that he too was very concerned about the spoliation of our crags. 'What I feel has not come across very clearly, at least to me, this evening is the connection between competition climbing and the bolting of our crags. I am still not sure whether the encouragement of indoor competition climbing poses a threat to our crags by example or whether, conversely, *not* encouraging competition climbing would have a worse effect.'

Ivor Delafield: 'What the young people see on television is not climbing on Cloggy, or on the Idwal Slabs. What they see, if they have cable satellite, is competition climbing, which relies totally on bolts. If young people grow up seeing this on television, as they do in France and other European countries, then that is all they see and all they know and if you say you mustn't do it, the more likely they are to do it. It requires careful management and a lot of work and I really ask you to think about this. What I would like to see is even more resources put into this kind of aspect. If you want to do it well, that is the route you are going to have to take. '

Ken Wilson: 'If competition climbing ever reaches mainstream television, then it will be a very pervasive propaganda influence indeed. The scene of young people going up cliffs, clipping into bolts and, the most important thing, being safe, and manifestly *being* safe, will commend itself to a vast swathe of vested interests that we haven't yet faced. The beautiful thing about the sport, that has kept it not only with its marvellous character that we all enjoy, is the fact that it's dangerous. It's the great thinner. If it's dangerous, not all that many people do it, because not all that many people want to take a risk. So it's very simple. There's a huge constituency out there that would like vast numbers of people to go climbing. One way they can achieve that, like France, is if they bolt everything up to make it safe. And then the sport will triplicate, will quintuplicate, overnight.'

The President brought the debate to a close by pointing out that most of it could have been conducted by putting five or six people in a ring and treating them as gladiators and cheering them on! He thanked the three lead speakers for their valuable contribution to this important debate, and suggested that it should continue around the bar.

ALAN BLACKSHAW

Competitions in Mountain Areas

Alan Blackshaw is Chairman of the Mountaineering Commission of the International Union of Alpine Associations (UIAA). This article is based on a paper he presented to the UIAA General Assembly at Santiago on 1 October 1993.

Introduction and Background

At the UIAA Council meeting on 29 May 1993, there was discussion about the competitions of all kinds that are taking place in the various mountain regions of the world, for instance solo-climbing, hang-gliding, ski-mountaineering and a number of combined competitions. The danger is that they may develop from small single competitions into mass events and championships which add different aspects to the sport: mass media, traffic, investments, risks and many more.

It was recognised, therefore, that the UIAA needed to give very careful consideration to the implications of these developments for the future of mountaineering and the mountain environment; and, in particular, to the issue of whether or not the UIAA should itself organise or endorse ski-alpinism or other competitions in mountain areas as an extension of its existing responsibility for rock-climbing competitions on artificial structures.

The present policy of the UIAA is to promote rock-climbing competitions only on artificial structures and not on mountain terrain; and it could be that, after considering the issues involved, the UIAA might decide, as a matter of principle, to maintain only its present level of involvement. There is little doubt that such a decision would be opposed by some UIAA federations. But whatever was decided, the UIAA would need to develop comprehensive and consistent policies towards mountain competitions. A thorough analysis of the situation and of the policy issues arising was therefore considered essential.

Accordingly, a small Working Group on Mountain Competitions was set up and I was asked to produce a paper to shed some light on all aspects of these problems, to point out the positive and negative aspects, and to propose possible solutions that might be adopted by the General Assembly of the UIAA at its meeting in 1994. It was recognised that this task would present a challenge: to shape policy for the future without disregarding reality. Furthermore, my report would need to reflect the considerable amount of discussion of these issues that has already taken place within the Mountaineering Commission over the past two years (and now in the new Working Group). The UIAA Council asked for a fresh approach to be made, covering the range of opinions involved, and recognising the extent to which competitions in mountain areas already exist and are seen by some as beneficial to mountaineering. My report therefore proposed that the Working Group on Mountain Competitions, in collaboration with the UIAA Commissions and member federations, should continue to analyse the extent and effects of mountain competitions, make proposals for the UIAA's future policy, and suggest guidelines for member federations.

For the purposes of the paper it was assumed that the UIAA would continue to have responsibility, at international level, for the sport of mountaineering in all its aspects, including competitions on artificial structures; and to represent the worldwide community of mountaineers through its member federations. It would continue to be concerned with the protection of the mountain environment, while at the same time encouraging responsible use of the mountains and access to them. Questions of safety should also be taken into account. The UIAA would need to keep in touch with all current developments in mountaineering, so that it could remain in the main stream and not become a backwater.

It was also assumed that the UIAA would continue to conserve its limited resources for those tasks which were of greatest benefit to the majority of its members; and that any proposals for extending UIAA responsibilities in competitions would need to be justified against other priorities, especially if they involved relatively few member federations.

A useful starting point for considering future policy might be to assess whether the original arguments for restricting UIAA involvement have proved to be correct. For instance, although the current policy has been to promote competition in rock-climbing only on artificial structures and not on mountain terrain, it has to be recognised that competitions are in fact occurring on natural sites also. We need to determine what are the main lessons to be learnt from the successful and widespread popular development of this form of competition.

We also need to recognise that competitions in mountain terrain of one kind or another have existed for a long time: mountain marathons, for example, together with triathlons, downhill ski races, long-distance ski races, ski-alpinism races and high-altitude mountaineering in the former USSR. In many cases these have been organised or sponsored by member federations of the UIAA, usually at Club or regional level, but sometimes also nationally or internationally.

It would seem, therefore, that there is, and has traditionally been, some tolerance of the use of mountain areas for competitions, especially those of limited impact or on lower mountain terrain. So it would not be realistic to suggest that there should be *no* competitions in mountain areas; we must recognise that competitions are in fact likely to increase, in some cases sponsored by member federations, whether or not the UIAA decides to endorse them.

However, the growing number and scale of competitions, especially in higher mountain terrain, raises legitimate questions about their impact on the sport of mountaineering, on the mountain environment, and on mountain safety, which undoubtedly need to be addressed.

Mountaineering-related sports and other sports

In considering whether or not the UIAA itself might take responsibility for competitions in mountain areas, or influence them in other ways, it is helpful to distinguish between mountaineering-related sports, which might in principle come within the ambit of the UIAA, and sports not related to mountaineering, over which UIAA does not have any possibility of control.

In principle the UIAA could regard the international aspects of any branch of mountaineering as being within its responsibility; and therefore become involved, if it so wished, in the provision for competition within it. On that basis, the following branches of mountaineering would be eligible for consideration: mountain walking or running, climbing in any form (including ice-climbing), high-altitude mountaineering, ski-mountaineering, snow-shoeing, canyoning, and possible other forms of the sport that might be developed in the future.

Conversely, the following independent sports, among others, do not fall directly within the UIAA responsibility, although they might be of considerable concern to member federations: mountain-biking, hang-gliding, parapente, cross-country skiing, downhill skiing. In each case these have their own international or national governing bodies; and it would be for the UIAA, or member federations, to discuss with them any issues of concern that impinge on the sport of mountaineering or on the mountain environment.

In dealing with these other sports, we must recognise that we do not have a monopoly of the mountains, nor indeed a greater right to them than other users, though we should do everything possible to maintain the interests of mountaineers, especially as regards aspects of the environment important to mountaineering.

Further development of the UIAA dossier

The Working Group recognised that there may be other sports which are of concern (positive or negative) to UIAA members and member federations were invited to supply information about them.

The kind of information sought was as follows: the status of the sport; its international organisation; its impacts (positive or negative) on the sport of mountaineering, the mountain environment and mountain safety; any proposals for UIAA involvement; and the policies of member federations.

It should be possible for the Working Group to present to the General Assembly in 1994 a more comprehensive analysis of the different mountain competitions of relevance to the UIAA, together with a summary of the issues (positive or negative) identified by member federations.

Proposed UIAA guidelines

It was hoped that, by 1994, sufficient detailed information would have been collected from the member federations to make it possible to compile UIAA guidelines on competitive sports in mountain areas. These might consist of broad guidelines covering the agreed approach towards competitions in general, and more specific guidelines covering the practical implications of particular forms of competition in mountain terrain. In both cases they should cover the impact of the sport on mountaineering and on the mountain environment, and they should also include safety considerations.

Such guidelines might assist member federations in formulating their own attitudes towards particular forms of competition in mountain areas; and, in the case of the independent sports, might form the basis for discussions between the UIAA or member federations and the international or national governing bodies involved.

The assessment of proposals for UIAA involvement

The UIAA is at present considering proposals relating to two projects. The first is concerned with ski-alpinism; it has been suggested by the Club Alpin Français and others that the UIAA should take responsibility for the present European Cup.

The second proposal relates to the annual competition on Kang Tengri; the Federation of Alpinism and Rock-climbing of the Republic of Kirghizstan has proposed that the UIAA should recognise this as a model for the organisation of high-altitude competitions.

In support of the first proposal it is argued that, although the situation remains fluid at present, the international organisation of ski-alpinism competitions could become divorced from the UIAA in the near future unless some indication is given of our willingness to consider possible integration. It should be noted, however, that a number of delegations have already expressed opposition in principle to the UIAA becoming involved with the organisation of ski-alpinism competitions; while yet other delegations have expressed themselves in favour. It will be important, before the meeting of the General Assembly in 1994, that the main arguments for both of these opposing viewpoints should be identified.

The Kang Tengri proposal is different in kind from that for ski-alpinism, involving as it does a single country, a relatively small number of participants, and the special issues (particularly medical and safety) associated with high altitude; conversely, the area concerned is relatively remote and unfrequented.

It is suggested that in specific cases such as these, the UIAA should, in conjunction with those concerned, carry out an in-depth assessment of the practical functioning of the proposed competitions. But the Mountaineering Commission also wishes to emphasise the importance of avoiding undue delay in reaching decisions on both these proposals.

Basic questions to consider in making assessments

The issues for consideration have been identified as follows:

- Is the branch of competition concerned compatible with the sport of mountaineering? And how important technically is it to the future development of mountaineering?

- How far can the UIAA be involved with such competitions without compromising its stands on mountain protection or mountain safety? Conversely, can any impact on the mountain environment, or the risks involved, be reduced to acceptable levels?

- Would UIAA involvement be welcomed by a significant number of member federations? And conversely, would it be at least acceptable to other members in the UIAA overall interest?

- Would the competitions be potentially world-wide and thus needing world-wide control? Or would they be of more limited coverage and thus perhaps more suited to a regional or Continental body?

- Could UIAA afford the time and resources required, as against other priorities?

It would be the objective of each assessment to provide answers to such basic questions.

The status of the sport
The assessment should also cover in some depth the various aspects of the sport's current status, including, for example, historical development, current organisation at international and national levels, financial issues, acceptance or otherwise of Olympic principles, levels (eg local, regional, national, international), geographical extent (how many countries? how many continents?), popularity (numbers involved at various levels), and its importance for member federations.

The assessment would also need to provide an objective and well-informed analysis (positive and negative) of the sport's impact on mountaineering, the mountain environment, and mountain safety. The guidelines for such assessments would need to be determined in consultation with the Mountaineering Commission, the Mountain Protection Commission and the Safety Commission, with assistance, as necessary, by the Medical Commission.

In general, the more widespread or important the particular branch of the sport, the more urgent it will be for the UIAA to decide how to deal with competitions within it, including the question of UIAA involvement and/or control of one kind or another.

Possible levels of UIAA involvement
There could be scope for several progressive levels of UIAA involvement.

Firstly, the UIAA could accept that a sport is appropriate for competition and recognise a particular body or bodies as being responsible for the sport on an international basis (always provided that the bodies concerned accepted, where relevant, the UIAA guidelines outlined above).

Or secondly, the UIAA could adopt rules for the competitions, incorporating whatever conditions and safeguards the UIAA considered appropriate; but leaving it to national federations or others to organise the competitions.

Or thirdly, the UIAA could take full responsibility for organising competitions, in the same way as we already do for rock-climbing on artificial structures.

It would always be important to ensure that conflict with other UIAA objectives was avoided or minimised.

Working towards solutions

Following detailed future work by the Working Group on Mountain Competitions, it is hoped that some analysis of the different mountain competitions, together with proposed guidelines, can be presented to the1994 UIAA General Assembly. Preparatory meetings of this Group have already been held, but in future it would be helpful if additional representatives of the Mountaineering Commission and of the Mountain Protection and Safety Commissions could also attend.

The UIAA should then be in a position to decide its attitude towards competitions in mountain areas and whether or not to agree to the present proposals for involvement in ski-alpinism competitions and the Kang Tengri competition on the basis of the necessary factual analysis.

I am indebted to the Fédération Française de la Montagne et de l'Escalade which has hosted two meetings of the Working Group at Chamonix. I would also like to thank Paul Brasset, Vladimir Komissarov, Robbert Leopold and Louis Volle for their help in preparing the paper on which this article is based. Thanks are also due to those federations which have written to set out their official views on these issues.

Looking Back

From Lauterbrunnen to Mürren 7's troubles begin, the ladies are not yet in training.

ROSEMARY GREENWOOD

A Mountaineering Heritage

(Plate 50)

In 1802 my great-grandfather Francis Tuckett was born at Frenchay, now a suburb of Bristol but then a country village. It had long been a Quaker enclave and the Tucketts were among a number of Quaker families, such as the Frys and the Barclays, who lived there and worked in Bristol. In those days certain professions were closed to them and many Quakers went into business, manufacturing and banking where they prospered and established a reputation for scrupulous fair dealing and a caring attitude to their employees.

Francis was a leather merchant and a keen traveller. He married Mariana Fox in 1833 and had four children: Frank, Lizzie, Mariana and Charlotte. Born in 1834, Frank inherited a love of travel and a keen interest in natural science. He first visited the Alps with his father in 1842 at the age of eight, and an excursion to the Mer de Glace kindled his passion for mountains. In 1853, aged 19, he returned to the Alps with his future brother-in-law, my grandfather Joseph Hoyland Fox, and they walked and scrambled prodigiously, covering enormous distances all over Switzerland. Three years later they started climbing. In Chamonix they engaged Victor Tairraz, three other guides and a porter for the Col du Géant. Their provisions consisted of three fowls, a joint of veal, two large loaves and four bottles of *vin ordinaire*. No wonder they needed a porter. Later, Frank Tuckett did a number of seasons with Victor Tairraz; he scarcely ever climbed without a guide and usually took two and a porter. In those early days guideless climbing was rare, and my grandfather remarked on the great feat of a party of well-known English mountaineers who had climbed Mont Blanc without guides in 1855.

Although Frank Tuckett worked in the leather business in Bristol and walked there every day from Frenchay to keep in training, he was able to go climbing most summers for two months or so, starting much earlier in the season than we do nowadays. In 1859 he and my grandfather were elected to the Alpine Club which had been formed two years earlier, and they often climbed together during the following years. As far as I can ascertain, none of my forebears in the last century ever did any rock-climbing in Britain. But in 1865 an Easter party of 13 Alpine Club members, including my grandfather and great uncle, stayed at Pen-y-Gwryd and climbed Snowdon and the Glyders!

The Tucketts often made up parties for their summer holidays – Frank and his sisters, cousins and Alpine Club friends. Some of these holidays were recorded by my great-aunt Lizzie, a gifted artist, who sketched their adventures amusingly in *Voyage en Zigzag*,* *Zigzagging in the Dolomites*, and other books. They toured from place to place – several times in the Dolomites and Tyrol – Frank and his climbing friends going over the tops of the mountains and meeting up from time to time with the ladies and the less energetic men, who went round by road or mule track either riding or walking or in primitive conveyances. The accommodation was often extremely poor and verminous and food sometimes hard to come by. Sunburn was a menace, particularly for the climbers, and they protected their faces with veils and masks when on the snow. Umbrellas were carried in the rain. Lizzie wore what she described as a 'waterproof habit' and Frank wore a plaid. The ladies looped up their skirts and the porters carried their hoops (one cannot ride in a crinoline).

On the Joch Pass.
They prepare for dirty weather

* The drawings on these and following pages are from Lizzie Tuckett's sketchbook, *Voyage en Zigzag*. Longman (London), 1864.

A doubtful footing.

Tradition has it that Frank always wore elastic-sided boots for climbing; a small room at Frenchay used to be filled with his climbing boots.[1] They often met other English parties on their travels, and there were more English tourists in the Alps in those days than any other nationality. Large hotels were built in the second half of the century, not only at the resorts but also at isolated viewpoints such as Riffelalp, Belalp and Eggishorn.

Between the years 1856 and 1874 Frank Tuckett made no fewer than 57 first ascents or new routes on mountains and high passes. Notable among these were:

1856   The first tourist ascent of the Mettelhorn.
1859   The first ascent of the Aletschhorn.
1861   The first direct ascent of Mont Blanc from St Gervais by the Dôme du Goûter and Les Bosses, with Leslie Stephen.
1862   A new route on Mont Pelvoux by the Tuckett Couloir. The Col des Ecrins.
1864   First ascents of Piz Kesch, Monte Confinale, Gran Zebrù (Königsspitze) and Ortles.
1867   The first ascent of Civetta.

During these years he climbed 165 peaks and crossed 376 passes. Many of these expeditions are recorded in *Peaks, Passes and Glaciers* and the *Alpine Journal*. He also contributed articles of geological and scientific interest. He made a study of glaciers and made observations from mountain summits, boiling his thermometer to calculate the altitude and sketching the neighbouring mountains. In the Dauphiné and Ortler he did extensive surveys with equipment that included a mercury barometer and water-boiling apparatus which also came in handy for brewing up Symington's dried soup.

Verandah. Hotel Bellevue. Thun July 5ᵗʰ.
Breakfast, versus mountains.

Frank always carried with him a bottle of his 'cure all' – a mixture of tincture of rhubarb, sal volatile and brandy – and very effective it was. We were all brought up on it. He designed a sleeping-bag with a mackintosh outer, the top of which could be unbuttoned to provide ventilation, and a red blanket bag inside, plus an extra red blanket which could be buttoned on and a woollen hood. This only weighed 8½ lbs. In 1869 Frank and his future brother-in-law Eliot Howard brought from Styria what are believed to have been the first rucksacks to be seen in Switzerland, and they were soon to replace the old Swiss knapsack. Frank also carried a conjuring set. He was an accomplished conjuror and wherever he went he delighted the villagers, especially the children, with his sleight-of-hand. He also used to take out his teeth, to their mystification.

t is not absolutely necessary to master the tight rope before joining the Alpine Club.

Frank was extremely tough and strong and often exhausted his companions, but he treated his guides with great consideration and was always on the best of terms with them. He spoke German well, so communication was no problem. In 1864 he organised a fund among Alpine Club members for the mother of his guide J J Bennen who was killed on the Haut de Cry, and went personally to Lax to help deal with the family's finances. He was one of the founder members of the Austrian Alpine Club in 1862 and in 1898 he was made an Honorary Member of the Club Alpin Français. From 1866 to 1868 he was Vice-President of the Alpine Club but refused the presidency more than once, as he felt that he lived too far from London.

By 1874 Frank Tuckett was still only 40 but he did no more serious climbing in the Alps; however, he was always ready to advise and encourage younger climbers. He travelled widely and continued to do so until his death in 1913 at the age of 80.[2] Between 1877 and 1886 he travelled in Greece, Corsica, the Pyrenees and Turkey, making many ascents. Later he travelled all over the world, with frequent visits to Egypt and Italy where he indulged his archaeological interests. He went three times round the world. Family legend has it that the first time he had not enough courage to propose to the beautiful Alice Fox, who was living at that time with her brother, a sheep farmer in New Zealand. The next time round he proposed and was accepted and they were married in 1896 when he was 62.

Alice was the sister of Harry Fox who was lost in the Caucasus with W F Donkin in 1888. I can just remember Aunt Alice, a handsome lady in widow's weeds and veil, and my elder sisters have fondest memories of Uncle Frank. There is a charming photograph in the *Alpine Journal* of him sitting in the garden at Frenchay in 1910.[3]

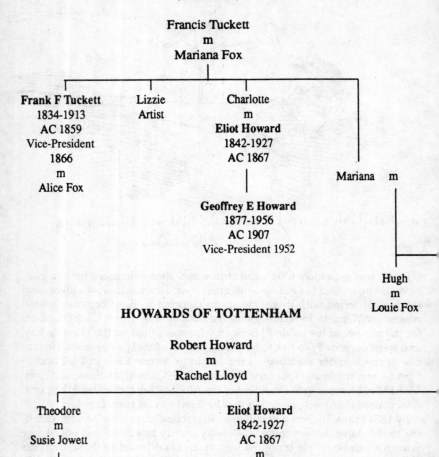

TUCKETTS OF FRENCHAY
(BRISTOL)

Francis Tuckett
m
Mariana Fox

Frank F Tuckett
1834-1913
AC 1859
Vice-President
1866
m
Alice Fox

Lizzie
Artist

Charlotte
m
Eliot Howard
1842-1927
AC 1867

Mariana   m

Geoffrey E Howard
1877-1956
AC 1907
Vice-President 1952

Hugh
m
Louie Fox

HOWARDS OF TOTTENHAM

Robert Howard
m
Rachel Lloyd

Theodore
m
Susie Jowett

Florence   5 daughters
m

W H Somervell

T Howard Somervell
1890-1975 AC 1921
Vice-President 1954
President 1962

Eliot Howard
1842-1927
AC 1867
m
Charlotte Tuckett

Geoffrey E Howard
1877-1956
AC 1907
Vice-President 1952

FOXES OF WELLINGTON
(SOMERSET)

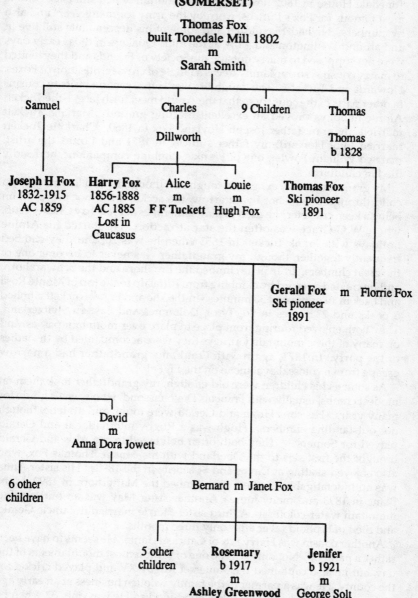

Thomas Fox
built Tonedale Mill 1802
m
Sarah Smith

Samuel   Charles   9 Children   Thomas

Dillworth   Thomas b 1828

Joseph H Fox
1832-1915
AC 1859

Harry Fox
1856-1888
AC 1885
Lost in
Caucasus

Alice
m
F F Tuckett

Louie
m
Hugh Fox

Thomas Fox
Ski pioneer
1891

Gerald Fox   m   Florrie Fox
Ski pioneer
1891

David
m
Anna Dora Jowett

6 other
children

Bernard   m   Janet Fox

5 other
children

Rosemary
b 1917
m
Ashley Greenwood

Jenifer
b 1921
m
George Solt

The Foxes of Wellington are all descended from Thomas Fox who built
Tonedale House in 1802 next to the woollen mill, which still exists and is
most famous for Fox's Puttees, worn by the army for many years and also
by climbers. He had 15 children and some of his descendants still live in
and around Wellington and work at the mill. Quakers in those early days
were not supposed to marry outside the Society of Friends and they tended
to marry cousins, so our family tree is a tangle of cross fertilisation of Foxes,
Howards and Tucketts. The daughters were often sent on visits to cousins
in other parts of the country so that they could meet fresh faces – the Tuckett
Alpine holidays proved an excellent meeting ground. Mariana Tuckett
married my grandfather Joseph Hoyland Fox in 1860. Charlotte Tuckett
married Eliot Howard, my father's uncle, in 1871 and Lizzie, the artist,
married William Fowler, one of Frank's climbing companions, and sadly
died in childbirth.

My grandfather was extremely tough and though he had lost an eye as a
child through being shot by an arrow, the accident did not prevent him
being a keen cricketer; he used to play sometimes at Frenchay Cricket Club,
where W G Grace was often the star attraction. He started his Alpine
holidays with Frank Tuckett in 1853 when he was 20, and they climbed
frequently together, though my grandfather was never to become one of
the great climbers. In 1859 he climbed the Breithorn and the Schwarzhorn;
and he created a record by climbing from Riffelalp to the top of Monte Rosa
and back in 10 hours and 50 minutes. In 1863 he and Frank Tuckett climbed
5 peaks and 23 passes in the Tyrol, Dolomites and Eastern Switzerland.
They both enjoyed touring from place to place over mountain passes, and
on many of these mountain journeys they were accompanied by the ladies
of the party. In 1871, again with Frank, my grandfather had a narrow
escape from a colossal avalanche on the Eiger.[4]

As soon as his children were old enough, my grandfather took them on
modest climbs, usually with François Dévouassoud, who was his guide for
many years. His sons Hugh and Gerald were tough and athletic, though
not outstanding climbers. Hugh was a Rugby international and Gerald
played for Somerset. They both often holidayed in the Alps and Gerald
brought the first skis to the Oberland with his cousin, Thomas Fox, who
also enjoyed skating at Davos and St Moritz in the 1890s. His sister Anna
was an indefatigable climber. She climbed the Matterhorn in 1890, Mont
Blanc in 1893 and many more. Another sister May was an outstanding
mountain water-colourist. A third sister Florrie married my uncle Gerald
and died of typhoid fever after only three months.

Another cousin was Harry Fox of Caucasus fame. He seems to have been
rather a paragon. Not only was he one of the foremost mountaineers of the
day, but he also captained the Somerset Rugby XV and played cricket for
the county. He was a partner in the family woollen business at an early age
and ran Sunday schools and other good works. He was only 32 when he
died in 1888.[5] He and W F Donkin, with two Swiss guides Kaspar Streich
and Johann Fischer, were exploring and surveying in the area of Dychtau
and they must have been killed in an attempt on the mountain. Their last

Frank F Tuckett, 1834-1913.
(From Rosemary Greenwood's family album, by permission) (p171)

51. John Muir, 1838-1914. (*W E Dassonville*) (p201)

Muir Glacier, 1971. (p208)

Yosemite: view of E side of Half Dome from Olmsted Point,
on the way up to Tuolumne Meadows. (*Sylvia Wyatt*) (p203)

Left
54. Mt Cook: High Peak before the avalanche in December 1991. (*Nick Groves*) (p221)

Below
55. High Peak photographed from almost the same place after the avalanche. (*Nick Groves*) (p221)

Kamet, 1920. (*Dr A M Kellas*) (p215)

57. On the summit ridge of the Grands Charmoz, July 1937.
(*J M L Gavin*) (p182)

Above
The Ruinette and the ridge leading to
Mont Blanc de Cheilon, August 1937.
(*A M Greenwood*) (p182)

Right
Traversing the Ruinette–Mont Blanc
de Cheilon ridge, August 1937.
(*A M Greenwood*) (p182)

60. The Obergabelhorn summit, August 1937.
   (*A M Greenwood*) (p182)

61. Near the top of the Mönch, August 1937.
   (*A M Greenwood*) (p182)

bivouac was found the following year, but their bodies were never found. One of Harry Fox's sisters married my uncle Hugh. Hugh's daughter Cecilia, a GP in Wellington, was another keen climber for many years. Her father always insisted that she took two guides. She was also a gifted painter of Alpine scenes and flowers.

My mother, Janet Fox, was a sister of Hugh and Gerald. The first time she went to the Alps with her father she was 12 and he was 61.[6] She went up the Brévent with François Dévouassoud and was also taken onto the Findelen glacier. My grandfather climbed the Petits Charmoz with cousin Anna. Another year in Grindelwald, climbs were arranged for my mother with Christian Jossi junior, son of one of my grandfather's guides. Thirty years later, on one of our family holidays, my mother arranged for Christian to repeat the climb of the Rötihorn with the next generation. Jen and I were too young to go, but Jossi had become a fat old man and thereafter his place was taken by his nephew Peter Bernet with whom all my siblings climbed.

My father's family, the Howards, did not have such a strong mountaineering tradition, though my father's uncle, Eliot Howard, was an Alpine Club member and married Charlotte Tuckett.[7]   Their son, Geoffrey Howard, was made a Vice-President of the Alpine Club in 1952, and it is said that this was on account of his witty after dinner speaking rather than his prowess as a climber. He was instrumental in bringing my parents together as he was first cousin to both.[8] My Howard grandparents often took Alpine holidays and walked energetically. My grandmother and aunts would visit the poor and hand out tracts. Nowadays this would be considered presumptuous.

My father first went to the Alps with his parents in 1899 at the age of 19. Starting from Argentière (pension rate 5 francs, about 20p), they trekked round Mont Blanc to Courmayeur where their pension was considered expensive at 8 francs, *vin compris*. They had terrible weather and thick snow on the Col du Bonhomme. They took two guides and three mules, two for the luggage; my grandmother rode the third with grandfather hanging onto its tail. Father was an energetic walker rather than a climber and took pleasure in forcing his body to the limits of endurance. In Scotland and Norway he did some incredibly strenuous walking and climbing, covering huge distances.

My parents were married in 1905, Geoffrey Howard being my father's best man, and from then on they had Alpine holidays usually on alternate years when there was no new baby to keep Mother at home. As most of our birthdays are in the spring we like to think that some of us were conceived in the Alps. In 1907, leaving their first baby with our nanny, my parents joined the Fox grandparents in Grindelwald and climbed the Wetterhorn with Christian Jossi. They stayed at the little Hotel des Alpes at Alpiglen, halfway between Grindelwald and Kleine Scheidegg and nowadays the starting point for attempts on the Eiger Nordwand. It was fantastically cheap and became our base for family Alpine holidays until 1934, when my parents rented a chalet in Grindelwald where we had glorious holidays and took up skiing. Ashley, my husband, who was a Cambridge friend of my elder brother, was a frequent visitor to our chalet and he climbed from there with various members of the family. Before we were old enough to accompany them, many of my parents' holidays were spent hut-to-hutting in Austria and the Dolomites, and even after we had the chalet they usually went off for a few days touring on their own.

Perhaps the most distinguished of my climbing relations was my cousin Howard Somervell. His grandparents were brother and sister respectively to my Howard grandparents. For us, as children, he was a very approachable and entertaining hero and a darling man. We saw him rarely as he was a medical missionary in South India. He qualified as a doctor in 1915 and served in France throughout the war, becoming a very expert surgeon and with a distinguished career ahead of him. His home being in Kendal he had walked and climbed in the Lake District since boyhood, and he soon developed a taste for the Alps as well, where he spent all available holidays. He was therefore a natural choice for the 1922 Everest expedition, as there were so few fit and experienced young climbers left after the war. Though the expedition ended in disaster, with the death of seven Sherpas in an avalanche, Howard Somervell had attained an altitude of 26,800ft.

It was after this expedition, while visiting a mission hospital in Travancore, that Somervell felt the call to use his skills in the service of God and the poor of India. In 1923, having renounced a very tempting offer of an appointment in England, he took up his post in Neyyoor, where he remained for 22 years. He worked incredibly long hours but believed in taking enough holidays to keep himself fit for work. He joined the 1924 Everest expedition and, with Lt Col E F Norton, attained the record height of 28,000ft, in spite of almost suffocating from a frostbitten larynx.[9] Mallory was a particular friend of his – they shared a tent – and his death was a great sorrow to Howard. While living in India, Howard had a number of Himalayan holidays, sometimes trekking with his wife and sometimes climbing in the areas of Nanda Devi, Kangchenjunga and Nanga Parbat.

Howard Somervell was a considerable artist and some of his mountain pictures are familiar to Alpine Club members. Most of his Everest sketches were done on brown paper in pastel or water colour, which shows up the luminous quality of the snow. He was also a keen musician and while in Tibet collected folk songs which he arranged for the musical accompaniment to the film of the 1922 expedition. He was President of the Alpine Club from 1962 to 1965 and was also President of the Fell and Rock and Vice-President of the Himalayan Club

Since 1859 there has always been at least one Alpine Club member among my relations, and my sister Jen and I are very proud of our mountaineering heritage.

REFERENCES

1 Geoffrey E Howard, 'A Mountaineering Family and Other Memories'. *AJ55*, 136, 1945.
2 Obit of F F Tuckett. *AJ27*, 340-346, 1913.
3 Photograph of F F Tuckett. *AJ27*, 346, 1913.
4 F F Tuckett, 'A Race for Life'. *AJ5*, 337-349, 1872.
5 F F Tuckett, his obituary of Harry Fox. *AJ14*, 132-134, 1889.
6 Joseph H Fox, *Holiday Memories*. Privately printed 1908.
7 Geoffrey E Howard, his obituary of Eliot Howard. *AJ40*, 150-151, 1928.
8 Obit of Geoffrey E Howard. *AJ61*, 197-199, 1956.
9 Theodore Howard Somervell, *After Everest: the experiences of a mountaineer and medical missionary*. Hodder & Stoughton, 1936. 'Mr Somervell's Story' from the Mount Everest dispatches of 1924. *AJ36*, 211-215, 1924.

Perseverance conquers every difficulty; a flag on the Höchste Spilze.

ASHLEY GREENWOOD

The Alps in 1937

(Plates 57–61)

A mixture of good and bad luck prefaced my climbing holiday in 1937. I was due to meet Edmund Wigram and Charles Rob at Montenvers on 24 July. At Lausanne station early that morning I lost my wallet. Luckily I had enough money in my pocket to get me to the rendezvous. The previous day Edmund and Charles, descending roped from the Requin, had both fallen into the same crevasse but had managed to get out. Next day the weather was bad and we mooched around at Montenvers. Two famous guides whom we knew by sight were doing the same: Josef Knubel and Alexander Graven. Edmund innocently enquired of them whether they would like a nice *promenade* on the Mer de Glace. They took it well.

The weather cleared and we three plus Jim Gavin and Charles Nicholls left to traverse the Grands Charmoz. After a long dry spell the Nantillons glacier was in atrocious condition (why did people say that there was only rock-climbing among the Aiguilles?), and the Rognon in its middle was alarmingly overhung by séracs. On reaching the Grépon/Charmoz couloir we soon traversed out into the middle of the face of the Charmoz to tackle somebody's chimney – not Burgener's but more difficult, 50 metres of it. Carrying the abseil rope as well as my rucksack on my first climb of the holiday, I found it exhausting and was nearly sick at the top. The rest of the climb was delightful and, after a rest on the tiny summit, we descended the Charmoz/Grépon couloir in ready-cut ice steps, Charles in *Kletterschuhe* and axeless (we had three among us five) bringing up the rear. On the Rognon I loosed a small stone and the language which rose from Josef Knubel below was intimidating.

Next day saw us at the Charpoua hut for a traverse of the Drus. The glacier and bergschrund were in a difficult state, but a single tongue of ice hanging down close to the rocks enabled us to cross the latter – just. Edmund, Charles Rob and I were two-thirds of the way up the Grand Dru when a shout from behind caused us to turn back, to find that Charles Nicholls had dislocated a shoulder while crossing 'La Pendule', a slab with a short fixed rope hanging from a piton. Edmund and Charles Rob were both newly qualified doctors, and Edmund, slightly the senior, rotated the shoulder back into place – his first patient after qualifying. The weather looked set fair so, leaving Charles Nicholls on a sunny ledge with food and water, the rest of us climbed to the top of the Grand Dru and then descended to help him down. With his shoulder immobilised and with assistance where necessary, we got him down all right and, after a roped glissade down the glacier, we reached Montenvers in time for dinner.

The weather now became unsettled again, so we started from Argentière for Zermatt, minus Charles Nicholls. The weather was too bad for the Aiguille d'Argentière, so in poor visibility we crossed the Col du Chardonnet and in pouring rain made a beeline for the Saleina hut, though this involved crossing a lot of crevasses. On arrival at the hut we were duly reproved by Marcel Kurz (guru and guidebook editor), who was inspecting the hut, for not following the proper guidebook route. But we had no guidebook and merely wanted to get out of the rain as soon as possible. The rain persisted (as so often on 1st August, Swiss national holiday) and we reached Orsières soaked. Our hotel there was being run in festive spirit by two young girls – but I retired to bed, sickening for a cold.

Next day Edmund departed for England and Charles, Jim and I reached the Valsorey hut via Bourg St Pierre in thick, low cloud. The clouds sank during the night, however, and soon after dawn we were at the foot of the Valsorey ridge of the Grand Combin. But this looked uninviting, with a layer of fresh snow and a cold wind from the north. We were far above the Col des Maisons Blanches and, loth to descend to reach the Corridor route, we consulted our postcard, which was our sole guide to the mountain. From this it looked as if we could cut horizontally across the N face and join the Corridor higher up. At this period we did not carry crampons, so step cutting it was, beneath the same séracs which threaten the Corridor, until a rib of rock with a steep cliff beyond barred further progress. Luckily, this coincided with a gap in the séracs and, cutting steps steeply upwards, we gained the gentler upper slopes and the summit. Many years later, I saw an article in *Die Alpen* by a Swiss party who had just done this route and claimed it as a new route. We descended by the Corridor and reached Fionnay at 6pm and the Chanrion hut the following afternoon. From there we aimed at Arolla, via the Ruinette, Mont Blanc de Cheilon and possibly the Pigne d'Arolla. Armed with vague directions from the hut guardian, we left at 3.30am, but soon lost the path. However, we reached the top of the Ruinette soon after 8am and roped up for the long traverse ahead. After an abseil down the big gendarme on the E ridge (on which I ended upside down), we embarked on the long snow ridge leading to Mont Blanc de Cheilon. Being cramponless, we eschewed the hard-frozen snow on its N flank and traversed the steep soft snow on the south below the cornice, where we found rock belays or secure stances frequently enough for safety. But it was hot and tiring and on the col below the NW ridge of Mont Blanc de Cheilon we renounced any further traverse and, leaving our rucksacks, climbed to the top and back. After dreamlike glissades to the Col de Cheilon we began the long trek to Arolla. We unroped on the dry glacier, and in my continued state of lassitude I soon fell far behind and had to climb the (ladderless) Pas de Chèvres alone, which I found alarming. Later, I caught the others up resting and we arrived together at Arolla at 6.30pm.

It now remained to get to Zermatt via the Bertol hut and the Dent Blanche. The hut was crowded and with all the windows shut the dortoir was stifling; so we did not need awakening at 1am. It was a relief to step out into the cold bracing moonlight and, ignoring Geoffrey Young's 'generally accepted rule that there shall be no talking before dawn', we chattered our way merrily across to breakfast at the Dent Blanche hut. The S ridge was in splendid condition and it was warm and sunny; after an hour and a half on top we reached Seiler's tearooms in Zermatt, with its light orchestra and smart clientele, by 5pm, and devoured five exquisite patisseries each.

Jim departed now for army manoeuvres. Charles and I dragged ourselves away from Zermatt full of friends and interesting strangers, among the former Brian (B K) Harris who had taught me climbing at school and who was climbing with Alexander Taugwalder, and among the latter a party whom we called the Himalayan Bivouackers (they bivouacked as high as they could get, near the top of Monte Rosa) led by 'Cooke of Kabru'. We left the village at 11.15pm to traverse the Wellenkuppe and Obergabelhorn to the Schönbiel hut. There was no Rothorn hut at that time, and the Trift Inn was expensive and low down; so we walked to the foot of the Trift Gletscher and stopped there for a good rest and food, while guided parties from the Trift passed by, only one of them bound in our direction. The ascent to the Wellenkuppe was simple and we roped up after a short rest just below its summit. The traverse north of the Grand Gendarme was pure ice, so we climbed it by the fixed rope – strenuous. After a long rest on the top of the Obergabelhorn we made a quick descent of the Arbengrat to the Arbenjoch; but between us and the Schönbiel hut lay the Arbenhorn, a steep and exhausting climb of 500ft, and a long descent to the hut where we arrived at 4.30pm. We had intended to traverse the Matterhorn by the Zmutt and Hörnli or Italian ridges next day but it was a relief when I awoke at daylight to be told that there had been a thunderstorm in the night. A party of Czechs had nevertheless started for the Zmutt ridge. They were last seen high up in the Galleries at 4pm and their bodies were later found on the Tiefenmatten glacier.

Next morning, having reprovisioned in Zermatt, we left the hut at 2am well ahead of three guided parties also bound for the Zmutt ridge. It was a bit cloudy with flickers of lightning around. On reaching the foot of the cliffs which fall westwards from the snowy part of the Zmutt ridge we continued till we heard running water, the clue which B K Harris and Alexander Taugwalder had given us for finding the easiest way onto the cliffs. It was still dark and, being still unroped, we soon lost sight of each other but kept in touch by shouts. Eventually we joined up near the foot of a slope of hard-frozen snow up which Charles cut steps. Easy rocks followed, but then came an ice slope covered by a thin layer of frozen snow, which Charles started to climb relying solely on his front *tricounis*. I demanded a rope or steps, but soon we needed both. Meanwhile, the first of the other parties, skirting the snow, gained the snow ridge first. It turned out to consist of Otto Furrer, famous guide and world skiing champion, with a young American woman, Mrs Coles, and a porter (we never saw the two other parties). We were annoyed to have lost the lead, but it paid off higher up. The snow ridge, the teeth of Zmutt and the ridge beyond were in good condition and, moving together, we soon caught up with the Furrer party who moved separately – Furrer first, then the other two.

At the top of this ridge, where it abuts against the nose of Zmutt, we all rested, and Charles and I fortified ourselves with brandy and condensed milk. We now reaped the benefit of Furrer's knowledge of the Galleries and the way onto Carrel's Corridor. The going was delicate, belayless but not difficult, with very little verglas. On regaining the ridge Charles and I were waved ahead and we soon reached the Italian summit where, though cloudy and breezy, it was warm enough for a long rest; but we were denied the wonderful view.

On the suggestion of Furrer we descended the Italian ridge, so full of landmarks of Whymper's and Carrel's early attempts. Below the Col du Lion we strayed from the best route but a shout from Furrer, far above, put us right. In thick cloud we might have missed the hotel/hut but for the loud noise of Italians (and their dogs) so characteristic of Italian huts. We were escorted in by a smartly dressed Italian in a dark suit and, after a meal and plenty of red wine with Mrs Coles, we left for Zermatt. We had no map and no idea of the route over the Furggjoch, but in a brief spell of clear weather we saw the way. We knew that B K Harris and Alexander Taugwalder had completed the same round in time for dinner in Zermatt at 8pm, but it was the pouring rain rather than competitive spirit which drove us, faster and faster, to reach Zermatt and a bottle of Bouvier, in true Mummery style, by 7pm.

The weather now deteriorated. We crossed the Bernese Oberland from Brig to Grindelwald in cloud and rain, unable to climb a single peak. Charles went home but, in a brief clearance, I climbed the Mönch via the Bergli hut with Tom Howard and got soaked once again on the way down.

Sad to say, both those fine guides, so helpful to young guideless climbers, died within a few years on their local mountains – Furrer when Jordan's ladder on the Italian ridge of the Matterhorn broke and Alexander Taugwalder in a crevasse while skiing on Monte Rosa. Edmund Wigram fell to his death on the Idwal Slabs soon after the end of the war. Happily, my mentor, B K Harris, lives on in Shropshire, well into his eighties.

TED MADEN

Climbs with John Longland

(*Plate 88*)

I first met John Longland in the dissection room of the Department of Anatomy at the University of Cambridge during the autumn of 1954. We were first-term medical students; John noticed my CUMC tie and strolled across for a chat. Neither of us was destined for distinction in human anatomy, but the burden of learning that subject was lightened by Mike Ball, then a trainee surgeon doing a year's demonstratorship in anatomy, and also wearer of a CUMC tie.

At that early time I had boundless but naive enthusiasm for mountaineering, with several Frank Smythe books voraciously devoured, limited background in hill-walking and a sum total of two afternoons' rock-climbing at Widdop. John, by contrast, scion of a distinguished climbing family, had climbed for several years and seemed to know everyone and everything. He had a naturally outgoing personality and we soon became friends.

The CUMC held a beginners' meet at Helyg for a week that December. As not infrequently happens on such occasions, the top brass were having a meet of their own elsewhere and John was official Helyg meet leader. He arrived at nine o'clock on the first night of the meet, having walked from Betws with two rucksacks, one on his back, one on his front. He was completely happy and in his element and the meet came to life with his arrival.

There was snow overnight, but despite the resulting desirability of an early start there was no way a sizeable group of students, cooking communally, could prepare and consume porridge and sausages, which my diary records were breakfast, in under two hours. Thus it was 11.30 when several of us gathered on the Heather Terrace.

John set off to lead a rope of three up what was then called *First Pinnacle Rib*; now it is named *Overlapping Rib*, one of many changes that have swept the nation in recent years. I was second on the rope. Another beginner, Mike Clay, was third. We were followed by another rope of two, while yet another rope of three were starting up *Second Pinnacle Rib*, now alias *Pinnacle Rib*. The two climbs converge higher up. Snow lay a few inches deep on the ledges. In my innocence I little knew that the scenario held the makings of a Late Show.

As we progressed, the cloud base, which had hung near the Heather Ledge, also rose, giving spectacular views down into the cwm; while, above, the cliffs remained shrouded and mysterious. Undaunted, we lunched at the actual Pinnacle about halfway up the climb. Under the conditions the Yellow Slab, just above, was not on. Instead we went round by the easier corner to the right. Then John did an excellent job of first leading the long crack above the slab and then shepherding all seven of us up as day turned into night.

Two days previously I had scrambled up Tryfan's North Ridge. Thus when the first four of us joined John on the easier ground above the crack it was agreed that I should lead this group down the North Ridge. From the summit a streak of green sky in the west marked the end of the day, and distant lights twinkled in Bangor and Llandudno. Soon it was dark. My diary records: 'It was full moon, and gaps in the clouds were rapidly widening, so that the snow was well illuminated. We kept the rope on, carrying coils, but my rope got hopelessly tangled up, so we had to stop for 20 minutes to straighten it out by the light of the moon ... ' We got back to the hut sometime before 7pm. John and the *Second Pinnacle Rib* party were glad to have our footsteps to follow, as the moon had gone behind the clouds again when they descended an hour later.

At the time I did not think twice about John staying behind to help the entire group up the slippery and difficult crack at nightfall. He was totally in command, volubly cheerful and encouraging. Now I realise he showed excellent leadership under conditions where not all group leaders would have been so happy.

During the week the weather see-sawed from diabolical to not too bad, and various further climbs and walks were done. Now, more than 35 years later, my diary brings back not only the principal acts and players but also a wealth of supporting details. For example, we inevitably, on the Sunday, ran out of shillings for the electricity meter. John Harding, displaying talents which were later to lead him to success as a solicitor, managed to persuade the local vicar to open the Sunday collection box and extract therefrom 20 shillings in exchange for a pound note. At the end of the meet I visited an aunt in Llandudno from whom I secured a travel grant for the onward journey by train to Manchester.

Back at Cambridge John Longland persuaded various owners of transport to visit Derbyshire on Sundays for gritstone climbing, followed by tea at the Longland family house which was then at Crich. I went on one such trip after the June exams and we enjoyed a perfect day on Gardoms and Birchens. Plate 88 shows John on *Garden Face Direct*.

We had separate arrangements for the summer holidays; I climbed in the Pyrenees and the Dauphiné – surviving two narrow scrapes, one in each area; later in the summer John climbed with his father and others at Zermatt and Arolla. We both then did summer jobs to earn some money. We met again in Derbyshire for a weekend in mid-September for the novel (to me) experience of instructing at the White Hall Outdoor Pursuits Centre. Afterwards, on a short trip to Crich, John showed me his very own gritstone outcrop – a quarry tucked away in a wood with some smallish but entertaining and difficult routes. One of his creations was a VS with a large overhang which he named *Smaug*. At the time the name meant nothing to me. Now I realise John must have been well versed in Tolkien.

I drove to North Wales, John planning to follow for a rendezvous at Ynys a few days later. In the meantime I had a brief but memorable encounter with another John. I was in the bar of Pen-y-Gwryd when a short stockily-built person entered. 'Well John,' said Chris Briggs, 'What did you do today?' I was mildly curious as to whether this person was a walker or a climber. His reply dispelled any doubt: 'The third ascent of *Suicide Wall* and the second ascent of *Suicide Groove*.' John Streetly had been climbing with Don Whillans; Don had led the *Wall*, John the *Groove*.

After a couple of days at Helyg on a low-key CUMC meet I went to Ynys for the rendezvous with John Longland. He had not yet arrived, but Streetly was there, without Whillans but still wanting to climb. My climbing had not yet touched Welsh VS and I found the Llanberis atmosphere daunting. Streetly led me up *Nea* and *Trilon*. One of my worries on the latter was whether *he* might get into difficulties. I had a lot to learn! After *Trilon* he let me lead him up *Crackstone Rib*.

Across the valley the declining afternoon sun cast shadows in Cwm Glas. I did not yet know what lay in store there. John Longland arrived in the evening and clarified that point, a climb called *Main Wall* which was 'about V Diff' and which we would do tomorrow. I wrote the story of the next few days under the title 'Two Walls' in *Cambridge Mountaineering* 1956. That archive is not on everyone's bookshelves and is incomplete in some respects. I therefore reflect here again on that pivotal week.

If each of the few 100 moves on *Main Wall* were placed at ground level, then it is probably true that none of them would exceed V Diff. Zigzagging up a steep and imposing wall their cumulative effect is very different, especially if, as on that occasion, it starts to rain soon after the start of the climb, the party ahead has problems, and number two of the present party, in socks over bendy rubbers, is unable to cope with the additional impediment of a well-provisioned rucksack. Luckily the party ahead were able to help us out with the rucksack at a critical point. Drenched, we made it to the top after a few hours. There had been no doubt about John's commitment and his mastery of the conditions. He was hungry for a week's climbing.

In the next four days we climbed *Grooved Arête* and *Munich* on Tryfan; *Ribstone Crack*, *Unicorn* and *Wrinkle* on Wastad; *Houndshead Buttress*, *Olympic Slab* and *Helsinki Wall* at Tremadog; and *Avalanche* on Lliwedd. John led all the VSs. The landmark climb was the first ascent of *Helsinki Wall*. John had not declared this project as part of the Tremadog sportplan. When he sprung it on me after *Olympic Slab* I was, in modern parlance, gobsmacked. In the current guidebook the first pitch is graded 5a. At the time this seemed the less horrific of the two main pitches, offering the possibility of subsequent escape to the top pitch of *Olympic Slab*. When John ruled out this option and headed left to the steep upper wall I really got the jitters. It was both a fine lead and a good piece of prior line-spotting by John. Even now people tell me it is a quality climb. Why *Helsinki*? Because it is next to *Olympic Slab*, which John Disley had put up in 1952, the year of the Helsinki Olympic Games.

Two days after *Helsinki Wall*, and the day after the pleasantly unpressured visit to Lliwedd, John wanted to do *Great Slab* on Cloggy. The weather had deteriorated again and we reached the Big Cliff in a dense drenching mist. Undeterred, and with socks over rubbers, John cracked the short but difficult entry slab and led way up into the mist and the first belay point. I baulked, totally. I could see only too clearly the likelihood of a slip, a big swing under the overhangs – and then what? At first John thought he had insufficient rope to abseil, but luckily the ropes were just long enough. He rejoined me and we walked down the hill in awkward silence. As we did so the clouds cleared and our spirits rose. We would rescue the day on Grochan. Three climbs seemed quite feasible. I would take *Phantom Rib* as my first Welsh VS lead, John would lead *Brant* and *Slape*.

The first pitch of *Phantom Rib*, up the cracks, did not seem easy but we had a schedule to keep and I did not dally. John joined me at the belay and I continued with difficulty to the little ledge, fixing a line runner. The rib above looked blank but, with some wishful thinking that the previous move had already been the crux, I set off, unsure where I was heading but making irreversible, fingery moves. About 30ft above John I got into hopeless difficulties, to the left of the correct line and peering into *Hazel Groove*, but unable to reach that relative haven. John began to realise what was happening and prepared himself. I clung on until I could cling no more, and then zoom, thump, zoom, tug, tug! The first tug had been the line runner breaking, the second was John holding me perfectly, a few feet above the deck. His achievement had been all the more remarkable as the thump had been me hitting him on the way down. He was as shaken as I was, and probably a bit concussed. He lowered me the few feet to the ground and I went down to Ynys for help. Luckily Hugh Banner and party had just arrived and they quickly went to John's rescue.

We seemed to have escaped remarkably lightly, myself with strains and bruises, John with a cracked wrist bone. However, John told me on a later occasion that a skull X-ray, taken some years after the accident and for a different reason, had revealed evidence of a previous fracture. The only likely cause seemed to have been the *Phantom Rib* affair.

Thereafter we had some adjusting to do. Whether it was primarily due to the fall and its psychological effects, or whether mainly for other reasons, I shall never fully know, but the fact is that we did not from then on do any further hard climbs together. Undoubtedly a contributory factor was that my regional interests diversified, with visits to the Lakes and Scotland, whereas John continued to concentrate largely on Wales. Another factor was that I began to feel happier and more in control of situations as I increasingly took on a leader's role with primary responsibility for decisions, and John also was primarily a leader. We did, however, remain friends, and the friendship continued to be embraced by the Longland family after their move to Bakewell.

As the years went by I began to think it would be fun if John and I were to repeat the *First Pinnacle Rib* together one December day. I never followed the idea through and now it is too late, but I shall always remember with pleasure and gratitude those early, formative days and climbs with John Longland.

JERRY MURLAND

One Man's Climbing:
Recollections of a Mediocre Mountaineer

Like most of my generation I missed the hemp rope by a fair margin but started climbing with a hemp waist-length, always difficult to put on exactly right and bloody painful when you fell off. I never did understand all that stuff about leaders never falling off; the school of climbing I started with had one basic rule: don't sit underneath the bloke who's leading because he'll usually land on you when he falls off! This lesson was learnt sitting under the first pitch of *Cobweb Crack* on the Cromlech in 1966 and being quite surprised to find an annoyed leader inches above my head hanging off a groaning runner that we had found on Sabre Cut the day before. The other two equally dodgy runners had jumped out in surrender as he passed them on the way down to test the third. Those old machined nuts threaded onto hawser-laid nylon never did work that well when you wanted them to. Quite how this episode failed to end up in the casualty ward in Bangor I'll never know. The rope burns on my hands and arms were a painful reminder for weeks afterwards.

This early introduction to the art of climbing was interrupted by a spell of voluntary service with the Army in 1967 and, as luck would have it, I found myself attached to the newly formed RAF Mountain Desert Rescue Team based at Sharjah in the Trucial Oman States. The RAF lads, led by Harry Wragg, were keen to continue the Kinloss MRT traditions of hard days on the hill followed by even harder nights on the Tiger Beer. It was a sort of Kinloss in the sun. My previously peculiar climbing practices were soon swapped for the safer procedures of the professional Mountain Rescue Team: my apprenticeship had begun. These lads were a strange mixture of mountaineers in uniform, almost the equivalent of the modern climbing bum. Every opportunity was seized to get out on the hill and to escape the discipline of service life. Inspections, scrutiny by senior officers and guard duty were all avoided by sudden and hastily planned rescue practices which took us away for convenient periods of time into the mountains.

It was not long before we discovered acres of virgin rock hiding away among the vast wilderness that surrounded us. Our time was spent lowering stretchers, climbing the arid 'peaks' and making first ascents. It was almost impossible not to put up a new route – every crag for miles around was untouched and only frequented by spiders and the odd scorpion. My diary records a first ascent of *Savage Slit* – '180 feet and bloody hard'. I suppose it was in bendy boots; looking at the slides that were taken at the time I guess it was about 4a. Another climb is only recorded as *Wee Mac's Route*, named after the Scottish dynamo who led it, and described as 'quite hard'. Mac had run out of runners just before the final few moves but had managed to jam in the knot of a sling for protection before he climbed an overhanging crack. Considering it was 300 miles from the nearest anything it was a very bold lead indeed, despite the fact that there was a rescue team jeering and hooting at us from below!

After a spell of lunacy chasing bandits in Oman and getting shot at, I left the army and got a 'job' at Plas y Brenin for no money and very little anything else. I always seemed to be hungry and soon developed the art of being strategically placed when one of the students was buying a round. However, when my boots fell apart John (Jacko) Jackson, the director at the time, did take pity on me and bought me a new pair. It was at the Brenin that I first saw Joe Brown when he stayed for tea and gave a few of us a lift up to the Pass afterwards in his new Volvo and dropped us off at the Cromlech boulders. I couldn't bring myself to yell 'See ya Joe', like the others did. I only managed a feeble wave with lower jaw swinging open.

Those months at Capel Curig, working on winter courses under the direction of Rowland Edwards, were a whole new learning experience. Edwards I found to be the safest and most professional climber I have met. Not only did he spend his time working carefully with the students on the courses but he also spent time with the various voluntary penniless staff, turning us into mountaineers. Lessons I learned then I have never forgotten and safe practices he taught me have on at least one occasion prevented disaster in the Alps. With Rowland we climbed a verglased *Tennis Shoe* on the Idwal Slabs, learned to snow-hole, had epics on long winter climbs and improved our rock-climbing skills beyond recognition. By the time the summer arrived I was sharing a room with another penniless itinerant climber, Arthur de Kuzel. Arthur's socks had an awesome reputation, one which I could personally vouch for. However, he was planning to go to Chamonix and suggested that I went as well. Could I stand the socks for a month, I asked myself? But in the end it was a question of cash, of which I had none, and I reluctantly watched him depart. It was soon after this that we heard he had been killed with Richard Caine on the E face of the Grand Capucin, cruelly hit by lightning on the final pitch. That particular storm killed 16 climbers in the Mont Blanc massif that night. Had I gone with Arthur I might have ended up a statistic.

Towards the end of the summer Jacko had a conversation with me that ended with me applying to Bangor for teacher training. His fatherly advice may have been prompted by the fact that my boots were wearing out again and it was cheaper to get rid of me by supporting my application for higher education. However, that October I began life as a student with characters such as John Beatty who, at the time, only had a Box Brownie, and an ex-Swansea dustman who climbed under the name of Mike Sharp. Mike only had two shirts and wore them continually on alternate days in an attempt to convince us that the other one was being washed. Mike's most recent claim to fame was when he appeared in Michael Palin's *Pole to Pole* as the Antarctic base camp manager.

Climbing was the main focus of our attention, with scholarly activities well down on our list of priorities. The handy student accommodation also attracted others from afar, such as the Burgess twins who were constantly found in the female halls of residence and Cliff Phillips who attained the status of superhero when he fell off Dinas Mot on one of his soloing expeditions and crawled down to the road in a very smashed up condition. After a short spell of compulsory mending he shot off to the Alps and took part in that well known Eiger film with Pete Minks, Eric Jones and Leo Dickinson, where he fell off again. We watched the first showing of that film, with Cliff, in a flat in Menai Bridge, and his eyes lit up when he watched himself hurtling to destruction before he finally braked on the edge of the second icefield. I am still convinced he left it until the last minute for the sake of the film!

My first Alpine season, in 1974, was noted for its lack of climbing. Having arrived in Arolla we went off to do the Dent de Tsalion as a warm up. John Beatty had also arrived but unfortunately his gear had not – Geneva airport were most apologetic but could shed no light on its whereabouts. After a few nights shivering in a duvet and the odd climb with borrowed gear he finally went home to get warm. Next on the list was the N face of the Pigne. After a very cramped bivvy below the Louettes Econdoué ridge with four of us in a tiny bivvy tent, I staggered up to the snow shoulder at 3295m and promptly threw up. My climbing partner was disgusted, not with the unsavoury pile of vomit but with my suggestion that we go down. It was two years before I returned to complete the climb; the pile of vomit had disappeared but I recalled the look on Barry's face quite vividly.

It took a second visit to the Matterhorn to complete the Hörnli ridge solo. That same Alpine season we had moved from Arolla to Zermatt, waiting until it was dark before we drove like madmen up to the campsite in my old MG Magnette, threw all the gear out and abandoned the car in the car-park. It collected several threatening letters before we stole away again under the cover of darkness. Barry and Greg Smith had gone off to do the Zmutt while I wandered up to the Hörnli hut and bivvied below the start of the climb. Following the first party, I overtook them after an hour of listening to the American telling a blonde Barbie Doll what an easy route it was. I stopped at the Solvay in the face of gathering cloud. Several other ropes had appeared, including the Americans, and were clearly thinking the same - time to beat a quick retreat. Barbie Doll was keen to reach the top and they vanished into the gloom. A German climber and I teamed up for a quick roped descent which turned out to be a slow one amid all the congestion lower down. While still at the Hörnli hut that evening we discovered that two American climbers had fallen down the E face. I never did find out if it was Barbie and her companion.

The next time I found myself at the Solvay it was late in the season, the sky was clear and, although the route had been a bit crowded, above the shoulder there was only me. I stood on the top alone.

My first visit to Chamonix was more of a pilgrimage than a holiday. I had read *The Hard Years* so many times that the cover had fallen off. The place was everything I had expected it to be except the Mer de Glace, which was much longer. I had teamed up with a friend from the South East Essex Climbing Club and after doing the obligatory rock routes that the Brits tend to start on, we headed off to greater glory on the Frendo Spur, mainly because it didn't look too far from the campsite! We walked up to the Plan de l'Aiguille to save money, which was the first mistake, and arrived at the bivvy site on the Spur a bit late to grab a good spot. After a poor night shivering in duvets we got onto the ice crest feeling a bit jaded even before we started. There were two ropes ahead of us until the leader of the nearest fell off and slithered past us, while his second screamed at him in Italian. The flying Italian climber reappeared behind us and asked if they could join ropes with us. It might improve my Italian, I reflected, as I accepted their rope and watched Alan's face crumple with disbelief. 'It won't slow us down much and anyway we're quite near the top,' I argued. Second mistake. I thought we were slow but these two were winning awards for the slowest ascent of the decade. 'Get rid of them,' snarled Alan who was becoming fed up with our new-found friends. My gesture to untie their rope threw them into a fit of panic which rather confirmed my impression that they were very much out of their depth on the route. By now the other rope had vanished. 'Probably near the top and within sight of an expensive French beer,' I heard Alan muttering darkly. A second bivvy at the Midi was looking a strong possibility after a long delay waiting for one of the Italians to retrieve a crampon. I thought of untying and making a run for it but finally we got going again. Near the top we heard shouts in English: our epic had been watched with interest from below and two clubmates were descending from the Midi–Plan ridge to see if we were still alive. They took over the job of escorting the Italian lads to the Midi station and left us to complete the route. Completely knackered, we slumped in a tangled heap of gear amongst the ogling tourists and promptly fell asleep until the others joined us. We caught the last cable-car down, and the next day Juliano and his friend met us in the National for a drink and proudly explained that they were the first climbers in their club to climb the Frendo.

It was 16 years before I was in Chamonix again. This time my partner was a lanky 15-year-old who called me Dad. The place had changed – it was always overcrowded, but this ... ! Even the National had fallen victim and become trendy. A lot of climbs had taken place since the Frendo episode; Alan had died in the Hindu Kush, and yet here I was starting all over again with the next generation.

We decided to warm up on the Petite Verte. We had been warned that the route would be a little crowded – there was even a hint in the guidebook that the climb might occasionally be *unbelievably crowded*, adding that *the more romantic Alpinists will attempt an overnight bivouac in order to avoid the rush* ... 'You've got to be joking,' I muttered, 'it can't be that bad.'

Having arrived at the Grands Montets in time to catch the 7.15am cablecar, I was smugly delighted to see only a handful of climbers hovering about with intent – indeed there was even space enough inside to hold a conversation without being squeezed senseless against the perspex. It's almost impossible to see anything through those scratched panels that mascarade as windows, but at least there was room to look at the blurred panorama that was unfolding below us.

After clanging down the steps at the top station to the glacier below, I noted with some satisfaction that most of the contents of the cable-car were vanishing in the direction of the Argentière hut. There were only three parties roping up now and I looked forward to a quiet ascent and being back in the valley for a lunchtime beer or three. This dream was rapidly shattered with the arrival of the second and then, shortly afterwards, the third cable-car, both of which had obviously been crammed to the gunwales with the Petite Verte fan club.

This was Richard's second Alpine mixed route so we were certainly not going to be the fastest party on the grid. Sure enough, by the time we reached the shoulder to gaze across into the *niche* of the N face of the Petit Dru, we had been overtaken several times. However, refusing to be hurried with a novice on the rope, we traversed onto the direct route and allowed the traffic jam to inch its way up the ridge above us. Big mistake this. We were now showered with lumps of ice and the occasional brick from the now nose-to-tail queue building up from the summit rocks almost down to the shoulder! We traversed further over towards the NE ridge wishing we had taken the trouble to climb the Camère–Chevalier couloir instead. At least we were on our own now and enjoying the steep snow slope that led directly to the already crowded summit. Mistake number two. Suddenly a shout from above us and a prickly sensation on the back of my neck warned us of impending doom. A washing machine sized lump of instant death was bounding down from the summit pile and heading straight for a rope of three climbers some 200ft below us. With horror, every climber on the ridge watched them fail to respond to the chorus of shouts and yells from above them. Just at the point when we all thought we were about to watch something quite appalling, the last guy on the rope looked up and threw himself to one side with a spectacular dive that dragged the other two out of the firing line. The hiss of relief from the spectators was quite audible. The boulder must have missed him by inches and flashed off down towards Argentière – probably to land on our car in the Montets car-park, was the comment from Richard. The whole place was becoming rather dodgy and here and there helmets were being dredged up from the bottom of sacks and hastily buckled on in the hope that the next rock would be a little smaller. The problem was that there were so many climbers on the route that it was almost impossible not to dislodge loose rock and ice. Arriving at the summit was rather like reaching the checkout in a supermarket in Chamonix – a mixture of relief and foreboding. We pushed our way through and past various parties and cramponed our way over thrutching bodies, weaving intricate patterns with the myriad of ropes lying about until, ten feet from the top, we gave in to market forces. 'Sod this.' said a disgruntled 15-year-old, 'Let's go down.'

I looked up at the ten or so bodies cluttering up the small space that was the top and followed him down. What a contrast to the previous week when three of us, including Richard, had climbed the N face of the Pic La Grave in the Ecrins, and had traversed the whole mountain in almost total isolation. We had sat for some time on the summit watching Mont Blanc and the Grandes Jorasses slowly vanish behind cloud – a perfect introduction to Alpine climbing.

However, back on the Verte, dodging the airborne ice, we descended the NW ridge past increasing numbers of ascending ropes, including one rope of rather overweight Brits who thought they were on the way to the Argentière hut! In the circumstances, this was an almost understandable mistake.

A year later, after a superb day on the Grands Montets ridge with Richard, we finally arrived back on the Argentière glacier and headed down through that bouldery mass of glacial chaos that always manages to sap the last of your strength. Unexpectedly I found myself in the unfamiliar position of trailing behind after the first of the fixed ladders and, to my horror, as hard as I tried to move ahead of him, I was unable to match his speed and agility. I finally arrived at the cable-car some five minutes behind him. It had finally happened. 'Never mind Dad, you didn't do too badly.'

I looked across at his grinning face, my feelings in a confused jumble of envy and pleasure. Envy because he had it all before him, just as I had 25 years previously, and pleasure because I still had time ahead of me to share some of it with him. The doors of the cable-car clattered open and we headed off towards the valley and a beer or two.

RUPERT HOARE

Innocents Abroad:
An Alpine Season in the Eighties

(Plates 48, 49)

I am grateful to Charles Warren for allowing me to draw inspiration from his article 'Innocents Abroad: An Alpine Season in the Thirties' which appeared in the 97th volume of the Alpine Journal.*

It was in 1982 that two of us teamed up for what turned out to be a memorable summer season in the Bernese Oberland. My companion was Alan Winton, whom I had met in Scotland a few months previously while soloing on Salisbury Crags. Alan was a first-year student at Edinburgh University, aged only 17. He had never before travelled beyond Scotland, let alone overseas. I was therefore the only one with Alpine experience and had all the fun of planning the holiday; but Alan was extremely fit and enthusiastic and so an ideal companion.

We travelled to Switzerland by rail, still the most romantic way to travel to the Alps even in the 1980s. We each had two large rucksacks, one filled with climbing gear and the other with camping gear, and these took up an anti-social amount of space in the rather cramped six-man couchette. The total cost of our two weeks' holiday was about £250 each.

We started by camping at Grindelwald. From the door of the tent we had a fine view of the Wetterhorn, so this immediately became our first objective. For the first two days we walked in the valley during bad weather. I slowly realised that the poor weather at Grindelwald was very local, so on the third day we went up to the Gleckstein hut. I remember this as a very friendly hut. Outside there were several tame ibex and some clown managed to tempt one of the creatures all the way into the common-room by laying a trail of salt on the floor!

In the morning we woke up to a thick 'Scottish' mist. No other parties left the hut but, as Alan had never been on a glacier, we decided to go at least that far. We walked up a moraine path for about an hour and gradually the mist thinned and we started to glimpse the moon. It turned out to be one of those magical days with just the highest peaks emerging from a sea of cloud below. We had the entire mountain to ourselves. I remember arriving on the summit completely unexpectedly, just as Alfred Wills did on the first ascent. We descended back into cloud and it rained the whole way down to Grindelwald.

* AJ97, 189-190, 1992/93

Two days later we caught the train to the Jungfraujoch and climbed the ordinary route up the Jungfrau. On top we met an unhappy guide who was cursing that his client was very slow. We paid for our late start by finding very soft snow on the glacier as we plodded across to the Mönchsjoch hut

The next day we climbed the Gross Fiescherhorn by the NW ridge. This was quite a short day but a very enjoyable route up a beautiful snow arête. After a day hut-bound in thick mist we then climbed the Mönch by the NE ridge, another very enjoyable snow ridge with extensive views down to Grindelwald and the grassy hills beyond on our right-hand side. We descended the S ridge and continued down the Aletsch glacier to the Konkordia hut. Owing to the recession of the glaciers, the hut is reached up a long series of near vertical ladders. I was intrigued to find a chair there donated by the Eagle Ski Club.

The following morning we made a very early start, slipping quietly out of the hut at 2am, and climbed the Hasler Rib on the Aletschhorn, returning by the same route. It wasn't necessary to have made quite such an early start as we were back in the hut soon after midday! We plodded back up the Aletsch glacier next day and took the train back to Grindelwald.

Our final fling was an ascent of the Schreckhorn by the SW ridge. The six-hour walk from Grindelwald to the Schreckhorn hut must be one of the finest hut walks in the Alps. We took it leisurely and enjoyed the flowery lower slopes of the mountain. The ridge provided a splendid rock climb which I thoroughly enjoyed once a chilly early morning wind had died down. On the summit a balloon passed overhead at high speed with not much altitude to spare!

Looking back after ten years, I think that this was rather a fine excursion into the Swiss Alps. Having climbed five 4000m peaks and the Wetterhorn in less than a fortnight, I returned home far too conceited. Luckily this didn't last long: a few weeks later a friend and I set out to climb Bowfell Buttress in the Lake District and we got so completely, utterly lost that we couldn't even find the mountain!

Geography and History

EDWARD PECK

John Muir, Mountaineer
1838 –1914

(Plates 51–53)

One hundred years ago, in 1894, a book entitled *The Mountains of California* by John Muir was published in the United States. It was a collection of articles which had appeared in American monthly magazines over the previous sixteen years, captivating their mountaineering, and wider, audience. A contemporary reviewer wrote: 'We have here nature pure and unadulterated ... sixteen chapters, each a gem of landscape and animal painting.' The writer did not exaggerate; like John Muir's earliest diaries (published as *My First Summer in the Sierra* in 1911), the articles do indeed reflect with vivid freshness Muir's devotion to his beloved Sierra Nevada.

But who was John Muir – this Scotsman who has only recently been recognised in the land of his birth but who has long been a household name in the United States? Perhaps he is best known internationally for his part in inspiring the Californian and Yosemite enthusiasts who, on 4 June 1892, founded the Sierra Club, of which John Muir became the first president. Though its original remit was limited to the mountain regions of the Pacific Coast, the Sierra Club became America's leading environmental group, with a declared aim 'to explore, enjoy and preserve the nation's forests, waters, wildlife and wilderness'.

Although John Muir is often thought of exclusively as a conservationist, his interests were, in fact, uniquely wide-ranging. This remarkable Scotsman can be assessed, successively and sometimes simultaneously, as farmhand, inventor, shepherd, sawmill manager, mountain guide, geologist, glaciologist, ornithologist, philosopher, friend of Presidents, founder of the Sierra Club, advocate of the US National Parks concept. But he was, above all, a man whose delight in mountains was all-embracing, and I propose here to consider John Muir primarily as a mountaineer.

Brought up in Dunbar until the age of eleven, when his stern God-fearing father emigrated to the plains of Wisconsin, John Muir did not set eyes on anything resembling a mountain until, in the course of a thousand-mile trek from Canada to Louisiana in 1866-67, he crossed the Unaka hills of the Cumberland range on the Tennessee border. Arriving in San Francisco in 1868, he made for the Sierra Nevada – the 'Range of Light' as he later called it – for his first enthralling visit to Yosemite. The following year (1869) he was fortunate in being engaged as a 'sheep-herder' by one Pat Delaney. Impressed by the intellectual qualities of the young Scot, who had already made a name for himself at Wisconsin University with his inventive gadgets, Delaney agreed that, once Muir had helped the regular shepherd bring the sheep up to the Tuolumne Meadows for the summer grazing, he would be free to roam this wonderful area. His diaries record his early joy and enthusiasm for the mountains. When, in later years, he suffered ill-health or depression in the plains, a trip to the mountains never failed to restore his health and peace of mind. Once, vexed with himself after a minor fall, he addressed his feet severely: 'That's what you get by intercourse with stupid town stairs and dead pavements.' (One sympathises.) [1]

Yosemite

It was during this period that Muir acquired his close knowledge of the upper Tuolumne area and tested his steadiness of head and foot by climbing down the stream that leads to the Upper Yosemite Fall. At the 'brink of the tremendous cliff', he took off shoes and stockings, working his way cautiously down 'alongside the rushing flood, keeping feet and hands pressed firmly on the polished rock'. Beyond the obvious lip of the fall, he found an 'irregular flake of rock' which offered a view into the 'heart of the snowy, chanting throng of comet-like streamers, into which the body of the fall soon separates'. The telling sentence, 'I concluded not to venture farther but did nevertheless' betrays the mountaineer's perennial need to 'feed the rat' of excitement. Muir's diary for that day (15 July) sagely concludes: 'Hereafter I'll try to keep from such extravagant, nerve-straining places'.[2] But of course he did not and his subsequent solo exploits not only led to a number of close calls but also inspired some fine mountain writing.

The Yosemite valley enthralled Muir and for the next five years, working as manager of a sawmill owned by the first innkeeper in the valley and acting as mountain guide to early tourists, he acquired a deep knowledge of and feeling for the plants and birds of the Yosemite, the scenery and mountains and the effect of glacial action. He had little patience with young ladies with unsuitable footwear and clothing, or the 'blank, fleshly apathy of the ordinary tourist'.[3] However, Mrs Jeanne Carr, a friend in San Francisco who knew Muir from his Wisconsin days, sent him a succession of distinguished Americans, including the geologist Joseph Leconte and the great Emerson himself.

While camping in the Upper Tuolumne in 1872, Muir broke away from his companions on a solo mountaineering venture to Mt Ritter. This involved another close call in high, unexplored mountain country. Frustrated on one face of the mountain, where he found himself in 'danger of being shed off like avalanching snow', he crossed the divide into 'one of the most exciting pieces of pure wilderness that I ever discovered in all my mountaineering. There loomed the majestic mass of Mount Ritter'. There follows a splendid description of the forbidding face, which he surveyed for a possible route. Climbing up into a 'wilderness of crumbling spires and battlements', Muir found himself in the sort of situation familiar to many of us: 'Having passed several dangerous spots, I dared not think of descending.' Higher up, halfway up a cliff with minuscule holds, 'I was suddenly brought to a dead stop with arms outspread,' Muir recalled. 'My doom appeared fixed. I *must* fall.' But 'the other self, bygone experience, instinct, or Guardian Angel, call it what you will, came forward and assumed control.' His trembling muscles became firm again and, having regained strength, courage and morale, he overcame the bad step and made the first ascent of Mt Ritter (4010m). Muir's vivid account of that incident, followed by the description of the view south along the range past the Minarets towards Mt Whitney, belongs to the finest tradition of mountaineering literature. The crest of the Sierra Nevada, along which he was looking to Mt Whitney (4418m), is now closely followed by the John Muir Trail.

Muir's ascent of Mt Whitney in October 1873 was made within two months of the four previous parties. It was memorable because, having run out of food while heading for the 'false' Mt Whitney, Muir returned to Independence (a good deal further away than the present base of Lone Pine) and was back to climb by a difficult route to the summit two days later. 'For climbers,' he commented, 'there is a canyon which comes down from the north shoulder of the Whitney Peak. Well-seasoned limbs will enjoy the climb of 9000 feet required for this direct route, but soft, succulent people should go the mule way.'[5]

In his writings on Yosemite, Muir repeatedly referred to 'glaciers' and to the glacial action which formed the domes and canyons of the Yosemite area. Though he counted 65 glaciers in his day, many are now no more than névé. But Muir correctly read the signs, noting the striations, moraines and erosion caused by the passage of huge glaciers. His application to Yosemite of the theory of glacial erosion, in which he was supported by the American geologist Joseph Leconte, brought Muir into conflict with the traditional geologists, in particular the prestigious Josiah D Whitney who headed the Geological Survey of California in the 1860s. Whitney maintained that the Yosemite gorge had been created by earthquake or volcanic action causing the bottom of the valley floor to 'drop out'. The observations of the brash young Scot, branded as those of an 'ignoramus' and 'sheepherder', were later thoroughly vindicated by the detailed surveys of the French geologist François Matthes.

Among Muir's many climbs in Yosemite was his ascent of Half Dome, 2698m, (or, as Muir called it, 'South Dome'), that dramatic, shorn-away dome that has become Yosemite's trade mark (Plate 53). In 1872 the Yosemite trail-builder John Conway had tried, with the help of his sons who 'climbed smooth rocks like lizards', to forge by rope, hammer and spikes a way up the east shoulder of the Dome which, as Muir described it, 'rises in a graceful curve a few degrees too steep for unaided climbing, besides being defended by overleaning ends of the concentric dome layers of the granite'.[1] They failed, but, three years later in 1875, Anderson, the valley blacksmith, forged a set of eye-bolts and drilled his way to the top. Shortly afterwards Muir, though 'apprehensive of the slipperiness of the rope and the rock', made his ascent in a 'snow-muffled condition'[6] after a November storm. Though disappointed by the flatness of the view, he expressed the

Phimister Proctor on Half Dome in 1884
drawn by him from memory in 1945

hope that no one should implement Anderson's plan to make Half Dome accessible to litter-leaving tourists and to charge for his *via ferrata*. Soon afterwards the latter was partially swept away in a winter snowstorm.

There was a sequel which (though it diverges from the Muir theme) should amuse members of the Alpine Club. In the summer of 1884 a fire was seen on the summit of Half Dome. Fearing a possible accident, a rescue party set out – needlessly, since the two climbers, Alden Sampson (a painter from New York) and Phimister Proctor (a sculptor from Colorado) managed to descend unaided. While making a horseback trip through the area, they had learnt from Galen Clark (the grand old man of Yosemite) that he was waiting for 'some member of the English Alpine Club to come over and have the goodness to replace the rope'. The pair resolved that 'no foreigner will do that job till we have had a try at it'. Their method of ascent was to cast a thin, frayed 'picket rope', cowboy fashion, from spike to spike. When the spikes gave out, they roped down to return the following day to complete the climb; this involved standing for over an hour on a two-inch pin while trying to lasso the pin above. Proctor's sketch of himself precariously balanced on one toe above an arch of granite belongs to the collection of Alpine comic horrors.[7]

In his early years in Yosemite John Muir's climbing techniques were scarcely less primitive. Climbing alone, he usually scorned any use of the rope, took a minimal amount of food, and relied on a comfortable pine tree for a bivouac; he seems reluctantly to have admitted that a few hobnails in his boots would help. At the same time, Muir was developing his mountain philosophy and recording in his journals magnificent descriptions of mountain scenery and close observations of trees, birds and animals, in particular his favourites – the Water Ouzel (or Dipper) and the fearless and inquisitive Douglas squirrel. His articles on glacial action, published in *Overland Monthly* 1874-75, were collected as *Studies of the Sierra*.

Muir was naturally driven to expand his mountain experience beyond Yosemite. His first visit to Mt Shasta (4317m), the semi-active volcano in North California, was in November 1874, when he enjoyed magnificent views over the clouds while snugly tucked up through successive storms in his camp on the tree-line. He returned in April 1875 with Jerome Fay, an experienced mountaineer. On the summit ridge a tremendous thunderstorm blew up, followed by a heavy snowstorm. Seeking refuge in the sludge of the hissing and spitting fumaroles, they passed the night broiled on one side and frozen on the other. Stumbling down the next morning, they met their rescue party and were escorted down, not without Muir suffering some permanent physical damage. 'A Perilous Night on Shasta's Summit'[8] makes exciting reading as another of Muir's close calls.

Muir's passion for the study of glaciers could not be satisfied among the denuded glaciers of the Sierra Nevada. He wanted to see glaciers on the grand scale and spent three summer seasons – 1879, 1880 and 1890 – on the Pacific coast of the Alaska 'Panhandle', exploring, among others, the glacier that was to bear his name. On the way north, he made the ascent (probably the seventh) of Mt Rainier (4392m) by the Nisqually and Cowlitz glacier route, which has now become the normal way up this 'ice-crowned king of the North West'. Muir was accompanied by a veteran local guide and five ambitious young climbers. He did not find the ascent particularly difficult, though when the crevassed ice became too steep 'every one of the party took off his shoes, drove stout steel caulks about half an inch long into them, having brought tools along for the purpose and not having made use of them until now so that the points might not get dulled on the rocks ere the smooth dangerous ice was reached'.[9] They also carried 100ft of rope and one axe. The night was spent on a narrow ridge, at a spot now marked as 'Camp Muir' at 10,000ft, somewhat below Gibraltar Rock. All were in 'light marching order, save one who pluckily determined to carry his camera to the summit'.

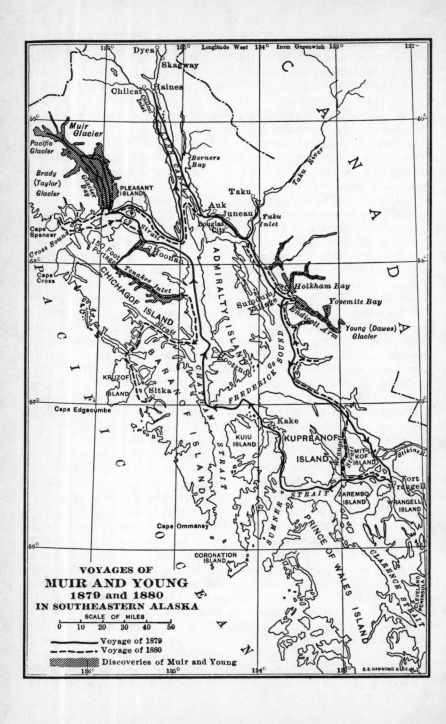

VOYAGES OF
MUIR AND YOUNG
1879 and 1880
IN SOUTHEASTERN ALASKA

SCALE OF MILES

0   10   20   30   40   50

—————— Voyage of 1879
– – – – – Voyage of 1880
▨▨▨▨ Discoveries of Muir and Young

Alaska

On arriving in Alaska, Muir enjoyed the friendship of Hall S Young, the missionary at Fort Wrangell. Their first expedition together, in July 1879, was up the Stickeen (now 'Stikine') river in the good ship *Cassiar* with a party of elderly clerics. Muir and Young played truant to climb Glenora Peak. Young was scrambling well and keeping up with Muir until, a few feet below the summit, he slipped above a thousand-foot drop, dislocating both his shoulders (weakened from a previous accident), and was left with his toes scrabbling in slaty grit. With great skill and strength, at one point grabbing Young's shirt collar in his teeth, Muir hauled him to the summit, thereby missing the spectacular sunset he had promised himself. He reset one of Young's shoulders on the spot and escorted him painfully and slowly back to the *Cassiar*, to endure the reproaches of the clerical party for having gone on a wild-goose chase.[11]

On his return down the Stikine river, Muir made solo surveys of two of the considerable glaciers flowing down into the Stikine gorge – the so-called 'Dirt' glacier and the 'Big Stikeen' glacier. After struggling through dense forest and sliding moraine he was thrilled to make his first direct contact with a really extensive glacier – kettle-holes, rumbling stream, crevasses and all – and to stand inside an ice-cave to study the debris accumulated under the ice.[12]

Meanwhile, Hall Young, nothing daunted by his accident, invited Muir to join him on a canoe trip in October 1879 to the glaciers of the Lynn Canal and the Fairweather Range north of Icy Strait. This was intended primarily as a missionary trip to the Tlingit, Chilcat and Hootsenou Indians, some of whom were inclined to Christian virtues, while others preferred the delights of Bacchus (thereby originating the word 'hooch'). The Stickeen Indians, already Christian converts, were reluctant to set off north so late in the year, but Young's missionary zeal, and Muir's eagerness to see even greater glaciers, carried the day. The party sailed up Chatham Strait and, after refuelling at a wooded island in Icy Strait, ventured into what the Indians called Sit-a-kay, (or 'icy bay'). This is Glacier Bay, now accessible to tourist cruise ships for over 50 miles inland. Vancouver, in his careful charting of this coast in 1794, had failed to note this entrance which was entirely filled with ice. Only 85 years later, Muir's party navigated 25 or more miles of sea before reaching the snout of what was to be known as Muir Glacier. It has since retreated as far again towards the Canadian border. As a result of the advancing winter and the somewhat fearful Indian crew who could not understand why Muir should wish to visit these icy mountains, Muir and Young only spent five days (24-29 October) in the area on this first visit. This was enough to allow Muir to name the James Geikie and Hugh Miller glaciers, after the Scots geologists of his day, and to climb as high as he could up the sides of the fjord. Through gaps in the mist and rain he obtained views over the huge glaciated expanse of mountains to the west – the Fairweather Range round Mt Crillon.

On their way down the east shore of Glacier Bay, dotted with icebergs, the party obtained the 'first broad view of the glacier afterwards to be named the Muir ... The spacious prairie-like glacier with its many tributaries extending far back into the snowy recesses of its fountains made a magnificent display of its wealth and I was strongly tempted to go and explore it at all hazards. But winter had come and the freezing of the fjords was an unsurmountable obstacle.'[13]

Back in California, Muir married Louise Strentzel in April 1880, but by October of that year he was already anxious to renew acquaintance with the huge glaciers around Fort Wrangell. On their second expedition, Muir and Young set out on 10 August up Frederick Sound where they first explored by canoe the SE branch, or Endicott Arm, where Muir described the 3500-4000ft 'granite walls of the very wildest, surpassing in some ways those of Yosemite'. He named the head glacier 'Young Glacier' after his friend, though later geographers have rechristened it 'Dawes'. In the NE branch, or Tracy Arm, they found 'stupendous walls of grey granite crowded with bergs from shore to shore with domes as lofty and as perfect in form as those of the California valley', and, at the head, 'a deeply and desperately hidden glacier'.[14]

Returning to Frederick Sound, they headed west along Icy Strait to Cross Sound and made a base in Taylor Bay, west of the entrance to Glacier Bay and in front of the immense moraine-strewn Brady glacier. Muir could not resist a solo expedition on this glacier, setting out on a cold and cloudy day, accompanied by his faithful little dog Stickeen. Moving up the east side of the glacier, he found it easy work crossing the narrow crevasses; he then decided to cross to the west side, enjoying the 'lovely colour and music [of the glacier rills] as they glided and swirled in their blue crystal channels and potholes ... '. Starting back across the glacier at 5pm towards camp about 15 miles away, he struck a maze of deep and wide crevasses, involving cutting steps across slivers of ice bridges. He flattened these knife-edges to allow Stickeen to follow, but to escape from one particular ice island was only possible 'over the very worst of these sliver bridges ... extending in a low, drooping curve like a loose rope'. This involved some tricky step-cutting and a lot of coaxing of the little dog, but eventually both reached camp, too tired to sleep and with nightmares about their 'dreadful ice bridge in the shadow of death'.[15]

Muir was able to persuade the Indian captain, reluctant to endanger his craft close to the calving bergs, to go round into Glacier Bay and let him land near the edge of the Muir Glacier and to camp there for a night or two. On climbing 2500ft up the hill behind, he was able to enjoy in fine weather the splendid sight of Mts Fairweather, La Pérouse and Crillon, and also to study his eponymous glacier. He compared it to a 'broad undulating prairie streaked with medial moraines and gashed with crevasses', comprising seven main tributary glaciers from 10 to 20 miles long. He boldly claimed that the area 'drained by this one grand glacier can hardly be less than seven or eight hundred square miles, and probably contains as much ice as all the eleven hundred Swiss glaciers combined'. He observed that 'the thundering ice-wall, while comfortably accessible, is also the most strikingly interesting portion of the glacier'.[16] In the past

110 years the glacier has continued its retreat up Muir Inlet, and the frontal ice-wall is still magnificent. (See Plate 52 showing state of the glacier in 1971.)

Muir was not to return to 'his' glacier for another ten years and by the time of his third visit, in 1890, tourist ship excursions were already plying to view this spectacular area. Leaving San Francisco on 14 June, he was able to set up his little base camp on the moraine at the snout of the Muir Glacier by 23 June. His one-room cabin is now no more than an overgrown heap of stones and the glacier snout is 25 miles further inland. Muir's exploratory excursions were largely on his own, and his delight in the glacier and its surroundings shines vividly out of the pages of his diary.[17] The climax was his memorable sled trip up the glacier to survey the seven tributary glaciers he had noted in 1880. He hauled his sled over hummocky ice, crossing 'many narrow nerve-trying, ice-sliver bridges, balancing astride and cautiously shoving the sled ahead of me with tremendous chasms on either side'. He enjoyed a long spell of fine weather which brought the unexpected discomfort of snow-blindness.[18] This extensive exploration of the Muir Glacier was rounded off by an adventurous canoe trip to the Hugh Miller Inlet. Muir's canoe was nearly nipped between two converging bergs. However, to his intense delight, he enjoyed several splendid displays of *aurora borealis*.[19]

Muir paid two visits to the Arctic. The first was in 1881 when he was invited to join the US naval vessel *Corwin* in the search for the US expedition ship *Jeannette*, which had been caught in the Arctic ice north of the Bering Strait and was drifting across the East Siberian Sea. The *Corwin*'s search did not succeed, as the *Jeannette* was crushed in the ice in June 1881; some of her crew reached the Siberian mainland near the mouth of the River Lena. The *Corwin* voyage, however, did enable Muir to make the first ascent, on 31 July, of Herald Island (now known in Russian as Ostrov Gerald), E of Wrangell Island and some 450 miles NW of the Bering Straits. The impetuous crew (no mountaineers, they) were anxious to get ashore on the steep-sided island, pronounced inaccessible by its discoverer, Kellett, in 1849. They rushed up a steep gully, dislodging rocks on themselves. Muir, as Captain Hooper reported, came over, axe in hand, and 'with the practised eye of an experienced mountaineer, selected a steep bank of frozen snow and ice at an angle of 50°, deliberately commenced cutting steps and ascended the ice-cliff'. Muir found an easy way to the top and spent the arctic midnight on the summit where he observed signs of glacial striation, proving that the hard granite of this 'fine glacial monument' had resisted the pressure of the northern ice sheet.[15]

Muir's final visit to Alaska and the Arctic was in much plushier circumstances, when his conservation activities had made him a national figure. Invited, along with 25 leading American scientists, to join Edward H Harriman's 1899 Alaska expedition in the railroad king's own steamer, Muir was able to point out and explain the Alaskan glaciers he knew so well.

Later life

Muir had spent most of the years from 1881 to 1889 rearing a family, managing his father-in-law's California fruit farm and starting some of his writing projects, based on his vividly written diaries. It was during this period that he began to take a keen interest in the conservation of wild areas. With others, he founded the Sierra Club in 1892 – the first and leading mountain club of the USA – and took an active part in the National Parks debate. This was another fascinating aspect of Muir's life, which there is no space to describe here save for one highlight. This was a four-day private visit to the Yosemite valley which President Theodore Roosevelt agreed to make alone with Muir (without the usual journalists and other hangers-on associated with Presidential tours). They visited Glacier Point and camped below the Bridal Veil Fall. Muir convinced the President of the need for conservation of the natural beauties of the US, especially its trees and mountains, by a policy of Federal National Parks. Would that mountain diplomacy could nowadays be conducted on such intimate terms with a Head of State!

In his later years, Muir, having achieved fame and a modicum of wealth, travelled to Scotland and the Alps in 1893 and to the foot of the Himalaya in 1902. Though tempted by the Alps, he achieved nothing higher than a view of the Matterhorn from the Gornergrat. In 1911, aged 73, he visited South America and went high in the Andes in search of the monkey-puzzle tree. He travelled thence to Southern and to East Africa where, though he did not see the Ruwenzori, he may have sighted the equatorial snows of Kilimanjaro or Mount Kenya.

Revered as a national figure in the USA, John Muir received scant recognition in his native Scotland or, indeed, in Britain until the foundation of the John Muir Trust in 1982 by a distinguished group of Muir enthusiasts. The Trust has acquired three fine mountain wilderness properties in Scotland in his memory. The first covers Li and Coire Dhorcaill, on the N side of Ladhar Bheinn on Knoydart peninsula; the second is at Torrin, on the SW coast of Skye, including part of the E slope of the black Cuillin; and the third, acquired in 1993, is the remote and desolately beautiful Sandwood Bay, on the NW coast of Scotland 12 miles south of Cape Wrath, with its prominent sea-stack Am Buachaille and tales of a haunting mermaid.

John Muir died in his California home on 24 December 1914, much venerated as the 'patriarch of American lovers of mountains' and, as James Bryce wrote at the time, 'one who had not only a passion for the splendours of Nature, but a wonderful power of interpreting her to men'.

A note on John Muir's writing

A list of John Muir's own writings occupies seven pages of Volume 10 of the *Sierra Club Bulletin* of January 1916, which is wholly devoted to him. A further six pages list associated articles and biographical notes up to that date. To these must be added the numerous subsequent biographical and other works to complete the *corpus* of John Muir literature. Much of his early writing was in the form of personal diaries or contributions to

Californian journals. He drew heavily on these when he began writing complete books, which he found a laborious task. Thus his first book, *Mountains of California*, was published in 1894, while *Travels in Alaska* only appeared posthumously in 1915. Subsequent compilations, such as *Mountaineering Essays*, may duplicate excerpts from other works, in particular *John Muir: The Eight Wilderness Discovery Books*, an omnibus edition published by Diadem Books in 1992.

REFERENCES

All the following references are from books, essays or letters by John Muir unless otherwise stated. Full details of the sources quoted are given in the bibliography on page 212.

1   Letter to Jeanne Carr, quoted in Margaret P Sanborn, *Yosemite, its Discovery, its Wonders and its People*, 124.
2   *My first Summer in the Sierra*, 71-72.
3   Letter to Jeanne Carr, quoted in Sanborn, 116.
4   'Near view of the High Sierra' in *Mountaineering Essays*; and *Mountains of California*, 44-45.
5   Quoted in Francis P Farquhar, *History of the Sierra Nevada*.
6   'The South Dome' in *Mountaineering Essays*, 93-93.
7   Francis P Farquhar, *History of the Sierra Nevada*, 192-194. The drawing of himself by Phimister Proctor is reproduced from Farquhar by courtesy of the University of California Press and Sierra Club.
8   'Perilous Night on Shasta's Summit' in *Mountaineering Essays*, 65-89.
9   'An Ascent of Mt Rainier' in *Mountaineering Essays*, 107-116.
10   Two accounts: Samuel Hall Young, *Alaska Days with John Muir*; 'The Stickeen River' in *Travels in Alaska*, ch 4, 44-46.
11   'Glenora Peak' in *Travels in Alaska*, ch 7, 75-80.
12   'Exploration of the Stickeen Glaciers' in *Travels in Alaska*, ch 8, 81-94.
13   'The Discovery of Glacier Bay' in *Travels in Alaska*, ch 10, 118-132.
14   'Sum Dum Bay' in *Travels in Alaska*, ch 14, 180-193.
15   'From Taku River to Taylor Bay' in *Travels in Alaska*, ch 15, 203-214.
16   'Glacier Bay' in *Travels in Alaska*, ch 16, 219-224.
17   'In Camp at Glacier Bay' in *Travels in Alaska*, ch 17, 234-246.
18   'My Sled Trip on the Muir Glacier' in *Travels in Alaska*, ch 18, 247- 261.
19   'Auroras' in *Travels in Alaska*, ch 19, 262-267.
20   'First Ascent of Herald Island' in *Mountaineering Essays*, 167. Also in *Cruise of the Corwin*.

The bibliography which follows is a short list of works drawn upon in writing the foregoing article, and does not include any of Muir's works relating to his pre-mountaineering days, such as *The Story of my Boyhood and Youth* or *A Thousand Mile Trek*. Where possible, reference is made to those few editions which are published in Britain.

BIBLIOGRAPHY

William F Badé	*The Life and Letters of John Muir* Houghton Mifflin, 1923-24.
Michael P Cohen	*The Pathless Way; John Muir and the American Wilderness* University of Wisconsin Press, 1984.
Francis P Farquhar	*History of the Sierra Nevada* University of California Press and Sierra Club, 1965.
Tom Melham	'John Muir's Wild America' in *National Geographic*, 1976.
John Muir	*The Eight Wilderness Discovery Books* Omnibus edition with an introduction by Terry Gifford. Diadem Books, 1992.
	Cruise of the Corwin (Ed William Badé, 1917) Houghton Mifflin, 1918.
	Discovery of Glacier Bay (1879) First published 1895; Outbooks, 1978.
	Mountaineering Essays (Reprints of essays in series entitled 'Literary Naturalists'.) Peregrine Smith, 1980.
	Mountains of California First published 1894; Penguin's American Library, 1988.
	My First Summer in the Sierra First published 1911; Canongate Classics, 1988.
	Studies in the Sierra (Articles on glaciation first published 1874- 75.) Sierra Club, 1950.
	Travels in Alaska First published 1915; Sierra Books, 1988.
Margaret P Sanborn	*Yosemite, its Discovery, its Wonders and its People.* Random House, 1981; Yosemite Association, 1989.
Chris Townsend	'John Muir Trail' in *Adventure Treks. Western North America* . (Series editor John Cleare) Crowood Press, 10-16, 1990.
Linda March Wolfe	*John of the Mountains, 1938* *Son of the Wilderness.* Alfred A Knopf, New York, 1945.
Samuel Hall Young	*Alaska Days with John Muir.* Revell, 1915.

Official National Park Handbook: Glacier Bay, 1983.
Official National Park Handbook: Yosemite, 1990.

MICHAEL WARD

Northern Approaches: Everest 1918–22

(Plate 56)

This is the third in a series of four articles, in consecutive volumes of the Alpine Journal, *describing some of the important events, both geographical and scientific, which preceded the first ascent of Everest in 1953.*

The First World War was hardly over before the subject of Mount Everest was raised at the Royal Geographical Society (RGS) on 19 December 1918. In an article in the *Geographical Journal* for 1970, T S Blakeney describes how Sir Thomas Holditch reopened negotiations by writing to the Secretary of State for India on behalf of the RGS and the Alpine Club. As Everest was now the central unsolved problem for both geographers and mountaineers, he urged that an expedition there should be mounted during 1919.[1]

On 19 March of that year Lt Col C K Howard-Bury wrote to A R Hinks, Secretary of the RGS, suggesting a preliminary reconnaissance that summer, followed at a later date by an attempt on the mountain. His plan was initially to approach the India Office for permission to travel to the north slopes of Everest, via Tingri Dzong. He would then proceed to Gyantse to seek permission from the Tibetan authorities for a full-scale expedition to Everest in 1920. That permission would be sought through the good offices of the trade agent there or, if possible, from the Teshi Lama himself.

Howard-Bury was well qualified to lead such an expedition. Although not at that time an Alpine Club member, he had visited the Tien Shan and the Karakoram and was an experienced Himalayan traveller. Moreover, he had valuable contacts amongst highly placed officials in India.

The choice of Tingri Dzong as a starting point for an Everest expedition was first suggested by Captain Cecil Rawling as a result of his survey of western Tibet carried out after the Younghusband mission to Lhasa in 1904.[2] It was known to be an important focal point, being the Tibetan terminus of a main trade route with Nepal via the Nyelam valley. The route from Sola Khumbu in NE Nepal and over the Nangpa La (the 'Pangu La' of the pundit MH) also ended there. Another possibility was that the Kyetrak glacier leading from the Nangpa La, which had a branch joining it from the east, might provide access to Everest itself. The more direct route by the East Rongbuk glacier was only discovered on the 1921 expedition after the Kyetrak glacier had been explored and found not to provide access to Everest, though it did suggest a possible route to the Tibetan side of Cho Oyu and Gyachung Kang. Tingri Dzong was also within the 'see' of the Teshi Lama, second only to the Dalai Lama in the hierarchy of Tibet.

In his letter to Hinks, Howard-Bury also mentioned the possibility of visiting Kathmandu to negotiate an approach from Nepal. In addition, he proposed seeing the Surveyor General of India in order to try to arrange, through him and the Director General of Flying, for an aerial reconnaissance of Everest. However, the Government of India objected to all these proposals because it feared they might prejudice a scheme of its own for installing wireless stations at Gyantse and Lhasa to counter possible Japanese activity in Tibet. At that time (1919) the Japanese were gradually taking control of China's telegraph and wireless communications and it was feared that their influence could spread to Tibet.

However, the matter was not allowed to rest. Following a lecture by Col John Noel on his attempt to approach Everest from the east in 1913, Sir Francis Younghusband and others spoke strongly in favour of a full-scale attempt on Everest. Previously Noel and A M Kellas had discussed a secret route from Tashirak, along a tributary of the Arun river to the Kharta valley and the eastern glaciers of Everest.

In the course of many years exploration in Sikkim, Kellas had trained a native in photography and sent him to Kharta and the Arun gorge to get pictures of the east side of Everest. As a result, he knew of a pass, the Tok Tok La, between Tashirak and Kharta and of a hide rope bridge across the Arun river which led on the far (west) side to the Langma La. This pass was used by shepherds of the Kama valley to gain access to the Kharta valley to the north. At the head of the Kharta glacier, which flowed into the valley, was the Lhakpa La, the col later crossed by Mallory and Bullock in 1921 on their first reconnaissance to the North Col. Kellas had worked out a plan to lay food depots, using his own Sherpas, in the high uninhabited valleys west of Kangchenjunga which he knew well from his own explorations, and this route would have evaded Tibetan surveillance. However, these plans were thwarted by the First World War.[3]

With the backing of the RGS, Howard-Bury visited India in 1920 and conferred with Charles Bell, Political Officer in Sikkim, who was responsible for the British side of Anglo-Tibetan affairs. His support would be needed for the expedition to pass through Sikkim on the way to Tibet, since access from Nepal was not to become possible until 1950. Howard-Bury also called on the Viceroy at Simla.

By this time the position with regard to Japanese infiltration into Tibet had improved and the main obstacle appears to have been Charles Bell himself who frankly admitted that he was opposed to the expedition. In addition, there was friction with Tibet over the British Government's refusal to allow ammunition to be sent to Lhasa despite the fact that rifles had already been dispatched. The Dalai Lama was friendly towards Britain but his *Tsongdu* (Council) favoured turning to China for support. Eventually it was arranged that Bell should visit Lhasa that winter (1920) and semi-official instructions were sent to him by the Government of India asking him to sound out the Tibetan Government about an expedition to Everest. The inference was that he should tactfully explain to the Tibetan officials that if no reason existed to fear serious objections on Tibet's part, the Government of India would be glad if permission were granted. This was done. On 15 December 1920 the Viceroy of India, Lord Chelmsford, telegraphed the India Office in London as follows: 'Bell telegraphs that he has explained to the Dalai Lama object of desired exploration and necessity of travelling through Tibetan territory and obtained Tibetan Government's consent.'

Meanwhile, Kellas and Morshead, backed by the Everest Committee in London, had mounted a reconnaissance expedition to Kamet in 1920 (Plate 56). Experiments were made with oxygen compressed in cylinders and oxygen obtained from mixing water with sodium peroxide in oxylithe bags, as suggested by Professor Leonard Hill at Oxford. Neither was satisfactory on the mountain, the cylinders being too heavy and the oxylithe bags only being able to produce oxygen at rest; Kellas was not impressed by either. The main discovery on this expedition was the importance of good cooking stoves. Neither adequate fluid nor food had been available at the high camps.[4, 5]

Kellas stayed on in India after this expedition and in November he trekked from Darjeeling along the watershed between Nepal and Sikkim. Near the Kang La he took some photographs of the Everest group and ranges to the north and sent them to Professor Collie for examination by the 1921 reconnaissance party.[6]

Because of the difficulty that Kellas had had with the Primus stoves on Kamet, sample stoves were sent to Oxford for tests in the decompression chamber in the laboratory of Professor Dreyer, FRS. Dreyer was a consultant to the RAF and had carried out a considerable amount of research on oxygen at altitude on airmen. He held strong views on the use of oxygen on Everest and commented: 'I do not think that you will get up [Everest] without, but if you do succeed you may not get down again.' His views impressed Farrar, a member of the Everest Committee, who expressed the wish to meet Dreyer.

The stoves were duly altered for use at altitude and Farrar, Finch (then a prospective member of the proposed 1921 Everest expedition) and P J H Unna went to Oxford on Good Friday in March 1921 to witness the tests. Unna was a civil engineer by profession and an experienced mountaineer and member of the Alpine Club. He was also recognised as an expert on alpine equipment and took a great interest in all the mechanical gear for Everest. While they were there Dreyer easily convinced Finch that the use of supplementary oxygen should receive serious consideration for an attempt on the summit. Finch stayed overnight in Oxford so that experiments could be carried out on himself in the decompression chamber next day. Finch was decompressed to 21,000ft and exercised both with and without supplementary oxygen. Obviously his performance was much better with oxygen, but the experiment was inadequate as a method of assessing performance on Everest, since it made no allowance for acclimatisation. It was later shown in the course of Operation Everest I in the United States in 1946 that, after acclimatisation over 30 days, man was indeed capable of an 'ascent' to the summit of Everest without oxygen;

whereas if he was taken too quickly to that altitude he would become unconscious and die. Finch was examined medically prior to the experiment and found to be perfectly fit. This finding was at variance, however, with that of a Harley Street doctor used by the Everest Committee, and Finch was rejected for the 1921 expedition. (The whole episode is dealt with in detail in Scott Russell's memoir of George Finch.[7])

This Oxford episode alerted the Everest Committee to the likelihood that supplementary oxygen should be taken for the attempt in 1922 (the 1921 expedition being a reconnaissance only, supplementary oxygen would not be required). Their view was supported by the extreme breathlessness of the climbers above 22,000ft in 1921. Though Mallory and Bullock climbed in that year to the North Col from the East Rongbuk glacier in only a few hours, in general the rate of ascent of most mountaineer's at altitude was slow.

The result was that in January 1922, Farrar and Unna, with Finch and Somervell, who were both prospective members of the 1922 party, visited Oxford again. Finch and Somervell were decompressed to 23,000ft and exercised at that altitude. Somervell nearly became unconscious and oxygen had to be forcibly administered to him. Immediately on return to London a detailed report was submitted to the Everest Committee to the effect that supplementary oxygen should be used on the 1922 Everest expedition. A considerable amount of work was carried out with the help of the Air Ministry and other organisations. A flow rate of 2.0 to 2.4 litres of oxygen per minute was decided on, and oxylithe bags for use at rest, together with other remedies for mountain sickness, were sent out. These included morphia and bicarbonate of soda, and also garlic either breathed through the nose or taken as a flavouring in soup. Liquid oxygen was also considered but dismissed as too expensive.

Before the departure of the 1922 expedition, the general feeling seems to have supported P J H Unna's view that 'an ascent [of Everest] is not likely to be made without an artificial aid to respiration'.[8] It was to be another 30 years before Griffith Pugh showed, in 1952, that a flow rate of 4 litres per minute was necessary to compensate for the weight of the set and provide a boost to climbing rate. How this discovery culminated in the successful ascent of Everest in 1953 was fully explained in 'The Contribution of Medical Science to the First Ascent of Everest' in the 1993 *Alpine Journal*.[9]

REFERENCES

1   T S Blakeney, 'A R Hinks and the First Everest Expedition 1921', in *Geographical Journal 136*, 333-343, 1970.
2   C G Rawling, *Military Report on Western Tibet including Chang Tang and Rudok*. Intelligence Branch of the Quarter Master General's Department. Simla, 1905.
3   J B L Noel, *Through Tibet to Everest*. Arnold, 1927.

4   H T Morshead, 'Report of the Expedition to Kamet, 1920', in *Geographical Journal 57*, 213-219, 1921.

5   A M Kellas, 'Expedition to Kamet in 1920', in *AJ33*, 312-319, 1921.

6   J N Collie, 'The Ranges North of Mt. Everest as seen from near the Kang La', in *AJ33*, 303-305, 1921.

7   G I Finch, *The Making of a Mountaineer*, with a Memoir by Scott Russell. J W Arrowsmith, 1988.

8   P J H Unna, 'The Oxygen Equipment of the 1922 Everest Expedition', in *AJ34*, 2235-250, 1922.

9   M P Ward, 'The Contribution of Medical Science to the First Ascent of Everest', in *AJ98*, 37-51, 1993.

Michael Ward's paper 'The first ascent of Mount Everest, 1953: the solution of the problem of the last thousand feet' was published in the *Journal of Wilderness Medicine 4*, 312-318, 1993. A reprint of the article is in the Alpine Club Library.

NORMAN HARDIE

Mountaineering by New Zealanders 1954 –1993

(Plates 54, 55)

This is the second of two articles on the history of mountaineering by New Zealanders. Scott Russell's article, 'The Centenary of the New Zealand Alpine Club', covering the period 1891-1953, appeared in AJ97, 161-163, 1992/93.

In 1954 the New Zealand Alpine Club sent an expedition to the Barun area in Nepal to attempt the first ascent of Makalu. Sir Edmund Hillary was the leader, Sir Charles Evans his deputy, and also from Everest 1953 was George Lowe. Seven others, all new to the Himalaya, made up the team. Among these was Mike Ball from Britain who, like Evans, was invited for his talents, but also as an expression of gratitude for past invitations to New Zealanders on British expeditions. Two had been on the 1951 Everest reconnaissance, two were on Everest in 1953 and three – Riddiford, Hillary and Lowe – were on Cho Oyu in 1952.

On the initial venture to higher altitudes in the Barun, Jim McFarlane fell into a crevasse and his hands and feet were badly frostbitten. After a few days it became evident that he would have to be carried to Kathmandu. Meanwhile, a not very spirited prod was made at Makalu by the route later used by the French. Three left with McFarlane and the remaining six formed three mobile groups which between them climbed 19 peaks over 6000m, the most notable being Baruntse (7129m) and Pethangtse (6730m). When the monsoon began most went home, but Evans and I travelled west to Kodari keeping near the Tibetan border. I was with Charles, two days north of Kathmandu, when he received the telegraphed invitation to lead the Kangchenjunga expedition the following year. I was delighted that he asked me on the spot to join him. The story of that highly successful expedition is well known.

Also in 1955 the Canterbury Mountaineering Club sent a strong group to Masherbrum. They were progressing well when a porter died of pneumonia. Unfortunately all the party came off the mountain for several days of mourning. By the time they regained their higher camps the good weather had departed. They were never close to the summit.

It is interesting that these two expeditions, to the Barun and to Masherbrum, were the only ones sent out by the main climbing clubs in 40 years. Subsequent scores of groups to the Andes and Himalaya went on a private basis. The clubs gave their blessing and generally some small financial support but distanced themselves from the selection of personnel or policy, to the approval of the climbers.

Antarctica

For several years after 1955 the Antarctic became the objective of most New Zealanders seeking overseas experience. As part of the preparations for the work of the International Geophysical Year (1958), Hillary and Lowe joined a reconnaissance visit to the South Atlantic in 1957. Afterwards Lowe went to England where he joined the team aiming to complete the first Antarctic crossing. Hillary led a large contingent to the south shore of Ross Sea. Here they built Scott Base, some four miles from Captain Scott's 1903 Discovery hut. The New Zealand base, although later enlarged and then rebuilt, has continued to house a wide range of scientific projects.

Hillary and his small team were part of the Commonwealth Trans-Antarctic expedition. Their main task was to put in depots from the New Zealand side in the direction of the South Pole and to restock the party currently on its way from the South Atlantic. The depots were placed successfully. However, Vivian Fuchs and his party were several weeks behind schedule. It was clear to Hillary and the four others waiting in the furthest camp that if they stayed for the crossing team they would be forced to consume the other team's supplies. The simplest solution was to go on to the Pole and from there fly back to Scott Base on the coast. The press put all sorts of interpretations on this action and on intercepted radio messages, apparently trying to stir up the notion of a race to the Pole.

When Fuchs was near the Pole, Hillary flew back to join him. The TAE vehicles then completed the whole crossing on a higher route, which was proved by Hillary to be considerably better than the Beardmore glacier and the near sea-level ice shelf of the Scott and Shackleton journeys.

Since 1956 the New Zealand Government has financed the continuing Antarctic research work, while not formally encouraging mountaineering. However, there are always climbers at Scott Base for rescue work and for giving the two days' introduction courses which all new arrivals must undertake. Most people arrive unacclimatised and are often inexperienced in the necessary techniques for field work in Antarctica. Scott Base has some 95 beds and about 350 people pass through each season. Now, with improved air transport, it is less than six hours away from Christchurch and quite short projects are possible. Only the wintering party of ten has to stay more than five months. Field parties going to these hazardous areas have to include technical assistants who are capable on the local terrain. Consequently, at the end of the season, one finds that an increasing number of summits have been climbed by the technical assistants, often accompanied by the scientists. But this type of mountain activity has to tolerate an enormous amount of bureaucratic tape, nor can one get there with one's usual companions. Some field assistants may return for a second season, but seldom more, unless they are climbing the scientific qualification ladder and therefore obtaining other benefits from the experience.

One break in the red tape occurred in 1967 when Ed Hillary managed to have a group flown to the Cape Hallett area with a mountain as their chief objective. This was Mount Herschel which rises in one steep ice and rock face from the sea to its 3335m summit. It is a very formidable prospect. Two pairs did reach the summit by an easier route, away from the sea face. I joined the team as deputy leader and surveyor. Two geologists studied this significant location which is by one of the main fracture lines where the Godwanaland breakup occurred. Continental drift theory was still fairly young in the 1960s. The expedition had some successes but the two snowmobiles for pulling sledges were greatly underpowered on the wet snow which occurs on that very stormy coastline.

School expeditions

A 1958 visitor to Antarctica, Dr Griffith Pugh of the 1953 Everest expedition, convinced Ed Hillary that much high-altitude physiological work still needed to be done. Their discussions resulted in the large research expedition to Nepal in 1960. American finance was obtained for a one-year programme involving medical men from New Zealand, USA and Britain. The sponsors also added a 'yeti search' to the party's objectives. For the extent of the work and the altitudes contemplated, mountaineers were needed. Great advances were made in research, Ama Dablam was climbed and a retreat was made from just under the summit of Makalu.

For once, an expedition had surplus dollars at its conclusion. After long discussions with local Sherpas it was decided to build a school at Khumjung. A metal building was donated by ICI in India. The expedition paid for the porterage to the site and the construction. Although this first building was not ideal, the teaching began with a full roll and a waiting list.

Soon, other villages began pressing Hillary for schools, medical assistance and larger buildings suitable as high schools. The situation drifted for three years while the first school was making its impact on the community. Over the same period, a 50 mile-wide access prohibition area was in force, while the Indians and Chinese had frontier confrontations.

By 1966 the situation had stabilised and a series of school building ventures began. Since then a small party has gone to Nepal every year for school, medical or maintenance work. There has always been a strong New Zealand input, but in recent years the main sponsorship has moved from the USA to Canada and more Canadians are being seen, particularly in the field of medicine.

Andes

New Zealanders began their considerable activities in the Andes in the early 1960s and the pressure continues. There were many reasons for this. Obtaining places in Government Antarctic expeditions was difficult and frequently frustrating. The closure of Himalayan frontier peaks kept people away from these areas and some of those who had a particular desire for Himalayan involvement were able to get there with the school building groups. Moreover, the Andes have many positive attractions, such as the shorter acclimatisation required, the steeper and more stable rock - and, of course, their great beauty.

In Peru, Huascaran (6768m) was climbed in 1959 and the following year Nevado Cayesh (5721m), the latter a first ascent. In 1962 Brian Hearfield led a party to the Vilcabamba, where they completed five new climbs and the third ascent of Pumasillo (6070m). Another group made the second ascent, with two Britons, of Rondoy (5882m).

Every year since 1962 there have been New Zealand climbers in Peru, Chile or Bolivia. They have succeeded on major routes of all types, including many first ascents. The list is long and it reflects the raising of technical standards which has occurred in recent years. The event which seems the most outstanding to me was the 1988 climb of Cerro Torre and Fitzroy by Nick Cradock and Russell Braddock. Then in 1993 two New Zealand guides made a winter ascent of the Super Couloir of Fitzroy. They were Erica Beuzemberg and Gottlieb Braun-Elwert, who also were the first to climb all the New Zealand 3000m peaks in winter in one season. There have been many other fine climbs, just short of these achievements.

New Zealand

Travelling has become much easier in the last 40 years and this has enabled climbers to gain immense experience in a shorter time. If one constructed a list of the top 50 or so New Zealand climbers of 1993, practically every one would have had an Antarctic season and have been to the Andes or Himalaya. Many have also been to Europe and North America.

Since 1953, equipment has become better and lighter, as have food and fuel. Clubs use highly qualified instructors to steer young climbers in the right direction. There are a number of artificial climbing walls in the main cities. The crags within a day's range of most cities have route guide booklets.

During this period every one of the 20 highest NewZealand peaks had several face routes made on them. The E face of Mt Cook was first ascended in 1962, the longest and most unrelenting of the big features. In 1992 a colossal rock fall of some 14 million cubic metres spilled from Cook, and the summit is now some ten metres lower. The newly exposed fragile precipice has daily rumbles and climbers do not go near it. (Plates 54, 55)

Two kilometres south is the Caroline face. This is a uniformly severe ice problem which tops at the ridge between the low and middle peaks of Cook. Peter Gough and John Glasgow waited in the district for weeks and eventually climbed it in November 1970. Two days later Graeme Dingle and George Harris repeated it. This climb was shortly followed by Dingle and Murray Jones making the first ascent of the S face of Hicks, which has subsequently had a host of variations on it.

Dingle and Jones had previously accomplished a brilliant Alpine season with the climbs of six major north faces. They began with the Matterhorn, the Bonatti Pillar, and the Croz Spur of the Grandes Jorasses. Next was the Dru, the Piz Badile, the Eiger and, finally, the Cima Grande di Lavaredo. Graham Dingle has been on many of the most successful Himalayan and Andean expeditions. He has just returned to NewZealand after taking three years to complete a round-the-world journey, keeping north of the Arctic Circle. He is also a regular competitor in 'iron man' racing, combining cycling, kayaking and mountain running.

The spectacular E side of Mt Sefton, the nearest big peak to the road-end at Mt Cook, has had several brilliantly successful options taken on it. Mt Tasman, the second highest, has numerous ribs and faces, almost all involving steep ice, all of which have been climbed by a variety of routes.

During the 1950s several new huts were built in the main ranges. With glacial shrinkage often removing the lower support of lateral moraines, many of these hut sites have recently become unstable. Some have received severe damage and others are in a poor state. With so many sites being fragile, there is a reluctance to spend much reconstruction money on high risk situations. Generally the main base huts, with road access, are in good condition.

Himalaya

Apart from school related work, New Zealanders were relatively quiet in the Himalaya until 1975 when Margaret Clark led a joint Indian and New Zealand women's group to climb Hardeol (7151m) in the Garhwal. In a year of exceptionally heavy snowfalls, four of the party were killed when an avalanche from high on the mountain swept out across the level glacier floor where they were walking. Although Margaret suffered a setback, she has now returned to the mountains of India every year since 1980.

The extraordinary N face of Jannu (7710m) was ascended by a strong party in 1975, but they did not go to the summit, which is some distance from the face. One year later an Everest attempt was made by a group which had strength but little money. They employed no Sherpas and wore themselves out on the lower slopes, reaching no higher than the South Col. Not long after that Nick Banks, while part of a German expedition, stood on the top of Everest. As an instructor at Plas y Brenin, he has become a familiar figure in the UK climbing world.

In May 1981 eight New Zealanders summited on Molamenqing (Phola Gangchen, 7661m), while a mixture of New Zealand climbers and Australians succeeded on Changabang. Many other teams did well on smaller objectives in subsequent years. A team of four very nearly climbed Kangchenjunga, but were forced to turn back owing to their lack of strength when one member returned to base with an injury. Everest was tried again from Tibet in 1986, but in that year of bad snow the team was repulsed at 7000m on the W ridge and the N face. Two years later Russell Brice climbed the 'Pinnacle' NE ridge with a British Everest expedition.

In 1992 Martin Hunter's expedition climbed a new route on Cholatse and not far away John Nankervis and David Bamford completed a new route on the Rowaling peak Chobutse (6689m). In the same year three men, Rob Hall, Gary Ball and Guy Cotter, hit headlines when they took a party of 14 to the top of Everest. Back in 1981 Hall had climbed Ama Dablam and Numbur and recently Hall and Ball climbed the highest peaks in seven continents in seven months. They were also prominent on many new routes in New Zealand. There seemed to be an abundance of wealthy customers for their Everest operations. But they cared about the environment and were praised for the way they brought out all their expedition rubbish. In 1993 they again took a large commercial group to Everest. Sadly, in October of that year, the death was announced of Gary Ball, at the early age of 40, after he had developed altitude sickness near the 8167m summit of Dhaulagiri. He was brought lower down the mountain by his climbing partner Rob Hall, but despite medical attention he died from pulmonary oedema.

Karakoram

In 1957 Allan Berry and Hugh Tyndale-Biscoe had a successful month in Swat and Chitral, but after that there was very little activity for many years. The first big return was by a strong party which attempted Gasherbrum I in 1986, but bad weather turned them back at 7772m. A 1989 expedition to Uli Biaho led by Nick Cradock climbed its impressive E face, with the summit pitches and descent being made in a snow storm.

During July and August 1991 a party of five New Zealanders – Dave Bamford, John Cocks, Matt Comeskey, John Nankervis and John Wild, with liaison officer Major Arif Khan – made a number of climbs in the Lukpe Lawo (Snow Lake) region during an ambitious Biafo–Hispar ski traverse. Though they failed in two attempts to climb virgin Hispar Sar (c6400m), they succeeded on four peaks including the highest and most elegant peak (c6500m) above the East Khurdopin glacier via its SE spur. They were unimpressed by a persistent hungry bear which occupied rocks near their base camp.

Rob Hall and Gary Ball made three attempts on K2 via the Abruzzi ridge. Their turnback points were at 7300m, 7800m and 8300m respectively, foiled by atrocious weather and snow conditions.

Other mountains

New Zealanders have appeared in all sorts of remote places. Back in 1964 the highest peak on Heard Island in the South Indian Ocean was climbed after a most precarious landing on an exposed beach. H W Tilman was the skipper of the expedition's yacht, Warwick Deacock was the leader and participants included Colin Putt and Philip Temple. Putt sailed with Tilman again off Iceland and in 1990 he sailed a yacht to Antarctica for the climb of Mt Minto (4000m), the highest peak in N Victorialand, a long way inland from Cape Hallett. Temple, now a very successful author, climbed most of the highest summits in New Guinea with Heinrich Harrer. Dr David Lewis, better known as an Atlantic solo yachtsman, has also sailed four times to Antarctic waters. He was prominent in New Zealand mountains in his student days. Colin Monteath is another New Zealander who seems to have climbed almost everywhere. He works as a freelance guide on Antarctic peaks and on polar ship voyages; he writes well and is an accomplished photographer.

The Alps have had many visitors and several New Zealanders have climbed in the old Soviet Union since the days when George Lowe was there in 1962 with John Hunt. At about that time George also climbed in Greenland and in Ethiopia.

The *New Zealand Alpine Journal* of 1988 stated that fifteen expeditions went overseas in that year. For many other years the number has been about ten, which is astonishing for a country of only 3.5 million people and where sponsoring firms are small in both number and size.

A brief summary of New Zealand mountaineering must include a paragraph on Paddy Freaney. He arrived here in 1969 after eleven years in the SAS. He has been involved in outdoor education as a career, mixing it with numerous mountain exploits. He climbed Ama Dablam and went very high on two Everest expeditions. With Russell Brice, he climbed in one season all 27 of the local peaks over 10,000ft. These facts are not well known to the general public, though his claim to have seen a moa, a bird believed to have been extinct for 400 years, made him headline news for several weeks.

Both men and women have been climbing in New Zealand for more than a century. Although the New Zealand Alpine Club has always admitted women as members, the Christchurch-based Canterbury Mountaineering Club barred them from membership until 12 years ago. But now the latter club is booming since its change in the rules. In recent years women have been climbing big-face routes, are leading overseas expeditions and are scientists and technical assistants for Antarctic parties. In February 1893 New Zealand women were given voting rights in parliamentary elections (a world first). To celebrate the centenary of this breakthrough, there was a 'Summits for Suffrage' week in February 1993. 4000 women reached summits, even if these were sometimes just local hills. But four women stood on top of the still crumbling Mt Cook.

Forty fascinating years have passed since 1953. May the next forty be just as good.

HARISH KAPADIA
The Himalayan Mountaineering Institute Darjeeling

The foundation stone of the Institute was laid by
Shri Jawharlal Nehru on 4 November 1954

(Plate 87)

We sat around a roaring campfire. Raymond Lambert was visiting Sikkim as a special guest of Tenzing Norgay, and we, the students of the basic training course of the Himalayan Mountaineering Institute, were entertaining the guests in exchange for superb Scotch whisky. The Indian pre-Everest expedition was also there. Students and Sherpas mingled with leading mountaineers of India, taking in the ambience of food and fun. As the fire turned to embers, the night passed into memory; but the bonds of friendship forged on that evening back in 1964 have lasted me a lifetime.

This would probably be the experience of many students of the Himalayan Mountaineering Institute (HMI). The training for the basic or advanced courses lasts for about 35 days and includes lectures on many aspects of mountaineering, trekking to the base camp and learning various skills. Adventure courses for young people aged between 12 and 17 are also available. To round everything off there is a 'graduation ceremony' at which a specially invited guest presents a badge and a certificate to each successful student. Like the question 'What do you do after climbing Everest?', it is important to ask what you do after completing your course at HMI.

For me, the HMI provided far more than physical training alone. Meeting famous Sherpas, hearing their stories and being exposed to the world of mountains has had a lasting spiritual effect on my life.

When Tenzing Norgay and Edmund Hillary climbed Everest in 1953 the whole of India was in raptures. To commemorate that historic event, India's then Prime Minister, Jawaharlal Nehru, agreed to create this Institute. Nehru realised the great potential of the Himalaya as a training ground for Indian youth to help turn them into self-reliant, disciplined and courageous citizens. He said: 'There will be no lack of adventures of the mind and body for those who are prepared to venture into uncharted seas and climb unknown peaks.' With advice from Arnold Glatthard, Principal of the Swiss Mountaineering School, Tenzing Norgay chose Darjeeling, home of the Sherpas, to become the home of the HMI. The Institute was sited on the western spur of Darjeeling where it commands a panoramic view of Kangchenjunga and its famous range. Dzongri in

Sikkim was selected as the training ground, and Nandu Jayal, one of the foremost mountaineers of the time, became the first Principal, with Tenzing Norgay as the first Director of Field Training. Jayal and Norgay, along with six experienced Sherpas, were sent to Switzerland for training, and by the winter of 1954 HMI was ready to receive its first students. The list of instructors included veterans like Angtharkay and the youngest of the lot, Nawang Gombu. Others were Topgay, Gyalzen, Ang Temba and Da Namgyal. Between them they were the living history of Himalayan mountaineering.

For many years Tenzing Norgay remained the most powerful influence on the HMI. With his Tibetan dogs, he accompanied most of the courses and took a keen interest in the training programmes. Without him the HMI might not have made such a flying start. But despite international recognition after climbing Everest, Tenzing remained a simple Sherpa at heart. He was the rallying point for the Sherpa community, who looked upon him as their leader; he acted as the father figure of the HMI until his death in 1986.

Today, the Institute carries on basically the same type of courses in the same area. The advanced course climbs a high peak (around 6000m) as part of the training. The HMI has a well-stocked library and a museum, and the courses are highly subsidised by the government. But it is always the men who make an institution, and the HMI has seen many famous names on its rolls. Nawang Gombu, Tenzing's successor, has climbed Everest twice and is one of the most celebrated Sherpas today. I cherish the talks I had with Sherpa Wangdi during my course, way back in 1964. He talked about his first ascent of Jannu with Lionel Terray, and about climbing on Makalu and a near-death experience with the Swiss on Kedarnath. On that course, we had famous instructors like Ang Temba, Da Namgyal, who almost climbed Everest in 1953, and Gyalzen who had climbed many mountains. By their mere presence and talk, this great band of Sherpas conveyed the benefits of their experience to young students like us and this was another major attraction of the course. We were able to lay the foundations for a life-long climbing passion.

Sadly, there have been losses, and some of the instructors who joined climbing expeditions have lost their lives. Ang Kami, who, in 1965, was the youngest to have climbed Everest, joined my expedition to Bethartoli Himal in 1970. He was a well-loved instructor at the HMI and charm personified. Perched in a high camp on the mountain, we discussed many aspects of Darjeeling, the HMI and Sherpa life. Little did I know that the next morning Ang Kami would be killed in an avalanche. The entire Sherpa community was plunged in gloom. This was perhaps the worst jolt to the HMI. Earlier, its first Principal, Nandu Jayal, was delayed on his way to Cho Oyu after finishing a course. He double-marched to catch up with the main team and died of pulmonary oedema; not much was known about this disease in the 1950s. Phu Dorje, another instructor at the HMI, slipped on Nanda Devi East and was killed instantly. And in 1993, Lopsang, one of the most charming personalities of the HMI, was killed on Everest.

Age and time have also taken their toll of many senior and well-known Sherpas; many have passed away, including Pasang Temba, Nawang Phenjo and Chewang Tashi.

But the HMI continues to be active and energetic. In addition to Nawang Gombu, the present Director of Field Training, there are two deputies, Dorjee Lhatoo and Nima Tashi. Both have excellent climbing records and a high calibre of technical expertise. Lhatoo has climbed Everest and kept himself abreast of the latest technical developments. He has also climbed Chomolhari, Nanda Devi and other peaks. From his regular contacts with the world climbing scene, he is well placed to keep the HMI updated. Among the younger instructors are Pasang Namgyal, Nima Norbu and others. All of them will help to keep the HMI in the forefront of the Indian climbing scene.

The Principal of the Institute looks after the administrative aspects and generally controls the HMI. Some well-known personalities have occupied this chair: Col B S Jaswal, Col N Kumar, Brig D K Khullar and Col Amit Roy, amongst others. All of them have contributed to the growth of the Institute in large measure. The present Principal, Col Ajit K Dutt, has been guiding the Institute for the past three years.

No institute worth its name would be without its critics, and the HMI also has its share. There are those who believe that it needs to revise its courses and regularly update the training schedule. What was good four decades ago, they say, may not be useful for the future. And there is concern that many Sherpas who retired after a long tenure of service to the HMI (Da Namgyal and Gyalzen, for example) received no help from the government and were reduced to selling sweaters in the streets of Darjeeling for their meagre needs. It is also felt that the HMI should look into the future, particularly as the traditional role of Sherpas as instructors is now changing. These are the views of well-meaning people who have the good of the HMI at heart, and the Institute can learn from them.

The HMI has played a wider role in developing the entire Indian climbing scene. It sends out instructors all over the country to train youth for rock-climbing nearer their homes. The first and the longest of such a series of courses was held around Bombay, and I know of many climbers there who have enormously benefited from their interaction with the Sherpa instructors. The HMI instructors have participated in various national and international events and the Institute has held mountaineering conferences. Also, literally millions of tourists have visited the HMI and its museum and have come to know something about the Himalaya through their visits. In the future, there is an abiding and fruitful role to be played by the Institute, with its experience, maturity and a young generation of instructors. Life, as they say, begins at forty, and the HMI will continue to fulfil its famous motto: 'May You Climb From Peak To Peak.'

EVELIO ECHEVARRÍA

Pioneers of the Paine: A Supplement

In the 1992 volume of this Journal Sir Edward Peck made a valuable contribution to the exploratory and climbing history of the Paine massif in southern Chile.[1] These brief notes are offered as a complement to that article.

The name Paine originated in Argentina and is therefore not local. The Cerros Paine are a range of lesser hills located in southern Argentina and the name, in the original Tehuelche language, meant 'blue' or 'light blue'. Argentine armymen, hunting for fleeing Indians, somehow decided that the Chilean rock and ice massif bore a resemblance to the lower hillocks of their country and gave it the same name.[2] This probably happened around 1880. The border controversy between Chile and Argentina that began around 1885 was solved when both nations agreed that their common borderline should run over the highest summits that form the continental watershed. Between 1896 and 1910 *comisiones de limites* (boundary commissions) were specially created to establish exactly where this boundary would run. Their work represented the first attempt to map the Andes running from parallel 22° to 55° S.

The Chilean commission was headed by the remarkable mathematician/engineer Luis Riso Patrón, who can justly be called the main mountain explorer in South America. He led the mapping of the entire length of the Chilean Andes from southern Peru to Cape Horn. In the course of their task, the members of the commission climbed many peaks, baptised even more and placed iron landmarks on the international border passes. Riso Patrón and his crew erected, along the Chilean Andes, a total of 488 two-metre-high iron landmarks, which are still there.

It was Riso Patrón and his second-in-command engineer Alvaro Donoso who measured the Paine. In a preliminary survey (1902) the Chilean surveyors established a height of 2734m for the highest point in the massif. In the first national chart of 1910 and its reprints of 1928 and 1945, as well as in his excellent *Diccionario Jeográfico de Chile* (1924), Riso Patrón quoted a corrected figure of only 2670m for the highest point and much lower ones for the other peaks of the massif. Low as that figure may appear, it was accepted unhesitatingly by Father Alberto de Agostini and by Dr Federico Reichert who were the two principal explorers of Patagonia before the 1950s.[3]

Why modern climbers insist on a figure of 3050m is something I have been unable to determine. Perhaps it originated with the French glaciologist Louis Lliboutry in his book *Nieves y glaciares de Chile* (1956),[4] where he stated that he was quoting this height because it so appeared on the maps of the Chilean Boundary Commission. But none of these maps in fact quoted a

Paine height above 2734m. The official Chilean chart of the Instituto Geográfico Militar cited (in 1966 and 1970) only 2730m. During the last few years the Instituto, the major geographical authority in the country, has undertaken the resurvey of the entire country at a scale of 1:100,000 and 1:25,000, and we will have to await their results concerning the Paine district. However, there should not be too much optimism, since nearly all the heights recently produced by that institution have closely confirmed the old figures that Riso Patrón's men obtained almost a century ago.[5]

It is my opinion, therefore, that when the new surveys have been completed by the Instituto Geográfico Militar de Chile, all Paine heights will be below 2750m. Moreover the lesser peaks, horns and towers of the massif will have to be lowered accordingly, since their heights have generally been obtained by estimates based on the former 3050m for Paine Grande.

Additional pioneer climbing and related events in the Paine area, to complement those quoted in AJ97, can be briefly summarised as follows:

1938, 8 March
The Club Andino de Chile, section Punta Arenas (capital of Patagonia, population 58,000) was founded.[6]

1947, December
Two members of the Club, José Floegel and Henning Willumsen, climbed the two highest points in the Cordón (chain) Barros Arana, 2250m. Willumsen, a Chilean of Danish ancestry, was instrumental in developing skiing, hiking and national parks in southernmost Chile.[6]

1954, January
An expedition of the Club Andino Bariloche, Argentina, attempted Cerro Paine, losing two men in an avalanche. Two others ascended Paine Medio, 2460m. This massive peak had been ascended in 1937 by the Bavarians Zuck and Teufel and was subsequently repeated by Chileans and Czechs.[7, 10]

1955, January
The subsidiary southern and central peaks of Paine were ascended by a Chilean team under Eduardo Meyer. The Chileans named the former peak 'Punta Bariloche' to honour the two Argentines who had perished the previous year.[8]

1968, January
Two Italians climbed El Escudo (shield), probably 2400m. A Chilean group of four, led by Eduardo García, a veteran instrumental in organising Eric Shipton's expeditions to Patagonia and Tierra del Fuego, climbed the Cuerno Principal del Paine (probably 2100m).[10]

1969, January
The strikingly difficult peak called by climbers Paine Norte was ascended by a strong Japanese party under Yoshimasa Takeuchi. Three Japanese also climbed Cerro 2265m, highest in the Cordón Olguín.[9, 10]

During and after the seventies came several daring new routes and at least one important first ascent, that of Cuerno Norte (c2000m) by South Africans. As late as January 1991 a French expedition made the first ascent of the Peineta (comb), also called Nido Negro de Cóndores (black nest of the condors), the spiky north tower attached to the Torre Norte.

Of all the mountain names that climbers mention in their reports, only Paine, Torres and Cuernos, Cordón Olguín and Cordón Barros Arana are official. The Instituto Geográfico Militar de Chile has refused to sanction any name so far imposed by climbers. There is no doubt that the poor quality of the names chosen by climbing expeditions in Patagonia and Tierra del Fuego has prompted that institution to remain firm in its decision.

REFERENCES AND BIBLIOGRAPHY

1 Edward Peck, 'Pioneers of the Paine', in *AJ97*, 222-225, 1992/93.
2 Araucanian mythology says that a part of Paine is actually the petri-fied body of chieftain Huincamal, killed, like so many inhabitants of their land, in a giant deluge. Rock peaks, peaklets and crags are called by them *huintralcún* and represent the many warriors that perished in that universal disaster.
3 Alvaro Donoso, *Demarcación de la línea de la frontera en la parte sur del territorio*. Imprenta Cervantes (Santiago) 1906. Luis Riso Patrón, *Diccionario Jeográfico de Chile*. Imprenta Universitaria (Santiago) 1924.
4 Louis Lliboutry, *Nieves y glaciares de Chile*. Editorial Universitaria (Santiago), 402, 1956.
5 The cherished figures of over 7000m for Aconcagua were always contested by Riso Patrón (and by the famous alpinist Paul Güssfeldt) as early as 1896, since Patrón had obtained a height of only 6960m (and Güssfeldt, 6970m) for that mountain. When the Argentine engineer Eduardo Baglietto finally resolved the controversy in 1959, he determined a final height for Aconcagua of only 6959.7m.
6 *Revista Andina 62* (1948) was wholly devoted to the mountain sports of the Punta Arenas district.
7 Vojko Arko, *Un pionero de Bariloche: Otto Meiling*. Imprenta Bavaria (Bariloche, Argentina), 70-90, 1991.
8 Luis Krahl, 'Primera expedición chilena a los Andes patagónicos', in *Revista Andina 81*, 5-9, 1955.
9 Eduardo García, 'Expedición universitaria a los Cuernos del Paine' in *Anuario de Montaña*. Federación de Andinismo de Chile, 72-77, 1972.
10 In general, the following publications provide good coverage of activity in the Paine area:
   Gastón San Román, *Historia del andinismo en Chile*, Imprenta Quickprint Ltda (Santiaga) 1989.
   Mountain 16, 11-22, 1971.
   Club Andino Bariloche, *Anuario* 1955 and 1956.
   American Alpine Journal, section 'Climbs and Expeditions', 1955 to date.

C A RUSSELL

One Hundred Years Ago

(with extracts from the *Alpine Journal*)

(*Plates 81-84*)

From the visitors' point of view the season has been charming. The snow came early and stayed long. This in itself was a complete contrast to last year, when it refused to put in an appearance before the end of January, and had almost melted by the middle of March. The only fault we have to complain of this year is that the snow has been too persistent in its kind attentions, and has, on the average, generously visited us once a week since November. In consequence of this the tobogganing has been extraordinarily good, and the far-famed "Cresta Run", which is composed entirely of ice, has been open for a longer period, and has been used by a greater number of visitors than in any preceding year.

The frequent snowfalls experienced in the Engadine and many other parts of the Alps during the early months of 1894 did not deter the climbing parties staying at the principal centres and several new expeditions were completed. On 13 January in perfect weather Sydney Spencer, accompanied by Christian Jossi and Adolf Schaller, made the first winter ascent of the Dom. After climbing for several hours through deep snow from the Dom hut to the Festijoch the party followed the NW ridge to the summit where a wonderful view was enjoyed in clear but intensely cold conditions. The descent to the hut was completed by moonlight and on the following day the party returned to Zermatt where Spencer, to his embarrassment, was serenaded by the village band. Another notable achievement, on 27 March, was that of Charles Simon who with Alexander Burgener and Alois Pollinger succeeded in making the first ascent under winter conditions of the NE, Hörnli ridge of the Matterhorn. The day was 'warm and wind free. On the shoulder the steps cut the preceding summer were quite visible and much facilitated the ascent.'

In contrast to the magnificent conditions of the previous year the weather was cold and unsettled for much of the climbing season. Severe storms and long periods of rain affected many regions and most expeditions were completed during occasional fine spells of limited duration. In the Mont Blanc range the Montenvers Hotel was again the principal base for a number of outstanding climbs. On 2 August A F Mummery, J N Collie and Geoffrey Hastings arrived in Courmayeur having crossed the range from the Argentière glacier by way of the very steep approach to the Col des Courtes – the first occasion on which this route had been taken – and the Col de Triolet. Three days later, from a camp on the Brenva glacier, Mummery and his companions set out to climb the Brenva ridge route on Mont Blanc. After crossing the famous ice ridge à *cheval* and cutting steps for several hours they reached the séracs at the top of the climb too late in the day to continue and descended to pass an uncomfortable night near a rock buttress on the lower section of the route. Addressing the Alpine Club in the following year Hastings described the bivouac site.

> The place we had chosen for the night was sheltered on one side by an overhanging crag; and when we had scraped off the snow from a big stone on the terrace below, we found there was sufficient room for the three of us to sit, and we proceeded to make ourselves as comfortable as our circumstances would allow. The rock we were sitting on did not afford comfortable seats. We could not even sit in a row; we formed three faces of a square, the centre man with his back to the rock. We thought there would be less chance of our feet being frostbitten if we put them into the rücksack, which was a large size and windproof. Now, this gave a very comfortable position to the middle man, but was an extremely irksome one for each of the outside men. Mummery's feet would only just reach into the rücksack, and required a great deal of attention to keep them there; on the other side, when I swung round and put my feet into the sack, I had, to prevent myself sliding off the rock, to embrace Collie by the waist, or prop myself by an outstretched arm against the wall behind.

On 6 August after reclimbing the ridge and forcing a way through the séracs the party completed the sixth, and first guideless, ascent of the route. J P Farrar, who in the previous year had made the fifth ascent, later wrote that 'this was the greatest of this famous party's ice-climbs in the Alps. No finer exhibition of determination and skill has ever been given by any amateur party.'

After returning to the Montenvers to enjoy 'an eternity of breakfast and an everlasting afternoon tea'[1] Mummery, Collie and Hastings completed another fine expedition on 11 August by making the second ascent of the Moine ridge on the Aiguille Verte, a route which they had believed to be unclimbed.[2]

Mummery then moved to Zermatt and on 27 August, accompanied by the Duke of the Abruzzi and Collie and under the lead of 'young Pollinger' – the great guide Josef Pollinger of St Niklaus – made the third ascent of the NW, Zmutt ridge of the Matterhorn, the scene of his celebrated first ascent 15 years earlier.

On 31 August three strong parties were in action on the Zmutt ridge:

Miss Lily Bristow accompanied by Josef Pollinger and Mattias Zurbriggen traversed the peak, ascending the Hörnli ridge and descending the Zmutt route; Paul Güssfeldt with Emile Rey completed the traverse in the reverse direction; and Farrar with Daniel Maquignaz climbed the Zmutt ridge, descending by the same route. Miss Bristow, who had climbed with Mummery's party during the previous season, achieved by a narrow margin the distinction of making the first descent of the Zmutt ridge, Farrar having completed his descent later in the day.

Although conditions were far from ideal several expeditions of note were completed by other parties during the occasional spells of fine weather. In the Arolla district the S peak of the Bouquetins, which had been attempted on many occasions, was finally reached on 18 July by A G Topham with Jean Maître and Pierre Maurys. A month later, on 18 August, the first ascent of the SW ridge of L'Evêque was completed by R A Robertson with Howard, Edmund and Miss Agnes Barrett and the guides Joseph Quinodoz and Alois Templ. Elsewhere in the Pennine Alps E F M Benecke and H A Cohen reached the summit of Mont Gelé by way of the unclimbed SE ridge on 16 July and five days later made the first recorded ascent of the Combin de Tsessette, at the E end of the Grand Combin massif. On 20 September the first ascent of the NNW ridge of the Hohberghorn, above the Hohbergjoch, was completed by F W Oliver with Alexander Burgener and Albert Supersaxo.

In the Graian Alps two ridges were ascended for the first time: the SW ridge of the Torre del Gran San Pietro, the highest point of the Apostoli group, on 19 August by P E Lord and George Yeld with François and Sylvain Pession; and the NW ridge of Ciarforon on 29 August by the guideless party of Orazio de Falkner and D Escoffier. In the Bernese Oberland on 5 July W A B Coolidge and Walter Larden, with Christian Almer junior and Rudolf Almer, made the first recorded ascent of the upper section of the WNW ridge of the Aletschhorn. Further east, in the Dolomites, W L Brodie with Giuseppe Zecchini reached the summit of Cima di Canali on 13 July after completing a new route on the NW face.

The principal undertaking of the season was W M Conway's journey through the Alps 'from end to end'. Conway, whose account[3] of his expedition to the Karakoram two years earlier had been widely acclaimed, explained[4] that it had occurred to him

> that it was now possible, taking the whole range of the Alps, to devise a route, or rather a combination of climbs, the descent from each ending at the starting-point for the next, so that a climber might begin at one extremity of the snowy range and walk up and down through its midst to the other extremity over a continuous series of peaks and passes. The Alps, of course, though spoken of as a range, are not a single line of peaks, but a series of locally parallel ridges covering a region. There is no continuous Alpine ridge stretching from one end of the region to the other.

The route selected had to be capable of execution within three months of average weather, which is a mixture of good and bad, with the bad predominating. It was also essential that it should lead as continuously as possible through snowy regions and that it should traverse as many of the more interesting and well-known groups as possible.

Although as Coolidge noted 'the weather was far below the average' and plans for a number of climbs including a traverse of the Matterhorn had to be abandoned, the journey, which began at the Colle di Tenda in the Maritime Alps and ended on the Ankogel to the east of the Grossglockner, was a considerable success. Accompanied throughout by two of the Gurkhas who had taken part in the Karakoram expedition and, for varying periods, by E A FitzGerald and the guides J B Aymonod, Louis Carrel and Mattias Zurbriggen, Conway covered on foot a distance of some 1600km in the course of 65 days on the march. During this time the party climbed or traversed 21 peaks, including Monte Viso, Mont Blanc, the Nordend of Monte Rosa, the Jungfrau and the Grossglockner, and 39 passes. On 27 June Conway and his party reached the summit of Mont Blanc – the first ascent of the season – where they were able to evade the wind by sheltering behind the observatory which had been erected for Dr Jules Janssen during the previous summer.

The panorama was complete and included the Pennine and Oberland ranges besides those we had already seen. It was however the clouds that fascinated us most, the flocks of little ones on the hills at our feet and the lines of soft white billows as it were breaking far away on a wide and shallow shore, with blue between and beneath them. The sky for a quarter of its height had parted with its azure to the valley-deeps and was striped all round with finest lines, incredibly numerous, like the lines in a wide-stretched solar spectrum, and each edging a new grade of tone.

Two weeks later, on 12 July, when approaching Monte Rosa, Conway was surprised to notice a large number of mule footprints but soon discovered that the animals were engaged in transporting materials across the Gorner glacier for the Monte Rosa, or Bétemps, hut which was then in course of construction.

The experiences of Conway and his companions, who at one stage were treated as probable spies and on another occasion were surrounded by hundreds of sheep urged by a longing for salt, aroused great interest. Four years earlier Conway had initiated one of the great debates of the time in climbing circles by attacking 'centrism' – the practice of climbing habitually in the immediate neighbourhood of a chosen centre. His journey through the Alps represented a further protest against the practice and provided an opportunity to demonstrate his own style of 'excentric' wandering through different mountain regions.

In Norway, where snow conditions were excellent throughout the summer, many parties were active in Jotunheimen and the other principal areas. Store Skagastølstind (2403m), the peak first climbed by W C Slingsby 18 years earlier, was ascended by ladies on three consecutive days, the honour of making the first ascent by a lady falling to frøken Therese Bertheau on 30 July. In August Slingsby returned to the Jostedalsbreen region where he carried out further exploration and crossed a number of passes.

In July F W Newmarch and G A Solly, again without guides, returned to the Caucasus accompanied on this occasion by Joseph Collier. Although the weather was, if anything, worse than that experienced in the previous year they climbed peaks to the south of the central region and made another attempt to ascend the S, higher peak of Ushba (4710m), reaching an estimated height of 3650m before being forced to retreat.

In the Pamir region Sven Hedin, the Swedish explorer, made several determined attempts to climb Muztagh Ata (7546m) in the Kashgar range. On 6 August, assisted by a number of Kirghiz nomads and several excellent yaks, Hedin reached a height of some 6150m before conceding defeat.

In New Zealand exploration of the Southern Alps continued and many notable expeditions were completed. Several peaks were climbed for the first time: Mount De la Bêche (2994m) on 17 February by T C Fyfe and George Graham; Malte Brun (3159m) by Fyfe, solo, on 7 March; and Mount Darwin (2913m) on 22 March by Franz Kronecker, with Fyfe and J M Clarke. Later in the year, on Christmas Day, Clarke, Fyfe and Graham made the first complete ascent[5] of Mount Cook or Aorangi (3764m), reaching the summit by way of the Hooker glacier, Green Saddle and the N ridge, a climb still regarded as a serious undertaking, after exploring the western approaches to the peak.

In the Canadian Rockies the guideless party of S E S Allen, L F Frissell and W D Wilcox reached the summit of the unclimbed Mount Aberdeen (3151m), then known as Hazel Peak, on 17 August and on the following day made the first ascent of Mount Temple (3543m) – the first peak in Canada exceeding 3350m (11,000ft) to be climbed – by way of Sentinel Pass and the SW face.

Further south, in Oregon, a well-known club was formed on 19 July when the Mazamas[6] were organised on the summit of Mount Hood (3421m) after 155 men and 38 ladies had ascended the peak despite a storm early in the day. The objects of the club included 'the exploration of snow-peaks and other mountains, especially those of the Pacific Northwest'; to qualify for membership it was necessary to have 'climbed to the summit of a snow-peak on which there is at least one living glacier, and the top of which cannot be reached by any other means than on foot.'

In Britain the development of climbing continued apace with many strong parties in the field. During the year Aleister Crowley, accompanied on two occasions by his cousin Gregor Grant, completed a number of routes on the chalk of Beachy Head. In Wales J M Archer Thomson began his exploration of the mountains of Snowdonia, completing two new routes on Lliwedd: the Intermediate with H Hughes and H Edwards in October; and the Bilberry Terrace with Edwards and H R Smith in December. On 25 November Archer Thomson turned his attention to Glyder Fawr, leading Hughes and Edwards during the first ascent of Central Gully. In the Lake District a new route on the Napes Needle, the Arête, was climbed by W H Fowler on 17 September and in Scotland Collie, Collier and Solly completed two outstanding climbs: in Glencoe on 24 March the first recorded ascent of the SE face of Stob Dearg, Buachaille Etive Mor; and on 29 March the first complete ascent [7] and the first ascent under winter conditions of Tower Ridge on Ben Nevis.

An event of great importance was the publication of the first volume, dealing with England, of *Climbing in the British Isles*, the famous guide-book written by W P Haskett Smith and illustrated by Ellis Carr. The work[8] was well received and was reviewed in the *Alpine Journal* where it was considered to mark 'a distinct epoch in British holiday-making. It admits publicly, if not proudly, that there is a class of travellers who "climb for climbing's sake." '

The guidebook, which was soon in demand, aroused considerable interest.

> There is an idea in regard to the pursuit of mountaineering that it is necessary to go abroad to break one's neck – to the Alps, to the Caucasus. Of course that is a mistake. How much of a mistake, however, I did not altogether realise until I talked yesterday with Mr W P Haskett Smith, a well-known mountaineer and member of the Alpine Club. He is preparing a series of little books on "Climbing in the British Isles", which Messrs Longmans and Co will publish.
> "Altogether, considering our size as an island, we are not so badly off for mountaineering facilities?"
> "Not by any means. Before ever he goes to the Alps, a man can by practice at home have grown into a by no means contempt-ible mountaineer."
> "How does mountain climbing as a malady – forgive me so putting it – generally take a man?"
> "Oh, it's inborn, or he goes to Switzerland and catches it, or he gets it by contagion from a friend who is already a climber. If he has not opportunity to repeat his first sweet impressions of the mountains for a year or two he may forget them, and after all miss becoming a mountaineer. But let him repeat the experience within a reasonable time and the malady becomes permanent, and the man is a mountain climber as long as his legs will carry him."
> Even to interview Mr Haskett Smith is to run the risk of catching the mountaineering fever, so I thought I had better come away.

A malady for which, fortunately, there is as yet no cure.

REFERENCES

1   A F Mummery, *My Climbs in the Alps and Caucasus*. London,
    T Fisher Unwin, 1895.

2   The first ascent had been made by G C Hodgkinson, the Rev Charles
    Hudson and T S Kennedy with Michel Croz, M A Ducroz and Peter
    Perren on 5 July 1865.

3   W M Conway, *Climbing and Exploration in the Karakoram-Himalayas*.
    London, T Fisher Unwin, 1894.

4   Sir W M Conway, *The Alps from End to End*. Westminster,
    Archibald Constable and Co, 1895.

5   A point close to the summit had been reached from the Linda glacier
    by the Rev W S Green with Ulrich Kaufmann and Emil Boss on
    2 March 1882.

6   Derived from the Spanish name of the mountain goat 'which makes
    its home among the glaciers and pinnacles of the cordillera of
    Western America'.

7   The ridge had been ascended to the foot of the Great Tower by John,
    Edward and Bertram Hopkinson on 3 September 1892.

8   W P Haskett Smith, MA, *Climbing in the British Isles. I. England*.
    London, Longmans, Green, and Co, 1894. (*Editor's note: a facsimile
    edition, bound with Vol II, was published by the Ernest Press in 1986*.)

Area Notes 1993

COMPILED BY ROY RUDDLE

The Alps	*Lindsay Griffin*
Tibet and China	*Józef Nyka*
Bhutan	*Józef Nyka*
India	*Harish Kapadia*
Nepal	*Bill O'Connor*
Pakistan	*Paul Nunn*
Central Asia	*Józef Nyka*
North America	*H Adams Carter*
South America	*David Sharman*
Middle East	*Tony Howard*
New Zealand	*Richard Thompson*

LINDSAY GRIFFIN

The Alps and Pyrenees 1993

In preparing these notes Lindsay Griffin would like to acknowledge the assistance of Patrick Gabarrou, Alison Hargreaves, Mireille Lazarevitch, Neil McAdie, Giuseppe Miotti, Brendan Murphy, Michel Piola, Andres Lietha, Simon Richardson, Ian Roper, Franci Savenc, Pierre Tardivel, John Sumner, Dick Turnbull and Dave Wilkinson. He would welcome further information and any new route descriptions for publication in these pages at: 2 Top Sling, Tregarth, Bangor, Gwynedd LL57 4RL.

The year saw AC members involved in several important winter ascents, a continuous crossing of all the 4000m peaks in the Alps, plus a fine series of first woman solo ascents. It also saw the demise of two outstanding continental activists: Romain Vogler, one of the greatest Swiss Alpine rock-climbers and full-time guide, died at the age of 34 in a rappelling accident on a crag at Maladière. It appears that he was making a long rappel and had not set the ropes equally, his weight coming on to a single strand as he neared the bottom. In May Fred Vimal, France's most promising young Alpinist, was killed whilst trying to solo a hard mixed free/aid route on the Grand Capucin. He was held by his ropes after a 20m fall, but appears to have hit his head and probably died of hypothermia.

THE WINTER SEASON

The official season spans the period from 21 December–20 March inclusive and hence events taking place in December 1992 have been noted.

Pyrenees

Winter conditions in the Pyrenees were exceptionally good this year, with stable weather keeping enough snow and ice on the routes, whilst leaving the approaches well consolidated and relatively safe from objective danger.

In the Cirque de Gavarnie, one of the best known venues for water-ice climbing in Europe, ideal conditions allowed the opening up of the upper, shorter tier. Many worthwhile new routes in the 4/5 catagory were created during January.

Pic du Midi d'Ossau This dramatic mountain offers numerous rock climbs, with several well-established classics that compare in quality with anything else in the range. The heavy buildup of ice during the winter allowed two new routes to be created in the area of the *Classic 1896 route* on the N face. On 19 January Benoit Dandonneau and Juna Carles Griso started up the *Classic route*, then moved left to reach a series of narrow runnels. These gave pitches of 70°- 80° and led straight up to a hard mixed exit (5+) onto the left end of a prominent easy ramp leading to the NE ridge.

NE ridge On 21 January Didier Berger and Remi Thivel, followed by Dominique Perrin and Rainer Munch, climbed a direct start (80°/5+) and continued to the summit, giving the route the name *Ya du Grisou dans l'Tempo* and a grade of TD+. On 18 March Thivel returned alone and climbed a parallel line about 100m to the right. Crossing the *Classic* after about 250m of climbing, the route swings left near the top to finish up the last 75° ice pitch of *Ya du Grisou*. Christened *Canaleta Santa Coloma* and graded TD+/ED1, the route was sustained at 55°-70° with plenty of icy rock from 3 to 5+.

The *Ravier route* on the SW face was soloed for the first time in winter on 20 January by Remi Thivel. The first 400m is a snowy 45° couloir and the final, 250-300m buttress is a TD rock climb.

The first solo winter ascent of the complete N spur of the **Grand Pic (Pt de France, 2878m)** was made from 17-19 March by Joan Jover. Despite sections of poor rock, it is now considered one of the best and certainly the longest route on the Ossau. In recent times the route has been climbed completely free at 5+/6a.

Pena Talera This major peak lies entirely in Spain and has a N face that gives excellent winter possibilities. On 23 January, Javier Alonso and Roman Bascunana climbed the 250m high gully immediately right of the prominent *Y Couloir*. The crux was a 70m icefall which steepened to the vertical and an overall grade of D+ was proposed. Just to the north the modern ski complex of Formigal offers numerous first-class icefalls close to the resort.

Cirque de Gourette At the beginning of January an impressive narrow couloir on the E Face of the **Pene Medan** received its first ascent, and was repeated several days later. It is 500m and graded TD, with ice pitches of 80° and some mixed climbing (moves of V on rock).

Vignemale: the N face – the biggest rock wall in the Pyrenees – is an obvious goal for Alpinists during the winter season. The rarely climbed *Y Couloir*, that branches left from the *Couloir de Gaube* at one third height, received at least six ascents during the winter. All the parties were able to climb the bed of the couloir directly, following a line inaugurated some years ago by Serge Casteran which features sections of vertical ice and rock steps of V+ (600m TD+/ED1).

One of the most impressive achievements throughout the Pyrenees occurred on 28-29 January, when French Alpinist Remy Thivel made the highly sought-after first solo winter ascent of the N spur on **Pique Longue**.

Another notable first winter and first solo ascent on this wall was made from 7-9 March when Jerome Thinière climbed the 1964 N dièdre (500m and nowadays largely free at 6b+, with one section of A2/3 in friable cracks). Earlier, Thinière soloed the classic N face of the **Piton Carré** (the *Ravier brothers' route*) in a day.

Tour de Marboré After fixing the first (and most difficult) couple of pitches on 28 January Javier Olivar made the first solo winter ascent of the classic N Face on 29th-30th. The face was icy and the crux pitches were climbed on aid.

Troumouse On the N face of the highest peak, commonly known as the **Pic de la Munia (3085m)**, Patrick Gabarrou and Pascal Girault put up a new direct route (TD).

Ernest Blade and Nestor Bohigas made a winter ascent of the classic *Ravier route* on the **Pic Blanc de Troumouse**: although a rock climb in summer, the pair front-pointed the whole route except for a mere 20m of mixed ground, and offer the new winter grade of V/5.

Monte Perdido (Ordesa National Park). A new *Direct route* on the N face was climbed by Patrick Gabarrou and Pascal Girault on 19 March and was only possible owing to the considerable glacial recession over the years and the subsequent diminished height of the two principal sérac barriers. Currently there is talk of a proposal to limit the number of climbers visiting this region at any one time.

Pic de l'Esquella The unusually good snow conditions on the Andorran border peaks saw enough buildup of ice for the lower section of the unclimbed narrow right-hand couloir on the 200m N face to be attempted. An initial pitch of 70° was followed by a 25m pillar of ice steepening to the vertical. Above, the angle eased giving 55°-65° snow/ice to the summit. Christened the *Henar Couloir*, the first ascent was made by Albert Querol climbing solo.

Ecrins

In common with the Mont Blanc range, activity here during the season was intense, with such routes as the famous and rarely climbed *Raie des Fesses* on the N face of the **Pic Sans Nom**, one of the hardest ice-climbs in the range, receiving at least a dozen ascents.

L'Olan In this very wild corner of the range, Lionel Daudet made the first solo winter ascent of the *Bouilloux/Villemare Directissima* on the NW face from 18-19 March. Daudet finished via the variation taken by Jean Marc Cambon and Bernard Francou in 1981. Despite the season and orientation of the wall, the harder pitches were climbed free at 6c.

Christophe Moulin reached the summit of **La Meije** on Christmas Eve having made the second winter ascent of the 1962 *Girel-Renaud Direct route* (ED2 VI/mixed), and then travelled (on foot and ski) to the base of the 1100m NW face of **L'Ailefroide**, where he was able to spend a prearranged night inside a tent with a group of friends. After a further three full days and two cold bivouacs he completed the first solo winter ascent of the classic 1936 *Devies-Gervasutti route* (ED1 VI).

Dome de Neige des Ecrins At least three winter ascents were reported of the narrow *Boivin/Diaferia/Vionet-Fuasset couloir* on the W face, first climbed in 1979 and thought to be at least ED2 in standard.

Pic Sans Nom On the right side of the N face the *Pilier de Souvenir*, a hard and rarely repeated rock route put up in 1980 by Pierre Farges and the late Vincent Fine (and later soloed by Farges), was climbed for the first time in winter from 6-13 January (including time spent on the approach) by E Fine and O Laborie.

Les Bans On the popular summer rock-climbing arena of the SE face, Gerard Lepreux and Pierre Teyssier made a winter ascent of the *GUM route* (Bellino/Clouet).

Pelvoux In February M Monnier and N Thibault made the first winter ascent in eight hours of the *Boivin/Poencet route* on the Momie Triangle. This rarely climbed 800m ice gully lies to the left of the *Couloir Chaud*.

Le Rateau In January Mollinati, Rizzardo and Robach made the second ascent in 14 hours of the *Cambon/Francou route* on the (generally) despicable rock of the N face – a route first climbed in winter.

Le Sérac In January D Crabières and A Guillaume made the first winter ascent of the *Biju Duval route* (TD-) on the NW face – slabby granite with considerable verglasing in parts.

Vanoise

The **Croix des Têtes** are formed by two magnificent limestone pillars which overlook the Arc valley. On 17-18 January Marc Almonte and Gilles Enrich made the first winter ascent of *Happy Birthday* on the huge W face (ED3 630m 6c obl). They had problems with any friction moves as the rubber on their rock boots had become far too hard in the low temperatures.

Mick Burke in the Khumbu Icefall in 1975 shortly before he disappeared somewhere on the summit ridge of Everest. (*Chris Ralling*) (p116)

63. John Hunt *(Chris Ralling)* (p121)

64. Edmund Hillary *(Chris Ralling)* (p121)

65. George Lowe *(Chris Ralling)* (p121)

66. Charles Wylie *(Chris Ralling)* (p121)

'he Magnificent Six' *From L:* Charles Wylie, Edmund Hillary, John Hunt,
eorge Lowe, George Band, Michael Westmacott. 3 April 1993. (*Susan Band*) (p89)

:hris Ralling, director of the
ilm *Return to Everest*. (p121)

69. John Davey, cameraman.
(*Chris Ralling*) (p121)

70. Local child below Hardi Lagna
pass in the foothills of W Nepal.
(*Chuck Evans*) (p81)

71. Bhotia girl outside Simikot,
capital of Humla. (*Chuck Evans*) (p81)

72. Humla shepherd descending from Sankha Lagna to the Kerang Khola.
(*Julia Wood*) (p81)

Saipal E face, looking S from above Chala. (*Chuck Evans*) (p81)

Visitor to Saipal Base Camp in the Kuwari Khola. (*Chuck Evans*) (p81)

75. Man with prayer wheel in Chala, a remote Humla village. (*Chuck Evans*) (p81)

Above left
The village of Mud, Pin valley, NE of the Pin-Parvati Pass.
(*Harish Kapadia*) (p71)

Left
Eastern Carpathians: the meadows above Zembronya.
(*J W Gajewski*) (p144)

Above
The Chornogora range: on Mt Smotrec, 1896m.
(*J W Gajewski*) (p144)

79.   Ian and Loretta McNaught-Davis in 'The Valley of the Moon', Atacama Desert, Northern Chile. (*Jim Curran*) (p133)

80.   Atacama Desert with Volcan Laskar (5690m). (*Jim Curran*) (p133)

Mont Blanc Massif

The season was blessed by superb anticyclonic weather which produced some of the best climbing conditions on record. Both open couloirs and the narrower *goulottes* were stacked full of first-class ice, with the easily accessible couloirs of Mont Blanc du Tacul coming in for a real hammering. On occasions teams were found retreating across the Vallée Blanche having been unable to start any of the more popular routes owing to the sheer volume of traffic.

Mont Blanc The first winter ascent of the 1984 Gabarrou/Profit/ Tavernier route *Abominette* was made on 14 March by Jean-Marc Genevois, Philippe Moine and Patrick Pessi. Although seldom in condition and very rarely repeated, this is probably the easiest of the modern ice climbs on the S Face.

Grand Pilier d'Angle *Divine Providence* received its second winter ascent (but first to the summit of Mont Blanc) from 24-28 December by the Irish–New Zealand team of Brendan Murphy and Dave Wills.

There are now in-situ pegs, especially on the crux corner, but many were found to be loose. The party climbed sections of A3 where sky-hooks, RPs and a selection of pegs were essential. Fortunately, the route gets the early morning sun, but with only one good ledge system (at half-height) on the tower, bivvies were a touch uncomfortable. On one, Murphy spent the whole night hanging in his harness in the middle of a 7a pitch.

From 10-14 February Alain Ghersen made the first solo winter ascent, but placed a bolt on the first hard (7a) pitch. This pitch was aided by Murphy and Wills, using sky-hooks on quartz rugosities after both had taken falls when nut placements ripped. Like the rest of the route, it has been climbed free in summer. It is particularly regrettable that such a talented climber should lower himself to this level simply in order to make a winter solo.

During the New Year period Tony Parks and Dave Wilkinson climbed a hybrid line which started up the *Dufour-Fréhel*. After a chilly bivouac half-way up the mixed ground below the sérac, they made a rising traverse right, roughly following the rambling line taken by Baumont and Becker in 1976 (which finishes up the *Japanese route*). Parks and Wilkinson turned the right edge of the sérac barrier to finish up the *Bonatti-Zappelli* and an icy, windswept Peuterey Ridge.

Aiguille Croux The first winter ascent of Romain Vogler's brilliant line *Que cherches-tu Jean-Marie?* (6c) was made by Francesco Arneodo and Daniele Caneparo on 23 January.

Grand Capucin Giovanni Bassanini and Pietro dal Pra made the first winter ascent of *L'Elixir d'Astaroth* and felt that this ED3 route represents the most demanding outing on the 'Cap' to date.

This March the German Alpinists Robert Jaspar and Malte Roeper made the fourth overall ascent and the first winter ascent of the Boivin/Piola 1983 route *Flagrant Délire* (400m ED3) – a hard aid route which finds a way up the smooth walls immediately right of *Gulliver's Travels*.

Aiguille du Tacul Patrick Gabarrou, in the company of Jean-Michel Asselin and Fred Vimal, climbed an ephemeral gully on the NE face, reaching the top on New Years Eve. The 550m couloir (350m of difficult climbing) was graded TD+ and christened *Goulotte à Eric* after Eric Mariaud, an aspirant guide killed in January after falling into a crevasse.

Grandes Jorasses Relatively amenable conditions on the Jorasses allowed a four-man Polish team (Jacek Fluder, Janurz Golab, Stanislas Piecuch and Bodgan Samborski) to make the first winter and second overall ascent of *Manitua* on the left flank of the Croz Spur (VII+ A3).

From 1-5 February Frank Connell and Dick Turnbull climbed the **Walker Spur**in almost perfect winter conditions. The rock was generally clear and dry except for a little powder adhering to the corners and the last 200m or so which was covered in rime. Odd marks of passage pointed to ascents earlier in the winter. They were followed on 8-10 by Catherine Destivelle who made the first solo ascent by a woman in any season.

Shortly afterwards, Hughes Beauzile soloed the route in four days. A crag-climber with four years experience, he had never previously tried a proper Alpine climb on a high mountain in any season, but completed the route with little damage other than minor frostbite. Later, Stevie Haston made a rapid solo ascent with only one bivouac.

Petites Jorasses Undoubtedly one of the finest achievements of the winter was the first ascent of the amazing ephemeral couloir, situated immediately to the right of the W face, by François Bernard and Antoine Cayrol on 5-6 January (600m ED2).

Germans Stephane Debryne and Tobias Heymann made the first winter ascent of the very steep couloir on the NW face of **Pt 3607m** first climbed in June 1978 by Richard Baumont and Gordon Smith.

Heymann, this time with Philip Jaerschky, made the first winter ascent of what is now considered the finest climb on the W face, *Anouk* (21 pitches, 108 bolts and 6b/c). They took just nine hours for the climb on 11 March, rappelling the route in the last flickers of daylight.

Patrick Gabarrou and Fred Vimal climbed a 450m gully to the left of the *Baumont/Smith route*, but just right of a rather less sustained line (TD) taken in 1981 by Lambert, Perroux and Sanchez which finishes close to **Pt 3576m**. The climbing was decidedly delicate and the route, dedicated to the late Alexis Long, was named *In Memoriam*.

Switching to the Italian side, normally a difficult area to reach in winter, Bruno Ferrari, Bill Ramella and Bruno Satinmade the first winter ascent of Piola's quality modern rock route on the E face, *Gargantua*.

Aiguille du Midi On this popular winter arena Martha Mercier and Bruno Robert have discovered a new line on the N face. *Wanda* (named after the late Polish climber Wanda Rukiewicz) lies to the right of the *Carli/ Chassange route*. Breaking with tradition, the pair have quoted a modern icefall grade of III/4 for their climb, despite a length of 1000m.

Col des Deux Aigles The SW side of the Col is a 550m couloir, first climbed by Collie, Hastings, Mummery and Slingsby in August 1893 and rarely ascended since (D). Directly above the start (a rightwards traverse into the main couloir) a thin gully rises for 150m before meeting the original line. This was climbed on 14 February by M Cereuil, H Defline, G Pareau and J Tafforeau, and for the most part was only a couple of metres wide. A rather competitive grade D was offered.

Petit Dru Although not mandatory for admission into the realms of high-standard Alpinism, spending a considerable amount of time alone on the W face of the Dru appears to be quite fashionable these days. This winter it was the turn of Chamonix guide François Marsigny, who made the first solo winter ascent of the *French Directissima* (ED2 6b/A2). Added fun was provided by dropping his sack high on the route and a subsequent bivouac with the rope wrapped around his body for protection. He persisted alone as far as the shoulder and was subsequently lifted off by helicopter after eight days on the face.

André Rhem and Fred Vimal narrowly failed to make the first winter ascent of *Absolu* (6c+ and A2) on the left flank of the Bonatti Pillar. Having climbed 19 of the 22 pitches, the pair were preparing their third bivouac when a small volley of stones caught Rhem directly in the face and they were forced to make an involved self-rescue.

Les Droites André Rhem and Fred Vimal reported climbing a fine new route on the N face in early December '92. However, their line appears to be similar to that followed by the Czechs, Semon and Slavick, in 1979 and has comparable technical difficulties (6a/6b and A2, plus hard mixed climbing).

Aiguille du Triolet Steve Coneys and John Sumner made a worrying ascent of the N face on 1-2 February. They bivvied alongside the lower sérac barrier which avalanched during the night, and the day after their ascent two French climbers, following them on the route, were hit by an avalanche from the upper ice wall and swept down the face.

Aiguille Dorées The first winter and almost certainly the second overall ascent of *Le Chevauchée Fantastique* (300m 6b+) on the SW face of the **Aiguille de la Varappe** fell to Amstutz and Vogler in mid-March.

Valais

Dent Blanche The classic ENE or Viereselgrat (1100m D-/D) received its first solo winter ascent on 21 January by the Swiss Alpinist Christian Portmann.

Breithorn Portmann again, this time with Patrick Torrent, made the first winter ascent of the *N Face Direct* of the central summit (Gabarrou/Steiner September 1979 850m TD-) on 5 January.

Liskamm Although it has received few repetitions, the *1982 Directissima* to the W summit is considered a superb outing and only really threatened by ice fall at the start (1050m TD+/ED1). Stephane Albasini and Christian Portmann made the first winter ascent this season, confirming the excellent quality but finding the conditions at the time decidedly difficult.

Gobba di Rollin Alessandro Jacod, Paolo Marselli and Rolando Nicco climbed another worthwhile *goulotte* on the steep mixed E face, which they rated TD.

Monte Rosa The two experienced Slovenian climbers, Vanja Furlan and Zvonito Pozgaj (who subsequently suffered serious amputations from frost-bite injuries sustained on K2), made the first winter and probably the second overall ascent of the 1991 *Francesca Schranz route* on the 'Himalayan' E face (ED1 1600m ice pitches of 70° and rock of IV). Italians, Walter Berardi and Claudio Georgia, have made the first winter ascent of the *Restelli route* (1600m TD-) in a continuous push of 27hrs, finishing on 20 January. *The Shroud Directissima* (2300m TD+/ED1), first climbed in July 1984 by Patrick Gabarrou and Christophe Viard, was probably unrepeated until this winter when it was climbed by Albasini and Portmann. They completed the ascent with a marvellous traverse over the summits of Monte Rosa, Liskamm, Castor and Pollux to finish at the Klein Matterhorn in a total of two days.

Bernese Alps

Eiger The N face was in excellent condition: there were a number of ascents of the classic 1938 route and at least one by a solo Alpinist. The naturalised Swiss Michal Pitelka (Czech born) climbed the face in only nine hours from the Stollenloch window at the end of January.

Mönch The *Damokles Couloir*, which falls 500m to the Guggi glacier from the lowest point between the Sphinx and the start of the SW ridge of the Mönch, was climbed for the first time by Peter Gobert and Beno Horner in February (TD+ ice pitches of 75° and mixed/rock at IV+).

Klein Wellhorn The two neo-classics on the Klein Wellhorn are *Adlerauge* (VII) and *Gletchersinfonie* (VII+) and both the work of the prolific Swiss pair Ruth Baldinger and Kaspar Ochsner. In a rapid time of 5hrs 30min on 6 February, German climber Frank Jourdan made the first solo winter ascent of *Adlerauge*, a route of 670m (20 pitches). Jourdan had originally hoped to combine *Adlerauge* and *Gletchersinfonie*, but was only able to complete a third of the latter before it got dark. British parties climbing *Adlerauge* in the summer had mixed feelings about the quality of the route, some commenting on the very repetitive nature of the climbing.

Wenden/Graustock From 12-14 March German Alpinists Robert Jasper and Molte Roeper climbed a very demanding new route on the N face above the Engelberg valley. The route (*Schwarzwaldklinik* ED3) involved rock pitches of VI and A2/3 (sky-hooks), 90° ice and mixed climbing of Scottish 4/5.

Bregaglia/Bernina

Winters here are not what they used to be and, with the long periods of stable weather and little snowfall that typified this season, local activists were able to bag a number of plums. Notable was Gianluca 'Rampikino'

Maspes, who over the last five years or so has been putting up many new high-quality routes throughout the range.

Piz Badile Maspes, together with fellow Italians D Fiorelli, D Grossi, S Mogovero and B More, was successful in making the first ascent of the 350m *Central Pillar* on the SW face. The climbing involved 60° ice in the couloir, followed by grade VI climbing on the crest of the pillar above.

Punta Allievi Although perhaps an unlikely target for a winter ascent, *Filo Logico*, the wildly exposed crest of the E pillar to the left of the classic *Erba route*, was in good condition in February and was climbed by D Fiorelli and C Perlini on the same day as the ascent of *Electroshock* reported below.

Punta Baroni On the right side of this face Maspes and M Fiorelli made the second ascent (first winter) of the recently created *Isippazzo*, which gave rock difficulties up to VI/VI+ and ice-climbing at 65°.

Picco Luigi Amedeo On this dramatic spire of golden granite, often referred to as the Grand Capucin of the Bregaglia, the ferocious *Electroshock* (VIII+ and A0, with 12 bolt-protected pitches) received its first winter ascent during February from D Bernasconi and M Ricotti. To the right D Galbiati and friends made the first winter ascent of the rarely climbed *Czechoslovakian route*.

Punta Chiara The first winter ascent of the classic S ridge of this rock pyramid, which lies close to the Manzi bivouac hut, was made by Maspes and C Gianetti at the end of December. On pitch seven the pair climbed the crest direct (VI), a harder variation that is usually avoided on the right.

Torre Darwin Ivo Ferrari, climbing alone, made the first winter ascent of the hard mixed free and aid route, *Memorie del Futuro*, on the quasi-vertical SE face (330m VI and A2).

Ago di Sciora A slightly different ball-game was being played on the sombre and sunless side of the range, where on 7-9 January Arturo Giovanoli and Franco Dellatorre made the first winter ascent of the infrequently climbed *NW Ridge Direct* (TD V+/VI).

Sentiero Roma Taking advantage of the very stable conditions in February the well-known local guide and guru Giuseppe Miotti, together with Sergio Salini, made the first winter crossing of the *Sentiero Roma*. Their odyssey, partially aided by cross-country skis, took five days and included ascents of the Badile and Disgrazia.

Monte Lobbia Maspes and Perlini were able to make the first ascent of the Grand Couloir on the E face – a 1100m gully – with plenty of mixed climbing and water-ice pitches up to 85°/90°.

Monte Disgrazia On the icy 700m NE face of **Punta 3483m** Benigno Balatti, with Giovanni Cavalli, made the first winter ascent of his own TD direct route, *Antonello Cardinale*, on 7 February.

Piz Argent The most noteworthy event of the season was the first winter ascent of the rarely climbed S ridge by A Marini and Maspes. Conditions were perfect, with the difficult pitches (V+) free of snow but hard névé covering all the sections of loose rock. This fine 700m route (but twice that amount of actual climbing), first ascended in 1944, was completed in a 19-hour round trip from the Bignami hut.

Dolomites

Civetta Leaving work in Munich on a Friday evening, Georg Kronthaler and Nico Mailander spent the weekend of 13-14 February making the first winter ascent of the *Haupt-Lompel route* on the N face of the Piccolo Civetta (3207m), one of the longest and most serious routes on the wall.

Marmolada The Italians Pietro Dal Pra and Alessandro Lamberti completed the first winter ascent of Igor Koller's route *Fram* (IX- or French 7c) over two days (8-9 February). They climbed the the exposed sunlit limestone walls free, dressed only in lightweight 'Lifa wear' and wearing rock boots with no socks. However, as with Dal Pra's winter ascent a month or so earlier on the Grand Capucin, fixed ropes were used.

Pala Routes on the Cimon della Pala can present quite feasible winter objectives. Franco Corn, Renzo Corona and Mauro Fronza made the first winter ascent of the 1968 *Reali/Vinco route* on the SW face, which is VII+ if climbed completely free. Close by, Corona, this time with his brother Giacomo and Tullio Simoni, climbed a new route on the Pala dei Cantoni. Despite the chilly conditions, this 350m route involved pitches of VII and A4.

Sassolungo Corn, Renso Corona and Fronza, together with Ivo Rabanser and partner, were quick off the mark to snatch the first winter ascent of the 1992 route *L'Ultimo dei Balkani* (650m VI).

Tofana Massimo da Pozzo, together with Pietro dal Pal, made the first winter ascent of his own route, *Agenti di Scorta dei Giudici Falcone e Borsellino*, on the Tofana di Mezzo (IX-).

Austria

Massive publicity was given to Thomas Bubendofer's solo winter ascent of the *Indirekten route* (VI) on the great S face of the Dachstein in a little over two hours. However, prior to his ascent there had been an uninterrupted eight weeks of sunshine, almost entirely clearing the face of any snow or ice.

THE SPRING/SUMMER SEASON

Older climbers, used to the summers of the 1970s, would have felt completely at home in 1993. For most of July the weather was unsettled with heavy falls of snow, and although the first three weeks in August appear to have been generally fine throughout the Alps, high temperatures led to a very rapid melt and considerable rockfall.

At the beginning and end of the season, breaks in the weather allowed several parties to tackle some of the big ice/mixed routes in excellent condition – a situation that has not occurred for many a summer. Most others kept to fast ascents of hard and generally short free rock routes.

As more people find enjoyment in climbing pure rock in a mountain setting, new crags are being 'discovered' in the Valais close to Alpine huts and are subsequently well equipped to cater for all climbing standards. This procedure also allows a couple of short rock routes of good quality to be slotted into an afternoon, prior to embarking on the main Alpine peak the following day.

The 4000m peaks

On 13 August Simon Jenkins and Martin Moran completed the first ever non-stop traverse of the Alpine 4000m peaks. Their journey took a mere 52 days. (*See 'Alps 4000: A Non-Stop Traverse', pages 7-15.*)

There have been various serious but unsuccessful attempts on this project in the past, generally made by competent amateur mountaineers. This time the considerable Alpine and Himalayan experience of the team allowed the programme to continue almost uninterrupted, despite unusually un-settled weather. The pair were well supported by friends, who established food dumps on some of the more lengthy stretches. However, no mecha-nised transport was used – only bicycles.

North Face Solos

Very considerable but well-deserved publicity was given to a remarkable series of solo ascents by Alison Hargreaves during the summer. After a lengthy period of mental and physical preparation Hargreaves set out to solo the six classic 'great north faces'. (*See 'The Big Six', pages 16-23.*)

The fact that only five of the six 'north faces' were completed (bad con-ditions forced her to climb a variation of the *Lauper route*, not the N face, on the **Eiger**) was subsequently of far less importance than the times, which showed a high degree of competence, and that each ascent was the first solo by a woman. The crowning achievement was an impressive solo as-cent of the *Slovenian route/Croz Spur* on 10 November in full winter condi-tions. Unable to cross the snow-covered and heavily-crevassed Leschaux glacier on her own, she was helicoptered over the rimaye and lifted from the summit, but only spent eight hours on the face.

Ecrins

A number of instances of excessive route development in the National Park have resulted in the authorities taking certain measures to limit wide-spread bolting. From now on, all development and equipping of routes in the Park are subject to prior approval. However, one of the positive effects of re-equipping can be seen on **La Meije** where, during a major clean-up, all the old tat and rappel gear that used to cover the mountain has now been removed and sound anchor points established exactly where necessary.

The weather, as normal in this region, was good for most of the summer (in contrast to the major massifs further north and east) with few storms in July and August. Unusually adequate snow cover from early summer kept most of the loose material, for which much of the range is well known, in place until towards the end of the season.

Aiguille de Sialouze On the steep and popular walls of the Sialouze, which hold some of the best granite in the range, Jerome Rochelle made the first solo ascent of *Jour de Colère* (ED2) and *Watatanka* (6c obl).

Crête de Palavar On one day in July Rochelle enjoyed 1600m of climbing by linking three routes on this popular granite area above Ailefroide – up and down the 400m classic *Palavar des Flots* (4+); then a combination of *La Vie devant Soi* (5+) and *Les Predateurs* (6a), finally descending *Palavar des Flots* again.

Upper Veneon Valley Highly developed and very popular are the superb granite slabs that lie close to La Bérarde. The two main areas are the **Tête de la Maye**, where there are routes of all grades (12-14 pitches), and **L'Encoula** which is quite a large area above the west bank of the river south of La Bérarde and below the Glacier de L'Encoula. Topos are available locally.

Briançon New routes and important developments continue on the dolomitic walls of the **Tête d'Aval de Montbrison,** the **Tenailles de Montbrison** and the walls close to the popular **Aiguillette du Lauzet** (where more work in the form of retro-bolting has been carried out on existing, but so far unpopular routes). Probably the hardest route in the whole Briançonnais was completed during the summer on the superb 300m pillar right of the classic *Voie du Grand Dièdre* (5+) on the **Crêtes du Raisin**. This extremely sustained offering gives obligatory 7b climbing with moves of 7c+ if climbed completely free.

Mont Blanc Massif

Unusually heavy snow cover on many of the north faces during June allowed a number of impressive ski descents. The **Aiguille du Midi** became almost over-populated with extreme skiers. Pierre Tardivel's descent of the *W Couloir* (Chassagne/Schmutz D+ in an upwards direction) on 1 June was perhaps the most technical, but there were also other notable achievements. Tardivel also made the first ski descent (his 43rd first descent on skis) of the central spur on the remote Miage face of **Mont Blanc**. Skied 'on-sight', the descent of this 1100m face was completed without incident in less than an hour. Sadly, the guide Alain Moroni was killed attempting to surf the N face of the **Aiguille du Plan**. It was thought that he fell victim to a windslab avalanche.

Mont Blanc This June 45 people had to be rescued from the Vallot hut. Having climbed the peak, they were overtaken by a storm and ended up marooned in the hut when not one of them felt capable of finding the descent in poor visibility (no one possessed either map or compass).

Grand Capucin There were several important repeats of routes on the E face as well as some very fine attempts, and in some cases successes, at aid elimination. The main protagonist was the very talented Italian guide, Giovanni Bassanini. With an ascent of *Flagrant Délire* in the summer Bassanini has now climbed the 'Cap' 30 times since his first introduction to the face in 1982, and by 10 different routes (including *Gulliver's Travels* eight times).

Le Trident After placing protection on rappel (micro-Friends and Friends up to one-and-a-half) Bassanini flashed a 30m pitch (*Chase the Morning*: solid 8a) to the left of the already supremely difficult crux crack of *Les Untouchables*.

Le Clocher An 'on-form' Bassanini, on his sixth ascent of the route, managed to free the third pitch of *L'Empire State Building* (Piola/Strappazzon, 1989 7c 6b obl), a boulder-problem move that had never previously been led.

Clochers de la Noire A prominent narrow ice gully on the N face has always looked a fine objective; one which would simply require the correct conditions and someone with the enthusiasm to go and ascertain its feasibility. François Damilano and Patrick Gabarrou were the team and the date of their successful ascent was 5 June.

Les Périades Climbing on these pinnacles was very fashionable in the early part of the century and although nowadays they hold great appeal for lovers of solitude (it's a long way to walk for 50m of climbing), the last decade has witnessed a fair number of new climbs created in the numerous steep and ephemeral ice gullies of the W face.

Early in the year Patrick Gabarrou climbed a trilogy of routes with various partners. Conditions were not generally favourable and several sections of these routes were climbed on aid. However, the finest route came in June when with Pascal Aruta he climbed the thin ice spear right of the *Puiseux Couloir* to reach the col right of **Pt 3517m**. This fine spear had never been climbed, so one week later Gabarrou returned with Jean Michel Assalin, despatched the remaining 80m of granite and so completed *Connection 3517*.

Tour des Jorasses Daniel Anker, Michel Piola and Benoit Robert have added another technically demanding line to the superb SE face. *Abysse* (ED3 7b+ 7a obl), climbed on 8-9 July, starts to the right of the *South Dièdre* and crosses *Etoiles Filantes* on pitch five.

Grandes Jorasses Patrick Gabarrou and the young, up-and-coming Alpinist Benoit Robert climbed out right below the third icefield of the *Colton/MacIntyre* to the steep rock on the N face of **Pt Whymper**. They reached the summit of the latter via a difficult snowed-up groove on the left flank of the prominent pillar high on the left of the buttress.

A major tragedy occurred when eight climbers were killed in an avalanche at 4.30 one morning in early August. They were crossing from the Rocher du Reposoir to the Rocher Whymper on the normal route.

At the end of August Polish climbers J Fluder and J Gotab made the second ascent of Jean-Marc Boivin and Gerard Vionnet-Fuasset's route *Extreme Dream* (first climbed on 29-30 December 1987).

Two ascents of the *Colton/MacIntyre* (1200m ED3) took place almost immediately after. On 1st September it was climbed by a party from Switzerland, who were followed a day later by the British team of Dave Heselden and Simon Richardson. The route was climbed again in late September by two Spaniards. The British party found the climbing bold, very steep and technically worthy of Scottish 6.

Petites Jorasses Bassanini, climbing on both occasions with a client, made the second ascent of the 1982 Piola/Steiner offering, *Le Pilier Inconnu*, and the first free ascent of *La Beauté du Monde* (ED2 and now 7c).

The superb rock of the E face came under further scrutiny this summer, with the result that three more fine routes were added. From 25-27 June Michel Piola and Benoit Robert created *Pantagruel* (450m 7a+ all-free, 6c with one point of aid, 6b obl) to the right of the original *Bonatti/Mazeaud route* and a finish up the previously unclimbed headwall.

Pure et Dure (Manlio Motto and Romain Vogler on 6 August) takes a direct line up the huge blank slabs to the left of the *Manera/Meneghin route* (ED3 300m 7a 6c+ obl).

The next day the pair, together with Gianni Predan, completed their 1992 project to the right of *Gargantua. Piano, Sano e Lontano* (420m and 12-pitches) gave sustained climbing and was allocated an overall grade of ED3 (6c+ 6c obl).

Monte Gruetta On the wonderfully remote E face, Motto and Vogler added *La Roue de la Fortune* (ED2 6b obl), which lies on the front of the large rounded pillar already taken by the superb 1982 Ferrero/Manera route *Pilastro del Sorriso* (TD V+ and a little A0). The new route takes a line to the right of the latter and was attempted by the Vogler brothers in 1982 before they turned their attention to the prominent slanting dièdre on the left, which eventually became the line of *Le Karma* (TD+ 6a/b). The latter is wrongly marked in the current edition of the Alpine Club *Guide to Mont Blanc*. The line shown is actually that of the 1982 Manera/Meneghin/ Ribetta route, *Via della Conca Grigia* (400m TD+ 5/6a and A2). *Le Karma* takes the shorter corner to the left and ends at the gap behind the first tower on the SE ridge.

Aiguille du Midi Gabarrou sniffed out a slim ice runnel of around 300m in the very centre of the Frendo Spur rock buttress. Climbed during a period of bad weather, the crux was a very hard ice pitch of 85°, submerged under a cascade of freezing cold water.

Aiguille des Pèlerins Jean Christophe Moulin made the first solo ascent of the classic Piola/Sprungli route, *Nostradamus* (ED2), on the N pillar. Bassanini and Armand Clavel mistakenly created a new five-pitch direct variant at the top of the pillar. This is probably a good deal more logical, though significantly harder (6a/b), than the original.

Aiguille du Fou Philippe Batoux, Lionel Daudet and Benoit Robert have added a sixth route to the S face during 18-20 August. *Le Bon, la Brute* *et le Truand* is situated on the right side of the wall and has a crux pitch of A4 and 7a obl.

Aiguille des Oiseaux To the right of the classic *Original route* on the slabby SE spur Philippe Batoux and Benoit Robert have added *Le Festin de Babeth* (6b). It now provides the best line of rappels for parties completing any of the routes on the spur.

Pt des Nantillons On the somewhat austere E face that is clearly visible from the Envers hut, Marc Batard, Vincent Delestre and Damien Girardier have put up a new route called *Désir d'Alan* (TD 5+/A0).

Aiguille de Roc On the E face a new line was added by Jacques and Stephane Dreyer. *Pêche de Genèse* lies to the right of the increasingly popular *Charlotte for Ever* and has maximum difficulties of 6a+.

Grands Charmoz Americans Scott Bakes and 'local' resident Mark Twight solved a longstanding problem on the W face, when they made the first ascent of a steep, ephemeral ice runnel (*Birthright* TD+). This 10-pitch route had some very bold run-outs on thin ice at half height.

Aiguille de la République Christophe Bodin and Olivier Ratheaux have created the excellent *Marianne et les Grimpeurs*, a 600m TD (6b) on the E face above Trélaporte glacier, and on the NE face of the Aiguille du Trélaporte, *Va Doucement, c'est Toubon* (240m 6a).

Aiguille du Moine The old partnership of Michel Piola and Pascal Strappazzon completed one of the rare 'modern' rock arêtes in the massif when they climbed along the fine crest of the Pinnacles at the base of the S ridge (Tyrolean traverses, short rappels and free climbing up to 6b).

Aiguille Sans Nom From the 27-28 October, a week after their ascent of the Charmoz, Bakes and Twight climbed a hard new route on the icy N face, finishing right of the 1978 *Gabarrou/Silvy Directissima. Here goes the Neighbourhood* is 900m in height and ED3. There were sections of vertical ice plus some aid (A3).

Flammes de Pierre Ridge On **Pt Michelle-Micheline**, *Michelle Angelo* takes the left flank of the prominent pillar to the left of *Guerre de Feu* starting with an obvious crack. The route is 550m and ED2 (6c 6b obl), and was climbed by Italian, Manlio Motto, and Romain Vogler on 27 June.

Aiguille d'Argentière Bodin and Ratheaux knocked off the previously unclimbed line of the W spur of **Pt 3352m** (slightly over one-third of the distance up the Charlet-Straton ridge). The 250m spur gave interesting TD climbing despite sections of broken rock.

Monts Rouges du Triolet Vogler climbed three routes here which all face the sun, lie at a relatively low altitude and can be tackled well after the end of a normal season. On **Pt 3289m**, which lies immediately north of the E peak, he created with Motto two routes on the steep diamond-shaped SE face. On the right *Mal Partiti* is 7a (6b obl), and *Tout Fou*, climbed as a threesome with Gerard Long, is 6c+ (6c obl). The face is around 270m high and can be reached in 1hr 30min up broken ground above the Triolet hut.

On the SW face of the N peak, *Le Fond de l'Air*, climbed on 5 September by Motto, Vogler and Christian Schwartz, starts to the left of the classic 1979 SW spur and is 6c (6b obl).

Aiguille de l'Encrenaz Devotees of the Aiguilles Rouges will be annoyed to have missed this one. Oliver Ratheaux has put up a pleasant new route on the W face, solo. With pitches of 4, an overall grade of AD was considered about right.

Valais

The Swiss Alpine Club are preparing to spend over SF2 million in 1994 on refurbishing seven of their huts. Included are the Orny, the Moiry, the Mischabeljoch bivouac hut, the Schönbiel, and the tiny Piansecco bivouac hut which is situated south of Pizzo Rotondo – an easy 3000m peak in the more gentle mountains of the Ticino Alps. The total hut revenue to the Club in 1992 was more than SF1.3 million.

Dent Blanche A new 900m mixed line on the right side of the NW face was created by Patrick Gabarrou and Tobias Heymann. The pair followed a succession of ice-glazed slabs, then finished up wonderfully sound rock to the crest of the Arête de Ferpècle in the region of the Grand Gendarme.

Monte Rosa On 27-28 June 1993, two Slovenians, Matjaz Jamnik and Bojan Pockar, climbed what may well be the most demanding route in the range to date, when they added a hard new line to the NE face of the **Signalkuppe**, cutting through the 1971 *Gardin route*. With sustained ice/ mixed climbing and rock of VII- and A2, an overall grade of ED3 was considered appropriate.

Bernese and Urner Alps

Eiger Two parties, Christophe Germiquet and Gino Merazzi, plus Nicolas and 14-year-old Julian Zambetti, made the second ascent of the 1992 Anker/ Piola route *Le Chant du Cygne* (900m ED3), which takes the true crest of the Geneva Pillar on the N face.

Jungfraujoch Robert Jasper has created a demanding new route on the NE side of the 3475m Jungfraujoch. Climbing alone and on his second attempt at the route, Jasper completed the ascent in 8hrs 30min on 18 May. The climb was graded ED3 and had 90° ice, grade VI- and A2/3 rock, plus Scottish 6 mixed climbing. Phew!

Grimsel/Furka The extreme southern section of the Urner Alps is a sub-Alpine chain with granite climbing to rival any other in Switzerland. The venues range from valley crags to 3000m peaks and are generally accessible from the main road, thus avoiding overnight bivouacs or hut usage. A good valley base is Innertkirchen, which has three campsites and a small grocery store: shopping is best done in Meiringen.

This is an increasingly popular region holding great attraction for the modern Alpine rock-climber, and many British parties were active here during the summer. Recommended are *Schnaggarsiider* and *Steiwaspi* on the **Raterischbodensee** which give a good introduction to the 'Etive style' climbing of this area. However, all pitches are generally a full 50m and there are only two bolt runners per pitch.

In the Urbachtal the Gauli hut is now modernised, fully equipped and occasionally guarded. There are some very big granite walls in this valley, but the latter can also be used by the Swiss Army and possibly subjected to live ammunition from time to time.

Despite first appearances, even the popular roadside classics are not quite as safe as one might imagine. Several days before one British party climbed the well known *Quartzriss* (VI) on the central section of **Oelberg**, the whole slab was swept by an enormous rockfall from the mountainside above.

Further afield, British parties climbed on the **Grauwand** and **Salbitschijen**. On the latter, a route on the Second Tower plus an ascent of the superb W ridge (often considered one of best rock climbs on a ridge in the Alps) should be high on anyone's list; similarly the classic *Neidermann* (VI) and, for competent parties, *Kalypso* (VII+) on the former. Both venues have recently been the scene of extensive retro-bolting, which is unfortunately likely to continue with the current policy towards fixed protection in Switzerland.

Wendenstock On the wall to the right of the SW pillar of the **Tallistock** the Remy brothers put up *Taimud* (7a 6b obl) in 1992. At the same time they started on another route to the right again, which on 7-8 July of this year became *La Trashion* (16 pitches of excellent limestone: 7a 6b obl).

At the west end of the chain the first Swiss *via ferrata* was opened in September. It uses 1300m of cable and lies to the left of the Horlaui Pillar on the **Gadmerflue**.

Fribourg Range On the 2236m **Dent de Ruth** the Remys have put up a very fine new line at an accessible standard to the left of Hans Peter Trachsel's classic *S Pillar*. *Dealer* is 5+/6a with around 10 points of aid on its 17 pitches.

Miroir d'Argentine The Remys have also been hard at work creating two more routes which start up the steeper walls right of the Miroir. *Mamba*, at 550m, is one of the longest on the cliff and relatively sustained at 6a (obl) and A1 (all-free at 6c). To the left and sandwiched between the *Super Direct* and *Zygofolis* is *Divine Martine* (450m fine and varied climbing at 5+/6a obl with several points of aid)

Bregaglia/Bernina

Monte Qualido / Precipizo degli Asteroidi Spanish climbers Josechu Jimeno and Juan Luis Monge made the first one-day ascent of *Celeste Nostalgia* (VII and A3) on the E face, home to some very impressive Big-Wall climbs.

They followed this with the third ascent of *Il Paradiso puo Attendere* (950m); originally VII and A4 with the A4 pitch on an expanding flake. Jimeno climbed this pitch free and the route is now regraded at VIII and A1. The pair then climbed *Mellodrama* in three days and finally, down in the valley on **Stella Marina,** completed *Bratamato Ye Ye* (400m VIII), one of the neckiest routes climbed to date.

Just to the right of *Il Paradiso puo Attendare,* two parallel routes were completed in the spring by the perennial Paolo Vitali and companions. The lines, which have been christened *I Melat* and *Artemisia,* each involve 20 pitches of hard free climbing, with maximum difficulties of VIII.

On the famous **Precipizo degli Asteroidi,** *Non sei piu della mia Banda* is the work of Gaffuri, Pizzagalli, Romano and Soldarini. It offers 15 pitches with obligatory moves of VIII+ and is probably the hardest route to date on the wall.

Piz Badile Gianluca Maspes made the first solo ascent of the 1973 *Bottani/Ciapponi/Dell'Oca route,* commonly referred to as the Third Pillar, on the sunny SE face (mainly IV-V with a pitch of VI).

Pizzo Cengalo Maspes (again) and Paolo Cucchi have climbed a new route on the E face. *Dalle Via* takes the crest of the pillar that lies immediately right of the large couloir separating the Punta Angela from the main body of the mountain. This eight-pitch route has crux sections of VII.

Albigna Valley The second edition of the Albigna valley guide – Albigna II – covers climbs close to the dam such as those on the Punta da l'Albigna, the Bio-Pillar, Piz dal Pal and the Spazzacaldeira. There are now nearly two dozen routes on the Spazza up to grade VIII. Of the more recent, *Lasciami Li* (VI+), which is situated towards the left side of the wall, has been particularly recommended.

Torrone Occidentale The ever productive Maspes has added another route facing the Allievi hut on the popular playgound of **Punta 2987m**. With Cristiano Perlini he climbed *Ciota Cicoz*, which is six pitches long and has a crux of VII+.

Monte Disgrazia Two speedy climbers, Paolo Maffazzini and Luca Salini followed the crest of the ridge above the Preda Rossa, over the Corni Bruciati and the Cima di Corna Rosso to the summit of the Disgrazia in eight hours. This is a notable performance on a ridge that is 8km long, has a total ascent of more than 1700m, traverses 10 summits and climbs rock, which is frequently poor, up to a standard of grade IV.

Piz Bernina Gabarrou and Heymann climbed a new route on the edge of the W spur, probably right of the ground taken by the 1899 *Burton-Alexander/Schocher/Platz route*. The team reported sustained climbing on very fine rock with pitches of V+/VI-.

Adamello

There is still plenty of scope for first ascents in this enchanting coarse-granite massif. On the S face of the **Pra Vecchio (2812m)**, a jagged aiguille standing to the NE of the Caro Alto, Carlo Care and Luigi Sauda put up *Zito parla 'l Granito* (TD VI), a 10-pitch route that climbs over a series of towers and compact slabs, similar to those found in the Bregaglia.

Tibet and China 1993

There was a long period of fine weather in late September. A Polish-Italian-Portugese expedition led by Krzysztof Wielicki climbed a new route on **Cho Oyu**. They started up the 1986 *Zakopane route* on the W Pillar and, from 7100m, continued direct. Wielicki and Marco Bianchi summited on 18 September and Piotr Pustelnik and Joao Garcia six days later.

The expedition members then climbed **Shisha Pangma**. Pustelnik and Bianchi climbed the 1982 British descent route (summiting on 6 October), while Wielicki soloed a fully independent new route on the 2000m S face, right of the 'Scott Gully'. He summited on 7 October after a 16hr climb. A 300m rock wall in the upper part was particularly difficult. Wielicki has now climbed ten 8000ers, including four by new routes and three first winter ascents.

One of the worst accidents of the year occured in China's **Province Sechuan**. An eight-member Japanese team attempting the virgin **Pt 4900m** were avalanched near 4700m. Four members, including leader Shinichi Tsushima (41) were killed.

Ascents of **Everest** from Tibet are reported in the Nepal Area Notes.

Bhutan 1993

Masa Gang (7194m) Julian Freeman-Attwood and Sean Smith (UK), Steven Sustad and Ed Webster (USA) and John Lecky (Canada) hoped to attempt the unknown SW face but miserable weather made this impossible. On the E side of the mountain they reached 6100m on the *Japanese route* but turned back owing to a combination of serious objective danger higher up and persistent bad weather.

The Royal Government of Bhutan has decided to open three new peaks for expeditions: **Masa Gang (7194m)**, **Jichu Drake (6794m)** and **Khang Bum (6494m)**. In addition, royalties for virgin peaks will differ from those for peaks already climbed, as follows:

Height	Virgin US$	Already climbed US$
7001m+	25,000	20,000
6501m – 7000m	20,000	15,000
6100m – 6500m	15,000	10,000

Other peaks will be considered on an individual basis.

India 1993

This was an active year in the Indian Himalaya, though a heavy storm in August troubled many expeditions. The Government of India has shifted the 'inner line', opening up many new areas for mountaineers. The major new areas opened up are in Kinnaur and Spiti, where the entire area west of the road is now approachable. This includes many good climbing areas like Bara Shigri, Tos nala, Dibibokari and the Western Spiti glaciers. Other good news is that the Milam glacier is open with peaks like **Hardeol (7151m), Tirsuli (7074m)** and **Chiring We (6559m)** now approachable. All the peaks of the North Sanctuary Wall of Nanda Devi can also be approached from the Milam valley which is to its east. This approach has not been tried before and should provide some excellent climbs.

Arunachal Pradesh also saw one foreign expedition this year, which is the forerunner of much good news to come, one hopes. The bad news is on the Sikkim front. The Government of Sikkim has decided to impose royalties on mountaineers, in addition to those to be paid to the IMF. Also two liaison officers, one each from the IMF and the Government of Sikkim, will have to be taken and provided for. The additional royalties are:

Kangchenjunga	US $20,000
Peaks above 8000m	$8,000
Peaks 7501m – 8000m	$3,000
Peaks 7001m – 7500m	$2,000
Peaks 6501m – 7000m	$1,500
Peaks below 6500m	$1,000

Charges are double for virgin peaks. For Indians 50% of the fees must be payable in hard currency. Various other 'environmental' fees have been levied, per day, for trekkers both from abroad and India and insistence has been made that Government agencies and travel agents are used. For the first time Indian mountaineers are to be charged in their own country. It is hoped that all Indian mountaineers and the international mountaineering community will protest against this policy to the IMF and the Governments of Sikkim and India.

The IMF has elected a new President, Dr M S Gill, who is also India's Election Commissioner. Hari Dang and Col Balwant Sandhu are the new Vice-Presidents with Sudhir Sahi as Hon Secretary. This new team will look into various aspects of climbing in the Indian Himalaya.

Reprints of old books can often be found in the book stores of India and gazetteers of Kashmir, Himachal and Garhwal are now available containing a wealth of information. *High Himalaya Unknown Valleys* by Harish Kapadia, published in 1993, contains information on trekking and climbing in almost all parts of the Indian Himalaya .

Sikkim

Kangchenjunga (8586m) An 18-member Indo-Ukraine team climbed the NE spur route from E Sikkim in May. They were led by Prajapati Bodhone and Vadim Siviridenko.

Twins (Gimmigela, 7350m) An attempt was made by a 15-man Japanese expedition, led by Tsuguyasu Itami, in October. Their summit attempt stopped at 7000m when Masanori Sato was killed in a crevasse fall.

Pathibara (Pyramid Peak, 7123m), Pathibara N (7100m) and **Pathibara E (Sphinx, 6837m)** An Indo-Japanese team, led by Harbhajan Singh (Indo-Tibet Border Police) and Yoshio Ogata (Himalayan Association of Japan), climbed these peaks in April. Neither Jill Neate's *High Asia* nor H Adams Carter's list make any mention of the N peak.

Kokthang (6147m) An Indian team led by Dilip Kolhatkar had the dubious distinction of becoming the first Indian expedition to run into trouble with the new Government of Sikkim rules. They were stopped at the local police check post and extra payment was demanded. The Sikkim authorities were apparently highly unco-operative and the expedition lost many valuable days before they could make any progress.

Garhwal

Bhagirathi III (6454m) A six-member Czechoslovakian team led by Trefil Pavel climbed the *SW Pillar route*. Climbing in two-member teams they reached the summit on separate days in mid-August.

A four-member team from Czechoslovakia, led by Miroslav Coubal, stopped at 5800m in September owing to heavy snow.

Satopanth (7075m) A seven-member Japanese team summited on 16 August, via the icefall and N ridge. The leader was Shigeyoshi Kido. A nine-member Norwegian team led by Jan Westby stopped at 6200m in September after heavy snow.

Shivling (6543m) Hans Kammerlander and Hainz Christoph (Swiss) climbed the N pillar on 31 May. A French expedition led by Yves Le Bissonnais ran into trouble on the W ridge at 5900m when Odile Lonclé was killed in a fall from fixed ropes. John Dunlop and James Keily attempted the peak in late November. An early winter storm deposited a lot of snow, forcing them to abandon their attempt.

Thalay Sagar (6904m) A Korean team, led by Choi Byung Soo, reached 6400m on the N face when bad weather in late June stopped them. A Spanish expedition, led by Jordi Sivila, was defeated by heavy snow in August.

Swargarohini I (6252m) A five-member Swedish team led by Ake

Nilsson climbed a new route up one of the rock ridges on the S face. They fixed rope on the prominent rock pinnacle in the central part of the face to reach a gap on the sérac barrier. From there they climbed steep ice to reach the easy snow ridge leading to the summit.

Meru S (6660m) A Spanish team led by José Luis Arnaiz was defeated by bad weather in August.

Meru N (6450m) A four-member American team, led by Tom Kimbrell, attempted the E face, but stopped at 5800m. A British team consisting of five members and led by Noel Crane reached 6050m on the same face. They were defeated by three heavy storms in September after climbing pitches as hard as E5.

Manda II (6568m) An expedition from Czechoslovakia, led by Maroko Vervc, also suffered bad weather in August and had to give up.

Chaukhamba II (7068m) The first expedition ever to attempt this peak was from Italy and led by Carlo Farina in August. They tried the W pillar, reaching 6200m and were stopped by the August storm. Alberto Tegiacchi fell and was killed when the fixed rope he was climbing was cut.

Chaturangi (6407m) Toshiko Ishino led a four-member Japanese team on the SW face. They stopped at 6200m on 29 August, finding snow conditions too dangerous.

Nilkanth (6596m) A multi-national army team (India, USA, UK, France and Italy) climbed a new route, gaining the NE ridge from the E face. Organised by Lt Col H S Chauhan (India) the team fixed rope almost unbroken from Base Camp to the summit and put 36 people on top.

Also attempting the NE ridge, six members of a Japanese expedition (leader Yuichi Sasaki, Kobayashi, Yoshinori Wakabayashi, Haruo Takano, Gen Masuda and Takeshi Namba) were killed in an avalanche. The one survivor made an epic retreat to report the tragedy.

The southern approaches still remain unclimbed and problematic. Duncan Tunstall and Chris Pasteur (UK) attempted the SW ridge. One of them fell sick at 5400m, coughing blood, and could not recover so the expedition was abandoned – the perils of two-member teams!

Trisul (7120m) E Radehose led a German team, climbing over the Ronti saddle from the west and reaching 6270m. The route's difficulties forced them to give up on 21 October.

Kedar Dome (6831m) A French expedition led by Christian Dejax was forced to give up at 6640m by sickness and injury.

Lamchir (5662m) Eight members from an American National Outdoor Leadership School expedition reached the summit on 5 October.

Nanda Devi (7816m) After many years' closure a large Indian Army Corps of Engineers expedition was permitted to climb from the Nanda Devi Sanctuary. Led by Lt Col V K Bhatt they studied the scientific and ecological aspects of the Sanctuary's closure. Five members summited.

Nanda Devi Sanctuary Recently the Government of India has instructed the State Government of Uttar Pradesh to allow trekking parties to visit the Sanctuary. It is not clear whether climbing expeditions will be allowed. Full details are available from the Himalayan Club.

Nanda Devi E (7434m) Seven members of a team from the Border Security Force, India, led by S C Negi, summited on 5 October. They approached from the Milam valley, going over the Longstaff Col.

Matri (6721m) An Indian expedition led by N H Shelar established four camps up to 6100m, but failed on 17 October after bad weather.

Sri Kailash (6932m) An expedition led by Basanta Singha Roy established seven camps and was successful on 20 September.

Gangotri II (6577m) Five members of an Indian expedition from Gujarat, led by Salil Joshi, climbed this peak on 30 May.

Kamet (7756m) Four members of an Indian Armoured Corps team led by Capt S P Malik climbed this peak on 5 October.

Bandarpunch W (6102m) Indian teams led by Rajiv Midha (Haryana) and Amar Biswas climbed this peak on 5 June and 15 August respectively.

Ronti (5956m) An expedition from Bengal climbed this peak on 29 September. They were led by Kani Bhattacharji.

Jogin I (6465m) and **Jogin III (6116m)** A Bengal expedition led by Animesh Bose climbed these peaks on 31 May and 4 June respectively.

Tirsuli (7074m) An Indian expedition from Bengal, led by Mrs Sarbani Chatterji, failed on this high peak on the Milam glacier.

Arunachal Pradesh

In November 1993, after a closure of many years, a five-member Dutch expedition led by Ronald Naar was the first foreign party allowed to climb in this area. After many bureaucratic delays, they climbed **Pt 6300** near **Gori Chen (6858m)**, and photographed the unclimbed **Kangtö (7090m)**.

Himachal Pradesh

Papsura (6440m) and **Dharamsura (6420m)** The Korean team led by Bo-Seong Hong was stopped by avalanche danger. Revised heights for both peaks are given.

Menthosa (6443m) Three parties from a Japanese expedition climbed this peak in mid-August. They were led by Tsuneo Suzuki.

Mulkila IV (6517m) This peak was climbed by an Italian expedition led by Renzo Gemignani on 25 August.

CB II (6044m) Allen Armstrong's ten-member British team attempted this peak from the north and reached 5925m in poor snow conditions.

Deo Tibba (6001m) A British expedition led by Harpur William failed on this peak. A Indian expedition led by S Sudhakar was successful on 29 July. Four members also climbed nearby **Norbu.**

KRI An Indian team climbed this peak on the Koa Rong glacier on 2 September. Leader P N Haldar and seven others reached the summit.

Chau Chau Kang Nilda II (6158m) An Indian team led by P K Barwan climbed this peak above Langja village in Spiti on 14 September.

Gangstang (6162m) On 1 August five members of an Indian team climbed this peak near Keylong, Lahul. The leader was N C Paramik.

Sanakdenk (6044m) and **Pt 6070** In August an Indian team from Bengal failed on these peaks near Milling, Shipting nala in Lahul.

Fluted Peak (6122m) This peak near Losar in Spiti was climbed by an Indian expedition from Bengal on 27 August. The leader was Tarit Das.

Tambu (5790m) and **Jori (5790m)** Heavy rains in July defeated a Bombay team led by S M Sawant on these two peaks.

Khamengar (5760m) and **Parahio (5920m)** Harish Kapadia and Kaivan Mistry climbed these two peaks during a 220km trek in the area. (*For full details see 'Exploration in Western Spiti', pages 71-75.*)

Kashmir, Zanskar and Ladakh

Cerro Kishtwar (6220m) Mick Fowler and Steve Sustad made the noteworthy first ascent of this peak on 19 September (Scottish 6 and A3). (*For full details see 'The One That Nearly Got Away', pages 48-53.*)

Dzo Jongo (6120m) This lovely peak situated in the Markha valley, Zanskar was climbed by Frank Seubert and Birgit Rossberg on 17 August. They followed the N ridge.

Kun (7077m) A six-member team led by Trippaceur Hermann was successful in August.

Pinnacle Peak (6930m) A French team led by Christian Julien established three camps on the SW ridge of the peak near the Nun-Kun massif. They were defeated by heavy snow in early August.

Bobang (5670m) On 7 August a team from Kashmir, led by Shawket Hussain, climbed this peak which is situated in the Panikhar valley on the Suru river.

Eastern Karakoram

Aq Tash (7016m) The first ascent of this prominent peak rising above Saser La was achieved by an Indo-Japanese expedition, led jointly by Hukam Singh (Indo-Tibet Border Police) and Minoru Nagoshi (Hiroshima Alpine Club). After setting up Base Camp on 18 July the Japanese and Indians climbed separately on the SW face and S ridge respectively. Both routes proved difficult. After fixing 1500m of rope Nobuo Yamamoto and Yasufumi (Japan) summited on 6 August. The Indians fixed 2000m and six members summited on 8 August. Though situated near the Central Asia trade route this peak had never been attempted before.

Mamostong Kangri II (7023m) An Indo-Austrian expedition led by N Ravikumar and Gunther Steinmair made the first ascent of this peak, 2km W of the main peak (7516m). After fixing 400m of rope, four Austrians summited in a 10hr push from Camp 3 on 14 August. Subsequent attempts failed, but the party climbed both the peak's two lower summits.

BILL O'CONNOR
Nepal 1993

Nepal notes this year are dominated by 'that mountain'. For some reason 40 became an auspicious number for Everest and Nepal although I am not sure what special merit there is in 40. The mind boggles at what is in store for us and Everest a decade down the road. Whatever mountaineers and the media conjure up for the half-century celebrations of the first ascent of Everest, the Khumbu will definitely be the place not to be.

Everest dominated the agenda. The Nepalese increased the peak fee to $50,000 and still they were climbing, literally over each other, to stand on top. With such a high peak fee only large commercial expeditions will be able to afford to go on the mountain. Inevitably such expeditions attract mountaineers with a low level of ability who 'buy in' with a high expectation of success, which means the South Col route is what they head for. It will be interesting to see how many, if any, lightweight, adventurous expeditions attempt new routes from the Nepalese side of the mountain over the next few years. It might mean that such expeditions will have to operate under the umbrella of a large commercial expedition, sharing the costs with guided clients but in fact acting independently once on the mountain by climbing new lines in lightweight style. Of course it is debatable whether it's possible to 'guide' anyone, in the traditional sense, above 8000m.

During the pre-monsoon period over half the 30 official expeditions were Everest bound. Apart from the shear tonnage of climbers and equipment on the mountain there were a number of firsts and even a double first for British Mountain Guide Dawson Stelfox, who made the first Irish and first British ascent via the North Col (he holds dual nationality). This is particularly interesting for lovers of mountaineering facts because it has taken 71 years for the first British ascent of the north side since General Bruce's expedition stirred our interest in the mountain. Harry Taylor climbed the 1953 route without bottled air and Rebecca Stephens became the first British woman to stand on top. Ms Stephens became one of 14 women to reach the summit pre-monsoon, including first female ascents for Nepal and Korea. Indian climber Santosh Yadav made her second ascent of the mountain in a year. Other memorable ticks included the first Finnish, Taiwanese and Lithuanian ascents. May 10 in particular stands out as something extraordinary with no less than 40 (1993's auspicious number) standing on top in a single day, rather more than reached the top between 1953 and 1973. Ang Rita Sherpa made his eighth ascent of the mountain with three Spanish mountaineers in his wake. Something close to 600 people have now reached the summit.

During the post-monsoon period, which was blessed by stable weather, a large commercial expedition, organised by British adventure travel company Himalayan Kingdoms ran into a spot of bother which rather took the shine off their summit successes. After confusion arose regarding verbal agreements about their permit, Himalayan Kingdoms were fined $100,000. Naturally an appeal has been lodged. It's all a far cry from the 'back of Bill Tilman's envelope'. Under the guidance of several British Mountain Guides, no less than seven members of the expedition reached the summit, including Ginette Harrison, the second British woman to reach the top, and Ramon Blanco, who at 60 became the oldest mountaineer to summit. The actor Brian Blessed reached an altitude of 8300m without supplementary oxygen.

On the north side of the mountain, another large commercial expedition, with 23 climbers, was successful on the North Ridge. Jon Tinker reached the summit for the second British ascent from this side. He and Polish climber Mariej Berbeka made a significant variation on the normal route by taking a direct line to the foot of the Second Step from a camp at 8100m. In fact their line is similar to that attempted by Norton in 1924 and has the advantage of being technically easier than the ridge between the First and Second Steps, with far less time being spent above 8000m. Climbing with oxygen, climbers averaged seven hours between a camp at 8100m and the summit.

Ama Dablam continues to attract a large number of expeditions, although the Nepalese are restricting the number of permits. Belgian, Japanese and Swiss teams were all successful on the SW ridge during December 1992. Multiple permits on a route like this where there is a lack of tent space at Camp 1 and Camp 2 on the Yellow Tower is a major problem. Stonefall above Camp 2 is also a problem. Belgium climber, Alain Hubert, had his arm broken by rockfall caused by the Koreans whilst evacuating one of their members with AMS. Japanese climber Yasushi Yamaroi climbed a new line on the right-hand side of the W face. This rib joins the normal route high up.

Cho Oyu was very busy pre-monsoon with eight expeditions on the W ridge, which is approached from Tibet or by crossing from Nepal. Several expeditions crossing into Tibet from Nepal have been visited by Chinese border police and had to pay a hefty fine to continue. A total of 26 climbers reached the summit of Cho Oyu between 29 April and 16 May. An eight-member Spanish expedition led by Manuel Gonzales put seven on the summit via the W ridge on 8 and 10 February. Roger Mear, leading a commercial expedition, also reached the summit from Tibet with three clients. Swiss Guide André George climbed the mountain solo. To date around 360 people are known to have climbed Cho Oyu of which 23 are women – only Everest has had more!

Dhaulagiri 1 A Russian expedition led by Sergei Efimov made the most important new route of the season on the N face. A total of six Russians and one Briton, Rick Allen, reached the summit without additional oxygen. (*Full details in 'Dhaulagiri on Cabbage Soup', pages 43-47.*)

A Chinese/Tibetan expedition led by Samdrup climbed the NE ridge on 30/31 May. Nine members reached the summit. The same expedition, which is attempting to climb all the 8000ers, reached the top of Annapurna I.

On 6 October Gary Ball died from oedema trying to climb Dhaulagiri. Climbing with Rob Hall he had had many successes on high peaks, including Everest. (*Further details in 'Mountaineering by New Zealanders', pages 222-223.*)

Gangchempo Tilman's 'Fluted Peak' in the upper Langtang valley was officially climbed by a joint Japanese/Nepalese expedition on 28 April via the SW ridge and S face. The mountain has had several unofficial ascents.

Kang Guru (6981m) This peak north of Manaslu in the Peri Himal had two more Japanese ascents, in May.

Langtang Lirung On 18 December 1992, two Sherpas and one South Korean reached the summit of this impressive and difficult peak, but sadly they died during the descent.

Machapuchare The wonderful 'fish tail' peak guarding the entrance to the Annapurna Sanctuary has been reopened for a Japanese expedition. First explored by Jimmy Roberts and all but climbed by Noyce and Cox in 1956 the mountain was subsequently listed as sacred.

Makalu Two expeditions were active on the mountain during the spring with the W face as their objective. The first was a strong Italian–Slav–Czech team led by Italian Oreste Forno, but they failed to siege the face, reaching 7600m at the start of the major difficulties. They then joined the normal route, reaching the summit on 22 May and making the 40th ascent of the mountain. Following the Italians, Jeff Lowe made a daring solo attempt on the W face, which has been the site of numerous failures and is fast growing the 'last great problem' tag.

Erik Decamp and Catherine Destivelle failed in their attempt on the W Pillar, first climbed by the French in 1971.

Manaslu An Austrian expedition led by Arthur Haid climbed the *Japanese route* on the N face pre-monsoon. Four climbers reached the summit.

Mera This popular 'trekking peak' between the Hongu and Hinku valleys south of Everest was attempted by Yasushi Yamanoi prior to his solo ascent of Ama Dablam. Again climbing solo he forced a way up the impressive W face of the mountain, but after 23 pitches and five bivouacs failed on the smooth headwall, having climbed several pitches of VI and A4.

Lobuje E (6119m) Janko Opresnik and Danilo Tic (Slovenia) climbed the *Lowe/Kendall route* on the E face on 9 December. Despite temperatures of -30° they climbed the 600m gully (UIAA V and Scottish 5) in 12 hours. Because of frostbite and a broken ice hammer they did not continue to the summit from the top of the route and instead descended the SE ridge.

New Peaks Added to the Permitted List

Api West	7100m	Byas Rikhi
Firnkoph	6697m	Saipal
Firnkoph West	6645m	Saipal
Nampa south	6580m	Byas Rikhi
Raksha Urai	6593m	Urai Lekh
Saipal East	6882m	Saipal
Surma-Sarovar N	6523m	Surma-Saravor Lekh
Tso Karpo	6518m	Kanjiroba

PAUL NUNN

Pakistan 1933

I would like to thank Taled Mohammed, Nazir Sabir and Lindsay Griffin for their help in preparing these notes.

This was an eventful year, with more expeditions than ever before and more action on sub-6000m peaks. Some good weather allowed successes on the high peaks, but it was punctuated by bad spells, especially in mid-July and August, which caused some expeditions to fail. On smaller peaks successes were rare.

Nine expeditions attempted **K2** and at least four succeeded in reaching the summit. Early in the season (Base Camp 25 May) Tomaz Jamnik (Slovenia) led a multi-national party on the **Abruzzi Spur**. A high camp was placed at 7850m and on 13 June Stipe Bozic (Croatia), Carlos Carsolio (Mexico), Victor Groselj and Zvonko Pozgaj (Slovenia) reached the summit. Support climber Bostjan Kekec died from cerebral oedema near Camp 4. David Sharman (UK) and Goran Kropp (Sweden) also made an attempt, but Sharman suffered a fall above Camp 4 and retreated. Kropp continued and reached the top on 23 June. Pozgaj and Boris Sedej had serious frost-bite and had to be evacuated by helicopter. It was Groselj's tenth 8000 metre peak.

In early July three climbers from an American party led by Stacy Allison reached the summit, but Dan Culver (Canada), slipped to his death descending, while filming near the bottleneck.

The German Northlight expedition, led by Dr Reinmar Joswig, climbed the **Abruzzi**. Joswig and Hans Peter reached the summit with fellow team members Anatoly Bukreev, an experienced Russian, and Andrew Lock (Australia). In descent above the Shoulder they separated and the Germans were not seen again.

Also on the **Abruzzi** Rafael Jansen (Sweden) and Daniel Bednener (Canada) summited on 31 July, after staying in a tent and snow-hole belonging to the British team Roger Payne, Julie-Ann Clyma, Alan Hinkes and Victor Saunders. Bednener developed cerebral oedema and Jansen spent a night trying to get him down, but then had to leave him. Later he appears to have fallen down the S face. In a weak condition Jansen met Alan Hinkes and Victor Saunders at 7600m. They, with Payne and Clyma, helped him down. A subsequent attempt by the British faltered on 13 August in deep, dangerous snow and the return of further bad weather. (*Full details in'Summer on the Savage Mountain', pages 54-57.*)

This group found clothing belonging to Art Gilkey, who died on the 1953 attempt, and, near Base Camp, bones believed to be the remains of Sherpa Pasang Kitar of the 1939 expedition.

Expeditions led by Wim van Harskamp (Holland) and Josep Aced Avda Abat were also unsuccessful on the Abruzzi. There appears to be some confusion about a possible repeat of the *Kukuckza-Piotrowski route* on the S face by Canadian Barry Blanchard and party (recorded by Pakistanis as unsuccessful).

An extended epic was played out on the *W ridge route* first attempted by Bonington's 1978 expedition and climbed by the Japanese Ohtani and Nazir Sabir (Pakistan) in 1981. Dan Mazur led a US/UK expedition comprising twelve climbing members and some trekkers. Base Camp was set up at 4900m on 24 June. A storm destroyed Camp 2 on 15 July and various members were avalanched and contracted oedema and frostbite. Camp 6 (8200m) was established on 18 August, but the party was by now too battered and the remaining climbers too tired to continue in the good weather that followed.

29 August saw a climb by Jonathan Pratt and Dan Mazur to Camp 3 in one push of 24 hours and three days later Camp 6 at 8200m was attained 'in light cloud and breeze'. The summit was reached in a long push of 31hrs 30min from 2 September (6.30am) to 3 September (2pm). A gully was climbed above Camp 6 and an old rope followed over slabs. 50m of steps and ledges followed, then a plateau, where some gear was left. Above was a gully, then a long traverse right on snow passing a wrecked Japanese tent. This ended in a six-metre vertical wall sporting an old piton. Mazur used two more for aid on this difficult section to reach the *Magic Line* (*S Pillar*) at 8350m. From there radio contact was made with Base Camp.

Pratt led a difficult mixed 200m section to 8550m, finding only two old pitons. After another brew behind a sheltering boulder at 8.35pm they took turns on the long easy-angled ridge which followed over false summits to reach the top in moonlight at 11.15pm There was wind and snow and they quickly retreated to bivouac at 8550m for an hour, to rest and make tea. Pratt fell off the ledge napping, luckily stopping in soft snow.

At 2.25am they resumed their descent, making short abseils from small rock anchors as they had only 12m of rope. The weather deteriorated, with a high wind and snow, but they reached the top of the S Pillar at 6.30am. From there they made radio contact with Base and rehydrated. There followed a long descent in blizzard conditions to Camp 6.

They had repeated the *1981 Japanese route* and used 4000m of fixed rope between 5700m and 7600m. Their account matches details and photographs shown by Nazir Sabir (Pakistan) of the 1981 Japanese expedition, of the section from the top of the S Pillar to the summit. Mazur and Pratt had previous experience of high altitude on Everest, but were advised in Britain before departure that most of their party seemed inexperienced for this difficult route, especially as they originally intended to finish the W ridge by a more difficult direct route to the summit, avoiding the original traverse right. (*A more detailed account of this expedition will appear in the* Alpine Journal *in 1995.*)

On the Chinese (Sinkiang) side of the mountain a Russian commercial expedition is reported to have reached 7000m on a new line left of the N ridge. A Spanish expedition exceeded 8000m on the N ridge before the weather defeated them. It seems that snowfall was even heavier this year on the north (Sinkiang) flanks of the mountain than in Pakistan.

On **Broad Peak** eight expeditions attempted the mountain. Four succeeded, including those led by Fausto de Stefani (Italy), Koji Sekine (Japan), Sergio Martini (Italy) and Tanabe Osamu (Japan). Unsuccessful were American, Andorran, Korean and Mexican parties.

On **Gasherbrum 1 (Hidden Peak)** one expedition succeeded. From Norbert Joos's Swiss expedition of 12, three climbers reached the summit. Japanese, Spanish and DAV Summit Club expeditions failed.

On **Gasherbrum 2** there was a different story. Six out of seven expeditions succeeded, several being commercial ventures. The proportion of the total membership reaching the summit possibly becomes significant on the more accessible 8000m peaks of the area, and could be a criterion of efficiency for commercial expeditions' clients.

The successful expeditions were led by Yasunari Yamashita (Japan – six out of seven summited), Yi Seok Yang (Korea – five out of six), Hirofumi Konishi (Japan – four out of four), Han's Kitel (Germany – four out of twenty), Lluis Bancella Nogue (Spain – three out of seven) and USA's Thor Keiser (Himalayan Kingdoms – twelve out of eighteen). Another three-member Spanish expedition failed.

Gasherbrum 4 (7980m) Danilo Valsecchi's City of Lecco (Italy) expedition failed, as did the strong British party, led by Andy Macnae, attempting the S ridge. The latter established Base Camp at the usual site on 25 June below the S Gasherbrum glacier.

The last day's approach was hampered by a snowstorm and porter strike. Better weather then allowed them to get through the icefall to a camp at 6000m in the upper basin under the S ridge. Like Steve Swenson's US party in 1992, they tried the slope between the icefall taken in 1957 (R Cassin G4 first ascent) and 1985 (G Cohen G3 expedition) and the S ridge itself previously tried by Dai Lampard (UK). Some of the American ropes were found. Ropes were fixed up big snow slopes to the ridge crest, avoiding the long rock ridge to the west, but July bad weather hindered their efforts. The party comprised Andy Cave, Chris Flewitt, Andy Macnae, Brendan Murphy, Andy Perkins and Kate Phillips. Murphy and Phillips reached 7200m on their sixth attempt in early August. Time and energy then ran out, presumably not helped by the long approach, but this line was thought to provide the key to the route for the future .

Hirofumi Konishi's four-person group (Japan) had permission for **Gasherbrum 4,** as in 1992, but appears to have been unsuccessful (if an attempt was mounted after climbing **Gasherbrum 2**). David Hamilton's four-man British team (José Bermúdez, Grant Dixon, Jerry Lovett and Hamilton) attempted to repeat the 1986 **Chogolisa** traverse. After much delay through bad weather crossing the Gondokoro La (5650m), where a porter broke a leg when avalanched and another became ill with altitude sickness and was evacuated from the E Vigne glacier by helicopter, they reached 6950m in deep snow close to the heavily corniced ridge. A joint

American–Pakistani expedition suffered the same problems and left in August, after helping the treatment of the porter with drugs and a Gamow pressure bag.

There were no deaths in the Gasherbrum range and a French group began to try to clean up the base camp on the Duke of Abruzzi glacier in early August 1993. This has been a mess for years, with little previous attempt at cleaning and 10 or more expeditions every year for about a decade. Several corpses remain on **Gasherbrum 2**'s standard *Austrian route.*

The worst pollution to the area continues to be caused by the military, both Pakistani in the Baltoro and elsewhere, and Indian in the Nubra and Siachen. A telephone line runs up the Baltoro, Paiju camp is reported a denuded desert, contaminating mule and pack-horse trains supply permanent military camps, and there are confirmed reports of the military shooting wildlife from vehicles and helicopters, including protected species like ibex, in the Trango region. Track and road building into the wilderness areas above last settlements is also proceeding on both sides, degrading the area solely for military purposes.

On a more positive note environmental projects at Askole and Hoto in the Braldu are attempting to improve water supply quality to villages, with inputs from Doug Scott, Roger Payne's sponsor Eastern Electricity and the Aga Khan Foundation, while Wilderness Experience and a French clean-up group have been active at Gasherbrum Base Camp and elsewhere.

Of 21 expeditions on peaks below 8000m, only three succeeded. Tagawa Yoshihisa's Japanese party climbed **Shayaz (6050m)**, three out of four climbers reaching the summit. Three out of five Koreans led by Chang Ho Kim climbed **Trango (Nameless) Tower,** and a large 29-member British RAF expedition led by William Batson from Lossiemouth succeeded when three climbers reached the summit of **Diran (7285m)**.

Sadly there were several deaths on unsuccessful expeditions, including Xavier Socies and José Marmul (Spain) on **Diran**, Philip Grobke (Bavaria) on **Baintha Brakk** and Mrs Anita Fendt and Klaus Gremer died on **Akher Chioh** near **Diran** during Alfred Fendt's expedition to that peak. Tetsu Ozasa and Satoshi Takahashi also died on **Sani Pokkhush (6885m)** in the Batura. An avalanche hit their top camp on 11 July, and injured a third climber. The five-man team led by Ozasa were seeking to make the second ascent of the mountain, which had been tried by a Japanese party in 1988 and climbed in July 1990 by Hubert Bleicher's German group via the NW ridge. In the same region a (mainly British)'trekking party' climbed a **5500m peak** south of **Baltar** via its N face (Stone Elworthy and Zoltan, a Hungarian student from Beijing) but failed on 9-10 August on **Darijo Sar (5600m)**, a beautiful wedge-shaped peak (David Anderson, James Howell, Stone Elworthy and Andy Riley).

Other enterprising but unsuccessful attempts were launched on **Koz-Sar (6677m)** in the Batura by an Anglo-Irish party led by Andrew Creigh, and on **Baintha Brakk (7285m)** by a Japanese party led by Hedeki Yosida and Carlos Buhler (USA). The Norwegian **Ultar (7388m)** expedition led by Jo Wang tried the route previously attempted by Mick Fowler and upon which Tsuneo Hasegawa and Kiyotaka Husino were avalanched leaving Nazir Sabir as sole survivor in autumn 1991. Though four climbers set up a well-stocked camp at 4900m by 13 July the team had only reached 5800m in dangerous snow conditions. More snow followed, and one member was frostbitten. One climber survived a 150m fall during the descent after 16 days on the mountain. Kitty Calhoun's (USA) attempt on **Latok 1 (7151m)** N ridge, Jack Tacklf's (USA) on **Uzzun Brakk (6422m)**, the Korean Alpine Club's attempt on **Rakaposhi (7785m)** led by Jae Heon Song and that by Japanese led by Tateshi Sudo all failed. Dai Lampard (UK) returned to the huge rock ridge on **K7** without success and Simon Yates failed on **Bobisghir peak (5415m)**. A Spanish party led by Jaume Campolier I Soy failed on **Malubiting W (7459m)**.

A refreshing sign was Gunter Schultz's Hamburg expedition to **Durban Zom (7110m)** in the Hindu Kush, long neglected because of the Afghan war.

Isolated and yet relatively accessible, **Nanga Parbat** attracted a two-climber French winter attempt on the *Schell route* on the Rupal flank which ended on 9 January 1993. The summer saw seven expeditions, less than of late (13 in 1992). A four-man Spanish party set up Base Camp on 6 June and were the first to try the *Kinshofer route*. They fixed ropes, set up four camps (Camp 4 at 7300m) and on 7 July Pablo Barrenetxea and José Luis Clavel reached the top. Three other members were later defeated by the weather. Two Catalan climbers from Girona on Joaquim Bover's expedition set off from Base by the same route on 7 July. At least one, Iniki Garijo, reached the summit. One Japanese climber reached the top from Tadakiyo Sakahara's group of six, as did four climbers from Richard Pawlowski's ten-person Anglo-Polish group.

Doug Scott's second attempt at the **SW 'Mazeno' Ridge** was to have been undertaken with Wojciech Kurtyka. For acclimatisation they were accompanied by Richard Cowper. After initially approaching the area via Astor and the jeep road to Tarshing and spending time thereabouts, they reached Mazeno high camp (4900m) on 30 July. This is near the easy link between the Rupal and Diamir valleys via the Mazeno Pass (5377m) frequented by trekkers. On 1 August Cowper and Scott climbed unroped on the rock spire at the S end of the W wall of the glacier. There was much scrambling, then a 200m section of VS on the S side. Scott climbed a final six-metre section (5a) to the summit, while Cowper waited below. There was no sign of any previous ascent of this **'Mazeno Spire'**. After bad weather all three aimed for **Mazeno W Peak (5700m)**, climbing by a 600m avalanche chute and final basin. There was no sign of previous ascent. Scott was avalanched in the chute during descent and fell 400m over rock and ice cliffs, but survived with severely wrenched tendons in the right ankle, which finished this second exploration of the **Mazeno Ridge**.

In Hushe region the Irish attempt on **Masherbrum 2** led by Michael Keyes was unsuccessful. After most climbers had left the Karakoram an international group led by the guide Edward Bekker (Holland) of the Expeditions Commission of the UIAA arrived, setting up a base in

Gondokoro Village at 3820m on 7 September. In 16 days of climbing the 25 climbers from 13 different countries split into small teams for climbing purposes.

First ascents claimed include **Glas Peak (c6000m)**, a serious three-day route (completed on 16 September) on 55°- 60° ice done with one bivouac by Bogdan Baciu (Romania) and Falk Leibstein (Germany), and the W ridge of **Gholon Peak (c6000m)**, a 1200m D/TD mixed climb done by Jorg Wilz, Evelyne Binsack, Edward Bekker, Andreas Daffner and Julian Neumeyer (Austria) and stopping 15m short of the summit because of avalanche danger and cornices (15 September). The same party climbed a rocky spire above their ABC (5700m), which was mostly ice with two TD–rock pitches. They called this **Sepp Jansen Peak**.

On **Balti Peak (5200m)** a 24-pitch rock route (TD IV-VI) on beautiful granite was done by Jorge Wiltze, Marrigje Hartmann (Holland), Hamid Olange (Iran) and Andreas Daffner (Germany) on 18 September, with one bivouac during the descent. Next day it was repeated by Federic de Wargny (France) and Neil McQueen (South Africa), and on 20 September by Evelyne Binsack, Julian Neumeyer, Brendan Waye (Canada) and Bekker.

On 15 September the **5700m Peak (Matzenspitze)** next to Laila was climbed by Hartmann and Wolfgang Rieder (Austria) by a classic AD snow and ice route, and subsequently by others. Its neighbour **Eiger Peak (5650m)** gave another classic ice route on 22nd (Wiltz, Wargny, Binsack, Olange, Rieder, Bekker and Ralph Hance from Ireland). Rock routes were also done above Base Camp. Kevin Tatsugawa (USA) and Hennie Niemand (South Africa) did a 9-pitch V and VI and a rock buttress above Saicho Camp gave two 15-pitch IV and V climbs, with some loose rock (Binsack, Wiltz Brett Pierce(USA) and A Daffner).

In September they were alone in the area and can be congratulated on a most successful international meet of younger alpinists. Guides Jorge Wiltz (German), Evelyne Binsack (Swiss) and British Doctor Ruth Howlett helped Edward Bekker, who also appreciated the logistical support from Mr Mohammed Iqbal and his staff. It seems likely from Edward Bekker's report and the discussions at the Pakistan Tourism Convention of November 1992 that some entry restrictions will be imposed on Hushe.

The aim of the Expeditions Commission of the UIAA in encouraging such events is to help younger alpinists to organise their own expeditions in future and to encourage good practice. There are plans for possible attempts on Gasherbrum 2, Gasherbrum 4, Broad Peak, Masherbrum 2 and possibly even K2 among young members of this expedition.

Jozef Nyka writes:

Two Polish climbers visited the still unexplored Lupghur S glacier and made the first ascent of a c6500m ice summit, called by locals **Borondo Sar.** Their ascent was via a 1500m face, the ice varying from 40° in the lower part (800m) to 60° in the upper (500m).

Central Asia 1993

Tien Shan

Khan Tengri (6995m) A party including A Pogorelov climbed the most impressive new route in the area this year, on the N face. Also, in July, an avalanche struck a camp on the col between Pik Chapayeva and Khan Tengri (c6000m) and killed Ukrainian guides Slava and Sergey and two Polish alpinists Marcin Hanzel (22) and Wojciech Krajewski (26). Other climbers in the camp survived and made a very dangerous descent.

On 4 August 1993 Robert Guy and Patrick West, clients of Himalayan Kingdoms, and two Russian mountaineers, Ilia Iodis and Valeri Khrichaty, were killed in an avalanche just below 5000m on Khan Tengri. Peter Potter, an aspirant guide, who was higher up, survived.

On the same day, Dave Wilkinson reached the summit alone after some other members of his party had turned back at about 6400m owing to the intense cold.

The American Himalayan guide Alex Lowe won the Speed Mountaineering Competition organised by the Tien Shan International Mountaineering Centre. Starting at 3950m he raced to the summit Khan Tengri and back again in a time of just over 10 hours.

Pik Alpinist (5492m) A team led by Mikhail Lebedev made the first ascent of this 'Matterhorn of the Tien Shan', climbing the NE face.

Pamir

Pik Sleslov (4240m) A team led by A Klenov climbed a five-day, 800m new route to the right of the other lines on this mountain. A considerable amount was aid climbing.

Pik 4810m R Karle, D Dumont and E Guy climbed a direct line on the NE face from 31 July to 4 August (6b ED+).

Pik 4520m A group including L and J-B Jourjon climbed the 1300m SE ridge.

Pik 3850m F Pallendre and team made the first ascent of *Le Paradis Artificiel* on the N face from 16-31 July (Abo 6b A4 720m). A Franco-Russian team added *Voie Papillon* (5b+ ED 800m) between the French and Russian direct routes on the W face.

North America 1993

Alaska

Apparently not much of note was done on **Denali (Mt McKinley)** in 1993. Mark Leffler and Robert Schneider made the second ascent of the route pioneered in 1991, solo, by the late Miroslav Smíd on the western side of the S face (Smíd died in a fall in Yosemite in the autumn of 1993). Four young Frenchmen, Xavier Cret, Robin Molinatti, Pierre Rizzardo and Paul Robach, made the second ascent of the *Ridge of No Return*, which ends at 4575m on the S buttress. Renato Casarotto had taken 12 days to do the climb solo. The French climbed the vertical 2000m in only three days. Speed ascents seem to be fashionable. Brad Johnson climbed solo to the N summit and back from the 5250m camp in 3hrs 40min.

Michael Kennedy and Greg Child made a remarkably fast ascent of the W face of **Mt Huntingdon** by the difficult *Quirk-Nettle route*, flying in on 15 May and out on the 19th. A party that landed a week later, hoping also to climb the route, was chased from its camp by a 'hopelessly misplaced bear', who ate up all their food.

Nearby, the SE face of **Royal Tower** in Little Switzerland, was climbed by Peter Haeussler and Lloyd Miller.

A British Armed Services party made the second ascent of the long and quite difficult Archangel Ridge of **Foraker**. Paul Edwards and David Peel got to the summit on 26 April, but because of frostbite they had to be helicoptered out.

British climbers Geoff Hornby and David Barlow made the first ascent of **Pt 10,920 (2765m, 'Thunder Mountain')**, just south of McKinley.

The SW ridge of **Hunter**, which had previously been climbed only twice, was ascended by Hornby and Barlow, as well as Britons Neil Main and Chris Schiller and two American pairs.

The SE face of **East Kahiltna Peak** was climbed for the first time by Pat Callis and Terry Kennedy.

Excellent new routes were done in the spires of the **Kichatna Mountains**. Michael Pennings and Jeff Hollenbaugh made a new route on the SE face of **Serenity Spire** and other good climbs despite terrible weather. Doug Byerly and Calvin Herbert made new routes on **Plumb Spire, Trinity Spire** and **'Hersey Tooth'**.

Germans Martin Göggelmann and Eduard Birnbacher made some good new climbs in the **Chigmit Mountains**, despite rotten rock.

Danny Kost was again active, climbing **Pt 7998** on the Thompson ridge of the **Chugach Mountains** and the **President's Chair** and **Pt 10,004** in the **Wrangell Mountains**, all with Harold Hunt.

The W summit of **Blackburn (4964m)** was reached by the SSE buttress by Peter Green and Daniel Culver on 23 June. Kaj Bune and Doug Barlow climbed above the Klutlan glacier in early June and got to the summits of **Bear (4526m)** and **Bona (5005m)**.

Before his tragic death soloing in Yosemite, Czech Miroslav Smíd, with Swiss Ruedi Hohberger, made an eight-day variant on the *boundary route* on St Elias **(5488m)**. Mike Daniel and Paul Netzband climbed the *Carpé Ridge* on **Fairweather (4669m)**. Bill Pilling and Carl Dietrich traversed **Mt Vancouver** from south to north over the S summit **(Good Neighbour Peak, 4785m)** and the main summit (4812m) to the Seward glacier. On the descent Pilling had a crevasse fall, severely injuring one leg, but the pair descended more than 2000 vertical metres and then walked 35km to the point where they were picked up by plane.

Canada

Mt Logan was attempted by 40 people and 22 managed to reach either the main or the E summit. One person was killed and another injured in an avalanche on the *Early Bird Buttress*. A Canadian all-female party climbed the difficult E ridge to the E summit. They were Mary Clayton, Sylvia Forest, Leanne Alison and Andrea Petzold.

Germans Stefan Winter, Stefan Vorderhuber and Ludwig Stitzinger climbed **Mt Baird** by its SE ridge, reaching the summit on 10 May. Americans led by Greg Collum made a new route on the S face of **McArthur Peak**.

Britons Paul Knott, Ade Miller, Paul Mead and Rob Wilson first attempted the E ridge of **Augusta** and then completed the first British ascent and the fourth overall, climbing the first ascent route, the N ridge.

In the NW Territories, Italians Mario Manica, Paola Fanton, Giuseppe Bagattoli, Danny Zampiccoli and Fabio Leoni made a splendid new route on the N face of **Harrison Smith** in the Cirque of the Unclimbables in the **Logan Mountains**. They also ascended **Lotus Flower Tower**. Further south, Greg Child and Perry Beckham made a new route on the E buttress of **Slesse Mountain**, a long and very difficult rock climb.

In the Canadian Arctic, on the Cumberland peninsula of **Baffin Island**, John Barbella, Kurt Roy, Alan Bills, Steve Hopkins and Dave Oakley climbed **Mt Thor** by its S ridge. Doug Cairns and Dan Cousins climbed **Mt Bilbo** by the NW ridge and **Mt Sigurd** by the SE ridge.

Continental United States

It would be difficult to give a list of all the remarkable rock climbs which have been done in many of the regions in the 'Lower 48'. I shall give only a few of possibly the most notable.

From 17 July to 5 August, Nancy Feagin, Hans Florine, Christian

Santelices and Willie Benegas did 20 of the climbs in *50 Classic Climbs in North America* by Allen Steck and Steve Roper. This took them from **Yellowstone** to the **Southwest Desert**, to **Colorado** and finally to the **Wind River Range** of Wyoming. They estimate that they climbed over 60,000 feet in the 19 days, walked 137 miles and climbed 241 pitches.

In **Yosemite**, Lynn Hill has taken one of the most coveted prizes in American rock-climbing with her totally free ascent of *The Nose* on **El Capitan** (5.13b). After working the route with Simon Nadin she returned to complete the whole route, from the ground, with Brooke Sandahl.

Todd Skinner with various partners took 61 days to complete the first free climb of the *Direct NW Face* of **Half Dome**. Charlie Fowler, Will Oxx and Swiss Xavier Bongard did a hammerless ascent of *The Shield* on **El Capitan**. John Middendorf and Oxx did a new route on the same mountain between *Magic Mushroom* and *The Shield*. Fast ascents were made on El Cap's *Nose*. Nancy Feagin and Sue McDevitt climbed the route in 17 hours – the first female pair to make the climb in a single day. The mixed team of Lynn Hill and Hans Florine climbed the route in 8hrs 17min. Florine had previously completed the climb with Peter Crofts in only 4hrs 22min. In August Florine made the fastest solo yet reported for *The Nose*: 14hrs 11m.

There was much climbing in the desert country of the south-west. Between Christmas 1992 and 30 May 1993, Rob Slater climbed all 23 of the **Fisher Towers** and the four **Mystery Towers** listed in Eric Bjornstad's *Desert Rock*. Many of these were desperate second ascents on crumbling rock and vertical dirt.

The biggest news in the **Canyonlands** in 1993 was Keith Reynolds's and Walt Shipley's free ascent of **Standing Rock** (5.11c). The tower was first climbed in 1962 by Layton Kor, Huntley Ingalls and Steve Komito and is considered one of the all-time classic desert towers.

In **Zion National Park** John Middendorf, Brad Quinn and Bill Hatcher climbed a new route on **Isaac**, a 1800ft high wall. Middendorf and Oxx later made the ascent of a 900ft tower, **Birdbeak Spire**. Roger Briggs and Steve Levin were active on the Diamond of **Longs Peak** in Colorado, completing a new route with four 5.12 pitches; the rest were mostly 5.11.

In Wyoming, Alex Lowe and Steve Koch did a new route on the NE face of **Cloudveil Dome** in the **Tetons**. Middendorf and Steve Quinlan made a third new route on the N face of **Mt Hooker**. They completed this very difficult 1800ft route after a number of sorties spread over three years.

A large number of notable members of the American climbing fraternity died in 1993. The American Alpine Club has lost four of its Honorary Members: Terris Moore, Walter Wood, Richard Leonard and John Salathé. Brilliant younger climbers Mark Bebie and Steve Risse died in an avalanche near the Columbia Ice Field in Canada. Julie Culberson, a remarkable guide with a splendid climbing record, was also killed in an avalanche accident. Stan Sheppard died in a car accident in his beloved Bolivia, where he had achieved an outstanding climbing record.

South America and Antarctica 1993

Thanks are due to Marcelo Scanu, Gerhard Feichtenschlager, Pavle Kozjek and Franci Savenc for their invaluable contributions.

Most of the activity this year has continued to centre on the developed countries of Argentina and Chile where an increasing number of teams are producing committing big-wall routes in a variety of styles. In Peru the situation continues to improve, with Slovenians notably active this summer.

Venezuela

Aratitiyope Paul Ridgeway, Todd Skinner, Paul Piana and a camera crew made a difficult approach through jungle to attempt the second ascent of Boivin's 1984 route up a prominent rib on the right side of the 600m E face of this flat-topped tower.

Peru – Cordilleras Blanca and Huayhuash

Both the weather and the security situation were considerably more settled in Peru this year with New Zealand climbers returning to the Huayhuash after a long absence following the 1988 shootout. They made an attempt on the W face of **Yerupaja**, stopping just short of the summit.

Slovenians dominated the new route scene in the Blanca where general levels of activity continued to rise.

Artesonraju (6025m) On 9 July 1993 Tomo Sbrizaj and Sebastian Semrajc climbed the SE face via a direct line up the triangular rock buttress to a junction with the normal route. On 18 July they returned with Borut Naglic and repeated the route, *Triangle*, continuing to the summit (TD+ 60°- 85° III 600m).

André Kecman and Dusan Kosir climbed the snowy SW face through séracs on the left side but it is not clear how this differs from previous ascents of this face.

Huascaran Sur (6768m) On 21 July 1993 Marjan Kovac, Bostjan Lozar and Tomas Petac summited after four and a half days climbing the obvious pillar which runs up the left side of the NE face to join the E ridge. In bad weather they completed 1300m up the pillar and then 570m along the ridge to the summit to give *The Road To Hell* (ED VI+ A1 60°- 90°).

Chacraraju Este (6001m) Pavle Kozjek and Gregor Kresal forged a stunning line up the uncompromising and unclimbed E face by linking the vague snow patches/slabs on the right side until reaching the *Terray route* on the NE ridge 250m below the summit. They summited on 19 July 1993, their second day, and descended the NE ridge where they noted frozen-in fixed ropes (ED+ VII A2 80° 700m). On 28 July they returned to climb the *Japanese 1979 route* on the S face in only 13hrs 30min up and down including crossing the glacier.

Bolivia

Nevado de las Virgenes Stan Shepard, Daken Cook, and Mario Miranda made the first ascent of this remote peak.

Cordillera de Potosí Evelio Echevarría climbed four unnamed peaks and christened them **Cerro de la Mina (4940m)**, **Cerro Cóndor Negro (5000m)**, **Cerro Sipuruni (4966m)** and **Cerro Maucatambo (4940m)** after local geographical features. He also climbed **Hembra de Andacaba (4980m)** and **Cerro Quellu Orco (4960m)**, the latter a first ascent.

Argentina and Chile

Chile is now requiring permission to be obtained before climbing in Tierra del Fuego, Paine National Park, Lauca National Park, or Ojos del Salado. Application should be sought from Chilean embassies or from: Director Nacional de Fronteras y Limitas del Estado, Ministerio de Relaciones Exteriores, Bandera 52, Piso 4, Santiago. There are increasing rumours that a fee of $750 will be imposed on expeditions to the Torres del Paine National Park which would certainly be prohibitive for many South American teams and less than welcomed by many others.

Argentina's experiment with a peak fee on Aconcagua seems relatively successful with the money being used to provide toilet facilities and generally clean up the area. In other Argentine parks the same tasks are carried out by rangers as their other duties permit and there is talk that if the environmental problems increase then they may be forced to follow suit in imposing a peak fee. The solution is in the hands of climbers.

The Argentine mapping authority has recently released the results of many previously classified surveys of heights. A partial list of the revisions has been filed with the Alpine Club Library. Additionally they are issuing new maps of the border regions which are reported to be excellent.

Argentine Northern Andes

Chusca (5512m) A large Argentine/Swiss group climbed the five summits of this massif in the **Cordillera de Catreal** from the E and found pre-

Columbian ruins on the highest summit, including the remains of a sacrificed deer.

Argentine Province of San Juan

Many summits here remain ujclimbed and various Argentine parties have been active in the area. Amongst these the more notable ascents were:

Cerro San Lorenzo First ascents of this unclimbed group in the **Cordilleras Agua Negra y Olivaros** by Martin Mattioli, Santiago Rocha and Marcelo Scanu on 20 January 1993 from the Quebrada San Lorenzo to the summits of **Chico (c5700m), Argentino (5700m+)** and **Este (5700m+)** from which they were able to see the Pacific.

Cerro Andres Costin/Peak 5 (5334m) On 13 April 1993 Humberto Campodonico and Roberto Pereira made the second ascent of this peak in the **Cordillera de Ansilta** by a new route following the 1000m ice couloir in the S face.

Argentine Province of Mendoza

Aconcagua (6954m) Patrick Berhault and François Pallandre abandoned a new route to the left of the Slovenian Pillar on the S face and settled for the second ascent of Slavko Sveticic's *SW Ridge Direct* on 29/31 January 1993, descending via the SE ridge and Polish glacier.

Ameghino (c6000m) Alex Lowe climbed a 150m ice couloir on the S face in one day from Camp 1 of the *normal route* on Aconcagua on 4 January 1993.

Sarmiento (5400m) A UK-based expedition composed of Susan Cooper, Greg Jones, Phil Swainson, and Henry Todd attempted the SE ridge in the southern summer of 92/93. After the 15-hour boat journey from Punta Arenas to this remote area they spent many days traversing difficult terrain to the base of the ridge. Lack of time forced them to abandon the attempt with only 1700m of steep but safe ice remaining before the W summit.

Patagonia - Northern Ice Cap

Cerro de Cristal Giuseppe Alippi, Benigno Balatti, and Enrico Cavalli climbed the W face of this peak which lies in the San Valentin range. The route which they named *Tocata e Fuga* has ice pitches up to 70°.

North–South Traverse A French team of Ilario Previtali and three companions made the first N–S traverse finishing on 25 March 1993 after 26 days. En route they made the twelfth ascent of **Mt San Valentin (4058m)** where they reported finding a large quantity of rubbish abandoned shortly before by an unsuccessful Italian team.

Southern Ice Cap Traverses

In 92/93 the Italians Joel Blumenburg, Paolo Cavagnetto, Paolo Falco and Alberto Guelpa planned to traverse from north to south along much the same route as Shipton's 1960/61 traverse, but continuing to the Paine group. In the event the terrain S of Lago Argentina proved unsuitable for skis and so they halted after 250km in 5 weeks.

On 28 February 1993 a Spanish team of José Luis Fernandez, Antonio Trabado, José Carlos Tamayo and the Argentine Sebastian de la Cruz began their attempt from Fiordo Calen. After 54 days they completed the entire N–S traverse of 400km at the foot of the Tyndall glacier on 24 April. Although self-supported they did use a helicopter to ferry gear past the broken-up glacier at Lago Argentina.

In February/March 1993 Australians Geoff and Steven Butcher, Graeme Hoxley and Alex McConnell explored the area around the head of Tempano Fjord and **Cerro Lautaro (3380m)** after finding the area to the E too crevassed to contemplate attempting the traverse. After ten days their boat failed to make its rendezvous and they were forced to walk out through difficult terrain for over a week before being able to hail a fishing vessel.

Fitzroy and Cerro Torre Groups

Aguja Saint Exupery (2558m) The *1968 Italian route* on the E pillar was almost completely freed by Michel Switter and Makoto Ishibe by difficult climbing on the wall rather than in the iced-up cracks (VII+ with one aid section versus VI/A3).

Cerro Standhardt (2730m)/Punta Herron In 1992/93 Adriano Cavellero, Ermanno Salvaterra, and Ferruccio Vidi repeated *Exocet* on the E face of Standhardt, abseiled down the S ridge to the notch connecting it with the NE ridge of **Torre Egger**'s N summit called Punta Herron and then climbed up this NE ridge by a new route of 400m V/VI+ 90°.

Punta Herron At the end of 1992 Maurizo Giarolli, Odoardo Ravizza and Andrea Sarchi climbed the prominent right-facing dièdre which splits the front face, summiting on 12 November. They called the route *Gracias a la Vida* and it is 750m of mostly A1/A2 with some VI+/A3 climbing.

Aguja Guillamet (2579m) In February 1993 Stephen Koch and Andy Parkin climbed the 600m central couloir of the SE face until it joins the NE ridge before the summit to give *Terra del Hombre* (ED1-2 VI 85°)

Aguja Mermoz (2732m) Andy Parkin soloed an impressive line up the SE face by the ramp line which starts from the right end of the face, slanting left to reach the right-hand end of the snowfield in the upper face. *Night Flight* took only 10hrs on 21 February 1993 (650m ED3 90° A2 V+).

Aguja Poincenot (3002m) Later Andy Parkin also soloed the original *Cochrane/Whillans 1962 route* on the E face. A route was reported on the summits between this and the Brecha de los Italianos by a Swiss/Japanese pair.

Aguja Bifida (2394m) The Austrians Tommy Bonapace and Gerold Dunser climbed a line on the E face summiting on 30 January 1993. Starting up the 800m crack system rising from the Torre glacier, at half height they traversed right over the ESE spur and original *1975 Swiss route* on the NE spur to reach the N summit (750m V/VI A1/A2).

Later two other Austrians, Paul Bruckner and George Schorghofer, climbed a 24-pitch route *Cogan* on the E pillar which may join the Bonapace/Dunser line in the upper section (VI+).

Aguja Cuatro Dedos/Aguja Bifida Ridge On 14 March 1993 Bonapace and Dunser traversed the three towers in the ridge joining these peaks, starting up the 200m snow ramp and rock wall to reach the col S of the Cuatro Dedos from the Torre glacier; 21 pitches of good climbing up to VI+.

Torre Egger (2673m) Americans Conrad Anker, Steve Gerberding and Jay Smith were unlucky not to complete a new line on the E face just right of the 1986 Slovenian line. Eventually they ran out of time just short of the summit after completing all the independent climbing.

Paine Group

The Shield In January 1993 Jerry Gore and Andy Perkins climbed the N ridge by a route they called *The Adventures of Don Quixote*. The 12-pitch approach up gullies of Scottish 4/5 was fixed with 200m of line before the pillar itself gave another 12 pitches of V+/A2 to reach the summit ridge. (*Full details in 'Windmills in the Mind', pages 58-63.*)

Cuernos Norte Mike Turner and Louise Thomas climbed the crack system of the W face in two days. The 21-pitch route is called *Caveman* (E5/A3).

Catedral José Chavarri, Lorenzo Ortiz, Javier Ballester and Santiago Palacios climbed the 1000m E face marginally right of the summit fall line to reach the summit on 22 February 1993 after 17 days. Most of the route required aid interspersed with free moves: *Cristal de Roca* VII+/A4.

Point 2000m Italians Raccamello Alessandro, Roberto Canzan, Valmassoi Mauro, Svaluto Moreolo and Renato Pancierre climbed the E face of this point S of the Catedral and overlooking the Frances valley. They climbed the prominent left-facing shoulder for 500m to stop at the summit ridge 200m below and right of the summit.

Torre Norte del Paine (2260m) The Italian group of Carlo Besana, Maurizo Garota, Emanuele Panzeri, Norberto Riva and Umberto Villota climbed one of several obvious cracklines on the NW face to give *Suarte para Manana* summiting on 30 December 1992, VII/A2.

Earlier, Argentines Ramiro Calvo, Diego Luro and Teo Plaza put up a 500m VI+/A1 new route on the W face climbing a crackline to the left of *Ultima Esperanza*, summiting on 3 December 1992. They called the route *Carapachin Tortola*.

At the end of February 1993 the British team of Celia Bull, Leigh McGinley and Paul Pritchard climbed another route at the right end of this face. They climbed the prominent SW rib to join the *normal route* at the S ridge with 500m of new climbing on fine granite. They called this *The Corn Wall* (TD+ VII V+).

On 4/5 March 1993 the Spanish team of José Chavarri and Lorenzo Ortiz climbed the 200m NW face to reach the easier crest of the N ridge at a prominent shoulder, which they followed for 150m to the top. They called the route *Armas y Rosas* (A2 VII).

On 21/22 November 1992 Bruno De Dona soloed the N tower via the normal *S ridge route*, then the N ridge of the central tower, and finally the N ridge of the S tower.

The first ascent of the 800m E face was made by François Bernard, Antoine Cayrol, Laurent Favre, Hubert Giot and Thierry Petitjean who reported it to be similar in standard to the E face of Cerro Paineta (VII A3).

Torre Central del Paine (2454m) A second route was added to the W face by the Italians Carlo Barbolini, Bruno de Dona, Angelo Pozzi, Alberto Rampini and Mario Veghetti in the 92/93 season. It is called *Via de las Mamas* (750m VII A2/A3).

The Argentines who climbed the N tower teamed up with Philip Lloyd and Peter Gaber to climb *A Fine Line Of Madness* on the E face. This begins left of the huge dièdre of the *1974 South African route*, crosses it after about 250m to reach the big dièdre on the right and follows this, moving right around the huge roof at two-thirds height to finish up the last 200m of the *1963 British route* (1000m VII with seven pitches of aid up to A3).

Paineta Lloyd and Gaber climbed a direct finish through the roofs at the finish of the *Original route* on the SW pillar (A2).

Cerro Almirante Nieto/Paine Chico Bruno de Dona climbed a 500m route of V+/A1 on the W face.

Antarctica

Mount Vinson (5271m) Dutch climbers Edward Bekker and André Hokke made the second ascent of a variant to the *normal route* on 14 December 1992. Above the Shinn-Vinson col they climbed mixed ground up the ridge on the left which runs W to the summit. An American team including Jay Smith may have made a first ascent on the S face.

TONY HOWARD

Middle East 1993

Oman

Amongst the best routes to be done in the Middle East in 1993 was what is known as the *French Route* on the 1500m S pillar of Jebel Misht. Originally sieged over four weeks and with considerable aid by French guides under the leadership of Raymond Renaud in 1979, a free ascent has since been attempted on at least two occasions. In January 1993 Jerry Hadwin, Sean Nelson and Garth Bradshaw finally succeeded in a two-day push and comment that the route should be climbable in a day. There is some E3 5c, but much of the route is Severe or below.

The end of the year was marked by the publication of Alec McDonald's guide *Rock Climbing in Oman* (Apex Publishing, distributed by Cordee), listing around 170 routes of all grades in all areas of the country and identifying areas for potential new climbs. The book is in traditional British style, easy to follow and essential for anyone considering climbing there, though a map of Oman identifying crag locations at a glance would have been useful.

Jordan

1993 seems to have been the year of the guidebook in the Middle East, for it also saw the publication of *Walks and Scrambles in Wadi Rumm* (Al Kutba), and the completion of the second edition of *Treks and Climbs in Wadi Rumm* (Cicerone), both by the author of this report.

The latter guide includes details of around 270 routes. The climbs in the early nineties by Austrian guides Haupolter and Precht are particularly notable and at the top end of difficulty, being serious undertakings on intricate big walls. Equally noteworthy was the ascent in 1993 of a new route on the 500m SW pillar of **Nassrani** by Bedouin climber Sabbah Eid with E Ratouis and a French team, at TD Sup, with a lot of 5b (English) and a 5c crux. (Plate 90)

With the assistance of the Ministry of Tourism, **Wadi Rumm** now has greatly improved amenities for visitors and climbers. The Rest House and surrounds have been extended to include a restaurant and bar, a climbers' self-catering kitchen, a campsite, showers and toilets, all within one hour's walk of most of the routes in the guide.

Elsewhere in Jordan, the author and Di Taylor are continuing trekking, climbing and canyoning explorations in the surrounds of Petra and the Dead Sea Hills where **Wadi Mujib** is situated – a magnificent 40km gorge descending from 1500m above sea level to 390m below!

A guide to this area is expected in the future, whilst the new Cicerone *Guide to the Wadi Rumm* should be in the shops for the spring '94 season.

Turkey

This country has also seen publication of a new Cicerone guide to Ala Dag by Ö B Tüzel entitled *The Ala Dag, Climbs and Treks in Turkey's Crimson Mountains*. It describes around 130 routes with both summer and winter ascents and indicates possible areas for exploration. (*The guide is reviewed by Sir Edward Peck on page 314.*)

This area and the S Med coast have also had a couple of recent visits by French guides Colonna and Domenech who report great potential for sport climbs and canyoning.

New Zealand 1993

The major focus of activity shifted from the high peaks of the **Mt Cook** region during 1993, with few of the classic faces, such as the Balfour and Hidden faces of **Tasman** even being repeated.

Rather, it was the valleys lying just to the south of Mt Cook village, the Mueller, Dobson and Hopkins, that attracted most attention . More attentive than anyone was the incomparable Bill McLeod, who put up 15 new routes, both in this region and further afield, many of which rank with the finest in the Southern Alps.

Hopkins Region

Vampire Peak (2623m) Although above the Mueller glacier, Vampire has been included in the Hopkins area for this review. On the E face, with Brian Alder, McLeod climbed *Nosferatu*, and with Andy MacFarlane *Bram Stoker*. The former is a particularly fine 14-pitch ice gully, comparable to Hick's S face routes.

Mt Sealey (2639m) *Prime Time* is an 800m rock route on the S face, climbed by McLeod and Peter Dickson. A better climb than Hick's N face central buttress, claims McLeod. On the same wall, but climbing to the peaks of **Jean** and **Marie** further west, McLeod climbed two more routes, the latter with Ross Cullen.

Mt Hopkins (2676m) One of the finest and most neglected peaks of the Southern Alps, to which McLeod has added two outstanding lines. The S ridge is so obvious, the dominant feature of the upper Hopkins valley, it seems incredible it was not climbed years ago. McLeod completed it with Dickson. In winter McLeod returned alone, struggling for several days through deep soft snow to reach the bottom of the SW face. *Gormenghast* is a formidable achievement. McLeod, who has soloed many of the test pieces of the Southern Alps, rated it as among the more gripping experiences of his career.

Mt McKerrow (2650m) Also in winter McLeod climbed the obvious line direct from valley floor to summit: *Orinoco Flow* .

Mt Percy Smith (2465m) On this landmark of colonial nomenclature (Stephenson Percy Smith was a 19th century surveyor-general and inventor of the 'great fleet' myth of Maori migration) McLeod and Dickson climbed on the S face. *On the Dark Shore* is a 23-pitch rock route with a crux of grade 17. Many New Zealand climbers were completely unaware even of the existence of the face until the completion of this route.

Westland

Mt Unicorn (2560m) On the very fine Strauchon face Bill McLeod and Peter Dickson did the rock route *Classical Gas* (rock, cruxes of 16).

Mt La Perouse (3081m) *Bill and Ted's Excellent Adventure* climbs the very steep ice on the S face. McLeod and Brian Alder bivouacked twice to complete the route.

'Kupe Peak' A small rock peak below the icefall of the Balfour glacier (visible on the spine of the Mt Cook guidebook). *Sinusoidal Ridge* (16), *Captain Incredible and the Naked Dancing Girls* and *Kupe Direct* (19) were climbed by Tony Ward Holmes, Bryan Moore and Erik 'the flatmate from hell'.

Darran Mountains

Cirque Creek confirmed its status as the pre-eminent ice-climbing venue in the country. *Southern Man* (Alan Uren and Clinton Beaven) and *Squealing* (Dave Vass and Paul Rogers) take lines on the lower wall of **Mt Crosscut**. The latter especially approaches the virtuosity of Scottish ice.

Mount Everest Foundation Expedition Reports 1992–93

SUMMARISED BY BILL RUTHVEN

After twelve years as author of these notes, Sir Edward Peck has decided to lay down his pen, and it has therefore fallen on me to try to maintain the high standard that he has set. The Mount Everest Foundation is extremely grateful for all his efforts: apart from writing these notes he served on the Committee of Management from 1974 to 1980, and on the Screening Committee from 1980 to 1991.

Each year, the Mount Everest Foundation supports a number of expeditions undertaking exploration in one form or another amongst the high mountains of the world. As well as 'Approval' – which in itself often has the effect of opening other purses – most expeditions also receive a grant, usually ranging between £200 and £1500. Whilst this only represents a small proportion of the overall cost of an expedition, the moral support and the offer of a few hundred pounds during the preparatory stages of an expedition can sometimes make the difference between it going and not going.

All that the MEF asks in return is a report. Once received, copies are lodged in the Alpine Club Library, the Royal Geographical Society and the British Mountaineering Council where they are available for consultation by future expeditioners. The following notes are based on reports that have been received during 1993, and are divided mainly into a number of discrete areas or countries.

America – North

92/37 British Alaskan Multi-Peak (May–June 1992)

The plans of this two-man team were badly affected by the weather and health problems, and the only new route attempted – the SW ridge of Mt Crosson (3900m) – was abandoned at c3200m owing to danger of avalanche. However, Mt Hunter (4442m) was climbed by its W ridge and Mt McKinley (6194m) by the W buttress.

93/29 British Mount Augusta (May 1993)

A four-man team achieved the first British ascent of Mount Augusta (4289m) by the 1953 N ridge route, after they had reached a long corniced section at c3000m on their proposed new route on the E ridge.

93/34 British Tokositna/Kahiltna (May 1993)

After making the first ascent of the central summit of Mount Thunder (3292m) via its S face, this two-man team spent a frustrating week waiting to be picked up and flown to Kahiltna Base. From here they achieved the second British ascent of the SW ridge of Mount Hunter (4442m).

93/50 Cathedral Spires (June–July 1993)

This four-man team achieved the first ascent of the S face of Sunrise Spire (2408m) in Kitchatna, Alaska in seven days climbing of which approximately half was aid climbing (Grade 6/5.10/A3).

America – South

93/3 Sarmiento (December 1992–February 1993)

This trip started with an invitation from the Federacion de Andinismo de Chile to form a joint British–Chilean expedition, but in the end no Chileans were available to join the four British climbers. The main objective, the first ascent of the SE ridge of Sarmiento (2404m) in Tierra del Fuego (second overall), was unsuccessful owing to lack of local support and bad weather. The secondary objective – a study of plants and birds in the area – was most successful.

93/7 British Extremely Chile 1992/93 (December '92–January '93)

This two-man team succeeded in climbing The Shield (c2400m) in the Torres del Paine National Park by a technical new route on the N ridge. This was the second overall ascent, and was achieved by climbing non-stop for 22 hours during the only window in the usual Patagonian weather. (*See article 'Windmills in the Mind', pages 58-63.*)

93/8 British Cerro Torre 1993 (January 1993)

A strong four-man team hoped to climb a major new route on the E face of Cerro Torre (3100m) in Argentine Patagonia. However, the weather prevented any appreciable progress being made on either this or the original *Maestri route*.

93/13 Bolivia 1993 – UK Apolobamba (July–September 1993)

A team of eight climbers achieved first British ascents of five named and four unnamed peaks between 5000m and 6000m in Bolivia. Plant material and seed was also collected for La Paz University and Kew Gardens.

93/23 British Salcantay 1993 (May 1993)

The team planned to attempt a new route on the very steep SW face of Salcantay (6271m) in the Cordillera Vilcabamba of Peru. Tragically both male members were killed in a fall on their second day on the route: their bodies were found by the two female members of the team.

Greenland and Arctic Europe

93/4 Jordanhill College East Greenland (July– September 1993)

This was a four-man team planning to make the first British ascent (preferably by a new route on the NE face) of Laupers Bjerg (2500m). That route proved to be too technical, but a successful ascent was made by the original SE face route. The party had an extra week's enforced stay in the area as their pick-up boat failed to arrive.

93/10 Arctic Research Group Svalbard 1993 (July– August 1993)

This was one stage in a project to develop a system of Continuous Automatic Monitoring of Mountain And Reticulated Glaciers (CAMMARG). Eventually it should be possible to use the system in the Greater Ranges, but in the meantime the ARG is proving it in the Paulabreen–Bakaninbreen glacier of Spitsbergen. Whilst on the glacier, the team was attacked by a polar bear, which was eventually shot at a range of 1 metre.

93/17 NI Greenland (July–August 1993)

This party of six planned to use sea kayaks to explore the area at the head of Sermilik Fjord, but heavy icebergs prevented entry to the fjord. However, they climbed a number of small peaks on the E shore, including some thought to be first ascents.

93/18 British Lemon Mountains 1993 (June– July 1993)

For three of the the four-man team this was a return to an area of E Greenland visited in 1992. This year they were rewarded with first ascents of Chisel (2320m), Trident (2350m), The Beacon (2262m), The Ivory Tower (2100m) and The Needle (1945m), as well as attempts on three other peaks. They also completed a survey of the area using a GPS. The leader sustained a fractured collar-bone (twice!) owing to rockfall.

(*See article 'Gneiss and Ice: Greenland on the Rocks', pages 64-70.*)

93/24 Greenland Sermersoq 1993 (July–August 1993)

The leader of this expedition had visited the uninhabited island off SW Greenland in 1977, and considered that it had great potential for a future visit. The four-man 'golden-oldie' party (sponsored by Saga magazine) confirmed this by climbing 12 peaks, 7 being first ascents.

93/40 1993 Tasermiut Fjord (August 1993)

This two-man team planned to climb new big-wall routes on the remote towers of Ketil and Ilamertorssuaq (both c2200m) near Cape Farewell. The NE ridge of the first was abandoned as being too serious after six pitches, as was the N pillar of Pt 2051m (aka Nalumassortok) after installing some fixed ropes. There was obviously plenty of scope in the area for a stronger team prepared to face man-eating mosquitoes.

Himalaya – Bhutan and China/Tibet

93/2 British Masa Gang (April–June 1993)
This was a five-man team planning to make the first ascent of the SW ridge (second overall) of Masa Gang, a 7194m peak on the Bhutanese border with Tibet. The proposed route proved impractical, and attempts on the NE face were stopped at 6550m by bad weather and objective danger.

93/19 Irish Mount Everest 1993 (March–June 1993)
The leader of this large mixed party of climbers from Northern Ireland and Eire achieved the first British/first Irish ascent of the mountain from the north. This was the route attempted unsuccessfully by all the pre-war expeditions.

Himalaya – India

92/8A Scottish Garhwal 1992 (October 1992)
A four-man team attempted to climb Nilkanth (6596m) by the SE ridge, a route that proved to be technically difficult and very committing, with much loose rock. A high point at the base of the 4th Pinnacle (c5600m) was reached – higher than any recent expedition.

92/24 Cambridge Gangotri 1992 (August–September 1992)
A four-man party hoped to achieve the first ascent of Manda III (6529m) by its NW face but gave up when they found that the snow was very avalanche prone. An attempt on Jogin III (6116m) was within 50m of the summit when they were hit by a slab avalanche: fortunately there were no injuries. Later, a high point (c6050m) was reached on the ridge between Jogin II (6342m) and Pk 6014m.

93/9 Cerro Kishtwar (August–October 1993)
A previous attempt to make the first truly alpine-style ascent of this 6200m peak had failed after 17 days when the team ran out of food. The summit was reached by two of this four-man team in a little over a week by means of a very steep route slanting left to right on the NW face and then crossing the N ridge to reach the summit via the NE face. By the time that they had abseiled to the bottom of the climb, three of their four ice tools had broken. (*See article 'The One That Nearly Got Away', pages 48-63.*)

93/39 Meru Shark's Fin 1993 (August–October 1993)
This five-man team included some of Britain's strongest rock climbers, and aimed to climb the *Shark's Fin* on Meru (c6600m) in the Gangotri. However, after climbing pitches of E5/6b one of the party dropped a boot whilst getting dressed at c6000m, necessitating an urgent descent to prevent frostbite. It also meant the end of the expedition.

Himalaya – Nepal

92/7 TWTCC West Nepal (September–October 1992)

A team of five planned to make the first British ascent of Api (7132m) in the Gurans Himal, hopefully by a new route. Two major storms, each lasting several days, forced the attempt to be abandoned some distance above Camp 2 (c6000m).

92/36 British Khumbu Alpine (October–November 1992)

A two-man team hoped to achieve several new routes on a number of 'trekking' peaks, but suffered from bad weather. Hence, the only route climbed was the SW ridge of Imja Tse (aka Island Peak), 6189m. Although no earlier ascent by this route is known, being such an obvious line the team would be surprised if it had not been climbed.

92/47 British Peri Himal (October–December 1992)

Six climbers attempted a new route on the S face/ridge of Himlung Himal (7126m) in the area N of the Manaslu range: the peak had only had one previous ascent. Heavy snow forced a diversion from their planned route and meant lost time, so the attempt was abandoned at c6250m.

Rolwaling Ski-mountaineering (February 1993)

Lack of snow prevented this six-man team from carrying out much of its intended exploratory winter journey in the area W of Namche Bazar, and none of the planned summits were attempted.

Gangchempo 1993 (March–April 1993)

A very strong seven-person team planned to make the first official ascent of this 6387m peak in the Langtang Himal by means of the NW face, but in view of apparent objective danger attempted the W ridge instead. A high point of 6000m was reached before unseasonal bad weather and lack of time brought the expedition to an end.

93/32 British Mera Peak West Face 1993 (October–November 1993)

A two-man team hoped to put up a new route on the W face of this 6476m 'trekking' peak in Nepal, but succeeded on the ordinary route. They also climbed the SW face of Pk 6091m.

Karakoram – Pakistan

92/17 British Nanga Parbat 1992 (July–August 1992)

A seven-man Anglo–Russian–Sherpa party planned to traverse the 8-mile long unclimbed W ridge from the Mazeno Pass to the 8125m summit: half of the distance is above 7300m. After placing food/fuel caches at 7000m and 7300m from the *Hans Schell route*, several members of the team were caught in a massive rock avalanche which caused injuries to two of them.

A reduced team of four commenced the traverse, and climbed over several of the pinnacles, reaching Pt 6970 before abandoning the attempt owing to high winds. (*See also 93/49 below.*)

93/16 British K2 1993 (June–August 1993)

Early onset of the monsoon with heavy precipitation and strong winds prevented this team of seven from getting higher than 7700m on the Abruzzi ridge. They assisted in the evacuation of an injured Swedish climber from this height and found the remains of the American, Art Gilkey, who disappeared in an avalanche in 1953. Their secondary objective of installing a hydro-electric system at the village of Mango was completed satisfactorily. (*See article 'Summer on the Savage Mountain', pages 54-57.*)

93/25 1993 Anglo-Irish Koz Sar (May–July 1993)

This five-man team experienced poor snow conditions throughout their expedition and aborted their attempt some 900m below the summit of the unclimbed Koz Sar (6677m) in the previously closed Batura Muztagh area.

93/27 British Gasherbrum IV (June–August 1993)

This team of six planned to climb a new route on the S ridge to make the first British ascent of this 7980m peak, but once on the mountain they decided to try the S face route attempted by an American team in 1992 instead. After fixing some rope, a storm and high winds ended the climb at c7300m. This was higher than the Americans had reached.

93/28 British K7 1993 (June–August 1993)

This five-man team hoped to make the first ascent of the SW ridge of this 6934m peak in the Hushe valley (2nd overall) but experienced appalling weather, with 26 days of snow. They also suffered malfunctioning stoves and had food stolen by ravens, so they did well to reach 6300m (after 32 days on the face) before abandoning the attempt. One member of the team sustained a knee injury but 'was made to continue'.

93/31 Batura 1993 (July–August 1993)

A five-man team hoped to make the first ascent of Dariyo Sar (c5600m) by its SE face, but were dissuaded from making an attempt owing to bad weather. However, they climbed a nearby peak (c5500m) by its N face – probably the first ascent. The MEF warning, that few people visited the area because the locals were violent, proved to be far from the case and good porters were obtained from the village of Bar.

93/41 British Kukua 1993 (August–September 1993)

This was a ten-man Service trip to a rarely visited glacier area in the Karakoram with the intention of exploring and climbing peaks up to 6000m as preparation for an expedition to Gasherbrum III in 1994. No peaks were climbed owing to bad weather/avalanches/rockfall, and the greatest height reached was only 5340m.

93/45 Karakoram Conquest 93 (July–August 1993)

A very large party from RAF Mountain Rescue teams planned to celebrate the 50th Anniversary of the Service with this expedition to the Hunza valley. Whilst many went trekking, a hard core attempted 7266m Diran Peak (aka Minapin). The NE ridge was abandoned owing to adverse snow conditions, but three achieved the summit via the N face.

93/46 British Shani North Face (July–September 1993)

This six-man team hoped to make the first ascent of the N face of Shani (5885m). After climbing Sentinel (5260m) by the Ordinary Route to acclimatise, heavy snow prevented them from attempting their main objective. However, they climbed two new TD+ ice routes in the cirque just S of Shani.

93/48 Chukatan '93 (July 1993)

A mixed team of six hoped to climb Peak 5753m from the Barpu glacier, but in view of continuous bad weather they switched their objective to Girgindil II (5750m), on which they reached 5500m before avalanche danger made further progress impracticable. They then climbed Rash Peak (5430m).

93/49 Nanga Parbat 1993 (July 1993)

After an abortive attempt on the Mazeno Ridge last year (92/17) the leader returned with one Polish companion in the hope of completing the ridge. After making first ascents of Mazeno Spire and Mazeno West Peak (5700m) he was hit by an avalanche whilst descending unroped, and was swept some 400m over rock and ice cliffs, badly damaging his already-pinned ankle in the process. No attempt was made on the main objective.

93/51A British Muchichul Glacier 1993 (July–September 1993)

This five-man team explored the S cwm of Hachinder Chhish, and one reached the summit of Majun Chhish (5800m) from Mandosh glacier.

Central Asia and the Far East

93/20 British Tien Shan 1993 (July–August 1993)

This was a multinational team, with five climbers from Britain, nine from Belarus and two from Switzerland. Attempts on several of the lower peaks in the area were thwarted by heavy snow, but on the clearest day of the whole trip one of the British climbers achieved the summit of Khan Tengri (7010m) by the ordinary route. The extreme objective danger was made clear when a massive avalanche was witnessed which killed four people from another group.

93/26 Asan Pamirs (July–September 1993)

Local fighting and a cholera outbreak added to the hazards that this four-man team faced before attempting big-wall climbs from the Asan valley. They succeeded in climbing Yellow Wall (TD) and the W face of Asan (ED1), but withdrew from a new route on Pyramidalny (5509m), the highest peak in the area, one of the team sustaining a broken arm in an avalanche. He was successfully evacuated by helicopter.

93/30 Welsh–Scottish Tien Shan 1993 (July–August 1993)

Heavy snow prevented an attempt on the S face of Khan Tengri by this four-man team, but one man achieved the summit via the W ridge.

93/42 Cambridge University Caucasus 1993 (August 1993)

A two-man team achieved possibly first British ascents of NW route on Pik Kavkaz (4037m), Sybartovich route on Peak Free Spain (4200m) and the Ablakov route on Nakra–Tau (4277m), all from the Baksan valley. They then moved to a valley near Arkhiz, from which they made the first British ascent of the W ridge of Sofia (3637m).

Book Reviews 1993

COMPILED BY GEOFFREY TEMPLEMAN

Everest
The Best Writing and Pictures
Edited by Peter Gillman
Foreword by Sir Edmund Hillary, Picture Research by Audrey Salkeld
Little Brown 1993, pp208, £25

This is a superb, monumental and lavishly illustrated book. As a Russian courier, I played a tiny part in securing some of the material before the publisher's deadline. When, in return, I received and opened an early complimentary copy, I was totally absorbed for two hours, oblivious of my bedtime. So I was happy to be invited to review this book for the *Alpine Journal*.

Publication was timed to coincide with the 40th Anniversary of the first ascent. It's all there, from Claude White's photograph taken from Khamba Dzong during the British Mission to Tibet in 1903-4, to the novelty stunts of the last five years: Boivin's parapente descent of 8000ft in 11 minutes to the Western Cwm; Batard's round trip from Base in 22½ hours; the 1991 hot-air balloon flights; and Tardivel's ski descent from the South Summit in September 1992. 'I am thankful,' says Sir Edmund Hillary in his Foreword, 'that I climbed Everest in the days of innocence, when everything was new and a constant challenge, and for me at least publicity was a bit of a laugh.' Now it's serious business!

The editor, journalist Peter Gillman, relates how he first fell under Everest's spell when, as a boy of eleven, he was taken to the film of the 1953 ascent and was transfixed by cameraman Tom Stobart's epic pan, seeming to last several minutes, from the snow-covered floor of the Western Cwm to the corniced crest of the Summit Ridge. That shot often returned to Gillman as he sifted through the hundreds of extracts, articles and photographs which he and Audrey Salkeld had gathered. In the end he resolved on a mix of old and new, of familiar icons and unpublished material with which to convey the awe he first felt 40 years before.

He has divided the material into four periods with appropriate captions: 'The finest cenotaph in the world' (Somervell) covering the British attempts before the Second World War; 'Ed, my boy, this is Everest' (Hillary's self-encouragement on the Summit Ridge) for the 1950s and 60s; 'All the world lay before us' (Scott), for the 1970s; and finally 'A dreamlike sense of disbelief' (Venables) from 1980 to the end of 1992.

The book ends with an incredible eleven pages of statistics, listing 485 ascents by 428 people over 13 different routes – over half the ascents having been made in the last five years. It classifies with Wisden-like accuracy and detail the 115 deaths, the 51 ascents without artificial oxygen (including an astonishing 7 by Sherpa Ang Rita), the 16 by women, the youngest person at 17, the oldest at 55, the 32 in a day on 12 May 1992. But the circus rolls on, as the number of ascents seems to rise exponentially. On 10 May 1993 there were 38 on top.

What can we learn from all this frenzied activity? I have an increasing respect for the scientific intellect of George Finch who, in addition to his well-known strong advocacy of supplementary oxygen, rejected the traditional Alpine clothing recommended for 1922 in favour of a quilted eiderdown jacket of his own design – an early duvet. On his high-altitude attempt he also had the good sense to take his boots to bed with him, unlike his companions who had to spend a further hour thawing them out over lighted candles. At 26,500ft he then watched carefully to see how his partner Geoffrey Bruce (the General's nephew) coped with the slippery sloping slabs on the N face on 'his first mountaineering expedition'. The fact that such indifferently chosen teams could get so high so early, surely contributed to the long delay in climbing Everest? It took the spur of international competition, the scientific deductions concerning oxygen rates, dehydration and acclimatisation, clearly reported by Dr Griffith Pugh in 1952, and the outstanding planning and leadership of a well-knit team by John Hunt, for Hillary and Tenzing to achieve ultimate success in 1953.

It is a sad reflection that, despite these basic lessons, so many parties still push on regardless for their moment of glory, and return by the slimmest of margins or suffer severe frostbite or death from exhaustion on the descent.

After 1953 there was a gap of 25 years before Everest was climbed without supplementary oxygen by Messner and Habeler in 1975. Since then the proliferating climbing population has produced a significant number of mortals of Olympian physique and fitness capable of this feat. But the number of successful ascents seems unlikely to continue at the recent rate. In the autumn of 1993 the Nepalese government increased the peak fee substantially to $10,000 per climber passing through the Khumbu icefall. This should reduce the number of expeditions sharply – a measure which I fully support, particularly if some of the income is ploughed back to improve the lot of the Sherpas and other hill people and to conserve the fragile Himalayan environment.

In conclusion, Peter Gillman and Audrey Salkeld are to be congratulated on their series of partial glimpses which together interpret the whole. Mallory's first awesome view of Everest on 13 June 1921: 'Gradually, very gradually, we saw the great mountainsides and glaciers and arêtes, now one fragment now another through the floating rifts, until far higher than imagination had dared to suggest the whole summit of Everest appeared. And in this series of partial glimpses we had seen a whole: we were able to piece together the fragments, to interpret the dream.'

George Band

The High Mountains of the Alps
Volume 1: The Four-Thousand-Metre Peaks
Helmut Dumler and Willi P Burkhardt
Diadem Books/The Mountaineers, 1993, pp224, £30.00

Once again, Ken Wilson has given great service to mountaineering by having the vision to introduce Dumler and Burkhardt's sumptuous publication to the English-speaking Alpinist. The collection of giants by their standard routes, whether it be 8000m Himalayan mountains, the highest points on the seven continents, or the 4000m peaks of the Alps, is becoming an increasingly popular, and many would argue a rather unimaginative, part of our sport.

Karl Blodig is generally accepted as the first person to have climbed all the Alpine 4000m peaks, and in the early part of this century he wrote a guide to these ascents – *Die Viertausender der Alpen* – which listed the 57 summits he had climbed. In 1932 Eustace Thomas became the first British climber to complete Blodig's original list (though by this stage Blodig himself had completed 76 summits), and as the years progressed even more 'tops' were added.

Not surprisingly, there are now a number of lists of 4000ers in existence, from as few as 52 (the total number of completely separate mountains) to around 150 peaks and tops (Goedeke). When Martin Moran and Simon Jenkins made their continuous traverse in 1993, the criterion was to include summits that had a height separation of 35m or more. This gave a total of 75. A couple of years ago a French guide listed 108 'summits', based on the number of individually named points with a height of 4000m or above. Recently, in an attempt to put an end to the endless arguments, a UIAA/CAI initiative came up with a list of 82, including the Grand Pilier d'Angle, and this may well be used as the bench-mark in the future.

The second edition of Blodig's original work was republished in 1968 with a considerable amount of revision. The new material was added by Helmut Dumler – one-time deputy editor of the famous German publication *Alpinismus* – who had himself just completed all the 4000ers. In 1989 Dumler co-opted the talents of Swiss photographer Willi Burkhardt, and between them they produced a new edition which formed the basis for Ken Wilson's translation. The recent version highlights 61 main peaks; yet to me it always seems dubious to draw up a list that includes all ten tops of Monte Rosa, yet only Pointe Walker on the Grandes Jorasses or just the Grafeniere on the Grand Combin. You see: the arguments are endless!

The majority of chapters are dedicated to a single 4000er and include mouthwatering plates which flatter its magnificent architecture, often from several different viewpoints. These are complemented by action photographs, taken most frequently, but by no means exclusively, on the normal route of ascent. In addition, there are many small topographical drawings detailing the various features and established routes that are visible in the main photographs, while Don Sargeant's excellent sketch-maps of the three main massifs form an essential aid to the geography.

The accompanying text neatly summarises the historic exploration that took place on the more obvious lines of weakness and then notes some of the more important subsequent climbs. Into this Wilson has subtly blended further information and anecdotal material extracted from reference sources of the period, notably early volumes of the *Alpine Journal*.

Valuable practical information is boxed at the end of each chapter in the form of a brief summary of the relevant valley bases, huts, routes, maps and guidebooks. Okay, we all have different opinions on gradings, and many of the route times seem a little generous, which is no bad thing, but the only real error, and one that occurs on many occasions throughout the book, is the misprint which reverses the Roman numeral IV. The middle-grade climber looking for slightly more ambitious ways up these noble mountains, will initially be horrified to find that many of his desired classics now contain rock pitches of VI or even VI+.

All this aside, the overwhelming impact must be the sheer magnificence of Burkhardt's photography. In this he has excellent subject material, for a high proportion of the 4000ers would probably be included in any list of the Alps' most beautiful mountains. However, he also has some material advantages: large and medium format cameras – many of the full-page plates are reproductions from original 10" x 8" transparencies – and a son with his own light aircraft, resulting in a number of original and interesting aerial views of the mountains cloaked in heavy winter snow. The shadows of a winter evening across the NW face of the Mönch, the dramatic double-page spread of the N face of the Breithorn and, possibly my favourite, an ethereal view of the shapely Brunegghorn, Bishorn and Weisshorn rising above a forested alp to the north, are just three of many technical masterpieces.

To these Wilson has added 150 photographs from various sources, and although some of these would appear outstanding in a different context, they inevitably take second place beside Burkhardt's pin-sharp, full page panoramas. Even so, Jim Teesdale's shot of the Nadelgrat at dawn, John Allen's crisp reproductions of the Rochefort Arête (the only monochrome print in the book), Teesdale's informative collection depicting the ascent of the Zinalrothorn, or some of O'Connor's and David Wynne-Jones's Matterhorn and Mont Blanc shots, certainly capture the essence of the climb in question.

The High Mountains of the Alps is thus a book primarily for the holiday Alpinist (and ski-mountaineer), who wishes to climb the traditional routes on the 4000ers. However, the middle-grade Alpinist will also find considerable inspiration, for who could not be moved by the fabulous panorama of the Paradiso range from Mont Blanc, or plates that include the delectable Weisshorn or Obergabelhorn? The more ambitious will, after a little research, be able to study in detail some of the modern technical offerings on the various faces, and the innovator, with a copy of the most recent definitive guidebook in hand, will be able to expose a few of the remaining secrets. In the case of one peak even this study is unnecessary, as two major unclimbed lines are duly noted in the text.

This is the first of a proposed two-part series, with the second volume looking at the best of the 3000m peaks. The potential for a work of even greater interest and significance to the Alpine mountaineer is staggering. I can hardly wait for its publication.

Lindsay Griffin

The Climbers. A History of Mountaineering
Chris Bonington
BBC Books and Hodder & Stoughton, 1992, pp288, £16.95

When Chris Bonington visited Bombay in May 1992 he carried a copy of *The Climbers*, his 12th book. When he returned in September 1992, he brought his 13th book: *Sea, Ice and Rock*. Not many writers, especially mountaineers, can boast of such prolific writing achievements. *The Climbers* deals with 'A History of Mountaineering'. There have been a few books in this genre, starting with the most celebrated of them all, Kenneth Mason's *Abode of Snow*. Mason's book covered the period from the earliest time till the first ascent of Everest in 1953. He covered only the Himalayan and trans-Himalayan ranges. Chris has a different line-up. He covers both the Alps and the Himalaya from 1881 to 1990, while Audrey Salkeld adds A Brief History of Mountaineering from 218 BC, ensuring a complete record of adventure.

If Mason's book is a thorough experience, like a symphony playing, with all the pieces, Bonington's book is to be read in an armchair with a cup of tea and a violin concerto playing lively tunes. The difference is obvious, But what is lost by way of complete coverage, Bonington makes up by way of extremely good reading and fun. He himself is part of the history, and he knows it:

> It is difficult for me to be completely objective since I have been closely and directly involved with the development of climbing in the last forty years. It has filled my life, given me that combination of joy, excitement, wonder and inevitably sorrow at the loss of all too many friends, but I hope that this has enabled me to empathise all the better with those early climbers who first explored the mysteries of the Alps and trace the course of this serpentine river of ours.

So, turning familiarity to an advantage, Bonington writes about the climbers (not explorers). For the younger generation, particularly, the first 200 pages tell all the well-known stories and weave different patterns. This is enjoyable and exciting with the right mix of events and stories.

The latter pages consider the last 37 years, a long period. The chapters present three main issues, leaving behind attempts to be exhaustive. The major climbs and development of climbing the mountains the 'hard way up' are considered. In the chapter entitled 'The Art of Suffering', extreme climbing is taken up. Exploits of Messner, Kurtyka and Kukuczka and the deaths of Boardman, Tasker and MacIntyre are covered in detail. But the last chapter is a stealer: 'Always a Little Further'. Here Bonington considers the major developments, which may affect the future attitudes. Sponsorship, commercial climbs, sport climbing and various developments in rock-climbing advancements are touched upon. We are left with a vision of the future.

In his opening sentence, Bonington declares the scope of the book: 'In writing a one-volume history of mountaineering I have had no choice but to be selective.' It is here that some can have a grouse against this book. To a lay reader it may appear that mountaineering is still a British preserve, or that only Americans and Europeans indulge in the sport. Not enough mention is made about the Japanese climbers or of climbers from many countries such as South Korea, India and others. This has led to specific achievements of these nationalities being ignored. For example, the traverse of the Nanda Devi peaks by the Indo-Japanese team; and climbs of many high peaks in the East Karakoram by the Japanese in the 1970s are not mentioned. They marched for weeks to reach the base camps over high passes and climbed giants like Singhi Kangri, Teram Kangri and others. One may not like the fixed-ropes but they are there, even as a style.

The personal selection necessarily misses out on some areas. Thus Paul Bauer's attempts on Kangchenjunga from Sikkim by the NE spur are taken up, but not the completion of the route in 1977 by the Indians. The 1979 British route by the N face also gets a mention.

The development of alpine-style climbing and the achievements of small teams and smaller, independent climbs, deserved a passing mention at least. Small expeditions like those of Shipton and Tilman still attract many. Stephen Venables' climb of Kishtwar–Shivling with Dick Renshaw, and even Bonington's own ascent with Jim Fotheringham of Shivling West, were trend-setters, and this brand of climbing should be emphasised. That would be really looking into the future.

But these are only small personal observations and do not detract from the merit and enjoyment of the book. To write *the* history of mountaineering someone would have to fill half a dozen volumes and the author would still not be able to include everything.

Bonington, even at his age and with his experience, refuses to be 'sidelined' and looks forward to the future with an open mind and welcomes change. I am sure readers will look forward to many more books from Bonington in future.

Harish Kapadia

(*This review first appeared in the* Himalayan Journal *in 1993 and is reproduced by kind permission of the Editor/author.*)

The Ascent
Ten Men and Two Women on the Brink of an Abyss
Jeff Long
Headline Features, 1993, pp370, pb, £4.99

When I am away on expeditions, I often read exciting thriller type novels. They are escapist and quite often a bit far-fetched, but enjoyable. I have not read many mountaineering novels and eagerly looked forward to getting stuck into this book which won the Boardman Tasker Memorial Award.

Objectively, I can see that Jeff Long has put a lot of thought and effort into the book, and perhaps an inner meaning – not that I found it. *The Ascent* tells the story of an attempt to climb the 'Kore Wall route' on the North Face of Mount Everest – an imaginary 'last great problem', loosely based on the West Face of Makalu. Fair enough so far; and changing the geography of a couple of passes on the north side of Everest is OK too – this is a novel. But, for me, the expedition described is massively unrealistic and the story corny and predictable, yet slightly baffling.

An opening sequence in the USA involves an accident and mountain rescue. The so-called MRT walks away and leaves a woman trapped in a crevasse! They do not even try to get her out. Where are the helicopters and media that would be involved?

The story then moves on to the nineties and reminds me of the film *K2*, which was pure 'corn'. It is peppered with military images, perhaps to make the action seem more sensational. After all, where is the fast-moving action in planning and preparing an expedition, plodding into Base Camp and setting up higher camps? At Base Camp '*JJ ... reached deep into the pile and extracted a 300 foot coil of orange rope and held it over his head, whooping, "Firepower!"*' I am surprised his team did not include Clint, Sly and Arnie, replete with helicopter gunships!

Later, when a camp is set up inside a cave on the mountain, the whole story loses any credibility I was trying to give it or, indeed, any enjoyment I was trying to get out of it. I have never seen or heard of a large cave, big enough for a camp, high up on a mountain. If such a cave existed, it would certainly not be calm inside. Spindrift would pour in and fill it up with snow!

The story then degenerates into a supposedly reader-gripping account of avalanches, retreat, a gory description of a leg amputation and inner meanings about the Chinese occupation of Tibet. Maybe I was missing some 'inner message', but *The Ascent* did not thrill me. It irritated me with its military comparisons, technical inaccuracies and American expressions. What, for example, is 'goosing'? One of the climbers '*was goosing his harness good and snug around his loins*'!

It has been reported that one reason Long wrote *The Ascent* was so that 'we not forget Tibet' and the genocide its people have suffered at the hands of the Chinese. 'I don't think climbers should climb in Tibet,' Long said at the annual meeting of the American Alpine Club (as reported in the American magazine *Climbing*). 'I've done it myself, but I won't be going again.' The genocide is undoubtedly true, but the western world has left its action a bit late; apparently more Chinese 'settlers' now live in Tibet than Tibetans. I first went to Tibet and Lhasa in 1984 and over the years I have been back several times and to Lhasa again in 1991. The changes and the Chinese development and building programme were marked. But by staying away from Tibet, climbers would only help to isolate the country and enable the Chinese to continue any oppression unseen. Visiting Tibet surely helps to mix our cultures and values, perhaps creating more understanding and openness. 'Sanctioning' Tibet would seem to serve no constructive purpose.

Perhaps non-mountaineers will love *The Ascent*, find it gripping and thrilling and think it shows Himalayan mountaineering as it is. It is not.

Alan Hinkes

This Game of Ghosts
The sequel to Touching the Void
Joe Simpson
Jonathan Cape, 1993, pp320, £16.99

A boyish face grins out from several of the illustrations in this book; it is frank, open, relaxed, engaging. Yet I found the impressions conveyed by the author's text often at variance with that image. Like anyone else enthralled by *Touching the Void* I was keen to know more about this apparently remarkable man, a survivor extraordinary, but Joe Simpson's third book left me faintly dissatisfied, even disappointed.

It begins with a flashback to the immediate aftermath of the traumatic events in the Peruvian Andes. However, although described as 'the sequel', it is much more an autobiographical account of his whole approach to mountaineering, and very readable too. Early chapters cover boyhood adventures when his dare-devil character emerges, clearly etched against a comfortable background of army family life, much of it in the Far East. Boarding school at Ampleforth merits scant mention except that there he discovers climbing before embarking on an honours degree course in English literature, at Edinburgh University. Once introduced to the University Mountaineering Club his life takes a new turn but later, within six months of his finals, he undergoes what he describes as a catharsis, drops out of his studies and takes himself off to Chamonix.

Much of what follows is gripping, hand-sweating stuff as Simpson survives a series of spectacular incidents, far more than his share to be still alive. Avalanched near the start of his descent of the NE face of Les Courtes, he is swept 2000ft, almost down to the Argentière glacier ... and limps back to the hut. A spine-chilling rockfall removes both boots and bivouac site high on the Bonatti Pillar of the Dru; the incredible series of events on Siula Grande, described so vividly in his first book; and yet more dramas in the Himalaya, including a long fall after a successful assault on Parchamo; not to mention a car crash and a singularly nasty incident with a Sheffield psychopath. Simpson emerges from all these if not unmarked at least undaunted, more or less. Yet one is bound to wonder why he continued, on the Courtes descent, when every nerve was screaming a warning and, occasionally, he does throw a reflective and more mature glance over these escapades.

Avoiding a repeat description of his ill-fated Peruvian expedition he gives us an absorbing account of the long road to recovery, first in a Lima hospital and later at home, with a sympathetic portrait of his surgeon with whom he slowly developed an unusually special relationship. Indeed, this is one of the best parts of the book. Similarly, he holds his reader's attention totally with the tingling suspense of the drama on the Dru: twelve hours dangling from a dodgy peg. Even so, the effect is somewhat spoiled by his technique of describing some of the scenes as seen through the eyes of other players, in this case the rescuer, a device he used to infinitely better effect in *Touching the Void*. Here it just seems artificial. Once or twice the English leaves something to be desired, perhaps more the result of hasty editing than sloppy construction; but his frequent use of simulative adjectives is as irritating as they are inaccurate. Whoever heard of "sodium yellow" torchlight? This and other tricks have the effect of lending some passages the style of a Jeffrey Archer novel – and Joe Simpson can do better than that.

Just how much better is clear from those pages in which he goes some way towards analysing his own attitude to climbing, to fear and, most importantly, the management of fear. He admits that not all his thoughts are original but the analysis is none the worse for that. Indeed, this part of the book is good stuff by any standard and will appeal to many a climbing reader. The introspection crops up elsewhere: his Roman Catholic upbringing and subsequent rejection of that faith, his dropping out of a privileged education and, albeit with tantalisingly little of his own views, his espousal of the Greenpeace cause. Perhaps he felt he should spare us the politics. His sheer boldness enables him to bivouac atop tall chimneys, abseil off bridges and even fly banners from Nelson on his column, all to publicise the cause. But, if there is little about the reason why, there is even less about the climbing techniques involved. Maybe they are a trade secret.

I find it all too easy to write about the man rather than the book and impossible to divorce one from the other entirely. With considerable skill Simpson portrays a maturing individual slowly coming to terms with himself, with his chosen pastime and with its unique demands, particularly the appalling attrition: so many of his friends have died within only a few recent years. Climbing accidents, stonefall, altitude sickness, even the Kathmandu air crash, all take an intensely personal toll. Hence the book's title, borrowed from one of Sassoon's war poems. Mountaineering is not war; but to Joe Simpson it must, at times, seem only too like it.

John Peacock

The Undiscovered Country
Phil Bartlett
The Ernest Press, 1993, pp183, £15.95

Why do we climb? In *The Undiscovered Country*, which reached the short-list for the 1993 Boardman Tasker Memorial Award, Phil Bartlett has had the courage to seek a definitive answer to that question, or as near to a definitive answer as it is possible to get. In attempting this task, Bartlett has not only drawn upon his own considerable mountaineering experience but has also spent ten years researching the entire range of mountain literature, from the pioneers of the Golden Age to the many contemporary mountaineers who have tried to define the motivation which impels them towards this magnetic activity.

But in spite of his wide reading Bartlett readily admits the impossibility of making an objective assessment of other people's experiences. He quotes Fred Hoyle who, 20 years ago, addressed the Alpine Club thus: 'Mountaineers are always being asked why they climb mountains and I am always surprised when they allow themselves to be trapped into offering reasons. The truth of the matter is surely this. Any purpose that can be precisely explained is always temporary ... It is a curious paradox of human existence that purposes which can be clearly defined and explained have a limited life-span. And conversely, the things in life that last indefinitely cannot be explained and defined.' Bartlett comments: 'This makes perfect sense. One of the reasons for thinking mountaineering a noble pursuit is that it defies our attempts to categorise it and explain it away.'

Nevertheless, Bartlett does make an in-depth attempt to arrive at a distillation of his own philosophical thought as it has developed through his wide reading but also, of equal importance, through the companion-ship of his climbing friends. He tells us that his experiences 'have been crucially moulded by all those with whom I have shared days on the hill'. In this book he seeks to define the attraction of that experience, 'to find not a single motive but a single underlying source of contentment which remains unchanged and unchangeable'.

Bartlett approaches his goal from a variety of directions. Broadly, the book is divided into eight chapters each dealing with a different aspect. For example, one chapter, entitled 'Ranges Beyond and Yet Beyond', describes how mountains offer 'a new perspective on life, a refreshed sense of its vitality and exhilaration'. Another chapter deals with the 'Return to the Primitive', and Bartlett uses the word in no derogatory sense: 'Primitive peoples may or may not be visionaries, but they are invariably less cluttered, both materially and mentally, than ourselves.' In 'Conditioning in Time' Bartlett demonstrates how the visual impression produced by a mountain is psychological and subjective rather than purely objective. In 'The Religious Symbol' he shows how 'mountains suggest the soaring of the human spirit and its expansion into new worlds'.

But Bartlett is also aware of the darker side of mountaineering, of writers who have turned away from the earlier idealism to deny both impersonal motives and even the existence of friendship and camaraderie in the mountains. In common with many of us, he fears that mountaineering may be reduced to its lowest common denominator – an Olympic sport, competition, glory, money – with the result that it will become 'a much lesser thing than Mummery, Shipton, Boardman and so many others have made it'.

Bartlett's wide reading enables him to come up with exactly the right quotations to illuminate his ideas and to set them in an historical context. Moreover, he reveals a talent for pinning down thoughts and feelings that have long hovered on the surface of one's mind without emerging as articulated concepts. I found that the further I delved into this book the more involved I became with Bartlett's way of looking at things. This is certainly not a book to rush through without thought. It demands an effort, but one that is amply repaid.

I have just two small reservations: occasionally I found Phil's train of thought a little hard to follow; possibly some discreet editing might have helped. Secondly, the unique set of carefully captioned photographs have been reproduced, probably for reasons of economy, on matt paper, which does not show them at their best. However, these are minor criticisms in the context of a book which provides a life-enhancing experience and the privilege of sharing the mind of a profound thinker.

People have tried before to get to grips with the motivation behind mountaineering but never, to my knowledge, with the insight and integrity that Bartlett has brought to this book. It is an outstanding achievement which deserves to become a classic of mountain literature.

Johanna Merz

Peaks of Glory
Climbing the World's Highest Mountains
Edited by Stefano Ardito
Italy: Edizioni White Star. UK: Swann Hill Press. £19.95

At first sight this is a lavish book, at second sight a most impressive book, but at third sight it's a bit ... well ... dare I say voyeuristic? '*Share the great climbers' passion for life at the borders of human daring,*' trumpets the jacket blurb. Sadly, this is the flavour of the book and my natural reaction is to run the other way.

Originating in Italy but obviously intended for multi-lingual, multi-national publication, this large-format volume (35mm x 25mm) contains 144 pages and no less than 121 decently reproduced colour photographs, 18 of them double-spreads and 53 at full page. The appearance is luxurious and the layout is excellent. Unusually, and to be welcomed in such a production, the captions are printed alongside the plates rather than gathered into an appendix. For what you actually get, this book is surely a bargain at today's prices.

After the main introduction, the book is divided into five territorial sections each with a short introductory essay: 'Himalayas and Karakoram',

'The Alps and Ranges of Europe' (which includes Ben Nevis), 'The High Peaks of Africa', 'From Alaska to Tierra del Fuego' and 'Oceania and Antarctica'. Nevertheless the actual coverage – both in words and pictures – is extremely shallow. One could be excused for thinking that the Himalaya consists of only Everest, Annapurna and Nanga Parbat, the Karakoram of K2 and something called Trango, while East Africa, despite stirring words, is represented by a snowy abseil off ... is it Glyder Fach? The chapter title notwithstanding, Tierra del Fuego figures not at all.

Despite the flavour and the purple prose that goes with it, most of the other sentiments and the historical coverage are acceptable, as one might expect from Stefano Ardito, who is a well-known Italian mountaineering journalist. But as a professional he should check his facts. For instance 79 separate summits in the Alps top 13,000ft, not 65. There are 277 Munros in Scotland, not 543. Norman Collie did not initiate winter climbing on the Ben around 1800. Tower Ridge was first climbed in 1894 not '92. Coolidge and the Dévouassouds had already bagged the Badile 51 years before 1918. And Harold Raeburn ('... a name never heard in the Alps') was in fact a distinguished alpinist who made, among other fine climbs, the first solo traverse of the formidable Meije in 1919. And so on and so on. Such errors challenge credibility.

I have worked with Stefano and he has previously written books in English, but this text has been translated by one Anthony Shugar who is obviously unfamiliar with mountains and mountaineering terminology. One assumes glacier climbers are what we would know as ice climbers, while surely North Slope is where BP found oil rather than a shadowed mountain face? With more in the same vein, credibility is still further eroded. An excellent feature, however, is the use of many apposite quotes in the page margins. Often quite lengthy, they range from writers as diverse as Whymper and Messner, Bonington and Cassin, to Rébuffat, Greg Child and Pat Morrow – genuine aesthetics at last!

But essentially this is a picture book. It could have been the ultimate coffee-table book of mountaineering, but it isn't. The success of such a volume depends on the folio of images being worth more than the sum total of the individual illustrations. And this folio has as little to do with real mountaineering as has a TV spectacular of an assault on the Old Man of Hoy. C'est manifique mais ce n'est pas l'alpinism.

Indeed, the title sums it all up: 'Glory'. Not the nothing-to-prove, primeval glory of the mountains themselves, though to be fair that does shine through in the occasional picture, but the very different kind of personal glory with which the captions typically invest the climbers portrayed. Most of these photographs are about apparently glorious people rather than glorious peaks. They show rarely-recognisable climbers going about their chosen business/pleasure in spectacular situations. Individually almost every image is a dramatic one but the drama is repetitive, theatrical and sadly unevocative. The reader remains uninvolved and becomes a mere voyeur.

The 45 photographers represented – I must admit to being one of them – are all either professional mountain photographers or well-known climbers with an eye of sorts. Most hail from the Alpine countries. Art and creativity are irrelevant in the situations portrayed here: situations where *any* photograph will be spectacular but where driving the camera *at all* is a tour de force. Not the peaks, not the climbers, but the photographers – in this book I reckon theirs is the real *glory*.

This book is such a paradox that I can only wonder at whom it is aimed. All praise nevertheless to the small imprint of Swan-Hill (Airlife Publishing) for breaking into the mountain genre with such an attractive and striking publication. Mountaineering, however, is a highly specialist subject and the employment of a draconian editor who really knew the game would have resulted in a far more credible – and a far better – book.

John Cleare

On the Edge of Europe. Mountaineering in the Caucasus
Audrey Salkeld and José Luis Bermúdez
Hodder & Stoughton, 1993, pp260, £18.99

It is curious how infrequently Europe's highest mountains, the Caucasus, have been visited by British climbers in recent times. It was not always so. In the heyday of the Alpine Club, Victorian mountaineers positively monopolised the early exploration of the range. This surge petered out at the end of the 19th century, since when there have been only sporadic visits, notably the Hunt expedition in 1958 and MacInnes in 1970.

Up-to-date literature on the subject has been sparse in comparison to that on the Alps or Himalaya. *On the Edge of Europe* therefore fills a vacant niche and is much to be welcomed. Here we have a well-researched climbing history of the region together with such useful addenda as a definitive bibliography and a concise, tabulated list of ascents.

After an introduction which sets the scene, the main bulk of the book is devoted to selected extracts covering the whole panorama of climbing in the Caucasus. This is where Salkeld's intimate historical knowledge pays off. Preceding each extract, the author and his achievement are placed precisely in context.

First we have a good helping of vintage Victorian fare: great names such as Freshfield, Mummery and Dent, with Longstaff just overlapping into the 20th century. Then the Germans and Austrians took over the initiative. The period of bagging virgin peaks ended at about the time of the Russian Revolution. Access by foreigners was not easy and from then onwards Russian climbers dominated the scene, adding scores of routes and demonstrating their taste for institutionalised climbing. There were no Western expeditions between 1937 and 1948. From Hunt's landmark expedition in 1958, the range was open to Western climbers but somehow the rush never took place. At about that time Western climbers were too preoccupied in polishing off the post-Everest virgin summits of the

Himalaya. Despite the fact that since the turn of the century the activity has been predominantly non-British, the extracts are all from British books. In this respect there is a lack of balance.

While reading the Longstaff extract I became somewhat baffled when I got to the foot of page 118. Some detective work with Longstaff's *This My Voyage* revealed that a whole page had been omitted. There must be egg on the proof reader's face!

Now, with the Berlin Wall long down, we should all be rushing to the Caucasus. Instead we see only a trickle. Admittedly post-Soviet turbulence on our TV screens largely concerns the periphery of the Caucasus – regions such as Georgia, Abkhasia, Armenia and Azerbaijan. Although things look a bit tricky at the moment, the time must come when, if for no other reason than the need for foreign exchange, we will see climbing and trekking made so easy that it will be little more hassle than going to the Alps. And before you go, *On the Edge of Europe* will be essential reading.

Mike Banks

My Vertical World
Jerzy Kukuczka
Hodder & Stoughton, 1992, 189pp, £16.99

Leaning on the bar at the Alpine Club, I overheard the following exchange: 'It's good, isn't it?' ... 'But it's not exactly literature, is it?'

I won't describe the speakers, it's not important. The point is: what exactly *is* mountain literature? Did the second speaker mean that, even in mountaineering, literature remains the province of those pursuing a hidden agenda? Did he understand by literature an intellectual game of semiotics accessible only to those sufficiently educated and willing to play? If so, I could not agree with the premise. If, on the other hand, literature means the use of words to convey the procession of emotions and the sense of place to enthrall and pull the reader convincingly into the story – the use of language that compels one to believe in a different reality for a while – then the second speaker was quite simply wrong. The book under discussion *was* literature.

They were talking about *My Vertical World* in which Kukuczka adopts a conversational style. He is, after all, only trying to tell a story. Andrew Wielochowski, a pretty useful mountaineer himself, has provided an admirable and seamless translation. From the first paragraph the writing is simple, honest and engaging: 'I touched rock for the first time on Saturday afternoon, 4th September in 1965. From that moment nothing else mattered ... ' His description of the discovery will ring echoes with all climbers. The first climb is as memorable as the loss of virginity. Yet, while he was undoubtedly addicted to climbing, there would always be the conflicting pull of the mountains against that of family. He turned down the first winter ascent of Everest to be with his wife for the birth of their son. He always recognised that there were '... more important things than climbing. The most important things'.

Kukuczka's story is set against the background of a crumbling dynasty. The expedition to his first 8000m peak, Lhotse, coincided with the rising of Solidarity in that famous summer of 1980, when the name Lech Walesa first gained international recognition. Throughout the next nine years, the Polish expeditions struggled to raise money from their own democracy. Towards the end of the decade there were also sadder homecomings. But all is not dour; like a loose thread in the pattern is Kukuczka's extremely understated sense of humour. Not many people have served both Messner and Doug Scott 'mountaineer's tea, slightly fortified with alcohol from the medicine box'. And introducing the great Wojciech Kurtyka, he asks: 'Who is Wojciech? Well, it is really hard not to know him ... '

It was really hard to know Kukuczka. He was quiet and did not interview well. This volume goes a long way to explain things he never seemed able to say. It gives an insight to the logic he adopted for his climbs and the reasoning that enabled him to become, along with Messner, the preeminent super-alpinist of his time. He does this in simple language because he has a story to tell. It works; the book is a communication.

Perhaps his death was inevitable; whereas Messner had promised his mother not to set foot on another 8000m peak after the collected set, Kukuczka said he had no choice but to continue climbing. In an interview for *On the Edge* in 1988, he said: 'I see a mountain, I see a route, I know that I must go there.' The following year he fell from the top of his new route on Lhotse South Face.

My Vertical World has a faded photograph for a cover and, like so many of my favourite volumes, the jacket does insufficient justice to the contents. But there are too few photographs inside and those that do appear only serve to tantalise. What other shots of MacIntyre did Kukuczka take? Where are the photos of that headwall pitch on Makalu West Wall? I do not criticise – the Kukuczka archives probably do not have the same photographic quality that Doug Scott's do. All that Polish film, and cheap East European cameras too. But do not be fooled by the presentation. Do read the book; you won't be disappointed.

Victor Saunders

In the High Mountains
Emil Zsigmondy
The Ernest Press, 1992, pp378, £125

We have had to wait over a century for this first English edition of Emil Zsigmondy's excursions *In the High Mountains*, but what we have now got is very much more than a good translation. Julius Kugy, who climbed with Zsigmondy for several years until he finally told him that he was too imprudent and that he was not going to climb with him any more, is said to have described the original German edition *Im Hochgebirge*, published in 1889 some four years after Zsigmondy's death, as one of the most beautiful books on mountains ever published.

Zsigmondy started climbing in his native Austria in 1874 at the age of 13 with his brother Otto and they were soon making notable ascents, mainly without guides. By 1884 he had progressed to some of the major routes in the Valais and the following year he climbed the Meije; but less than a fortnight later he was attempting a new route on its south face when he fell some 200ft before the rope broke and he then plunged another 2000ft to his death. Many of his climbs are described in this book, which includes additional material relating to his death, as well as John Stogdon's original review in the *Alpine Journal* of 1891. Much controversy surrounded the circumstances of Zsigmondy's death and indeed his whole approach to climbing, as Volume XII of the *Journal* testifies, not just on account of such contentious issues of the day as the use of crampons and the justification for guideless climbing, but his willingness to run risks of a much greater magnitude than his contemporaries. He was not only ahead of his time but also ahead of the improvements in technique and in equipment. It is therefore hardly surprising that there may have been insufficient demand to warrant an English edition in the 1890s, despite a favourable review by Stogdon.

The major part of the value of this new edition lies in its illustrations. These include some 190 vignettes above, below or embedded in the text, the great majority of which bear the monogram of E T Compton. No effort has been spared in seeking to reproduce them as closely as possible to the original and this has been achieved with remarkable success, the clarity and dramatic effect being wholly unimpaired.

The sixteen full-page paintings by Compton, copied from the original photogravures, must represent the most readily available collection of works by this leading English climber and artist of his day, quite apart from the vignettes. They include the Meije, Matterhorn, Bietschhorn and 'The Ortler from the Hochspitze', which Stogdon suggested was the best of them all. In the original edition two of the plates including the Meije were printed in grey-blue ink, the Bietschhorn in grey-brown and all the rest were in dull brown tones, but although the reproduction is once again of the highest quality the plates are now all printed in black. It is a pity that some of them lack the finer subtlety of shade apparent in the original.

The text sometimes retains German words unnecessarily, owing perhaps to the translator's unfamiliarity with the subject matter. Thus several English, French and American climbers still bear the title 'Herr', which would certainly have upset 'Herr Coolidge' had it been published a century sooner, particularly as his Alpine pioneering aunt suffers from the same complaint, with the title 'Fräulein Brevoort'. Another problem arises when Zsigmondy quotes from the German translation of an English book, and we are given an English translation of the German translation instead of the original English wording. It may mean almost the same, but when Whymper's drawing in *Scrambles* of his fall in 1862 is captioned 'As I was trying ... ' instead of the original caption 'In attempting to pass the corner I slipped and fell', there may be unnecessary confusion. These may seem somewhat minor faults, but they do stand out in marked contrast to the meticulous attention to detail apparent in the layout of the text and in the illustrations.

As for the unusual price, this limited edition of 300 copies is essentially a collector's item and there can be little doubt that had it been published a century ago a nice second-hand copy would have been likely to command even more today.

Alan Lyall

Personal Growth Through Adventure
David Hopkins and Roger Putnam
David Fulton Publishers, London, 1993, ppx+241, pb, £14.99

In the past three decades one of the unsung success stories in British education has been the widespread imaginative development of 'open country' or 'adventure' education for young adults. Many of the best initiatives have been by local authorities. This success story should be promoted by every political party. Yet it could quite easily be pruned to death by penny-pinching policies. The seed was planted and watered by Kurt Hahn, Geoffrey Young and Jack Longland. It has grown, often in the face of prejudice and difficulty, so that now, each year, many thousands of children get some first-hand experience of the challenges and beauty and the tempo of life which wild country can offer. This book gives a fine, concentrated account of the story, of the ideas behind it and of its present, rich expression.

About a third of the book comprises case histories which exemplify the impressive sweep of what is being done: expeditions for young people suffering from diabetes, spinal injury or epilepsy; special courses for ICI managers or for young delinquents. Of course there have been occasional sad failures. But what shines through this book is the number and dedication and imaginative competence of the many lovers of wild places who sustain this movement. What was, perhaps, the most impressive tale is that of the Toxteth Community College (Comprehensive) which has for 20 years built up a tradition of expeditions to the Atlas, Sahara and Hoggar – two weeks, ex-army trucks, careful budgeting, and no volunteer turned down on grounds of 'behaviour' at school!

The title of the book is slightly clumsy. It would not be worth a comment, except that it also indicates a significant, contemporary limitation on current views about adventure in education. I refer to the over-emphasis on 'personal growth' and personal autonomy. They are important but, if made a central aim, they can lead to a kind of macho individualism. Other, greater questions need to be at the centre: what is 'adventure' contributing to the community, to an enduring well-rooted culture, to the survival of the planet's rich endowment? Such questions are hinted at in several quotations from Hahn, Schumacher and others; and notably in a fine peroration by Tom Price. This is an excellent book. It will help that often endangered species which *must* survive: *good education.*

Robin A Hodgkin

Pakistan Trekking Guide
Isobel Shaw and Ben Shaw
Odyssey Hongkong, 1993, pp420, sketch-maps, pb, npq

This well-researched guide is the product of five years of travel across the mountain regions of Pakistan. Isobel Shaw has written two other guides to Pakistan, and she and her son's wide background knowledge has been gained by previous residence in the country. Beginning with an introduction to Pakistan's history, people, religions, languages, climate, flora and fauna, economy and politics, it goes on to inform potential travellers what to expect when they get there, from the authorities, from the local populations, and how to avoid the obvious and the less obvious pitfalls. Three principal trekking regions – Skardu, Gilgit and Chitral – are dealt with and journeys radiating in all directions from each are described in detail.

Practically all the treks mentioned are based upon personal journeys; otherwise, the information source is quoted. A great asset to these descriptions is the provision of adequate sketch-maps. There is not a route of the hundred or so described that cannot be found on one of them. The Guide scores full marks for this. The picture given of the current scene emphasises how far the country has moved ahead to meet the growing demands of modern tourism.

There is such a wide range of subjects covered that a few slips are inevitable. The Tibetan plateau, not the Deosai, is surely the world's largest. The Gilgit Scouts were raised in 1913. The nine small feudal states in the Gilgit region were merged into the Republic of Pakistan (some not without resistance) in February 1970. I do not believe that the existence of the Indus river prior to that of the mountains through which it flows has been sufficiently proved. A F Mummery was not killed on the Diamir face of Nanga Parbat, but in attempting to reach the north side of the mountain across the Diamir gap.

As well as an index and bibliography there are several useful appendices, including glossaries for four of the main local languages. Where better than in a work such as this to preach the need for good trekking practices and environmental awareness? The sense of urgency in the message does not seem to me to be quite strong enough. However, the many virtues of this handbook and its immense practical value far outweigh any minor shortcomings. It is a comprehensive information source for anyone contemplating a visit to Pakistan as a tourist, trekker or first-time climber. If it should help to swell the volume of trekkers visiting the country, turning the flow into a flood similar to that sweeping through Nepal, then it will bring great satisfaction to the Pakistan Tourism Ministry and to the proliferating numbers of trekking agencies. However, unless the changes that tourist growth may bequeath are wisely managed, the inheritance might turn into a mixed blessing for the mountain regions and the people who dwell there.

Trevor Braham

Ballooning Over Everest
Leo Dickinson
Jonathan Cape, 1993, pp160, £14.99

Although this book came out at the same time as several other anniversary Everest books, it celebrates a quite different achievement: the flight of two balloons over Everest in 1991, years after planes first flew over the mountain. It was an incredible adventure, and Dickinson tells the story well in a book that, as one would expect, is superbly illustrated.

The early part of the book recalls the tribulations of getting the expedition off the ground at all. The first attempt resulted in the balloon spending most of its time in Nepalese customs, being inflated in a field in Kathmandu, and then being packed away again, the pilot abandoning the project. Names such as Per Lindstrand, Richard Branson and Chris Bonington were involved at this stage. Later, a two-balloon attempt was agreed on by the sponsors, with one balloon filming the other. Chris Dewhurst and Andy Elson were the pilots, with Dickinson and Eric Jones filming.

The author had disagreements with most of the major participants at some time or other which, of course, makes for absorbing reading. But there were many lighter moments, as when one of the team dressed up as a yeti, apparently fooling both the other team members and the Sherpas.

Whilst the expedition was an undoubted success from the point of view of flying over Everest, it was very much less so from the author's filming hopes. The attempt was sabotaged at the start by Leo's pilot who jumped the gun and started ahead of the other balloon, thus eliminating at one stroke any chance of photographing it in flight. The author obviously never forgave him!

Both balloons had a somewhat traumatic flight. Dewhurst and Dickinson sailed high and swiftly, passing very close to the summit, but used a lot of fuel and came down fast, crashing onto the Tibetan plateau. Elson and Jones had burner trouble; they came down low and almost crashed into the SW face, burning through a quarter of their wire basket supports, but they gained height again and made a perfect landing.

This is a fascinating book with superb photographs. But the photos are not all that they seem. Three of the best double-page spreads show the second balloon sailing over Everest, and you wonder how they were taken since the two balloons were eight miles apart at the time. I was quite prepared to believe that Leo, with his usual inventiveness, had trained a vulture to fly alongside with a camera strapped to its back.

A fourth photo, which is also used for the dust jacket, is a close-up of the second balloon over Everest, with flames roaring from the burner and the basket at a crazy angle as if nearly all the wires had snapped. Fortunately this never happened. All four photos are the product of photographic trickery and computer graphics. But is such manipulation justified? Whatever you feel about the pictures, buy the book as an entertaining account of a great venture.

Geof Templeman

The Ala Dag, Climbs and Treks in Turkey's Crimson Mountains
Ö B Tüzel
Cicerone Press, 1993, pp280, £14.99

This carefully researched guidebook by Ömer Tüzel, a member of the Turkish diplomatic service and an experienced mountaineer, is a much expanded and very worthy successor to Haldun Aydingün's *Ala Daglar – An Introduction* (Redhouse, 1988).

Tüzel devotes his first 75 pages to the practicalities of access to the Ala Dag, its nomenclature, its geology and, in particular, to the history of climbing in this range. He pays generous tribute to the British mountaineering effort (pioneering and later) and allots one appendix to British first ascents and another to a chronology of British expeditions from 1943 to 1991. Turkish alpinism was slow to develop: at first an unimaginative group activity, organised nationally, it only took off as an individual sport in the mid-1970s under the impetus of Yalçin Koç and other hard climbers including, though he is too modest to admit it, Ömer Tüzel himself.

A useful vocabulary of Turkish mountain terms and peak names tidies up a confusion of local and foreign contributions to the nomenclature of the range. 'Ala Dag' itself is a bit of a puzzle since 'ala' can mean 'darkish' – scarcely applicable to these grey-white partly dolomitic limestone peaks rising out of the Anatolian plateau. Another, if rather dull, interpretation of 'ala' is 'high', but there can be no doubt that, on seeing the great wall light up as the sun sets, 'crimson' of the title is absolutely right, as testified by some of the colour plates.

Tüzel divides the climbers' Ala Dag into four sectors, each with ridge maps, topos, and detailed route descriptions. The northern sector lists 35 routes, one third on the highest and most prominent peak – Demirkazik ('Iron Stake'), 3756m. (The formidable N wall – Grade VI – was first climbed by an Australian/New Zealand pair in 1972.) The central – or Yedi Göl – sector has 32 routes centring on the monolith Direk Tas ('Upright Rock'). The southern sector, with 38 routes, covers the less prominent second highest peak – Kaldi Dag, 3736m – and includes the spectacular 120m high pinnacle Parmakkaya ('Finger Rock') – taking 7 hours of Grade V/VI on the first ascent in 1971. Finally, there is the remote south-eastern or 'Torasan' sector, a group seen from afar by British pioneers who called its highest summit 'Mystery Peak'. Originally only accessible across the main range from the west, access from the east is now somewhat easier. It offers 17 routes including the exacting N wall of Vay Vay, 3600m. All the climbing routes described are supplemented by trekking routes across the range, mainly from west to east.

The Ala Dag range has been thoroughly explored since Robin Hodgkin and myself were there in 1943/44, but the mountains have not, it seems, been spoilt. Tüzel is critical of the Demirkazik Mountaineering Centre – a mountain hut/hotel located too low on the western slopes to allow effective tackling of the high peaks in a single day. It is still a pleasant necessity to camp at one of the alps where the infrequent springs emerge from the foot of the high peaks, or else in the basin of the Yedi Göl ('Seven Tarns', but only two have water in high summer). Tüzel earnestly hopes that no hut or shelter will be built to spoil this fine, remote corrie. Indeed, modest as the Ala Dag is by Himalayan or even Alpine standards, a climbing holiday among the Crimson Peaks has the added attraction of constituting a small expedition.

Edward Peck

Beyond Risk: Conversations with Climbers
Nicholas O'Connell
Diadem, 1993, pp300, £15.99

Climbing is a totally daft activity, if you look at it honestly. It follows that we climbers inevitably have a decidedly dotty side to our nature which we are only too eager to explain. The most famous explainer was Mallory with his 'Because it's there'. But he also made a more profound statement when he said: 'If you ask the question, there can be no answer.'

Despite this, *Beyond Risk* devotes 300 pages in trying to utter the unutterable, it being a well-known fact that the superstars of mountaineering are more than willing to bare their souls at the drop of a cheque. Nicholas O'Connell interviews 17 of the most famous contemporary climbers including our own Chris Bonington and Doug Scott. Most of the predictable names are there: Cassin, Hillary, Diemberger, Messner, Destivelle, Cesen. The question and answer interview technique employed is not my favourite format but here O'Connell has gone far to overcome my reservations by starting each interview with a concise biography which clearly identifies the particular contribution the interviewee has made to the progress of mountaineering. I found this most elucidating. For instance I now understand exactly the roles played by Royal Robbins and Warren Harding in the development of Yosemite climbing; or what precisely Cassin and Bonatti each contributed to Alpine climbing. The author being American, American climbers are particularly well represented.

The deeper I got into this book, the more I enjoyed it. The successive developments in the history of mountaineering were obviously not achieved because the particular exponent had superior muscles. It mostly happens in the mind. This aspect is cleverly probed by O'Connell with his very accurately aimed questions, calculated to reveal the essence of the matter. In their responses the great climbers disclose their philosophy and their techniques, their dreams and sometimes their conceits. It all adds up to a fascinating testimony of the progression of mountaineering in our time.

The photographs are printed very flatly in black and white. No doubt this keeps the price down but it gives the book a dull feel which it does not deserve.

Mike Banks

The Mountains of Wales
Ioan Bowen Rees
University of Wales Press, 1992, pp299, pb £10.95, hb £25.00

This is a revision and considerable expansion of a book, a very beautiful one, first published by the Gregynog Press in 1987. It is an anthology of prose and verse, English and Welsh, on the mountains of Wales. Most of the Welsh is accompanied by translations; those verses which are not have explanatory notes.

The book is cast into sections related to the people who have come to the mountains of Wales. An introductory section sets the scene; it is followed by Heroes, from legendary ages to the time of Glyndwr, whose exploit in climbing the chimney on Moel Hebog to escape his pursuers is recounted. Discoverers takes us from the earliest days of tourism into the full flood of the late eighteenth and early nineteenth century. The Romantics take the experience seriously (rightly enough) while the native Welsh like Talhaiarn can afford to be more lighthearted. In Mountaineers readers will find themselves in company with J M Archer Thompson, Geoffrey Winthrop Young, Arnold Lunn, Dorothy Pilley, Gwen Moffat and Joe Brown, among many others. Neighbours, on those who live in the mountains, is especially appealing; we see them not as visitors, but from the inside. The warmth and security of Margaret Roberts' mountain farm, while outside a blizzard rages, are almost tangible. A section on Artists celebrates the extraordinary range of poets and draughtsmen who have worked in Wales and found unexpected beauty. T H Parry Williams, who was born and grew up right among the mountains at Rhyd Ddu, beautifully redeems what most take to be blots on the landscape: the slate tips. The final section, Pilgrims, is meditative, and touches on the exaltation of the spirit to which the mountains have led not a few writers.

Readers who have Welsh will be even more rewarded. That the rocky solidity of the Moelwyns should be no more than tissue paper stuck against the sky is a delightful conceit; while Nesta Wyn Jones on her farm combines description of fire, storm and mist with her own feeling superbly.

If you climb in Wales, and want your appreciation of both the mountains themselves and the people who live there greatly and very pleasurably enhanced, read *The Mountains of Wales*.

James Bogle

Look Back in Happiness
Michael Harmer
Cygnet Press, pp152, £12.95

Introducing this book to the *Alpine Journal* requires a short backward delve into Club history, when the author was a member of the Committee shortly before the Second World War. He was appointed spokesman for the group of members, known as the 'Young Shavers', who wished to modernise the Club at South Audley Street. This was opposed by the President, Col Strutt, but supported by Geoffrey Winthrop Young. Harmer, my friend from student days at Barts and on the hills, says that he told the Committee it was 'no longer possible for younger members to belong to the Carlton for its politics, the Reform for its cutlets and soup, the Ski Club for winter exercise *and* the Alpine Club for its snob-value'. He then proceeded with the Young Shavers' recommendations which were: 'Sell South Audley Street; buy premises near an Underground station in Paddington or the Borough and provide facilities to include sleeping accommodation even if of the simplest kind.' *Plus ça change* ... ! It is said that the day after hearing this General Bruce had a stroke and Col Strutt had Harmer sacked from the Committee.

Harmer's story, the memoir of a London surgeon, covers much else beside mountains and derives its own pleasure and charm from a pen which the author tells us he has 'dipt in honey'. The chapter 'Of Men and Mountains' gives us vivid thumb-nail sketches of his expeditions (he narrowly missed Wiessner's disastrous 1939 attempt on K2) and of his companions – from Professor Pigou who proposed him for the Club and whose AC tie, invariably worn for all occasions, had been reduced to a green bootlace, to climbers of the calibre of Wilfrid Noyce and James Joyce and the famous Zermatt guide Xavier Lochmatter. He tells us something of the difficulties and frustrations of a busy surgeon's life, but has far more to say about its rewards. He traces for us the National Health Service, which he thoroughly supported, from its inception under Nye Bevan to present times.

There is much debunking, for the most part gentle. *Bêtes noires* include contemporary art and, more regrettably and less convincingly to this reviewer, Christianity. Nor do the endless bureaucracies which impede progress in medicine and surgery escape castigation, especially in the field (now so topical) of cancer-classification. The family motto, 'Always contradict; it gives you time to think', remains in play throughout the book. But I would be prepared to offer a money-back guarantee to any reader who will not admit to having enjoyed it. On the title-page of my copy Michael has written '*Auf dem Bergen ist Freiheit*', and I recommend all mountaineers and other people to share the happiness of his pilgrimage.

Edward Smyth

Vascos en el Himalaya
Edited by Antonio Ortega
Pyrenaica, Bilbao, 1992, pp264, 5000 pesetas

The main thing that will strike readers will be the quantity and quality of the colour pictures contained in this massive book. It is actually a chronicle of the Basque achievements (and failures) in the high mountains of Asia. Areas visited have been the Himalaya , Karakoram, Hindu Kush and Pamir. The chronicle covers a total of 136 Basque expeditions that were fielded between 1974 (an attempt on Everest and an ascent of Shakhaur, 7084m) and the year of 1992, when Everest was ascended four times and Cho Oyu three times. The book closes with statistics of different kinds. And while it is true, as editor Ortega recognises, that Basques have preferred to head for the greater mountains only, thus disregarding exploratory work, it is also true that their activity in high Asia has been remarkable.

The book is in Spanish, with very short sections in Basque (a strange language unrelated to Spanish and a distant relative of the Finno-Urgric stock). Several climbers are interviewed and we thus receive an insight into their attitudes toward expeditionary climbing and ecology. But above all, attention should be drawn to the illustrations of this work; their quantity, quality and variety would alone justify its acquisition.

Evelio Echevarría

On the Edge of Silence: A Mountain Anthology
Compiled by Mary-Jane Selwood
Springbank Press, 1993, pp80, £8.95

Dr Mark Selwood worked in Pokhara in Nepal in 1986, and had a great desire to help the people of Nepal by improving health facilities. Tragically, he was killed in a climbing accident in the Cairngorms at the age of 27. A memorial fund was set up in his name and, in July 1993, the Mark Selwood Training Centre was opened in Pokhara.

A second project, to fund health education in remote areas, is now under way, and to help this Mark's mother has published this delightful anthology of prose and poetry. Only one or two of the pieces chosen are 'regulars', such as Winthrop Young's 'The Cragsman', the remainder ranging widely from Po Chu-i to Philip Larkin, and Emily Brontë to Louis MacNeice. The whole is enlivened by charming illustrations.

All proceeds from sales go to the Mark Selwood Memorial Fund, and copies can be obtained from the Fund, at 75 James Street, Helensburgh, Dunbartonshire, G84 8XH. (£8.95 + £1 p&p)

Tight Rope. The Fun of Climbing
Dennis Gray
The Ernest Press, 1993, ppvi+184, pb, £9.95

Dennis Gray was at his most active during one of rock-climbing's golden periods: that of the Rock and Ice, Creag Dhu and other star names of the fifties and sixties. He has already portrayed much of this in his two autobiographies. The present book covers the same ground but in a more anecdotal way, consisting of a string of stories about Brown, Whillans, Patey, et al. It is stories such as these that fill in the background to the whole era, so that the book becomes almost an historical document. It is also highly enjoyable reading.

The Reverend A E Robertson: His Life, Munros and Photographs
Peter Drummond & Ian Mitchell
The Ernest Press, 1993, ppx+133, £13.95

Now that Munro-bagging has become a national pastime, it is good to have a book that goes right back to the beginnings. Robertson was the first man to complete the list although there is some doubt as to whether he actually reached every top, one description in particular being rather ambiguous. Robertson's first Munro was climbed in 1889 and he made slow but steady progress over the next nine years, attaining about 100 summits. But he accelerated the programme in 1898 and 1899, adding another 150 in two long walking tours.

The authors split the book between them, Drummond dealing with The Man and Mitchell with The Background, which naturally includes much about early climbers of the time and the SMC. The two final sections of the book contain Robertson's own account of ancient tracks across the NW Highlands, with observations on access problems, a subject which occupied a lot of his time in later years. There is also a portfolio of his photographs.

Climbing Mount Everest. The Bibliography
Audrey Salkeld & John Boyle
Sixways Publishing, 1993, pp120, £15

This bibliography will be very useful to those interested in Mount Everest itself and also mountain literature in general. It is an obvious labour of love by the authors, carrying on the tradition of the late Jill Neate. There are 587 individual entries, each sub-divided into different issues and editions; for instance, John Hunt's *The Ascent of Everest* has 15 entries of editions in English, plus a staggering 43 further listings for those in foreign languages. It is in the complete listings of East European, Japanese and other less well-known Everest books that much of the importance of this bibliography lies but, whilst many of the books listed are old favourites, some eyebrows may be raised at the inclusion of Salman Rushdie's *The Satanic Verses* as an Everest book!

In addition to the main bibliography, there is a useful selective listing of magazine and journal articles, plus a chronological list of expeditions to Everest with their principal sources of reference.

Nothing So Simple as Climbing
G J F Dutton
Diadem, 1993, pp160, pb, £8.99

Another collection of 21 stories of the Doctor, the Apprentice and the Narrator, and their adventures in the Highlands. Some have appeared previously in the SMCJ and other publications, but the majority appear here for the first time and continue the tradition started by *The Ridiculous*

Mountains. Readers of that first volume will know what to expect: witty, humorous stories, beautifully written, of just the right length to keep by the bedside and dip into before dozing off. This latest volume includes what the blurb describes as 'a bizarre spectrum of contemporary mountain obstacles and activities' – they are all here: paragliding, sponsored walks, access, witches, mountain biking, and so on. Read them and have a good laugh.

Breaking Loose
Dave Cook
The Ernest Press, 1993, ppx+202, pb £9.50

Dave Cook was well known as a climber and communist, but not, until recently, as a cyclist. This changed after his decision to 'get away from it all' by cycling to Australia, climbing whatever turned up in his path. Setting out from Brixton in the rain in 1989, he met up with friends in Verdon, Orco, Mello and other rock-climbing shrines before finally feeling free, as he crossed the Bosphorus, to continue his journey. From then on, the story is obviously much more about the people he met and the social injustices he encountered. The long, long cycling stages were interspersed with train and air travel, either because of difficulty in obtaining visas, clashes with Saddam Hussein's police, or the sheer impracticability of travel by bicycle. A persistent thread is his love/hate relationship with the juggernaut drivers. He comments at one stage that you can get injected against everything except being run down by a lorry driver – a sad prediction for his Mediterranean trip in 1993. Whilst containing comparatively little climbing, this is a fascinating memoir by one of the sport's great characters.

The Best of Ascent
Twenty-five Years of the Mountaineering Experience
Ed. Steve Roper & Allen Steck
Diadem, 1993, ppxiv+384, £16.99

The publication *Ascent* has so far run to twelve issues in the past 25 years, changing after the first nine, in 1975, from the annual mountaineering journal of the Sierra Club to an infrequent publication in book form. In that time, it has ensured for itself a unique niche in mountaineering literature, not least in promoting climbing fiction.

For their 25th anniversary, the editors decided to reprint a selection of their favourite articles, mainly from the earlier out-of-print issues. Financial constraints resulted in a smaller book format and few photos, but the delight is in the writing. All the old favourites are here: Harding, Tejada-Flores, David Roberts, Jeff Long and the editors themselves. In addition, eight new articles have been commissioned to round off the anthology. There are nearly 400 pages of pure pleasure here.

The following books have also been received by the Alpine Club Library during 1993:

Encyclopaedia of Mountaineering Walt Unsworth. *Hodder & Stoughton, 1992, pp384, pb, £16.99.* Second enlarged and updated edition.

On Peak Rock. A guide to selected rock climbs on 100 Peak District outcrops Ed. Carl Dawson. *BMC, 1993, pp436, £15.95*

Walks in the Julian Alps Simon Brown. *Cicerone, 1993, pp176, £8.99*

Race Against Time. British North Geomagnetic Pole Expedition 1992 David Hempleman-Adams. *The Self Publishing Association Ltd/Hempleman-Adams, 1993, pp222, £14.95*

The Karakoram. Mountains of Pakistan. Shiro Shirahata *Cloud Cap, Seattle, 1990, pp192, $75*

Avalanche Safety for Skiers & Climbers Tony Daffern. *Diadem, 1992, pp192, pb, £11.99.* Second edition.

Bibliography of Colorado Mountain Ascents. 1977-1990 Joseph D Kramarsac. *Privately published, 1992, ppx+122, npq* Follow-up to the author's volume for 1863-1976.

Medicine for Mountaineering & Other Wilderness Activities Ed. James Wilkerson. *The Mountaineers, 1992, pp416, $16.95.* 4th edition

The High Mountains of Britain and Ireland. A guide for mountain walkers. Vol I. The Munros and Tops and other 3000ft Peaks *Irvine Butterfield. Diadem, 1993, pp320, £18.99.* Revised & updated.

Speak to the Hills Ed. Hamish Brown & Martyn Barry. *Aberdeen University/Mercat Press, 1985 (1993), pp528, pb, £9.95.* An anthology of poetry.

Andalusian Rock Climbs, including Tenerife Chris Craggs. *Cicerone, 1992, pp160, £6.99*

Northern Highlands. Rock & Ice Climbs Ed. Roger Everett, *SMC, 1993*
    Vol. 1 Knoydart to An Teallach *ppxii+372, £13.95*
    Vol. 2 Strathfarrar to Shetland *ppxiv+400, £14.95*

The Cairngorms, Lochnagar and The Mounth Adam Watson. *SMT, 1992, ppx+262, £17.95*

Die Alpenvereinshutten *DAV/OeAV/AUS. Rother, 1991, pp720, npq*

Ogwen and Carneddau   Iwan Arfon Jones.
Climbers' Club, 1993, pp418, £13.95

Chair Ladder and the South Coast   Des Hannigan.
Climbers' Club, 1992, pp308, npq

The Mountains of Ireland   Paddy Dillon.
Cicerone, 1992, pp220, £9.99

Hut-to-Hut in the Stubai Alps   Allan Hartley.
Cicerone,1993, pp120, £6.99

The Mountains of Greece. A Walkers' Guide   Tim Salmon.
Cicerone, 1993, pp176, £9.99

Classic Tramps in New Zealand   Constance Roos.
Cicerone, 1993, pp208, £14.99

Annapurna. A Trekker's Guide   Kev Reynolds.
Cicerone, 1993, pp176, £8.99

Central Switzerland. A Walker's Guide   Kev Reynolds.
Cicerone, 1993, pp208, £10.99

The Haute Route. Chamonix–Zermatt. A guide for skiers & mountain walkers   Peter Cliff.   *Cordee, 1993, ppvi+122, £10.95*

Selected Climbs in Adrspach and Teplice   Pavel Lisák.
JUKO, 1993, pp108, npq

Jersey Rock   Kevin Eloury.
Jersey Rock Climbing Club, 1993, pp136, npq

Southern Chalk   Chris Mellor. *ITI Guides, 1993, pp50, £3.25*

Clwyd Rock   Gary Dickinson.
Cicerone, 1993, pp220, £14.99

Mexico's Volcanoes. A Climbing Guide   R J Secor.
The Mountaineers, 1993, pp139, $14.95

French Rock   Bill Birkett.
Cicerone, 1993, pp304, £14.99

Zen in the Art of Climbing Mountains   Neville Shulman.
Element Books, 1992, ppx+118, pb, £6.99

Mount Temple, Canadian Rockies. (*Government of the Province of Alberta*) (p235)

85. Peaks on the SW branch of Khamengar valley:
    Left Peak 6507m, *Right* Peak 6410m. (*Harish Kapadia*) (p71)

86. View from the Upper Khamengar valley. *L to R:* Peak 6360m, Parahio Col,
    Shigri Parbat, 6526m. (*Harish Kapadia*) (p71)

Three famous Sherpas of the Himalayan Mountaineering Institute.
L to R: Gyalzen, Lhatoo, Da Namgyal. (*Harish Kapadia*) (p225)

88. John Longland (1936-1991) on *Garden Face Direct*, Gardom's Edge, June 1955.
(*Ted Maden*) (p186)

Sir William McEwan Younger, Bart., DSO. (1905-1992) (p323)

90. Wadi Rumm: the 500m W face of Nassrani Towers. Left to right: *Jolly Joker*, ED Sup, 1990; *l'Autre Dimension*, TD, 1986; *Tea on the Moon*, TD Sup, 1993; *Merci Allah*, TD Sup, 1986; *Aqaba*, ED Inf, 1988. *(Tony Howard)* (p283)

In Memoriam

COMPILED BY GEOFFREY TEMPLEMAN

The Alpine Club Obituary		Year of Election
Dame Freya Stark	LAC	1935 (Hon1935)
Lady Susi Jeans	LAC	1947
Jill Neate		1988
John Callis Hawksley		1940
Walter Abbott Wood		1930
John Raymond Fearon		1941
William Eric Radcliffe		1954
Charmian Longstaff	LAC	1939
Terence Dominic Leggett		1975
Penelope Storey	LAC	1954
Ronald James Wathen		1957-65, 1982
Roland Arnold Rodda		1960
Kevin Columba Fitzgerald		1973
Frederick Paul French		1961
Donald Ernest Lockhart		1973
Sir John Laurence Longland		1928
Louis Charles Baume		1952

In addition to the above, obituaries are included for Sir William Younger and Jo Kretschmer, who both died in 1992.

On a personal note, I remember the humorous letter I received from my predecessor when I took over the obituary section, packed with typical dos and don'ts and warnings of the pitfalls that might be encountered. It hasn't been as bad as he painted, nor has it been possible to achieve the literary heights of his marvellous introductions. In Kevin Fitzgerald the Club has lost a great writer.

Sir William McEwan Younger Bart, DSO 1905 –1992

Bill Younger, who died in 1992 after a long illness, outlived his climbing contemporaries, and it falls to me, who only knew him in the last 20 years of his life, to write his obituary. He was a great figure in the business world, especially in Edinburgh and in the Conservative Party in Scotland. He was elected to the Club in 1927 while still an undergraduate on the proposal of A M Carr Saunders and Geoffrey Winthrop Young, so totalling 65 years of membership.

On leaving Oxford he went straight into the family brewing business of McEwans and proceeded to build this up first by the acquisition of another family company, William Youngers, and later by the takeover of Newcastle Breweries and several smaller Edinburgh companies to form Scottish and Newcastle with about 10% of the market. He had an outstanding war record, enlisting in 1939 in a lowland anti-aircraft regiment of the Royal Artillery with which he served in the North African campaign, including the first siege of Tobruk, and in Italy, finishing up in command of the regiment. His double-barrelled name, evocative of beer, earned him the nickname 'Colonel Screwtop'.

After the war he remained chairman of his company until 1969 and was also active as director of a number of other Edinburgh companies. He was Deputy Lieutenant of Midlothian and later of the City of Edinburgh and, in the seventies, Chairman of the Scottish Conservative Party. Through his charitable trust he supported many good causes, notably his college Balliol, of which he became an Honorary Fellow, many Edinburgh charities including the Scottish Symphony Orchestra, the Mount Everest Foundation and the A C Irvine Travel Fund.

Bill Younger's mountaineering record is largely lost in the sands of time, but his companions in his Oxford days included Douglas Busk, A M Binnie and Carr Saunders. In the thirties and after the war he climbed with John Tilney and Claude Elliott. There is a splendid portrait in oils, now in the possession of his daughter, showing him as a young man against the background of the Cresta Rey on Monte Rosa.

When I knew him, in the seventies and eighties in Edinburgh, in Glen Lyon and then in his final home near Henley, we were both past anything more than walks on the Scottish hills. I remember him best in his beautiful house in Moray Place, a swell but quite without pomposity, easygoing but suddenly coming out with trenchant criticisms of the good and the great, casually dressed with a glass of whisky and a cheroot in his hand, enjoying life.

Peter Lloyd

John Martin Kretschmer 1916-1992

During the last fifty years I numbered the Kretschmers, first Nully and then Jo, amongst my closest friends. During the war years Nully and I and John Barford climbed a lot together in Wales and the Lakes. Eventually, as we were successively bombed out, we three coagulated in a flat in London, only to be broken up again in 1947 when Nully and John were both killed in separate accidents in the Alps. It was shortly after that that I first met Jo.

During the war he served with distinction in the Royal Engineers in Africa, India and Burma and also as an instructor in winter warfare in Scotland where his skills as a ski-mountaineer were invaluable for teaching others.

In the 1950s probably the most potent influence on his climbing activities was his friendship with Wilf Noyce. He could not fail to have been influenced by Wilf's qualities of leadership and climbing skills, so often concealed under a mantle of humility. Like Nully, Jo seldom left any record of his achievements, valuing them only for themselves or for the shared companionship they brought. In those days those of us in industry with our routine two weeks annual holiday had little chance to travel abroad, and air travel had hardly begun, so most of his climbing was in the UK. It wasn't until we were much older, and indeed after we had retired, that I made many expeditions with Jo and Mike Low (another AC member, who died in 1990), when we climbed in the Pyrenees or trekked in Nepal or had three or four geriatric walks, carrying some 40lbs, for four or five days through the wildest parts of the western highlands of Scotland.

We were all engineers of moderate success and mountaineers of no great distinction, yet active enough to value the experience of stretching our powers to the limit. We were lovers of wild places, especially when approached by sea on the wings of the wind and enjoyed seeking out the wild creatures and flowers we found there.

Jo served the Alpine Club as Treasurer for three years and the Mount Everest Foundation for sixteen years.

As John Hunt has said in his note, 'Jo was a wonderful companion and a person whom it was easy to love'.

Alan Pullinger

John Hunt writes:

I don't remember how or when I first met Jo. It must have been shortly after the War, when he had been demobilised. Probably it was Wilfrid Noyce who introduced us. However that may be, it marked the beginning of a friendship of over forty years. When I was appointed to launch the Duke of Edinburgh's Award Scheme, he was one of my first choices, among the many friends on whom I could rely to promote its growth, in the voluntary role of an Award Liaison Officer. I fancy that one of the first climbs we did together was Crib Goch Buttress. In the following years we skied together in the Cairngorms, climbed on Arran, Lundy and in North Wales. We climbed in the Alpes de Provence; we traversed the Haute Route from Argentière and, on two especially memorable occasions, climbed the Matterhorn and the Aiguille Méridionale d'Arves in very bad weather.

Perhaps the happiest memories which Joy and I shared with Jo and other friends were visits to various islands, partly to watch the sea birds at nesting time. Lundy was our favourite island, but Arran, Skomer Skokholm, Grassholm, the Farne Islands were all part of the repertoire, year after year, in late May or early June. Perhaps the most exotic of all those dream island days was a visit to the Galapagos archipelago. Sark, in 1991, was to be the last occasion, for when the time came to explore the Orkneys the following year, Jo was already too ill to accompany us. His love and knowledge of birds was considerable. I, who had first fired his enthusiasm, found renewed delight in learning from my former pupil. He rejoiced in coastal scenery, as he did in mountains; with friends, we walked several of the coastal footpaths.

As a climber, Jo made no pretension to be brilliant; one of his most appealing features was his modesty. But he had done some hard routes with Wilfrid Noyce, and on a rope he was solid, dependable, unflappable: an ideal second. Above all, he was a wonderful companion, relaxed, sensible, interesting in conversation, informed and enthusiastic about many matters. Jo was a person whom it was easy to love.

Dame Freya Stark 1893-1993

Freya Stark was famous for her adventurous travels in the Middle East, Arabia and Persia, and for the splendid books she wrote about them; these achievements were fully described in other obituaries. But years before she made her name as traveller and writer, she had proved herself as a mountaineer, and of the many honours she received in a long life she was particularly proud and happy to be an Honorary Member of the Alpine Club. It is this side of her life that it is appropriate to remember here.

Freya started to climb before the 1914-18 war, with her adopted god-father (who was also mine), the scholar W. P. Ker, later Professor of Poetry at Oxford and a member of the Alpine Club. In 1913 he took her to the Gran Paradiso range; in 1919 they were again on the Italian side of Mont Blanc, climbing from Courmayeur and walking over the passes between the valleys that radiate from Monte Rosa, ending at Macugnaga in the Val Anzasca. In 1923 they returned to Macugnaga, and as they were climbing towards a minor summit, the Pizzo Bianco, 'W.P. gave a sudden cry and died'. His heart had stopped. He was buried in the old church at Macugnaga, under the great east face of Monte Rosa. A few days later Freya, with the Macugnaga guide Tofi, traversed the Matterhorn – up the Swiss side, down the Italian, back to Zermatt over the Theodul, a 17-hour day.

Back in Macugnaga the following year she decided to attack that formidable east face of Monte Rosa which, so W.P. had told her, had seldom been climbed, and only once by a woman. She recalled her climb – again with Tofi – in the LAC Journal of 1964. The crux was the Marinelli couloir that runs right up the face – 'the highway for the avalanches of Monte Rosa, which pour down with a dull soft sound as if they were milk' – which they traversed at midnight when the surface was frozen. Then up the Loccie glacier, in places so steep that 'when now and then we took a few minutes rest, we would sit by merely leaning slightly towards the gigantic wall'. (When, to the packed congregation at her memorial sevice, Colin Thubron said she had learnt to 'overcome fear', I reflected that this day on Monte Rosa must have given her an early lesson.) With Tofi, she had ambitions to make a new route up the south edge of the Loccie glacier next season. Illness prevented this, and Monte Rosa by the Marinelli remained 'the only really big climb of my life'.

In 1931, when travelling in Persia, she had hopes of climbing Takht-i-Suleiman, but was foiled by a Hungarian climber who bribed her *shikari* to lead her to the unclimbable side of the mountain. After she settled at Asolo, she often went walking in the Dolomites, crossing passes and staying in huts. Her delight in just being in the mountains endured. 'Nothing will ever hold me like the mountains,' she wrote me in 1975; and in her eighties she went 'creeping round Annapurna – on a very peaceful pony'. In a letter of May 1979 she confessed to me that she was 'not up to much (86)' and old age meant 'one has to be treated like luggage', yet she had 'an unreasonable but happy wish to look once more on the Himalaya', and especially 'to ride from Indus source to Oxus across Pamirs'. Would she need a Russian visa, she asked me; and would her heart hold out? I think she half hoped it would not, and that, like her beloved W.P., she would end her life suddenly, among high mountains.

On her election as an Honorary Member of the LAC in 1935, Freya wrote to the President, Miss MacAndrew, that no honour could have given her greater pleasure 'since it is associated with mountains which have always meant so very much to me'. And after the merger with the Alpine Club in 1975 she told me 'I am so proud and happy to be with you in the Noble Club'.

In 1982 the province of Treviso organised an *Omaggio a Freya Stark* at Asolo – a splendid affair, with a banquet, concert, films of her travels, and the band of the Blues and Royals, flown out at the expense of a local bank. The crowning ceremony was the presentation to her of the Keys of Asolo; and as the 89-year-old Freya appeared at the top of the steps of the piazza, the tune the band struck up was 'The Maid of the Mountains'.

Janet Adam Smith
(Janet Carleton)

Jill Neate 1934-1993

The death occurred in May 1993 of Jill Neate, Alpine Club member and a leading mountaineering historian and bibliographer. She was 58. Her *Mountaineering Literature*, 1986, an enlarged version of an earlier work, is the internationally regarded authority on books about mountains and climbing in the English language. Booksellers the world over identify items in their catalogues by their 'Neate' numbers, and take immoderate delight when they are able to advertise some obscure piece of ephemera as 'Not in Neate.'

Jill Neate had been born William Neate in London and qualified as a chartered accountant, working in management consultancy and company secretarial services for the Institute of Chartered Accountants. On the deaths of her parents, she moved in 1970 to the Lake District and embarked on a career of mountain scholarship. Soon afterwards began the long, lonely process towards a change in sexual identity.

The patient accumulation of often obscure detail suited her temperament and the peculiar circumstance in which she found herself. Increasingly reclusive, she drew comfort from her correspondence with fellow biblio-philes, and set herself to chronicle the exploration and mountaineering history of those areas which receive little attention in the standard literature. *Mountaineering in the Andes* was published by the Expedition Advisory Centre of the Royal Geographical Society in 1987 as a source book for climb-ers. It was an astonishing assemblage of information that had taken seven years to complete. In order to track down elusive Spanish references, Neate had added a working knowledge of that language to the French and Ger-man she already possessed. A thorough revision of the work had just been completed at the time of her death.

In 1989 she brought out what many believe was her major work, *High Asia, an illustrated history of the 7,000 metre peaks*. It covered the mountains from the Pamirs to Assam, and all the little-known mountain groups of China and Tibet, listing their accessibility, history and climbing potential, and giving an extensive bibliography to each geographical section, with an even fuller general bibliography at the end of the book. It has been praised as a 'gem of research'.

Jill Neate translated many European books into English, including several Reinhold Messner titles and Friedrich Bender's *Classic Climbs in the Caucasus*, and she had produced a Readers' Guide to the Lake District. For several years she served on the Library Committee of the Alpine Club.

Audrey Salkeld

Walter Abbott Wood 1908–1993

Walter Wood died at West Palm Beach, Florida, after a long illness. He had been President of the American Alpine Club, the American Geo-graphical Society and the Explorers Club of New York. He was a notable surveyor of mountain country and, while training in Switzerland, had obtained his Alpine guide's diploma enabling him to wear the *bergführer* badge of the SAC. After a number of seasons in the Alps, his first expedi-tion was in 1929 on a mapping mission to the Kashmir–Tibet border.

From the thirties onwards, a private income enabled Wood to mount his own expeditions. These included the ascent of Mt Steele in 1935, and Mt Vancouver in 1949. Although Wood himself did not reach the summit of the latter, one of the four who did was Noel Odell. Whilst Wood was descending from the first ascent of Mt Hubbard in 1951, he received news that his wife and daughter had disappeared without trace whilst flying with the bush pilot Maurice King in the St Elias mountains.

From 1949 onwards, Walter Wood organised research projects in the Alaska/Yukon mountains, directing a programme of survey, geology, glaciology and mountaineering. In the early sixties, these programmes were extended to include a biological element which gave the Canadian Government much useful information for establishing the Kluane National Park.

Geoffrey Templeman

Charmian Longstaff 1907-1993

'Professional painter' was Charmian's description of herself on her application to join the LAC in 1939. She had won a scholarship to the Slade School, where she was a contemporary of William Coldstream and Claud Rogers, and highly regarded by Tonks, the Principal. She met Tom Longstaff through a Slade contemporary who had married Tom's brother. Immediately attracted to each other, in due course they married, and for all the 32 years difference in age, it was a most happy marriage. Tom used to say that Charmian, born in 1907, was his reward for his exertions on Trisul, climbed that year.

Charmian had enjoyed hill-walking and mild scrambling on family holidays on Deeside, but her serious climbing began with Tom. Before the war they had three seasons camping and climbing in the Carinthian and Julian Alps; in 1937 with the Courmayeur guide Adolph Rey they climbed the Grandes Jorasses and the Matterhorn, up and down the Italian side.

When Tom was discharged from the army in 1941, after the authorities, according to him, had discovered his real age (in 1939 he had cheated his way in), they retired to Achiltibuie, where they rented Badentarbat Lodge from the Cromartie estate. There they welcomed friends on leave from wartime duties, 'escaping to that heavenly spot and to the wonderful welcome they gave us' Peter Lloyd remembers. In those days Charmian was indefatigable – following Peter Bicknell and Tom Brocklebank across the trackless waste to Suilven, biking back to cook a huge dinner on a paraffin stove. After the war (and the welcome advent of calor gas and electricity) their hospitality to climbers, and to the children of climbers, made Badentarbat seem like an outpost of the AC and LAC.

In 1951 the Longstaffs visited his daughter Sylvia in Jordan, where her husband John Branford served in the Arab Legion. They all camped in the Wadi Rumm; and, though lacking boots or rope, Sylvia and Charmian decided to climb Jebel Rumm. Scrabbling in gym-shoes up screes and gullies and along fearsome ledges, they followed Sheikh Hamdam up to the white domes of the summit. 'I suppose it was very easy climbing,' Charmian wrote in the LAC Journal, 'but it was very exposed. This made us feel tremendously clever and accomplished.'

Back at Achiltibuie Charmian produced many paintings based on sketches made on the trip; she also painted their own hills, shores and islands, and portraits of her neighbours. Her portrait of Tom, painted for his daughter Jo Sancha, was given to the Alpine Club by Jo and hangs in the Committee Room. Charmian also drew the maps for Tom's *This My Voyage*.

After Tom died in 1964, in his ninetieth year, Charmian went on living at Badentarbat, entertaining family and friends in the spring and summer, making winter visits to the South to paint portraits, see her friends, renew her wardrobe and enjoy the opera. One of her last visits was in November 1990 when – Tom having been a member of the 1922 expedition – she was an honoured guest at 'The Everest Adventure' evening at the Royal Geographical Society.

They had been able to buy Badentarbat in 1957, in Charmian's name. So she became the laird, and took her duties seriously – she had to deal with planning permissions, fishing rights, the complications of the crofting laws. On Rent Days her crofter-tenants were offered hospitality which must have made a dent in the modest sums she received. After she died in a nursing home in Inverness in June 1993, a great contingent from Achiltibuie came over to the funeral; and for those who couldn't come to Inverness, there was a memorial service in September in the kirk at Achiltibuie. Her ashes were scattered on the hillside above Badentarbat, where she had scattered Tom's.

Janet Adam Smith
(Janet Carleton)

Penelope Storey d. 1993

My last memory of Penny is a fitting one. She asked me to lunch in her pretty Hampstead flat: it was a delicious lunch made festive by champagne. A few weeks later I heard that she had died.

She had to drop out of the climbing world (she was a member of the Pinnacle Club as well as the Ladies' Alpine and later the Alpine Club) after a stroke that kept her in hospital for several years and permanently disabled her. She had always been good company for a climb or a concert, or a meal and a talk. She worked at the Foreign Office for many years.

She had done climbs like the Bishorn and Weisshorn, Obergabelhorn and Arbengrat, Aiguille du Chardonnet by Forbes Arête. Her last climb was Mount Olympus.

Margaret Darvall

Ronnie Wathen 1934-1993

I must write warily: I feel there may be a 'most individual and bewildering ghost' glaring with mock ferocity over my shoulder, a restless shade who would never forgive me if I tried to bury him with platitudes. Ronnie Wathen was quite spectacularly different: unpredictable, provocative, abrasive yet stimulating in argument, generous with himself, always able to see and articulate the quirky side of life. What can I really say of a man who did his National Service in his father's smart cavalry regiment and passed idle moments in his tank knitting!

During our South Audley Street days I would know that Ronnie was in the club when a bicycle was chained to the railings and then, across the room, I would spy his tall, burly figure, a head torch in his tousled hair, hairy pullover and, sometimes, shorts. In a matter of moments mutual insults would be pinging between us, argument raging, friendship abounding. He was an endangered species: the true eccentric; in other words different by nature and not for effect.

Outside his family there were three thrusts to Ronnie's life: poetry, mountaineering and the Uilleann (Irish) pipes. He was differently good at all of them.

Ronnie was introduced to mountaineering by one of his Marlborough masters, pre-war Everest climber Edwin Kempson. Instinctively and correctly he spurned Oxbridge and went on to Trinity, Dublin, where the future pattern of his life took form. In Ireland he found what he had been seeking and it gave him a rich bounty. This powerful link once formed was never broken although he was to lead a wandering and gipsy life.

In Ireland Ronnie's first poems appeared and many slim volumes were to follow. He had a most splendid, if unruly, facility with words. Usually he employed them seriously but he also loved frolicking with them, standing them on their heads just for fun. He wrote about anything and everything that caught his fancy, as a poet should. However, there is curiously little about climbing although his later mountain travels in Greece and Turkey are well recorded.

He laboured long and hard with his Uilleann pipes and must be one of very few Anglo-Saxons to become really proficient with them. He was to give very entertaining one-man shows, playing the pipes and reciting his poems in his strong, clear, declamatory voice; in the same league as Dylan Thomas. He was blessed with a prodigious memory and could, for instance, recite vast chunks of the tortuously difficult *Finnegans Wake*.

Emerging from Trinity he tried work and marriage, both experiences lasting but a few weeks! He therefore opted for independence on his small private income, living life on his own terms. Some while later, working on an Israeli kibbutz, he met Àsta, a charming Icelandic woman of sterling mettle. This time the marriage was enduring.

As a mountaineer Ronnie had an early Alpine season with Chris Bonington and was a member of Simon Clark's expedition to Pumasillo (20,490ft) in the Andes in 1957. He took a nasty fall while supporting the summit push, damaging his ankle. However, his upthrusting urge was undented and, recovering, he made the summit. Other expeditions led him to the Karakoram and Mt Kenya. He was a very steady climber and an uncannily good route-finder. He remained constant to his Irish climbing and described Dalkey as 'my favourite climbing wall in the western hemisphere'.

Clearly Ronnie pursued his chosen activities with skill and dedication but it was the coruscating wit of the man himself that has left such an indelible impression on his many friends. The Ronnies of this world are of a rare and fugitive quality. He will be sorely missed and our condolences go out to Àsta and his children, Sunna and Sean.

My last and very typical memory of Ronnie was at the usual Sunday morning gathering of veteran Irish climbers at Dalkey, just a few weeks before his sudden and final illness. Ronnie was being Ronnie: controversial, assertive, entertaining, rumbustious. Frank Winder, at 65 still a powerful climber, was therefore assigned the task of sapping Ronnie's energy by leading him up as many climbs as possible that were known to be at the limit of Ronnie's ability to follow. To everyone's delight, including Ronnie's, this was duly done. Its success was only partial. After lunchtime drinks with Bill Hannon, the last I saw of Ronnie was when he strode off up the road to do a kindness to an old friend.

I must end with a grumble. Ronnie was an insomniac, never known to leave a party until very late. His parting prank was to quit the party of life far too early, at the age of 58, just to tease I like to think. It was a cruel jest. On Àsta's inspiration, he held his final party at the little church of Calary, below Sugarloaf Mountain, in the verdant lap of his beloved Wicklow Hills. On that sunny autumn afternoon many, many friends crowded the church, farewells were spoken in prose and verse, laments welled up from three of the finest pipers in Ireland and a lone fiddler knelt by the open grave and hauntingly played the restless Ronnie to his rest.

Mike Banks

GLENDALOUGH, COUNTY WICKLOW

> *Ronnie Wathen was a shaman.*
> *Only he knew what it was he blew*
> *From the mountains of his life*
> *Through his poems and his pipes.*

Waking to a bright morning of white houses
circling Dublin Bay, we rolled off the ferry
and into the cloud-clearing hills of Wicklow,
into the raised glacial arms of Glendalough.
We passed St Kevin's sixth century retreat,
its round tower, rounded Celtic crosses,
to walk through the Scots pines beside the lake
dancing with grains of gold from the mines above.
We pinched ourselves. Was this your latest trick?
The day was so bright we must be crossing
the water still, in some crag-walking dream.

Sweating up the big scree boulders we met
goats. I memorised your eulogy. We rushed
up a jinksy little slab climb of closed
cracks called *Expectancy*, then abseiled
off a metal ring against the *dead*line
of your funeral. (Are you writing this?)
You'd have laughed at the three of us changing
in the carpark toilets. We *heard* you laughing
as we circled round the Sugar Loaf Mountain
searching, cursing, asking for the right church
which was the first church we had passed.

Poems and poignant pipes, words and weeping,
a fiddle and bright flowers sent you down.
In the quiet sunlight and open fields
by the mountain, the crowd could not leave,
could not come to believe that it was you
under that mound of wet Wicklow earth.
How the Irish understand the circle.
Exile and return. A tower, a round cross,
a ring of a hill. What you gave us was
Expectancy, a life that leaped circles,
as full of surprises as your death.

Terry Gifford

Roland Arnold Rodda 1917–1993

Dr Roland Rodda, who died in England on 17 October 1993, was a New Zealander and a well-known and much respected member of the New Zealand Alpine Club for 54 years.

If there are two words which characterised Rodda's mountaineering career they are enthusiasm and perseverance: once he got a mountain in his sights he did not give up. But for all that he showed discretion. And you could be sure that, whether forced to retreat by unfavourable rock, snow or weather conditions, he would be certain to return and complete the climb.

Rodda did most of his mountaineering in the years between the mid-1930s and the end of the 1970s when there were still some virgin peaks in the remoter corners of the Southern Alps. It was in quest of such mountains that Roland Rodda did his best work and he became well known for his exploits among the peaks of NW Otago, the Central Darran and Milford Sound mountains of the Fiordland National Park. In his medical student days he made first ascents of peaks at the head of Lake Wakatipu. Later he climbed Mt Aspiring by the NW ridge and took part in the first ascent of the steep N buttress. These were only some of his Otago climbs. He led a party on a new route, predominantly snow and ice, up the Earnslaw Burn face of Mt Earnslaw. Perhaps the Darrans were one of his most favoured places, for there he climbed with Dr Lindsay Stewart, the doyen of the Southland Section of the NZ Alpine Club, on virgin Mt Patuki. In addition to the peaks such as Mt Christina in the Upper Hollyford valley, Rodda first ascended Mt Grave (named after the celebrated explorer of Western Fiordland) and made a pioneering ascent of the W face of Mt Tutoko, the highest peak in the Darran group. Roland Rodda did many climbs on New Zealand's highest peaks, among them Mt Cook and Mt Tasman, and in winter he ski-mountaineered on the Franz Josef and the Upper Tasman glaciers.

During the Second World War Rodda served as a medical officer with the Royal New Zealand Air Force in New Zealand and in the South Pacific, several times flying with RNZAF aircraft on bombing missions. At the end of the war he climbed on Bougainville, the largest island in the Solomons group, where he made the first complete ascent of Mt Balbi (8888ft) and Mt Bagana (5730ft). On his return to Dunedin, Roland Rodda not only went back to the hills but also served on the Otago Section Committee, the Central Committee of the NZAC, and on the board of the Fiordland National Park.

After graduation from the University of Otago Medical School, Dr Rodda specialised in pathology in which subject he gained a post-graduate degree and was a senior lecturer before he left Dunedin to become the foundation professor of pathology in the Medical School in Hobart. While in Tasmania he tramped and climbed extensively.

Retiring to Sale, Cheshire, Roland Rodda still kept up his interest in mountaineering through the Alpine Club, the NZ Alpine Club, the Alpine Ski Club and his frequent trips to the Lake District and the peaks of Snowdonia.

Roland and I were contemporaries and friends from our high school and university days; and we shared many mountains. We climbed together on the first ascent of Mt Grave in Fiordland. A remote rock peak of some consequence, we were overtaken on it during our descent by a nor'-west storm. J Ede, Rodda and I survived our enforced night out perched on the illusory and proverbial ledge.

To me, Roland Rodda's greatest attribute was his steadfastness under difficulties: I never knew him to flap. I was mindful of this when I wrote of him in one of my books: 'Rodda was a wonderful man for giving you strength on a mountain and you never had anything but the greatest confidence in him.'

Paul Powell
Dunedin

Kevin Columba FitzGerald 1902-1993

Kevin FitzGerald was a man of fine physique, 6ft 3in tall and strongly built. With names such as his he could hardly have been anything but an Irishman; and he might easily have spent most of his life in Ireland, where his father (whom, characteristically, he described as 'usually a rich man') had bought an estate in Tipperary which it was intended that he should manage and eventually inherit. But things worked out otherwise, and after four years at Seale Hayle Agricultural College he finally joined the Agricultural Division of ICI. He remained with that company in various capacities until his retirement after 33 years' service.

The first passion of his life was books. He was an immensely literary man, very widely read and with a retentive memory; and he possessed a library of several thousand books, of which he had read all but a very few. He was a master of words, whether spoken or written, humorous or serious, and during the Second World War, and in the years after it, he did a lot of casual broadcasting – readings and short talks – for the BBC. During the 1950s and early 1960s he wrote perhaps a dozen thrillers which were quite successful at the time, although they would nowadays seem fairly dated. Incidentally a mountaineering interest begins to appear in some of them, with occasional references to 'Christopher Higgs', the thinly disguised proprietor of Pen-y-Gwryd. Later, he wrote a book on the Chilterns (where he lived), and also an official history of the Farmers' Club on the occasion of that club's 125th anniversary. But it was not until he was over eighty, and his eyesight was failing, that he wrote *With O'Leary in the Grave*, which can fairly be described as a little masterpiece – a brilliantly amusing account of his own youth and a vivid picture of his eccentric father. Later still, when he was completely blind, he dictated a continuation of *With O'Leary*, which he called *Walking the Prodigal Way*; but this was never published.

Kevin did many good works by stealth; for example, he was once a prison visitor, and so long as he could drive a car he went into Oxford once a week as a helper at meetings of Alcoholics Anonymous. At one stage in his life, he himself had been so serious an alcoholic that he was warned that he had only a few months to live. It must be extremely rare to give up, as he did, without assistance or treatment of any kind.

Mountains meant nothing to him until shortly after the War when, already in his late forties, he had a spell as ICI's General Manager in Ireland. One member of his staff there, Brian Hilton-Jones, persuaded him to come with him on weekend trips on the overnight Dublin–Holyhead mailboat, and it was then that he was introduced to Pen-y-Gwryd. From that time he became a lover of the Welsh mountains, and even of Welsh rock-climbing, for which it is fair to say he had no aptitude whatever; and this improbable passion soon extended to anything to do with mountains or mountain literature.

He was an immensely entertaining after-dinner speaker, and naturally was in great demand at the Annual Dinners of different British climbing clubs. He was an Honorary Member of the Climbers' Club; and he must have been one of the few people to have been elected to the Alpine Club (I am not sure under what rule) without ever having climbed in the Alps or any other high range, in disregard of all the normal election qualifications, simply because of his great love of mountains. He contributed three or four characteristic articles to the *AJ* and for two or three years in the 1970s was in charge of its obituary section, which he introduced with a few apposite lines of his own writing.

He was married to Janet Quigley, the creator of the radio programme *Woman's Hour* which is still running, and it was a tremendous blow to him when she died six or seven years ago. By that time Kevin had become totally blind, and his deafness was becoming increasingly serious. He will be widely remembered for many reasons, and not least for the dignity and the courageous, uncomplaining way in which he faced the handicaps of his last few years.

David Cox

Sir Jack Longland 1905 –1993

Jack Longland died on 29 November 1993 aged 88. He joined the AC at the unusually early age of 22, proposed and seconded by Claude Elliott and Geoffrey Young. He was on the Committee in 1939, Vice-President in 1961 and President in 1974. He was President of the Climbers' Club 1945-48 and Honorary Member in 1964; he was made an Honorary Member of various north country climbing clubs. I was two years junior to him at Cambridge but since he stayed on after taking his degree, as a Fellow of Magdalene College responsible for the Pepys Library, we overlapped for four years and remained friends ever since. As to the last years at Bakewell, I have depended on help and advice from his daughter Jo and from Jim Perrin.

At Cambridge Jack was a brilliant all-rounder taking a first in the History Tripos and first-class honours with special distinction in English, while also winning an athletics Blue as a pole-vaulter and inevitably becoming President of the Cambridge University Mountaineering Club, a distinction which Basil Goodfellow used to equate to a Blue. In the mountaineering club he was contemporary with Lawrence Wager, with whom he did many of the major Alpine routes, and with Gino Watkins, Wyn Harris, Freddie Chapman and Ivan Waller, all names to conjure with. But the father figure for some of us, and certainly for Jack, was Geoffrey Winthrop Young whose house and whose Easter parties at Pen y Pass were great gathering places for the climbing fraternity. Jack was a dashing figure on these occasions, active on the hills, a witty and stimulating companion, excelling also with his compact muscular figure at such gymnastic contests as arm wrestling and climbing round an upright chair without touching the floor. But it would be a mistake to make too much of Geoffrey Young's influence, for the tradition of guideless climbing was already strongly established in the Club. He was incidentally also a roof climber but deplored the publicity which this activity later received. 'The whole point about roof climbing,' he said, 'was its quietness and anonymity and the University authorities would not take any strong action, such as sending you down, if you kept quiet.' This versatility was a foretaste of what was to come in his professional life.

The high point of Jack's rock-climbing achievement, and the most famous, was certainly the first ascent of the climb which bears his name and which he pioneered and led on the West Buttress of Clogwyn du'r Arddu over the Easter and Whitsun weekends of 1928 when he was still at Cambridge. The Easter visits to the cliff were essentially for reconnaissance, exploration and preliminary gardening, in which Frank Smythe and Graham Brown were also involved. They abseiled off in bad weather half-way up the climb and came back at Whitsun, Jack with Frank Smythe, Ivan Waller and Peter Bicknell. When they got to the foot of the climb a party from the Rucksack Club, led by Fred Piggott, were on the point of starting up it but they recognised that Jack's party had prior rights and encouraged Jack to lead a combined attack. He described what followed in an article he wrote in old age for the magazine *Crags* (*No 18*, p15): 'We had a sort of toss up to decide who was going up and who wasn't and Ivan Waller and Peter Bicknell stood down which was very gallant of them, and we linked together – myself, Frank Smythe, Fred Piggott, Bill Eversden and Morley Wood. I thought Piggott was going to lead it, but he said that I'd been on this one first, and I was simply flung the end of the rope and told to get on with the business.'

But Jack was no mere cragsman; he left the further exploration of Clogwyn du'r Arddu to others and turned his attention to the Alps, doing many of the classic ridge climbs and some new routes. Like the rest of us, he had his eye on the chance of getting to the Himalaya, and when the 1933 expedition to Everest was being planned his climbing record made him an obvious choice for it. Not having been at high altitude before, he was at a disadvantage compared with Frank Smythe, Eric Shipton and Wyn Harris and was not in either of the teams chosen to go for the summit. But he played a big role in establishing Camp 6 and had the formidable task of bringing down a party of exhausted Sherpas in a blizzard – a real feat of route-finding and leadership. Needless to say, he relished the whole experience of the expedition, the rivalry and companionship, the physical challenge of high altitude, and the mutual trust between sahibs and Sherpas.

Jack's next major project was, in contrast, a journey to the Watkins Mountains in Rasmussen Land, the biggest mountain mass in Greenland which had first been seen from the air by Gino Watkins in 1930 when on a survey flight in a moth aircraft. The expedition was under the leadership of Lawrence Wager and was very much a Cambridge party with August Courtauld, who had chartered Shackleton's old ship *The Quest* to get them there, Lawrence's brother Hal and Dr Fountaine, a geologist. Bad ice conditions forced them to land 70 miles short of their intended starting point and the approach to the mountain required a nine days march hauling sledges over very difficult country before reaching the peak which they successfully climbed, measuring its height at 12,250ft – the highest mountain in the Arctic. Jack described the expedition in his second paper to the Club (*AJ58*, 1936).

He was invited by Tilman to join the 1938 expedition to Everest but had just undertaken a new job and felt obliged to decline.

The course of Jack's professional life was decided in the depressed years of the early thirties when he was first a lecturer in English at Durham University and then director of the Durham Community Service Council. He took an immediate liking to the Durham mining community and was deeply moved by the injustice of their life and hardships. This caring idealistic side of Jack is one that, in my experience, he never made a show of. His motivation to enter the field of state education is best expressed in his own words from an address he gave in 1970:

'I came into educational administration at the end of the squalid and hungry 1930s after some years working with unemployed Durham miners and their families. I think that those underfed children, their fathers on the scrapheap, and the mean houses under the tip, all the casual product of a selfishly irresponsible society, have coloured my thinking ever since. They were one main cause of my entering the statutory education business. I had been shunting about in social sidings for long enough, helping men to move mountains with little shovels. I wanted the mainline express to a new world and fair shares all round.'

After a spell as Deputy Director of Education in Hertfordshire (1940) he moved to the top job in Dorset (1942) and then to Derbyshire in 1949, a post he held till his retirement in 1970. Despite his own elitist background he was an enthusiastic supporter of the move to comprehensive schools and played a crucial part in introducing them in Derbyshire. An initiative which was particularly his own was the establishment at White Hall near Buxton of an outdoor education centre run by the county. It was the first of its kind and its success led many, indeed most, counties to follow suit. This led, in turn, to the establishment of the Mountain Leader Training Board of which he was Chairman from 1964 to 1980 and to his active membership of many committees and commissions dealing with sport and outdoor education, notably the Outward Bound Trust Council, the Central Council for Physical Recreation and the Sports Council of which he was Vice-Chairman 1971-74. He was also a member of the Royal Commission on Local Government, 1964-67.

In parallel with all these activities, Jack had in effect a second career as a broadcaster on various brains trusts and similar programmes. His erudition, quick wit and sense of fun made him an immediate success in this role and, in particular, he was for no less than 20 years the chairman of the famous programme *My Word*, one of the high spots of sound radio.

The knighthood awarded on his retirement as Director of Education both surprised and gratified him but here I agree with another obituarist that the Establishment had missed an opportunity; for Jack had been a long time in the Derbyshire job and was surely overdue for a move to bigger responsibilities and opportunities. Perhaps he just didn't want to move on or maybe he had given offence in high places, for he had a sharp tongue and could be quite combative, ever ready to stand up for what he thought right even at the risk of unpopularity. Back in the thirties he had been active in the behind-the-scenes dispute over the leadership of the 1936 Everest expedition, a stance which effectively ruled him out from joining the party. In his valedictory address to the Club he spoke out strongly in a way that, to my knowledge, no one else had done against the decline in manners and moral standards among some young British mountaineers. Later still, in his last years as head of the Mountain Leader Training Board, he got at loggerheads with the BMC and a deadlock resulted which the Sports Council was quite unable to resolve. It fell to the President of the Alpine Club to intervene as honest broker to get the contestants to agree to an impartial enquiry.

After retirement Jack continued with his many activities and in 1974 was elected President of the Club. I have already referred to his valedictory address and at the end of it he recalled what Leo Amery had said on the same occasion: 'For myself I echo the voice of a more distinguished President, that he was prouder of being elected to that office than of being appointed Privy Councillor. I would put up the ante a bit and say I'd be prouder of the Presidency than if I were to become Archbishop of Canterbury.'

As to Jack's last years, he had a great circle of friends whom he saw at Bakewell or in the Savile Club or at North Country dinners and events. For a man of his active disposition old age was bound to be a frustrating time and two strokes further cramped his style, robbing him of the use of the car; but there were always friends at hand to provide company and transport. He had great inner resources and retained his mental activity almost to the end. Then, in the nineties, came the great sadness of the deaths in quick succession of his son John and his wife Peggy.

He will be sorely missed by many of us.

Peter Lloyd

John Hunt writes:

Jack was numbered among a small group of brilliant young men who emerged from the old universities with double firsts in the mid-twenties; they included John Wolfenden and John Redcliffe-Maud, who played leading parts in extending the perspectives and scope of formal education beyond the classroom and into outdoor experience beyond the confines of school playing fields. Those ideas had their genesis in the private sector of education; Abbotsholme and Gordonstoun both preached the equal and complementary values of academic or technical learning on the one hand, and outdoor activities additional to, or instead of, competitive organised sport on the other. This was a concept of education by no means generally accepted in the years immediately after the War.

Longland was fortunate in finding himself, on beginning his career as an education administrator, appointed to Durham Education Authority as deputy to another of the elite progressives, John Newsom. He followed Newsom to Hertfordshire and helped him to institute Kurt Hahn's County Badge scheme which, in turn, led to the creation of a far more successful project, the Duke of Edinburgh's Award. I count myself fortunate to have been associated with that small band of Chief Education Officers: Alec Clegg and Jim Hogan, Newsom and Longland; for they provided me with much help and encouragement in the difficult task of launching Prince Philip's challenge to youth. From Hertfordshire Jack was promoted to the post of Director of Education for Dorset and, in 1949, to the same senior position in Derbyshire where he remained until his retirement 21 years later. The establishment of the first local authority Outdoor Activities Centre in Britain, at Whitehall, is a monument to the inspirational lead which Jack Longland gave to a more holistic concept of education.

One consequence of this was the greatly increased numbers of people walking, scrambling and climbing on our British hills and crags. Jack described it as an 'avalanche'. As President of the British Mountaineering Council, he appreciated the need to set standards of safety and to establish levels of adult competence in hillcraft. He took the initiative in codifying standards of leadership, which would be operated by a training board. The Mountain Leadership Certificate was established which could be earned through the channels of mountain centres approved by the board. I was privileged to be closely involved in that work, and recall the disapproval and criticism which were voiced by some of our fellow climbers at the time. Happily, time and circumstance have proved its value and the need to enable all young people to experience adventurous activities in the hills, and to gain that experience with proper safeguards.

In these and other ways, Jack Longland rendered a great service to youth.

Charles Warren writes:

My memories of Jack, as he was always known to us, date from my Cambridge days in the late twenties in the heydays of the CUMC. With Lawrence Wager as our president, we were strictly brought up. Any form of notoriety in respect of our mountaineering activities was frowned upon and considered to be in bad taste. If you were involved in an accident, however trivial, you kept quiet about it. I remember an episode when I slipped off a hold on the bottom slab of Central Buttress on Tryfan and landed safely on a grassy ledge laughing, only to be soundly ticked off by Lawrence.

I also remember an occasion when a party of us in the CUMC dashed up to Derbyshire to climb on Black Rocks, near Matlock, under the direction of our member Ivan Waller. Here I was encouraged to climb a sandstone chimney, only to find that the exit involved a hand traverse and a pull up to safety onto a mantelshelf over rounded holds. As my hands slipped back, Jack, who had seen my predicament, tried to grasp them from above but could not secure me. I slipped through his fingers and fell some 50 feet or so through a small tree, landing on my back between the rocks on a grassy patch unscathed. In the CUMC tradition of those days, I was immediately taken up another hard climb.

But Jack will, of course, always be remembered first and foremost for *Longland's* on Clogwyn du'r Arddu – that classic and most original route up the cliff. I was not on the first ascent but have memories of my own of the 'faith and friction slab' and the following pull-up over the overhang – a wonderful route up the cliff in its day!

I was not with Jack on Everest in 1933; that year I was climbing around the Gangotri glacier. But all of us in the mountaineering world at that time knew about his famous descent with a group of porters from a high camp down to the North Col in bad weather.

Post-war I climbed with Jack in Zermatt on the Dent Blanche and on the Zinalrothorn at the AC centenary meet.

I am unable to dilate upon Jack's academic activities except to say that I knew that he was, for a time, the Pepysian Librarian at Magdalene College, Cambridge. But Jack, the great mountaineer and our very distinguished Past President, will always go down in my memory as Longland of *Longland's* on Cloggy.

Oliver Turnbull writes:

This may be the occasion to record an account of an accident involving my uncle, Professor H W Turnbull, later FRS, AC member and President of the SMC, and Jack Longland.

In a letter in June 1960 my uncle wrote to me:

' ... you have completed what the family vainly tried many years ago! It was March and there was some ice about on the bottom pitch of the slab. I remember it was hard, but nothing like the difficulty about halfway up the climb where one has to step across onto another slab on its right – the Faith and Friction Slab according to Smythe, who was in the party of the first ascent with Longland leading. I was third in a party of four, with Longland again leading in his second ascent. He went up all the pitches rapidly each time, until he reached that step: and he took a good quarter hour or more over that pitch, having first fixed a stone in a crack for a running belay. When my turn came I took even longer – in fact I missed my footing and came off, and dangled 70 or 80 feet below, about 15 feet from the nearest point of Wales, for 25 minutes before someone had time to climb up to my level and lassoo me with a spare rope. Then, as I beat a retreat, alas our number two Paul Sinker (now Sir Paul) badly burnt his hands with my running rope as he tried to save my fall. He and Longland had fixed a piton at the top of the pitch, which was a merciful safeguard, for they told me that their grass footing had slid down a good 12 inches during the tension on the rope ... '

There is a family tradition, recently confirmed as fact by my cousin Derwent, which throws light on a possible cause of the accident. Before setting out for the climb my uncle, being a competent but modest rock-climber, had no rubbers of his own so had to borrow from others. The best he could obtain consisted of two right-footed shoes, and these had to do. When he came to the crux move the curve of the shoe caused him to slip off as he swung up and round on his left foot. On my ascent in the 1960s I had the benefit of a pair of matching PAs, but it is not hard to see how he was inconvenienced by his ill-matched footwear.

The Professor at least was none the worse for his experience. He was known to carry a small flask of brandy in his sack and when asked later if he had felt in need of a reviving nip replied: 'Oh no, I only take the brandy in case of emergencies.' But I hope he offered the flask to his leaders who had saved the party from a catastrophe which would have devastated the climbing world.

Alpine Club Notes

OFFICERS AND COMMITTEE FOR 1994

PRESIDENT	M H Westmacott
VICE PRESIDENTS	S M W Venables
	J S Cleare
HONORARY SECRETARY	Dr M J Esten
HONORARY TREASURER	J M C Evans
HONORARY LIBRARIAN	D J Lovatt
LIBRARIAN EMERITUS	R Lawford
HONORARY EDITOR	Mrs J Merz
COMMITTEE: ELECTIVE MEMBERS	J L Bermúdez
	Ms J-A Clyma
	M W Fletcher
	D W Hamilton
	M H Johnston
	S A Jones
	R F Morgan
	Ms J A Turner
	P Wickens
EXTRA COMMITTEE MEMBERS	G D Hughes
	M F Baker
ACG REPRESENTATIVES	D Tunstall
	D Wills

OFFICE BEARERS

HONORARY ARCHIVIST	Miss L Gollancz
HONORARY ASSISTANT ARCHIVIST	Miss M Darvall
HONORARY KEEPER OF THE CLUB'S PICTURES	D J Lovatt
HONORARY KEEPER OF THE CLUB'S ARTEFACTS	R Lawford
CHAIRMAN OF THE FINANCE COMMITTEE	R F Morgan
CHAIRMAN OF THE HOUSE COMMITTEE	M H Johnston
CHAIRMAN OF THE LIBRARY COUNCIL	G C Band
CHAIRMAN OF THE PUBLICATIONS COMMITTEE	J N Slee-Smith
ASSISTANT EDITORS OF THE *Alpine Journal*	R A Ruddle
	G W Templeman

GUIDEBOOKS EDITOR	G L Swindin
ASSISTANT HONORARY SECRETARIES:	
ANNUAL WINTER DINNER	Mrs G D Bull
LECTURES	S M W Venables
INFORMAL EVENINGS	S A Jones
MEETS	M W Fletcher
MEMBERSHIP	G D Hughes
TRUSTEES	M F Baker
	J G R Harding
	P J Nunn
HONORARY SOLICITOR	S N Beare
AUDITORS	A M Dowler
	Russell Ohly & Co

ALPINE CLIMBING GROUP

PRESIDENT	D Wilkinson
HONORARY SECRETARY	R A Ruddle

GENERAL MEETINGS OF THE ALPINE CLUB 1993

12 January	Roger Mear, *Nanga Parbat 1991*
9 February	Wolfgang Stefan, *Mountain Odyssey: Forty Years' Alpinism*
6-7 March	North Wales Meet and General Meeting
	Lindsay Griffin, *Mongolia, Camels, Yurts and Yeti Tracks*
16 March	Simon Yates, *Patagonian Big Walls*
13 April	Gordon Stainforth, *Eye to the Hills*
11 May	George Band, Peter Mould and Patrick Limerick, *A Bhutan Evening*
15 June	Everest Anniversary Evening.
	Portraits of Everest by Rick Allen, Chris Bonington, Ed Webster and Michael Westmacott
24-25 Sept	Lake District Meet and General Meeting
	Jim Fotheringham, *Climbs in the Caucasus*
12 October	Robert Anderson, *Seven Summits*
26 October	A Debate, *Competition Climbing*
9 November	Martin Moran, *Alpine 4000 metres Marathon*
13 November	Annuual Symposium at Plas y Brenin, *Africa's Mountains*
6 December	Annual General Meeting
	George Band, *Return to Everest*

The Annual London Dinner was held on 7 December at The Great Hall, St Bartholomew's Hospital. The Chief Guest was Joss Lynam and the Toast to the Guests was proposed by Jim Milledge.

CLIMBING MEETINGS 1993

20-21 February	ACG/AC Winter Meet, Glencoe
6-7 March	North Wales Meet and General Meeting
26-27 June	Derbyshire Meet
24 July - 7 August	Alpine Meet based at Grindelwald
2-10 September	Cornwall Meet - joint meet with CC at Bosigran
24-25 September	Lake District Meet

THE ALPINE CLUB LIBRARY 1993

The Library continues to flourish under new management. Mrs Margaret Ecclestone has succeeded Mrs Pat Johnston who resigned at the end of 1993 after 15 years dedicated service. John Peacock also succeeded Jon Mellor as Treasurer during 1992. On being elected President of the Club, Michael Westmacott resigned as Chairman after guiding the Library Council for seven years through the difficult period of the move from South Audley Street to Charlotte Road, via the Ski Club, and the establishment of the Library in our new premises. I was invited to succeed him, and initiated a review of our objectives in order to develop a fresh operating plan.

Following the 1992 Appeal, which raised a very creditable £187,000, mostly from Club members, the most urgent and important matter was to safeguard the Library's financial future by prudent investment for both capital growth and some £15,000-£20,000 annual operating income. Accordingly, Fleming Private Asset Management were appointed in March to manage the portfolio, and the Charity Commissioners confirmed that we were not restricted in our range of investments.

A second aim was to increase the 'user friendliness' of the Library. An information leaflet was developed; regulations were reviewed and opening hours extended to cover the additional Club informal evening meetings. The policy for acquisitions was clarified.

The historical database for the Himalayan Index is largely complete, with references to 3700 expeditions to 1900 mountains over 6000m; so Anne Andrews has relinquished her role and the index is now maintained voluntarily, largely by Sally Holland.

The next major Library task is to update the Catalogue. Volume One, published in 1982, covered the period to 1979, with some 19,000 book entries. There is now scope for a similar sized Volume Two. A working group, drawing on the professional expertise of Margaret Clennett and Chris Gravina, was set up to consider how best to proceed.

Their recommendation was not to publish a further volume but to adopt a computerised catalogue system using a special Library package such as INMAGIC. Once installed with voluntary help, our Librarian could keep pace with new entries; but the 14-year backlog would require the services of a professional cataloguer. This approach was agreed in principle by the Council and at the end of 1993 additional funds were being sought from the British Library and various charitable bodies to pay for this exciting development, which falls outside the Library's normal operating budget.

During the year, three exhibitions were arranged: the first was of Everest photographs and memorabilia to commemorate the 40th Anniversary of the first ascent; the second showed some outstanding black and white photographs by our late member Douglas Milner, which he bequeathed to the Club; and thirdly, there was a display of the Club's many paintings and watercolours which are not normally on view.

As always, the Library is marvellously served by a dedicated core of members: those already mentioned, plus Bob Lawford, Jerry Lovatt, Peter Ledeboer, and Livia Gollancz as Archivist, assisted by Margaret Darvall. I thank them all.

George Band

HONOURS AND AWARDS

The New Year Honours List
Two members received the MBE. Congratulations to Dawson Stelfox and Rebecca Stephens. Congratulations also to Alan Blackshaw who received an OBE in 1992 for services to mountaineering.

Honorary Membership
In May 1993 Sir Edmund Hillary KBE was made an Honorary Member of the UIAA in recognition of his distinguished mountaineering career and long-term service to the Sherpa people. The following have been made Honorary Members of the Alpine Club: Michael Ward CBE in December 1992 and Janet Carleton OBE (Janet Adam Smith) in December 1993.

The Boardman Tasker Memorial Award for Mountain Literature
The 11th award ceremony was held at the Alpine Club on 21 October 1993. The judges were Terry Gifford (Chairman), Sheila Harrison and Paul Nunn. The winner was *The Ascent* by Jeff Long (Headline). Shortlisted were *The Undiscovered Country* by Phil Bartlett (The Ernest Press) and *This Game of Ghosts* by Joe Simpson (Jonathan Cape).

Medical Honours
Michael Ward was elected Master of the Worshipful Society of Apothecaries of London for the year 1993/94. Griffith Pugh was presented with an Honorary Diploma in Sports Medicine. Both awards were announced in *The Times* of 20 August 1993.

THE TYNDALL MEMORIAL

John Tyndall, FRS, 1820-1893, was one of our most distinguished members. He made the first ascent of the Weisshorn in 1861, attempted the Matterhorn from Breuil in 1860 and 1863, reaching the shoulder later known as Pic Tyndall, and made the first traverse of the Matterhorn from Breuil to Zermatt. He built a house at Belalp, near which is a memorial raised by his widow. The commune of Naters have cleaned up the memorial and added a centenary plaque in four languages saying briefly who Tyndall was. The plaque was unveiled on 11 September 1993 at a well-attended ceremony organised by the local *Gemeinde*. The Alpine Club was represented by Trevor Braham who has had the enthusiasm to stimulate the refurbishment of the memorial for this centenary year of John Tyndall's death. The plaque would not have been erected but for Trevor Braham's generosity in underwriting the cost.

M J Esten

UIAA COUNCIL MEETING AT PLAS Y BRENIN
27-29 May 1993

To coincide with the 40th anniversary of the first ascent of Everest the British Mountaineering Council hosted the council meeting of the International Union of Alpine Associations, the world body of mountaineering. Over 60 delegates from overseas converged on Plas y Brenin for a truly memorable weekend. They were joined on the Friday evening by members of the 1953 Everest team, staying at the nearby Pen-y-Gwyrd Hotel, for a splendid buffet reception during which Sir Edmund Hillary was made an Honorary Member of the UIAA for his distinguished mountaineering career and for his long-term service to the Sherpa people.

Apart from the obvious celebrations, the UIAA held two days of intensive meetings at Plas y Brenin. As is customary, the chairmen of the various commissions reported on the work of their commissions since the last meeting of the General Assembly in Japan the previous October. Among the important issues discussed were the reorganisation and restructuring of the UIAA, on which a working group is currently engaged. The level of UIAA involvement in mountaineering competitions (apart from competition climbing which the UIAA has organised at an international level since 1988) in areas such as ski-alpinism was also hotly debated. Opinions seemed to be equally divided, and there was much concern about the environmental impact of further competitions in mountain regions. A working group of the mountaineering commission, under the chairmanship of Alan Blackshaw, was given the task of studying the problem and reporting to the next General Assembly in Chile. [*See 'Competitions in Mountain Areas', pages 163-168.*] In addition, Alan Blackshaw's commission has been working on draft model standards for the training of mountain leaders and these have been circulated to all the Federations.

The British Mountaineering Council has a strong involvement with the UIAA at present. In addition to Alan Blackshaw and his Mountaineering Commission Secretary Roger Payne, Ivor Delafield has been Chairman of the Competition Climbing Committee, George Steele and Neville McMillan are on the Safety Commission, Dave Morris is Secretary of the Mountain Protection Commission, Michael Westmacott is Vice-Chairman of the Documentation Commission, while Charles Clarke is on the Medical and Paul Nunn on the Expeditions Commissions. Ian McNaught-Davis, President of the BMC, is proposed as the next UIAA Vice-President at the General Assembly in October, a great honour for himself and the BMC and the first time anyone from the UK has been offered this important post.

Altogether it was a highly successful and enjoyable weekend at Plas y Brenin and both the overseas guests and the 1953 Everest team were full of praise for the warmth of their welcome at the National Mountain Centre.

It is 25 years since the UIAA last visited Plas y Brenin. At that time, in 1968, Lord Hunt was President of the BMC and the UIAA General Assembly met at the Bonnington Hotel (especially chosen?) in London and then had the option to visit North Wales and see the various activities at the centre. It is interesting to reflect on the prices charged then, when bed and breakfast at the Bonnington was £2 15s per person, and the two-day visit to Wales, including all travel, railway sleeper, meals and hotel accommodation cost just £14.

Derek Walker
BMC General Secretary
August 1993

ALPINE CLUB SYMPOSIUM 1993: AFRICA'S MOUNTAINS

Plas y Brenin once again provided a venue for the Symposium held on Saturday 13 November. The large audience was made up of those who had been to Africa, those who wanted to go there and an indeterminate but welcome group who perhaps came in initially to avoid the evil weather that marked the transition from autumn to winter. The proceedings were introduced by George Band.

A Dark Continent

John Temple's introductory talk began with an apologia for the relative absence of 'serious' mountains in Africa. There had been commendable efforts to make up for the Continent's deficiencies in this respect, ranging from the construction of the Pyramids to the invention of the Kong Mountains, a 5000km range extending from Sierra Leone eastwards to the Mountains of the Moon. In Africa, heat and thirst were your fellow travellers in place of the cold and hunger of the Greater Ranges, and could prove equally lethal and even less comfortable. John Temple's talk concluded with a brief description of the first ascent of Mt Kenya's Diamond Buttress.

Footloose and Fancy Freelance

Matt Dickinson gave a wide-ranging account of the mountains and hill country of the quarter of the continent between the Mediterranean and the Gulf of Guinea. The Atlas, with their broad crests and rubble slopes, are trekking and ski-touring country. Much of their attraction is to be found in the valleys, where the architecture and lifestyle of the Berbers survive as a unique culture. In the heart of the Sahara the Hoggar offer trekking and high quality rock-climbing, some of which is remarkably accessible. The Tassili, a vast gallery of rock art, is more difficult to reach, its remoter gorges still probably unvisited. It was particularly satisfying to see and hear something of the rarely visited Mt Cameroun and Mandara range.

The Northern Highlands of Tanzania

In a talk prepared at short notice, Ian Munro described a line of volcanoes starting in the west with the huge caldera of Ngorongoro, its rim over 3000m, its floor a justly famous haven for wildlife. To the north the wide moorlands of the Crater Highlands end abruptly with the western scarp of the Rift valley, at the foot of which rise the currently active Ol Doinyo Lengai. Mt Meru, to the east, was active at the turn of the century, forming a neat recent conelet in the wild amphitheatre which rises in 1000m cliffs to the summit. On Kilimanjaro, the mountaineer should explore the dramatic southern slopes or the lunar landscape of the crater icefields to appreciate what is on offer.

A Tour of South African Crags

Evan Wiercx described how the combination of reliable good weather, varied and often accessible cliffs and a welcoming climbing community makes the region a most attractive destination for those seeking a climbing holiday. For variety there are *kloofs* (gorges) to be descended, with a combination of slides, jumps and abseils down the waterfalls. The reported 'Best Rock Climb in the Universe' in the Cedarberg must be an irresistible attraction for those in E2 mode.

The Ruwenzori

Andrew Wielochowski's first visit to the Ruwenzori was from the western (Zaire) side. A series of huts built in the colonial era were, like much else, neglected; the tracks were overgrown but the mountains when reached were as impressive as ever. The Uganda side displayed similar neglect until a UN-funded programme promoted by Guy Yeoman reopened the tracks and restored the huts, making the Mountains of the Moon more accessible than they had been for a quarter century. The snow-covered crowns of the main peaks, however, will take more than UN funds to preserve them against the threat of global warming.

The Rock-Climbing Scene in Central Africa

Zimbabwe's seemingly limitless rock-climbing possibilities kept Chris Field busy for the two years he was stationed there. The army exercises he was involved in constantly brought new areas to his attention. Conforming to local convention, Chris became a convert to bolt belays. Jerry Gore had only two weeks in the area and had to fit in a honeymoon as well as the rock-climbing. Judging from his slides he got his priorities right.

From Poi to Point John

Pat Littlejohn described the second ascent of the Wielochowski–Corkill route on Poi and the free ascent of the overhanging W face of Point John, Mt Kenya. Pat spoke of the debilitating effects of thirst and heat, and recounted how he and John Mothersele had been stuck in a storm on the W face of Point John, wet and cold, and how they had personally experienced Kenya's claim to be a land of contrasts.

The 1993 Symposium was organised by John Temple, Jerry Gore and Sheila Harrison, with help from Cotswold Camping of Betwys y Coed.

John Temple

THE SEVENTH INTERNATIONAL FESTIVAL OF MOUNTAINEERING LITERATURE
Bretton Hall, Yorkshire, 20th November 1993

When I dropped in at Doug Scott's house in 1986 he unrolled across the floor a plan for his autobiography. It was fifteen feet long. Doug opened the Festival by displaying this tatty scroll and reading from work in progress. Then he admitted that he had taken the advance from Hodder & Stoughton in 1976 and that life was outpacing the autobiography. Judging from the originality of his writing so far, it will be worth waiting for.

Mick Ryan had accepted this year's Festival challenge by offering to respond to the question 'Can sport climbing produce interesting writing?' After a thorough survey of the field, he admitted that it hadn't so far, but he then read two pieces of his own that revealed a sport climber who could write brilliantly, if not actually about bolted routes. It was Mick's bouldering piece which most impressed the audience.

When I realised that the title of Steve Dean's new biography of Colin Kirkus, *Hands of a Climber*, was taken from a poem by Colin's brother Guy who is still very much alive, I invited Guy to read three climbing poems to us, one of which was written over half a century ago. Guy was able to make a strong and moving reading from a pamphlet of his three poems published as a limited edition especially for the occasion by Jack Baines's Ernest Press. By contrast, three newly-commissioned poems were read by the young climber Kym Martindale. These were so widely admired that she has been commissioned to produce three more poems for the next event, on 19 November 1994.

The well known *Alpine Journal* contributor Phil Bartlett answered the question 'Why go on writing about it?' by discussing his recently published philosophical enquiry *The Undiscovered Country*. Probing questions from the floor showed what an important book this will become for clarifying the thinking of mountaineering readers.

The laid-back philosophy of Allen Steck disguised the meticulous approach of mountaineering editors in the USA when Al spoke about '25 Years of Ascent – The Inside Story'. Allen Steck had been flown over from California by the Wild Country Foundation in recognition of the work by the Sierra Club, publishers of *Ascent*, in protecting mountain environments.

A repeat of the adjudication address, originally given at the Boardman Tasker Memorial Award ceremony in October at the Alpine Club, preceded a reading from Jeff Long's winning novel *The Ascent;* a lively debate followed. The annual Festival writing competition, run in conjunction with *High* magazine, was judged by Doug Scott and Robin Campbell. David Atkinson's winning story 'Delayed on the Hill' was read by Ian Smith and published in the December 1993 issue of *High*.

The opening of an exhibition of Bill Maltman's Scottish mountain watercolours anticipated the appearance of Robin Campbell who had journeyed from Perth to give an erudite and witty lecture on Scottish Victorian mountaineering writing. Quoting from SMC Journals of the 1880s, Campbell demonstrated how hilarious some Victorian writing can be. Sir Hugh Munro yielded good examples of this. Campbell suggested that Munro often strode the hills alone 'because he was not much liked'.

Terry Gifford

To receive details of future Festivals write to Terry Gifford, Bretton Hall College, West Bretton, Wakefield, West Yorkshire, WF4 4LG.

THE HIMALAYAN MOUNTAINEERING INSTITUTE, DARJEELING

The foundation stone of the Institute was laid by Shri Jawharlal Nehru on 4 November 1954. To mark its 40th Anniversary the Alpine Club gave the Institute a leather-bound presentation copy of John Hunt's *The Ascent of Everest*, the gift having been funded by two Club members. We are grateful to Roy Watkins of Himalayan Kingdoms who kindly transported the book to Darjeeling and personally presented it to Col Ajit K Dutt, the Principal of the Institute.

'I was pleased to have the opportunity to present the book,' said Roy. 'It was very well received and the experience made a significant impact upon my own trip – well worth carrying the extra weight! I was accompanied by a group of eleven trekkers and we were made extremely welcome by Colonel Dutt, who made us all a cup of tea and spoke to us about the Institute. We were then shown a delightful film on the first all-Indian ascent of Everest. This was a great bonus for my group who were thrilled to be associated – even in such a small way – with improving the boundaries of international understanding and co-operation.'

(*See also 'The Himalayan Mountaineering Institute, Darjeeling', page 225*.)

WHYMPER'S TENT

Whymper's tent has been refurbished professionally at very considerable expense by the Royal School of Needlework, the work being made possible through the generosity of Frank Solari to whom the Club is very grateful. The refurbished tent, together with other artefacts, was displayed at the Club as part of the celebrations of the first ascent of Everest in May 1993.

The provenance of the tent has long been a puzzle, and a clue was discovered at the time of the 125th anniversary celebration of the first ascent of the Matterhorn (see *AJ96*) when discussions between myself and guides from Valtournanche revealed that the tent had found its way to the Club somehow from their valley, where it had remained in a barn since the days of Whymper's campaigns on the Matterhorn. Antoine Carrel, grandson of *the* Carrel, Mayor of Valtournanche, and a frequent visitor to the Club, has pursued these earlier discussions and we are very grateful to him for the following account:

'The tent was Whymper's present to the Alpine guide Angel Maquignaz, son of the famous Jean Joseph, who disappeared in 1890 on Mont Blanc. Angel Maquignaz, as well as climbing throughout the Alps, was with Freshfield on the trip around Kangchenjunga in 1899. He was also one of Guido Rey's personal guides. Angel left the tent to his brother, Jean Baptiste Maquignaz, who was one of the party, with Jean Joseph Maquignaz's father and Daniele Maquignaz, Jean Joseph's nephew, who climbed the Dent du Géant in 1882. Jean Baptiste left it to his cousin Daniele, Camillo's father and Piero Maquignaz's grandfather, who sold it to Guido Monzino who in turn presented it to the Alpine Club.'

When the Club was given the tent by Guido Monzino in 1965 or thereabouts, it was in a very dilapidated condition, consistent with the story from the Valtournanche guides. It must have been damp for some time as substantial areas of the material of the sides and floor of the tent had disappeared, the damage being worst at the entrance end. Frank Solari recalls that, at the time of receipt of the tent, the Club was not well organised in the custody of its various treasures and no one was delegated specifically for the task. The basement of 75 South Audley Street reflected a long period of neglect, and awaited Bob Lawford's arrival on the scene to catalogue and organise it. Memory of the action taken on receipt is dim, but the Rev Fred Jenkins made the box which has protected it ever since; no other attention seems to have been given to conservation or preservation at that time.

Prior to the Everest anniversary, the tent appears to have been publicly displayed only once – when the new Library Catalogue was published. The many gaps in the fabric made it difficult to erect and ad hoc supports had to be contrived, causing local stress and threatening to tear the edges of some of the voids. It was clear that the tent could not be displayed again without risk.

On the Club's departure from South Audley Street, Frank Solari sought advice from the Victoria and Albert Museum and the Royal School of

Needlework. The RSN recommended that a fabric similar to and compatible with the original material be stitched to the inside as a support. Frank Solari relayed the RSN proposal to the Committee, offering to bear all of the considerable cost of the work. The Committee initially took a very cautious position but, after discussion, authorised the work to proceed. A few Committee members expressed reservations at the time about 'interfering' with the tent but, so far as the Hon Secretary is aware, none of them is now other than most impressed with the result of the work.

The Club wishes to record its gratitude to Frank Solari for his generosity, both financially and with his time in studying the best means to conserve the tent. Surprisingly, no record is to be found in the *Alpine Journal* concerning the original generosity of the Count of Monzino and all the others who have helped to bring the tent to the Club and to unravel its history; it is hoped that this short article makes amends.

However, like all good stories, this one has not quite ended. Comparison made by Jerry Lovatt of the tent with descriptions to be found in Whymper's *Scrambles Amongst the Alps* reveals that the tent in our possession is not identical to the one described in detail and recommended in Chapter V. It is, however, a very considerable development beyond the tent described as unsatisfactory earlier in the book, and could reasonably be interpreted as a model produced shortly before the final one described in *Scrambles*. The puzzle now remaining is, bearing in mind the history of the first ascent of the Matterhorn, how did Whymper come to give the tent to the Maquignaz family?

M J Esten

CHARLES CLARKE STARTS MOUNTAIN BOOKSHOP

Charles Clarke has opened a specialist climbing bookshop in London. Called *The Second Step*, it sells rare volumes, photographs and prints, as well as more standard fare. The shop is at York Arcade, 80 Islington High Street, London N1 8EQ. Phone/Fax 071-359 6412. It is two minutes from Angel tube station and is open on Wednesdays and Saturdays.

ERRATA

Alpine Journal 1993 Vol 98 The following corrections have been noted:
Plate 26   The caption should read 'Tenzing in 1969, with his wife Daku and daughter Pem Pem.'
Plate 39   The small circle to the left of the arrow should be removed.
Page 91   Eight lines up from the foot, the years 1983 and 1982 should be reversed.
The Editor apologises to John Hunt and Kurt Diemberger for these errors.

Contributors

H ADAMS CARTER is a retired schoolmaster who taught foreign languages. He has led expeditions to the Himalaya, Andes and Alaska, and has been Editor of the *American Alpine Journal* since 1959.

PRINCE SADDRUDIN AGA KHAN is a leader in international environmental causes and the founder and chairman of Alp Action. Through the international corporate funding of concrete Alpine projects, Alp Action is helping to integrate the environment into companies' corporate culture.

RICK ALLEN attempts to combine expedition mountaineering with work as a petroleum engineer, married life and committed Christianity. He has made 11 trips to the greater Himalaya including two attempts on the NE ridge of Everest. Recent climbs in Central Asia with Russian mountaineers led to a successful joint expedition to Dhaulagiri in 1993.

ALAN BLACKSHAW OBE wrote the best-selling book *Mountaineering* in 1965 and edited the *Alpine Journal* from 1968 to 1970. He has climbed in the Caucasus, Greenland and Garhwal and extensively in the Alps. He led the first British ski traverse of the Alps and a N–S traverse of Scandinavia. A former President of the BMC, he is now a Patron.

JIM CURRAN, formerly a lecturer at the University of the West of England, is now a freelance writer and film-maker. He has taken part in 11 expeditions to the Himalaya and South America. Books include *K2, Triumph and Tragedy* and *Suspended Sentences*.

IVOR DELAFIELD has become deeply committed to competition climbing as an international judge, as British team manager for a time, as the BMC's representative on the UIAA's International Commission on Competition Climbing and now as President of the UIAA's Commission of Rock Climbing Competitions.

ED DOUGLAS is editor of *Mountain Review* and writes on mountaineering for *The Guardian* and *The Observer*. When not pursuing this Walter Mittyish profession, he climbs in Britain and the Alps and has been known to surface in the United States and Alaska. He is married and lives in London.

EVELIO ECHEVARRÍA was born in Santiago, Chile, and teaches Hispanic Literature at Colorado State University. He has climbed in North and South America, and has contributed numerous articles to Andean, North American and European journals.

CHUCK EVANS climbed Jaonli (6632m) in Garhwal in 1988 and Churen Himal (7371m), W of Dhaulagiri, in 1989. An early honeymoon to Island Peak preceded his recent attempt on Saipal in far NW Nepal. Club Treasurer from 1992.

MICK FOWLER works for the Inland Revenue and, by contrast, likes to inject as much adventure and excitement as possible into his climbing ventures. He has climbed extensively in the UK and has been on 10 expeditions to peaks in Peru, Africa, India, Pakistan and the (ex) USSR.

JERZY W GAJEWSKI, born in Cracow, belongs to the Mountain Tourism Committee of the Polish Tourist Association. He has written several books and many articles in tourist journals, and has wandered through mountains in Eastern Europe, the Alps and in Wales.

YEVGENIY B GIPPENREITER was born in Moscow and has climbed in the Caucasus, Pamirs, Himalaya and Britain. He is a member of the UIAA Medical Commission and Vice-President of the Int Society for Mountain Medicine. He has written two books: *Acute and Chronic Hypoxia* (1977) and *Physiology of Man at High Altitude* (1987). In 1993 he climbed in Kamchatka, a vast volcanic peninsula in NW Russia. Hon Member 1984.

JERRY GORE joined the Royal Marines as an Officer in 1981. After completing a Short Service Commission he gained a BSc (Hons) in human physiology at Loughborough. He now works as a marketing co-ordinator and, in between, has climbed extensively in the Alps, the Himalaya, South and North America, Arctic Norway, Pamirs and Gogarth.

ASHLEY GREENWOOD is a lawyer, formerly in the Colonial and Diplomatic legal services. He began climbing at school, has been President of the CUMC and the ASC and has climbed extensively in every continent during 63 years.

ROSEMARY GREENWOOD comes of a mountaineering family. In the last 57 years she has done many modest climbs and trekked in many parts of the world. She is also a keen skier.

LINDSAY GRIFFIN, after a lengthy Alpine apprenticeship, has concentrated on remote ascents in the Greater Ranges, including 42 Himalayan peaks. He intends to continue until increasing age, unfitness, accidents and a long-suffering wife call a halt to these activities.

NORMAN HARDIE, a civil engineer, has climbed in New Zealand since 1943 and in Switzerland, Japan, the Himalaya and Antarctica; in 1983 he was leader of Scott Base. He was deputy leader on Kangchenjunga in 1955, reaching the summit with Tony Streather. He is past President of the NZAC.

ALISON JANE HARGREAVES climbed her first mountain at the age of six and divides her time between two over-energetic young children and fulfilling ambitions on the world's mountains. Her first book *A Hard Day's Summer* was published in 1994.

HUGH HARRIS is the BMC's Development Officer with responsibility for Climbing Walls, Youth and Competition Climbing. He has played a major role in developing hard new routes in Northumberland and has run introductory climbing courses on the new Berghaus Wall in Newcastle. He enjoys winter mountaineering in Scotland.

RUPERT HOARE is a geophysicist who has climbed and ski-toured extensively in Europe, Africa, Asia, Australasia and Greenland. His favourite mountains are the Alps, where climbing can be maximised and suffering minimised on short holidays.

TONY HOWARD, a founding partner of Troll Safety Equipment, took part in the first ascent of the Troll Wall in 1965. His expeditions include Greenland, N Canada and desert mountains in Morocco, Algeria, the Sudan, Iran and Jordan.

JOHN HUNT (Lord Hunt of Llanfairwaterdine) has had a highly distinguished career in the army, the public service and as a mountaineer. He led the 1953 Everest expedition, and his classic book *The Ascent of Everest* was reissued with a newly-written Prologue in 1993.

HARISH KAPADIA is a cloth merchant by profession. He has climbed and trekked in the Himalaya since 1960, with ascents up to 6800m. He is Honorary Editor of the *Himalayan Journal* and compiler of the *HC Newsletter*. In 1993 he was awarded the IMF's Gold Medal.

GRAHAM LITTLE, marketing executive with Ordnance Survey, has been on eight expeditions to the Greater Ranges including the Himalaya and Andes. He is past President of the Mountaineering Council of Scotland and has made many first ascents in Scotland, with a particular affinity for islands.

JERRY LOVATT is the Hon Librarian of the Alpine Club and has a particular interest in early Alpine history. He has been climbing for 35 years, from the Alps, to Iran, Bhutan and the Karakoram.

ANDY MACNAE, one time astrophysicist cum painter and decorator, is now studying pollution control in Leeds. He enjoys regular Himalayan holidays including visits to Cerro Kishtwar, Latok and Gasherbrum IV. His favourite venue remains Africa. Currently editor of the *ACG Bulletin* and Alpine editor for *Mountain Review.*

TED MADEN started climbing with the CUMC in the 1950s. From a varied climbing career his happiest memories are of excursions combining physical effort, adequate safety margins and a successful outcome. He enjoys remote places and has completed the Munros.

MARTIN MORAN is a qualified mountain guide whose interests range from mountain running – he holds the record for the Cuillin Ridge traverse – to making new routes on technical peaks in the Garhwal. In 1985 he made the first winter traverse of the Munros and in 1993, with Simon Jenkins, the first continuous traverse of all the 4000m peaks in the Alps.

JERRY MURLAND is deputy head teacher at a Coventry school and has been climbing regularly for 25 years, apart from a short spell of fringe lunacy when he took up caving and cave diving. He enjoys following his children, now fitter and faster than he is, on classic Alpine routes.

PAUL NUNN PhD lectures in economic history at Sheffield. He has climbed for over 30 years in the Alps, Caucasus and Baffin Island and taken part in 14 expeditions to the Greater Ranges. His book *At the Sharp End* was published in 1988. AC Vice-President 1989-90.

BILL O'CONNOR, writer and photographer, has 28 Alpine seasons and 20 expeditions to the Nepal Himalaya under his harness. He currently runs his own adventure travel company and his books include *The Trekking Peaks of Nepal* and *Adventure Travel Nepal.*

ROGER PAYNE started climbing on south-east sandstone and the sea cliffs of Swanage. He has been on expeditions to Peru, Alaska, Nepal, India, Pakistan and Kazakhstan. He has worked as a teacher in the northeast of England and as a mountain guide in Britain and Europe. Currently he is the BMC's National Officer.

SIR EDWARD PECK GCMG was in the Diplomatic Service until 1975 and climbed in the Alps, Turkey, Kulu, Borneo and E Africa. Since retirement he has trekked in Nepal, Bhutan and Patagonia.

CHRISTOPHER RALLING OBE directed and narrated the film *Return to Everest.* In the course of a long career, with the BBC and as a freelance, he has won many international awards including two US Emmys and two British Academy Awards. He divides his time between writing, directing and broadcasting.

ROY RUDDLE researches the psychology of virtual reality and finds that third world bureaucracy is sometimes too frustrating to enjoy. His favourite high mountain area is Alaska, where it is possible to arrange everything in advance by telephone and pay by credit card. Asst Editor from 1972.

C A RUSSELL, who formerly worked with a City bank, devotes much of his time to mountaineering and related activities. He has climbed in many regions of the Alps, in the Pyrenees, East Africa, North America and the Himalaya.

BILL RUTHVEN has been Hon Secretary of the Mount Everest Foundation since 1985. A keen traveller and photographer, he finds that MEF work takes up most of his time, but remembers that in another life he was once an aeronautical engineer.

DAVID SHARMAN is an engineer in the oil and gas industry. He has climbed in North and South America as well as in the Alps.

NIGEL SHEPHERD is an international mountain guide who lived in Chamonix from 1986 to 1993. He has climbed extensively in the UK (including some notable new routes) and in the Alps, USA, Canada, New Zealand and Australia. He is President of the British Association of Mountain Guides and has written two text books on rope techniques.

GUY SHERIDAN OBE served in the Royal Marines and lives in the Pyrenees. He has completed long winter journeys on Nordic skis in the Indian Himalaya, Zagros, Yukon, Drakensberg and Iceland and has taken part in two Himalayan expeditions.

REBECCA STEPHENS MBE is a journalist. Her introduction to climbing was as a *Financial Times* reporter on an Anglo-American expedition to Everest's NE ridge in 1989. She has since climbed Mont Blanc, Mount Kenya, Kilimanjaro, Mount McKinley and, in May 1993, Mount Everest.

GEOFFREY TEMPLEMAN, a retired chartered surveyor, has greatly enjoyed being an Assistant Editor of the *AJ* for the past 18 years. A love of mountain literature is coupled with excursions into the hills which are becoming less and less energetic.

MICHAEL WARD CBE MD FRCS was Medical Officer on Everest in 1953. He is a consultant surgeon (retired) who has combined exploration in Nepal, Bhutan, Kun Lun and Tibet with high-altitude research. Honorary Member 1992.

MICHAEL WESTMACOTT was a member of the Everest team in 1953 and has since climbed in every continent except the Antarctic. On retirement from Shell International he set up the AC's Himalayan Index. Hon Secretary 1967-71, Vice-President 1977-78, AC President from 1993.

DAVE WILKINSON, a lecturer in mathematics, has been climbing in the Alps for 26 years. Expeditions include the first ascent of Rimo III (7233m) in 1985, a failed attempt on K2 in 1986, the first ascent of Chong Kumdan I (7071m) in 1991, and a new route on Pik KGB (5600m) in 1992.

NOTES FOR CONTRIBUTORS

The *Alpine Journal* records all aspects of mountains and mountaineering, including expeditions, adventure, art, literature, geography, history, geology, medicine, ethics and the mountain environment.

Articles Contributions in English are invited. They should be sent to the **Hon Editor, Mrs J Merz, 14 Whitefield Close, Putney, London SW15 3SS.** Articles should be in the form of typed copy or on disk compatible with Apple Macintosh LC III. Their length should not exceed 3000 words without prior approval of the Editor and may be edited or shortened at her discretion. Authors are asked to keep a copy. It is regretted that the *Alpine Journal* is unable to offer a fee for articles published, but authors receive a complimentary copy of the issue of the *Alpine Journal* in which their article appears.

Articles and book reviews should not have been published in substantially the same form by any other publication, nor subsequently be published elsewhere, without permission from the Editor.

Maps These should be well researched, accurate, and finished ready for printing. They should show the most important place-names mentioned in the text. It is the authors' responsibility to get their maps redrawn if necessary. This can be arranged through the Editor if required.

Photographs Only top quality photographs will be accepted. Prints (any size) should be black and white, with glossy finish if possible, and with the author's name, in pencil, on the reverse side. Colour transparencies, in 35mm format or larger, should be originals (not copies).

Captions These should be listed on a separate sheet and should give title, author and approximate date when the photograph was taken.

Copyright It is the author's responsibility to obtain copyright clearance for both text and photographs, to pay any fees involved and to ensure that acknowledgements are in the form required by the copyright owner.

Summaries A brief summary should be included with all 'expedition' articles.

Biographies Authors are asked to provide a short biography, in not more than 50 words, listing the most noteworthy items in their climbing career and anything else they wish to mention.

Deadline: copy should reach the Editor by 1 January of the year of publication.

Index

1994 Vol 99